The Legacy of Alexander

The Legacy of Alexander

*Politics, Warfare, and Propaganda under
the Successors*

A. B. Bosworth

OXFORD
UNIVERSITY PRESS

OXFORD
UNIVERSITY PRESS

Great Clarendon Street, Oxford OX2 6DP

Oxford University Press is a department of the University of Oxford.
It furthers the University's objective of excellence in research, scholarship,
and education by publishing worldwide in

Oxford New York

Auckland Bangkok Buenos Aires Cape Town Chennai
Dar es Salaam Delhi Hong Kong Istanbul Karachi Kolkata
Kuala Lumpur Madrid Melbourne Mexico City Mumbai Nairobi
São Paulo Shanghai Taipei Tokyo Toronto

Oxford is a registered trade mark of Oxford University Press
in the UK and certain other countries

Published in the United States
by Oxford University Press Inc., New York

British Library Cataloguing in Publication Data

Data available

Library of Congress Cataloging in Publication Data
Bosworth, A. B.
The legacy of Alexander : politics, warfare, and propaganda under the successors /
A. B. Bosworth.
p. cm.
1. Mediterranean Region—History—To 476. 2. Greece—History—Macedonian Hegemony,
323-281 B.C. 3. Hellenism. I. Title.
DE86 .B67 2002
938'.08—dc21   2002074913
ISBN 0-19-815306-6

1 3 5 7 9 10 8 6 4 2

Typeset by Newgen Imaging Systems (P) Ltd., Chennai, India
Printed in Great Britain
on acid-free paper by
Biddles Ltd., Guildford & King's Lynn

#499 76922

Preface

This book has had a long gestation. The idea was implanted
long ago when I was an undergraduate, wading through the
first chapter of Tarn and Griffith's *Hellenistic Civilisation*
with its dense and abbreviated summary of events after
Alexander. My friend Richard Hawkins remarked that there
had to be a more extended and lucid introduction to the
period, and the comment has been in the back of my mind
for nearly 40 years. I engaged more closely with the period
when I wrote my early article on the death of Alexander the
Great, and discovered to my chagrin that I knew virtually
nothing about the Babylon Settlement and its aftermath. A
long learning process ensued, and I became more and more
convinced that there was an urgent need for a full historical
coverage of the half century after Alexander, something that
did not exist, and still does not, despite the series of biographies which have been published over the last decade, devoted
to the careers of individual dynasts. There still remains the
difficult task of integration and collation, drawing out the
general trends and exploring the complex interrelations of
ruler and subject, city and empire.

The present work is a prelude to the larger project. There
is a strong narrative core, dealing with the conflict between
Eumenes and Antigonus the One-Eyed, which probably did
more than anything to define the shape of the Hellenistic
world but has been astoundingly ignored in modern scholarship. The central chapters amount to a history of the period
318–311, which saw the formation of the Antigonid and
Seleucid monarchies, and the Introduction provides an
analysis of developments in the five years after Alexander's
death. The early chapters set the scene. An intensive analysis
of the Babylon Settlement sheds new light on the power
groups as they emerged in 323 and the political interplay
which resulted in the overriding problem of the period, a
central monarchy with token kings, nominally exercising

authority over powerful regional satraps but with almost no practical control over their supposed subjects. The political setting leads to the main social issue, the practical dismemberment of what had been the Macedonian national army. A close investigation of the sources (often misinterpreted) illustrates the gradual dissipation of the central army group as it had served under Alexander. As early as 319 the bulk of the Macedonian troops had been transferred from the royal court, now in Pella, to serve under Antigonus (and provide the foundation for his future empire). As the army dispersed and Macedonians became less important, the kingship itself lost any authority it may have had, and a new type of dynast emerged. The final chapter accordingly addresses the problem of legitimation and explores the means by which power was maintained or—equally important—lost.

Source analysis bulks large in my work. The period is dominated by a shadowy literary colossus, Hieronymus of Cardia, who by common consent lies behind the narrative of the most detailed extant narrative, that of Diodorus Siculus. It is heady material, a colourful, well-documented exposition from a contemporary of events and a friend of successive kings. Information there is in plenty, as is generally acknowledged, but there must also be disinformation—as is increasingly realized to be the case with Hieronymus' closest counterpart, Thucydides. Chapter 5 is a historiographical investigation into the famous ethnographic digressions in which Hieronymus subtly intrudes his own social and personal commentary. That is paralleled by the discussion of the Babylon Settlement where (in the Latin account of Curtius Rufus) we have a counter-tradition embellished with late rhetoric and also affected by the political interests of the court of Ptolemy. Almost all our literary evidence comes from the entourage of the great dynasts, and propaganda is pervasive. There is little documentary evidence. What there is comes predominantly from Babylonia, in a large and varied corpus of cuneiform tablets that still awaits full investigation. I have tried to address this evidence throughout the work, and I must admit frankly that it would have been impossible without the help of two gifted young Assyriologists. Cornelia Wunsch worked with me as a Research Associate, funded by the Australian Research Committee and explained the multiple ambiguities of interpretation. I also had a very informative correspondence with Tom Boiy, whose comprehensive doctoral thesis has become an indispensable research tool. I am conscious that some of my chronological conclusions are not welcomed by cuneiform specialists, but they are the product of integrating the Hellenic and Babylonian evidence, and such dialogue is essential if there is to be progress in the field.

I have many other obligations. In 1998 I was a visiting fellow at All Souls College, enjoying its unparalleled hospitality and exploiting the resources of the Bodleian and Ashmolean libraries. Robert Parker suggested that I give a number of seminars on the post Alexander period, and with that stimulus I was able to write the first drafts of chapters 2, 3 and 6. I am grateful for the invitation and for the helpful comments made on those occasions by him, Robin Lane Fox, Robin Osborne, John Ma, and many others. An invitation to Stanford University in 1999 resulted in the final chapter. For detailed advice and guidance on the complexities of things Nabataean I am indebted to David Graf of Miami and to my colleague David Kennedy. I should also acknowledge the support of my university and department, for generous leave and financial support for travel. I am particularly grateful to Pat Wheatley for almost literally working through the manuscript with me and injecting much of his considerable enthusiasm, and also to Honours students in Perth and Newcastle who have been inflicted with working drafts of the individual chapters. Finally, and most importantly, I must pay tribute to my partner, Elizabeth Baynham, who has lived through the work from its outset, read and criticized the successive drafts, and been an unfailing source of encouragement and inspiration. I owe her more than I can say.

A.B.B.

September 2001

Contents

Abbreviations

ABC	A. K. Grayson, *Assyrian and Babylonian Chronicles* (Locust Valley, NY 1975)
ABL	R. F. Harper, *Assyrian and Babylonian Letters* (London and Chicago 1892–1914)
AC	*L'Antiquité classique*
AHB	*Ancient History Bulletin*
AION	*Annali dell'Istituto Orientale di Napoli*
AJAH	*American Journal of Ancient History*
Al. in Fact and Fiction	A. B. Bosworth and E. J. Baynham (eds.), *Alexander the Great in Fact and Fiction* (Oxford 2000)
AncW	*Ancient World*
ANRW	*Aufstieg und Niedergang der römischen Welt*
ANSMN	*American Numismatic Society. Museum Notes*
AS	*Antike Schlachtfelder. Bausteine zu einer antiken Kriegsgeschichte*, 4 vols. (Berlin 1903–31)
Atkinson i	J. E. Atkinson, *A Commentary on Q. Curtius Rufus' Historiae Alexandri Magni. Books 3 and 4* (Amsterdam 1980)
Atkinson ii	J. E. Atkinson, *A Commentary on Q. Curtius Rufus' Historiae Alexandri Magni. Books 5 to 7, 2* (Amsterdam 1994)
BaM	*Baghdader Mitteilungen*
BCH	*Bulletin de correspondence hellénique*
Beloch	K. J. Beloch, *Griechische Geschichte*, 2nd edn., 4 vols. (Strassburg, Berlin, Leipzig 1922–7)
Berve	H. Berve, *Das Alexanderreich auf prosopographischer Grundlage*, 2 vols. (Munich 1926)
BES	*Bulletin of the Egyptological Seminar*
Billows, *Antigonos*	R. Billows, *Antigonos the One-Eyed and the Creation of the Hellenistic State* (Berkeley 1990)

BM	British Museum (inventory number)
BN	*Beiträge zur Namenforschung*
Bosworth,	A. B. Bosworth, *A Historical*
HCA	*Commentary on Arrian's*
	History of Alexander i–
	(Oxford 1980–)
Bosworth,	A. B. Bosworth, 'Calanus and the
'Calanus'	Brahman Opposition', in W. Will
	(ed.), *Alexander der Grosse. Eine*
	Welteroberung und ihr Hintergrund
	(Bonn 1988) 173–203
Bosworth, 'History	A. B. Bosworth, 'History and
and Artifice'	Artifice in Plutarch's *Eumenes*', in
	P. A. Stadter (ed.). *Plutarch and the*
	Historical Tradition (London 1992)
	56–89
Briant, *RTP*	P. Briant, *Rois, tributs et paysans*
	(Paris 1982)
Brunt, *Arrian*	P. A. Brunt, *Arrian,* 2 vols., Loeb
	Classical Library (Cambridge,
	Mass. 1976–83)
BSOAS	*Bulletin of the Schools of Oriental*
	and African Studies
CA	*Classical Antiquity*
CAH	*Cambridge Ancient History,*
	2nd edn. (1970–)
CHIran	*Cambridge History of Iran*
CPh	*Classical Philology*
CQ	*Classical Quarterly*
CT	*Cuneiform Texts from Babylonian*
	Tablets in the British Museum
CW	*Classical Weekly*
Del Monte	G. F. Del Monte, *Testi dalla Babilonia*
	Ellenistica I (Pisa 1997)
DHA	*Dialogues d'histoire ancienne*
Droysen	J. G. Droysen, *Geschichte des*
	Hellenismus, 2nd edn., 3 vols.
	(Gotha 1877–8)
EA	*Epigraphica Anatolica. Zeitschrift für*
	Epigraphik und historische Geographie
	Anatoliens

FGrH	F. Jacoby, *Die Fragmente der griechischen Historiker* (Berlin and Leiden 1923–)
GB	*Grazer Beiträge*
GRBS	*Greek, Roman and Byzantine Studies*
Goukowsky, *Diodore xviii*	P. Goukowsky, *Diodore de Sicile, bibliothèque historique livre xviii* (Paris 1978)
HSCP	*Harvard Studies in Classical Philology*
Heckel	W. Heckel, *The Marshals of Alexander's Empire* (London 1992)
HM	N. G. L. Hammond et al., *A History of Macedonia*, 3 vols. (Oxford 1972–88)
Hornblower, *Hieronymus*	Jane Hornblower, *Hieronymus of Cardia* (Oxford 1981)
HSCP	*Harvard Studies in Classical Philology*
IEJ	*Israel Exploration Journal*
Inscr. Iasos	W. Blümel, *Die Inschriften von Iasos*, IGSK 28 (Bonn 1985)
ISE	L. Moretti, *Iscrizioni storiche ellenistiche* (2 vols.: Florence 1967–75)
IG	*Inscriptiones graecae* (1st edn. Berlin 1873–, 2nd edn. Berlin 1913–)
JEA	*Journal of Egyptian Archaeology*
JHS	*Journal of Hellenic Studies*
LBAT	T. G. Pinches et al., *Late Babylonian Astronomical and Related Texts* (Providence, RI 1955)
LGPN	P. M. Fraser and E. Matthews (eds.), *A Lexicon of Greek Personal Names* i– (1988–)
OGIS	*Orientis graeci inscriptiones selectae*, ed. W. Dittenberger, 2 vols. (Leipzig 1903–5)
OLD	*Oxford Latin Dictionary*, ed. P. G. W. Glare (Oxford 1982)
PACA	*Proceedings of the African Classical Association*
PCG	*Poetae Comici Graeci*, ed. R. Kassel and C. Austin i– (Berlin 1983–)
Pearson, *LHA*	L. Pearson, *The Lost Historians of Alexander the Great*, Philological Monographs 20 (New York 1960)

PEQ	*Palestine Exploration Quarterly*
PKöln	*Kölner Papyri vi.*, Papyrologica
	Coloniensis 7 (Opladen 1987).
RAL	*Atti della Accademia Nazionale dei*
	Lincei. Rendiconti. Classe di Scienze
	morali, storiche e filologiche
RE	*Realencyclopädie der classischen*
	Altertumswissenschaft, ed. Pauly,
	Wissowa, Kroll (Stuttgart 1893–)
REA	*Revue des études anciennes*
SBBerlin	*Sitzungsberichte der preussischen*
	Akademie der Wissenschaften,
	phil.-hist. Klasse
Schachermeyr,	F. Schachermeyr, *Alexander in Babylon*
Al. in Babylon	*und die Reichsordnung nach seinem Tode*,
	Sitzungsberichte der Österreichischen
	Akademie der Wissenschaften, phil.-hist.
	Klasse 286.3 (Vienna 1970)
Schober	L. Schober, *Untersuchungen zur*
	Geschichte Babyloniens und der Oberen
	Satrapien von 323–303 v.Chr.
	(Frankfurt 1981)
Seibert,	J. Seibert, *Untersuchungen zur Geschichte*
Untersuchungen	*Ptolemaios' I* (Munich 1969)
SO	*Symbolae Osloenses*
Tarn, *Al.*	W. W. Tarn, *Alexander the Great*, 2 vols.
	(Cambridge 1948)
TBER	J.-M. Durand, *Textes babyloniens*
	d'époque récente (Paris 1981)
TCL	*Textes cunéiformes du Louvre*
Walbank, *HCP*	F. W. Walbank, *A Historical Commentary*
	on Polybius, 3 vols. (Oxford 1957–79)
Welles, *RC*	C. B. Welles, *Royal Correspondence in the*
	Hellenistic Period (London 1934)
YCS	*Yale Classical Studies*
ZA	*Zeitschrift für Assyriologie*
ZPE	*Zeitschrift für Papyrologie und Epigraphik*

I
Introduction

1. A PERIOD OF DECLINE?

The period after Alexander is generally regarded as an anticlimax, a depressing anticlimax. It was characterized by destabilization and virtual anarchy, as the great king's marshals fought for the empire which he had allegedly left to the strongest of them. The army which he had led into Asia was dissipated in a sequence of futile civil wars, and the élite Macedonian troops were progressively reduced by combat, much of it against fellow Macedonians. Out of the conflict emerged a number of kingdoms, created by the ambitions of individual satraps, which gradually coalesced into hereditary dynasties. The main casualty was inevitably the ruling Argead dynasty of Macedon, which became extinct 15 years after Alexander's death, and Macedon itself ceased to be an imperial power. It became one—and not the strongest—of a number of successor kingdoms. The impression is one of decline and disintegration. That is somewhat misleading. Like the Achaemenid empire before it, Alexander's empire was far from a unified, organized whole. Even before his death ambitious satraps might disregard his authority when he was in distant parts and lord it over their subjects as monarchs in their own right.[1] And the process of disintegration had started even before his death. Alexander himself had tacitly admitted that the Indian lands were out of control, relinquishing the Indus provinces to native rulers.[2] In the west too, in Thrace, Cappadocia, and Armenia,[3] there were powerful forces in

---

*In this chapter I keep footnotes to a minimum, referring, when appropriate, to more detailed discussion later in the book.

[1] On the details see Bosworth, *Conquest and Empire* 147–8, 239–41; *Alexander and the East* 23–4; Badian, in *Al. in Fact and Fiction* 74–5.

[2] Schober, *Untersuchungen* 11–26; Bosworth, *Antichthon* 17 (1983) 39–45.

[3] On Thrace see Ch. 7, pp. 268–71; on Cappadocia see App. *Mithr.* 8.25–6 = Hieronymus, *FGrH* 154 F 3; Diod. 18.16.1–3; Plut. *Eum.* 3.3–5; Nep. *Eum.* 2.2–3; on Armenia see below, p. 10.

revolt or defying subjugation. That was largely the result of Alexander's own pattern of action. For most of his reign he was in constant movement, between 329 and 325 on the very periphery of the old Achaemenid realms; and the most effective military forces he possessed were with him. It was only in the last eighteen months of his life that he was relatively stationary, travelling between the central capitals of the empire as the Achaemenid rulers had before him. That was too short a time to create institutions of empire other than those he had inherited from the Persians, and at his death he was about to leave for another point on the periphery, the spice lands of southern Arabia. Further instability and satrapal insubordination was almost inevitable. His death, it could be argued, simply accelerated the process.

In contrast, the successor dynasts tended to be more constructive. This was largely because their regimes had originated in individual satrapies. They expanded outwards, but the administrative and military centre remained. Antigonus' power base was his satrapal capital of Celaenae.[4] From there he overran much of Asia Minor between 320 and 317. With resources from his expanded satrapy he pursued Eumenes into Iran and won the Battle of Gabiene, which gave him effective control of most of the central satrapies of the empire.[5] He was almost in the position of Alexander when he had pursued Darius III to his death, but he returned to the west, first to Syria and after a highly successful campaign of conquest there to his old capital of Celaenae. Power had focalized. Alexander had been wholly atypical, an absolute monarch without a fixed capital. Ptolemy on the other hand had his Alexandria, Seleucus his Babylon and later Antioch, Lysimachus his Lysimacheia. The competition for supremacy discouraged grandiose military adventures. To embark on an unlimited programme of conquest was to risk invasion and the loss of one's home base (as Demetrius was to discover in 288).[6] The practical imperative was to create the resources to protect one's territory against invasion and expand one's power base without overreaching oneself. For

---

[4] See the historical sketch below, pp. 17–19.
[5] Described in full in Ch. 4, pp. 112–68.   [6] See below, Ch. 7, p. 258.

all the glamour and charisma of Alexander his conquests could not be repeated.

In this respect the period can be regarded as one of creation rather than disintegration. The successor dynasts had to build their courts, recruit their armies and maintain an adequate economic base. Talented individuals, mostly of Greek origin, were attracted to the new courts to operate as 'friends', i.e. as advisers, administrators and commanders. At a humbler level, fighting men were recruited from the entire Mediterranean world, to be enlisted into the new armies or settled as colonists with the obligation to serve in person if called upon. Large-scale recruitment of this nature required considerable finance and, apart from booty acquired in war, the revenues were preponderantly gained through fiscal exactions, such as land and poll tax and dues on sales, and for the system to be operative it was necessary for the native population to accept its rulers and support, with resignation, if not enthusiasm what was in effect an occupation army. Hence the adoption of native institutions and native titulature in Egypt and Babylonia. The new dynasts proclaimed themselves the successors of the previous rulers, blessed by the native gods, whether Ahura Mazda, Bel Marduk, or Amon Re, and the indigenous population to some degree identified with the new regimes. When Ptolemy took to the field in 312 to attack the Antigonid armies in Syria, the majority of his troops were native Egyptian, not merely baggage handlers and camp followers, but front-line fighters 'useful for combat'.[7] Graeco-Macedonian settlers, however numerous, were not sufficient for a grand army, and all major battles from the death of Alexander were fought with an exotic blend of troops: Macedonians, natives trained in Macedonian style, mercenaries of all nationalities. Alexander may have won his major battles without using troops other than his Macedonians, but the situation had changed even before his death. Iranian cavalry were used in front-line situations as early as the battle of the Hydaspes (326), and after the dismissal of 10,000 Macedonian veterans in 324

---

[7] Diod. 19.80.4. On the use of native troops trained in Macedonian style see Ch. 3, pp. 80, 83 and Ch. 4.

Alexander was increasingly turning to Iranian infantry which had been trained in Macedonian weaponry and tactics. He even experimented with a mixed phalanx of Macedonians and Iranians, each using their traditional weapons.[8] His successors had no alternative but to follow his example. The last army that was wholly or almost wholly Macedonian was the expeditionary force which Craterus and Antipater led into Asia in 321. Four years later, in the great campaign of Paraetacene, both sides deployed composite armies with Macedonians, both infantry and cavalry, in a minority. This had an important consequence. The new rulers were Macedonians, commanders under Alexander, but their courts were more cosmopolitan, their friends recruited from the entire Greek world and their armies still more heterogeneous. And the entire structure rested on an agrarian population which had little or no part in the political and military establishment. These natives might be coerced into subjection by the military settlements created in their territory, but it was economical to attract their good will. In other words, the rulers were all things to all men. To their native subjects they were the legitimate kings, the successors of indigenous rulers, who like their predecessors had their power sanctioned by the local gods. For their armies they were naturally commanders, who proved their legitimacy by success in the field and by gaining spoils and land to reward their troops. For their courts they were benefactors, rewarding good service with material honour and wealth. The new regimes had no tradition, no established customs; rather they encountered a multiplicity of traditions which they absorbed and modified. For the populations of Egypt and Babylonia they were pharaohs or kings of the four corners of the earth. For Greek cities in their ambit they used the diplomatic language that had evolved to transact business between city-states and hegemonial powers.[9] The rulers had absolute power over these communities, but they courteously heard the representations of city embassies and gave grants of freedom, autonomy,

---

[8] Arr. 7.23.3, 24.1 (*FGrH* 139 F 58). See Ch. 3, pp. 79–81
[9] See now the subtle discussion by John Ma, *Antiochus III and the Cities of Asia Minor*, esp. 179–242.

exemption from tribute or garrison, and graciously received acclamations of saviour, benefactor, or even god manifest. This is in effect the relation of fifth-century Athens to her subjects, but the autocracy is less bluntly expressed than we find with the sovereign *demos*—and the gratitude of the subjects is more fulsome.

The new regimes were essentially the creation of individuals, who exploited the absence of any effective central power. It could be a relatively gradual process, when a more powerful satrap expelled or absorbed his neighbours, as Antigonus did in Asia Minor between 315 and 313. There were also what one might describe as defining moments, the most important of which was the winter of 317/16 when two warring coalitions of satraps fought it out in the Iranian plateau. Antigonus emerged victorious from the campaign, promptly outmanœuvred his fellow generals, Peithon and Seleucus, and became in effect master of a vast territory from Persis to the Hellespont. At Alexander's death there were twenty or so satrapies, in constant interplay with each other, and by 308 they had effectively severed contact with Macedon and coalesced into three separate groupings, under Antigonus, Seleucus and Ptolemy. The reality was recognized in 306, when Antigonus solemnly assumed the diadem, the insignia of kingship, and took the title of Basileus for all official purposes.[10] He gave his son Demetrius the same trappings, and his example was followed by Ptolemy and Seleucus, by Cassander in Macedon, and even by Agathocles in Sicily. It was the end of a charade. The new rulers had in theory received their original power base from the king of Macedon, from Alexander himself or the regents governing in the name of the two incapable kings who succeeded him. They recognized it in their public protocol. In Egypt and Babylon Ptolemy and Seleucus represented themselves as satraps, and even Antigonus merely styled himself 'royal commander' (*rab uqi*) when he was master of Babylonia. They were technically subordinates, but since Alexander's death there had been no effective power to impose discipline from above. The fatal step probably came in 319, when the

---

[10] On this see the exposition in Ch. 7.

regent Antipater returned to Macedon with the two kings, effectively renouncing the empire in Asia and delegating most of the royal army to Antigonus. It gave Antigonus the means to extend his power throughout Asia Minor and defeat the satrapal coalition in Iran.

This process, the unravelling of central authority and the creation of new monarchies, is the context of my book. It is in no sense a formal history of the period but a series of studies which explore the political and military background and lay some of the groundwork for a more comprehensive treatment. Some preliminary discussion is necessary, for the events of the period were tumultuous and confused. For the non-specialist they are frankly baffling, a kaleidoscope of exotic individuals engaged in complex military and diplomatic manœuvres on several fronts simultaneously. Some basic points of reference are clearly desirable, and I hope it will be of assistance to my readers if I now sketch in the early stages, the division of the empire and the first bout of internecine warfare which came close to defining the shape of the Hellenistic world. Subsequent events, in particular the period from 318 to 311, are covered in the central chapters (4–6) of the book. I also provide a chronological appendix correlating key events in Europe and Asia.

2. HISTORICAL ORIENTATION

Alexander's death on 10 June 323 left Macedonian resources divided between three widely separated areas.[11] The royal court and most of Alexander's staff were with him in Babylon at his death, as was a large army of Macedonians and native troops. This was one focus of power. Another was in Cilicia, where Alexander's most senior marshal, Craterus, was entrenched with a veteran army of Macedonians and controlled the arsenals which Alexander had been establishing for his future expansion in the west. Finally, in Macedon proper, Alexander's regent, Antipater, remained in power.

---

[11] What follows is a summary of the conclusions which I reach in Ch. 2, where sources and bibliography are fully cited.

He had been recalled by Alexander a year before the latter's death and commissioned to lead reinforcements into Asia, but neither he nor any military forces had moved, and he was still the dominant figure in Europe. We have evidence only for events in Babylon, where, it seems, the marshals were disinclined to make any radical decision. The first proposal was to await the birth of the child who would be born to Alexander's wife, Rhoxane, and in the unlikely event of its proving male and surviving it would have four guardians, two of the Bodyguards at Babylon, Perdiccas and Leonnatus, and Craterus and Antipater in the west. This cautious delaying of the issue was sabotaged by the infantry at Babylon, which demanded a present, living king and proclaimed the half-brother of Alexander, Arrhidaeus. He was mentally impaired and could not rule without a guardian, but that was no deterrent to the Macedonian rank-and-file or to their leader, Meleager, who saw himself as the king-maker. A tense period of confrontation between the infantry and cavalry eventually ended in compromise, with the cavalry accepting Arrhidaeus and the infantry agreeing to the child of Alexander as a second king. The key players retained their positions. Perdiccas remained as chief of staff (chiliarch), the position he had held under Alexander: Antipater was confirmed in Macedonia, while Craterus had a roving commission to promote the royal interests wherever he thought fit.

The situation changed a little later, when Perdiccas was able to dispose of Meleager and execute the chief mutineers in the Macedonian infantry. He felt strong enough to assume the regency, and he was hailed guardian of the kingdom by his troops and authorized to decide on the satrapies as he saw fit. It was in effect a coup. Antipater could do nothing about it. Once reports of Alexander's death had been authenticated in Greece, the Athenians and Aetolians made an alliance against Macedon and called the rest of the Greek world to the cause of liberty.[12] Within a matter of weeks Thermopylae was occupied by the insurgent forces, while

---

[12] For general bibliography on the Lamian War see J. Seibert, *Das Zeitalter der Diadochen* 92–8, and the extremely useful dissertation of Oliver Schmitt, *Der Lamische Krieg*. For a short, recent account of the war see Christian Habicht, *Athens from Alexander to Antony* 36–42.

Antipater himself, deserted by his crack Thessalian cavalry, suffered the first defeat experienced by Macedonian arms in 30 years and took refuge in Lamia. There was nothing he could do to effect events in Babylon, and Craterus also chose to remain in Cilicia and await the outcome of events. For the moment Perdiccas was the dominant personality, and he distributed the satrapies with a view to entrenching his domination. The most powerful of Alexander's marshals disappeared from court and were assigned to remote satrapies, where they had very limited forces at their disposal, too weak at all events to challenge the power of the centre. However, if the centre were to be weakened, then there was the opportunity for expansion. The monarchs-to-be had the bases for their future power. Ptolemy occupied Egypt, where he found a useful war chest of 8,000 talents, amassed by its administrator, the astute and unscrupulous Cleomenes of Naucratis.[13] Another Bodyguard, Lysimachus, occupied Thrace, where he was to hold sway for the rest of his long life. Yet another of the main actors in the period, Antigonus, was confirmed in Phrygia, where he had been installed by Alexander long ago in 334 and had distinguished himself by repelling the Persian counter-offensive after Issus.[14] Seleucus was the only future dynast who did not receive a satrapy in the distribution. He remained in Babylon, second in command to Perdiccas with Perdiccas' old position of chiliarch.[15] That left Perdiccas without a rival at the royal court: he was the guardian of Arrhidaeus (who now changed his name to Philip), commander of the army at Babylon, and the unchallenged head of a group of subordinate commanders who included his own brother Alcetas.

By the end of 323 the balance of power had changed. Antipater was in desperate straits, defeated and under siege at Lamia. He was awaiting reinforcements but it was uncertain

[13] Diod. 18.14.1; Just. 13.6.18–19; Arr. *Succ.* F 1a; Paus. 1.6.3. On the career of Cleomenes see Berve no. 431; Seibert, *Untersuchungen* 39–51; H. Kloft, *GB* 15 (1988) 191–222; G. Le Rider, *BCH* 121 (1997) 71–93.

[14] On Antigonus' career under Alexander see briefly Bosworth, *Conquest and Empire* 52, 62–3, 231; and at greater length Briant, *Antigone le Borgne* 53–74; Billows, *Antigonos* 36–48.

[15] Diod. 18.3.5; Just. 13.4.17. See the discussion in Ch. 2, p. 56 with n. 102.

who, if anyone, would come to his rescue. Craterus remained in Cilicia and made no move towards Macedonia. He may have been in genuine doubt what to do, and he was presumably aware that Antipater had also made overtures to Leonnatus in Hellespontine Phrygia.[16] In the event he was prepared to cede the glory of intervention. In Babylon Rhoxane at last bore a son, who received his father's name but not (at first) the kingship.[17] It was prudent to wait until he had survived the first year of infancy. But Perdiccas had the acknowledged king (Arrhidaeus) in his power and acted in his name. He also had an army at his disposal and proceeded to use it. The pretext was given by another of the powerful actors in our drama, Eumenes of Cardia. Eumenes was a Greek who had acted as chief secretary for both Philip and Alexander. As events were to show, he had a very considerable strategic genius, and in the last years of Alexander he commanded a unit of the élite Companion cavalry. At Babylon he was given the satrapy of Cappadocia, which had escaped conquest under Alexander and was dominated by an Iranian noble, Ariarathes. None of the other commanders in Asia Minor gave him military assistance, as they had been instructed, and Perdiccas took the royal army to break the power of Ariarathes and install Eumenes as satrap. In this he was strikingly successful. Ariarathes was defeated in a full-scale pitched battle and executed along with his family; Eumenes immediately took over the provincial organization of Cappadocia. Perdiccas, it would seem, now had the infant Alexander formally proclaimed king.

Meanwhile, in Macedonia Leonnatus had at last brought forces from Asia and Europe, to the relief of Antipater. Leonnatus arrived early in the spring of 322, and lost his life in a cavalry battle against the Thessalians. His infantry phalanx was untouched, however, and joined forces with Antipater, who was content to avoid another battle and return to Macedon. Now Craterus at last made his move. He led his 10,000 veterans from Cilicia across Asia Minor. There is no

---

[16] Diod. 18.12.1; Plut. *Eum.* 3.6–8; Just. 13.5.14–15.
[17] Arr. *Succ.* F 1a.1. On the chronology see Bosworth, *CQ* 43 (1993) 423–6.

record of his meeting Perdiccas, and it is most likely that the regent had invaded Cappadocia from the east, via Armenia where his lieutenant Neoptolemus is attested operating with a force of Macedonians.[18] These two principal actors in the drama seem to have avoided each other, and it appears that there was a real danger of conflict if they met in person. In Macedonia Craterus decisively shifted the military equilibrium. His veterans brought the forces at Antipater's disposal to over 40,000,[19] far outnumbering the Hellenic coalition, which was hamstrung by the absence of the Aetolians, preoccupied by their own concerns in the west.[20] The Athenians and their allies had no chance against this new army, led by arguably the ablest of Alexander's marshals. At the Battle of Crannon, late in July 322, the Macedonian phalanx proved its superiority yet again over Greek hoplite infantry, and almost simultaneously at sea Craterus' fleet won a series of victories over the Athenians, culminating in the Battle of Amorgos. The Lamian War now ended, as Athens surrendered and Antipater and Craterus dictated their terms to the Greek alliance. It was the (temporary) end of democracy in the city of Pericles, which now came under a restricted oligarchy, supervised by a Macedonian garrison in Peiraeus.[21]

Craterus had ostentatiously deferred to Antipater, the older man and friend of Philip II. But there had clearly been some friction, as Craterus dressed himself as a clone of Alexander (without the diadem) and his soldiers compared him very favourably with the small, unprepossessing figure

---

[18] Plut. *Eum.* 4.1–4 (cf. Briant, *RTP* 30–41; Bosworth, *GRBS* 19 (1978) 232–3). Armenia, like Cappadocia, was not under Macedonian control at the time of Alexander's death, and its subjugation was unfinished business. Perdiccas could have stamped his authority there on his way to Cappadocia, and after the defeat of Ariarathes he sent Neoptolemus to complete the conquest. He may have imposed Orontes as satrap before the outbreak of the first coalition war. See Ch. 4, n. 93.

[19] Diod. 18.16.4–17.2. On the numbers see Ch. 3, p. 79.

[20] Diod. 18.13.3, 15.2. On the murky evidence for war in the west see my forthcoming article, 'How did Athens lose the Lamian War?', in O. Palagia and S. V. Tracy (eds.), *The Macedonians in Athens 322–229 B.C.* (Oxford 2003).

[21] Diod. 18.18.4–5; Plut. *Phoc.* 27.5–28.7. On the settlement see Hammond, *HM* iii.114–15; Habicht, *Athens from Alexander to Antony* 44–6; L. Tritle, *Phocion the Good* 129–37, and most recently E. Poddighe, *DHA* 23/2 (1997) 47–82 and E. J. Baynham, 'Antipater and Athens', in Palagia and Tracy (above, n. 20).

of Antipater.[22] He married Phila, Antipater's eldest daughter, and prepared to return to Asia. That would have been a reversal of Alexander's instructions, which were to have Craterus replace Antipater as regent, as it was of the final settlement at Babylon, which not only distributed the satrapies but assigned Macedon to Craterus and Antipater together.[23] That was hardly an attractive prospect for either, and it is not surprising that Craterus was preparing for a return to Asia, where he might coexist or—more likely—conflict with Perdiccas. By the summer of 322 Perdiccas appeared dominant. He followed his defeat of Ariarathes with a punitive expedition against two cities of Lycaonia (Laranda and Isaura), which had resisted Macedonian rule and killed Balacrus, satrap of Cilicia under Alexander.[24] They were ruthlessly destroyed, to deter resistance elsewhere. It was at this peak of success that Perdiccas married Nicaea, a daughter of Antipater, whom he had requested shortly after Alexander's death. But she was not the only lady who had an interest in him. The queen mother Olympias wrote, proposing that he marry her own daughter, Cleopatra, Alexander's full sister; and there is a tradition of disagreement in the Perdiccan camp, Eumenes arguing that Olympias' offer should be explored and Alcetas insisting that the marriage agreement with Antipater should stand.[25] A third princess, Cynnane (also a daughter of Philip II), also entered into contention. She evaded Antipater's custody and fled to Asia Minor with her daughter. There she was killed in mysterious circumstances by Alcetas, apparently with Perdiccas'

---

[22] This was emphatically stated in Arrian's History of events after Alexander (below, p. 22): cf. Arr. *Succ.* F 19 (see also the new Göteborg palimpsest) with Plut. *Phoc.* 29.3.

[23] The planned return to Asia is attested by Diod. 18.18.7. The division of Macedon at Babylon is attested only in Arr. *Succ.* F 1a.7 (see Ch. 2, pp. 58–9).

[24] Diod. 18.22.1. Balacrus appears to have been the first husband of Phila, daughter of Antipater and wife of Craterus (Wehrli, *Historia* 13 (1964) 141; Heckel, *ZPE* 70 (1987) 161–2; Badian, *ZPE* 72 (1988) 116; Bosworth, *CQ* 44 (1994) 60). He had been a Bodyguard of Alexander (Arr. 2.12.2), and was clearly a noble of the highest distinction, whose death cried out for vengeance.

[25] Arr. *Succ.* F 1.21; cf. Just. 13.6.4–7. According to Diodorus (18.23.1) Cleopatra came in person to Lycaonia. That is unlikely; the intrigue would have been too obvious. Perdiccas later invited her to Sardes, where she had established herself by early 321 (Arr. *Succ.* F 1.26, 25.2–6). That was a prelude to formal marriage.

connivance.[26] It is clear that she was deeply estranged from Antipater, and neither Perdiccas nor his brother wished to cause a provocation by giving her sanctuary and support. However, her death was found intolerable by the troops, who came close to mutiny, and to calm the situation Cynnane's daughter was married to King Philip, his mental disability notwithstanding, and like her husband (and uncle) she assumed a royal name, Eurydice. This was a woman of a very different mould from her husband, deeply ambitious, calculating and hostile to Antipater; she was no cipher, to be manipulated at will.

This complex situation became even more entangled when Perdiccas intrigued against Antigonus, the long-standing satrap of Phrygia, who had kept up friendly relations with Antipater throughout Alexander's reign. Perdiccas is said to have been suspicious of his ambitions and summoned him to answer charges of conspiracy.[27] Antigonus accordingly fled to Europe, where he joined Antipater and Craterus in Aetolia. It was the winter of 322/1, and they were crushing the last of the insurgent powers. Antigonus' arrival saved Aetolia for the moment. He brought news, or rumours, of the intrigues for the hand of Cleopatra, and it was sufficient to push the two dynasts into open war.[28] At the same time Perdiccas had sent Eumenes to negotiate with Cleopatra in her residence at Sardes, and his arrival was duly passed on to Antigonus by Menander, the sympathetic satrap of Lydia.[29] That consolidated the impulse to war, and the spring of 321 saw Antipater and Craterus at the Hellespont at the head of a Macedonian army which could compare, in numbers at least, to Alexander's expeditionary force of 334. But Perdiccas had fatally overreached himself by alienating Ptolemy in Egypt. Late in 322 the immensely lavish catafalque which contained the enbalmed body of Alexander began its

---

[26] Arr. *Succ.* F 1.22–3; Polyaen. 8.60; cf. Diod. 19.52.5. See particularly E. Carney, *Women and Monarchy in Macedonia* 29–31, arguing that Cynnane intended her daughter to marry Philip Arrhidaeus; there is no warrant for this in the sources.

[27] Arr. *Succ.* F 1.20; Diod. 18.23.3–4; cf. Billows, *Antigonos* 58–9.

[28] Diod. 18.25.3–5; Arr. *Succ.* F 1.24. I take the winter of Diod. 18.25.1 to be that of 322/1.   [29] Arr. *Succ.* F 1.26; cf. F 25.2.

journey west from Babylon. Perdiccas, it would seem, intended to take control of the mortal remains, whether to keep them with him for the moment or to escort them to their final destination.[30] But he was forestalled by Ptolemy who met the cortège near Damascus and escorted it south to Egypt.[31] Perdiccas had lost the body with all the mystique it invested upon its owner, and he was set on recovering it. That meant war, not merely with Ptolemy but also the city kings of Cyprus who had allied themselves with him.

Perdiccas had to engage on several fronts, and he chose to concentrate his own efforts on Egypt. In Asia Minor Eumenes was commissioned to co-ordinate the defence against Antipater and Craterus. Unfortunately the other commanders in the area refused to co-operate. Alcetas, slighted at being passed over by his brother, stayed in Pisidia with his Macedonian forces, while Neoptolemus fought a pitched battle against Eumenes, losing the engagement thanks to the superior cavalry that Eumenes had recruited in Cappadocia. In the confusion Craterus and Antipater crossed the Hellespont unopposed. Despite the disarray in his camp Eumenes combined his and Neoptolemus' armies and faced Craterus in battle in the early summer of 321.[32] This battle was militarily inconclusive. The two phalanxes failed to engage (it would have pitted Macedonian against Macedonian) and the fighting was restricted to the cavalry on the wings. Here the great casualty was Craterus who died heroically; Eumenes on the other wing killed his bitter enemy Neoptolemus in single combat and routed his cavalry. The defeated force remained together, and Eumenes did not risk attacking its infantry.

[30] The consensus of the sources is that the body of Alexander was originally intended to be buried at Siwah (Diod. 18.3.5; Curt. 10.5.4; Just. 12.15.7; 13.4.6). If Pausanias (1.6.3) is correct, Arrhidaeus was instructed to take the body to the Macedonian capital of Aegae. That might have been a decision made through mutual consultation by Perdiccas, Craterus, and Antipater in the year after the king's death. In that case Perdiccas would have been unwilling to let the body pass into the control of Antipater and Craterus once hostilities had broken out, and he would have been eager to intercept it and dispose of it at his leisure after he had won the war.

[31] Arr. *Succ.* F 1.25, 24,1; Diod. 18.28.2–5; Strabo 17.1.8 (794); Parian Marble, *FGrH* 239 B 11. See in particular Badian, *HSCP* 72 (1967) 185–9; Seibert, *Untersuchungen* 96–102, 110–12.

[32] On this campaign see Ch. 3, pp. 81, 84–5.

The troops agreed to an armistice, but then withdrew by
night and joined Antipater, who had gone ahead to Cilicia.
Meanwhile there had been a resolution of the crisis. Perdiccas'
invasion had misfired, like so many previous invasions of
Egypt. He failed to break the coastal defences at Pelusium,
and he sustained an unacceptable number of casualties when
he attempted to cross the Nile near Memphis.[33] Alienated by
his autocratic savagery,[34] his chief lieutenants, notably Peithon
and Seleucus, conspired to kill him, and the war in Egypt
ended.

Ptolemy immediately entered the enemy camp and made
his peace. Subsequently a council of senior officers resolved
to appoint two regents in place of Perdiccas, and the choice
fell on Peithon and Arrhidaeus.[35] The murderer of Perdiccas
and the organizer of Alexander's cortège were associated
in the care of the kings, and, given equal power, each would
be a check on the other's ambitions. Ptolemy remained in
Egypt, in all probability with a contingent of Macedonians
to strengthen his satrapal forces. At the same time the army
passed a sentence of death on the most prominent members
of Perdiccas' faction. Those who had turned against him
were of course exempt, but Eumenes was condemned, as
were Alcetas in Pisidia and Attalus, who commanded the
Perdiccan fleet, still intact after the Egyptian campaign.[36]
In all some fifty Macedonians were sentenced, mostly in
absentia, and between them they controlled a significant
armament. It would not be easy to suppress them. And there
was an additional factor, Antipater. The commanders at
Memphis had acted independently of him, just as Perdiccas
had done at Babylon, and there was no guarantee that he

---

[33] The campaign is vividly described by Diodorus (18.33.1–35.6), on which see
Seibert, *Untersuchungen* 114–28. What particularly incensed Perdiccas' troops was
the needless losses by drowning and crocodile attacks (36.2–3).

[34] This is attested by Arr. *Succ.* F 1.28 and Diod. 18.33.3. It is a stereotype, contrasting with Ptolemy's magananimity and moderation, but there is likely to be
some truth behind the contrast of characters.

[35] According to Diod. 18.36.6 Ptolemy might have been given the regency but
did not canvass it. There is no hint of this in Arrian's parallel account of the
meeting (*Succ.* F 1.29–30).

[36] Arr. *Succ.* 1.30; Diod. 18.37.2–4: Plut. *Eum.* 8.1–4; Nep. *Eum.* 5.1; Just.
13.8.10.

would accept the new dispensation. He had a united army, little weaker than when it crossed the Hellespont and without doubt containing more Macedonians than the army in Egypt. There is no record of his reaction to the new regents, but he certainly held aloof for some time, maintaining his army in the natural fortress of Cilicia, exactly as Craterus had done in 323.[37]

Meanwhile the royal army, with two regents, two kings and a queen, moved north from Memphis and continued up the Syrian coast to the great triple game park named Triparadeisus, near the sources of the River Orontes, to the north of the Bekaa Valley.[38] Antipater had been summoned to court, as had Antigonus, who had been operating in Cyprus, but neither, it seems, had arrived when the army reached Triparadeisus. By then the royal army had become a mutinous rabble. The Macedonians, particularly the élite Silver Shields, demanded the donatives which Alexander had promised them at Opis, long ago in 324, and their truculent mood was exacerbated by Queen Eurydice who agitated against the regents and demanded to share the decision-making with them.[39] Antipater now appeared with his army. He was evidently well aware of the situation at court, and entered the stage when it had become uncontrollable. Even before he arrived, he had been proclaimed regent by the troops after Peithon and Arrhidaeus had abdicated. On arrival he pitched camp on the bank of the Orontes opposite to the royal army, and attempted to restore order. However, he faced the determined opposition of Eurydice who stirred up the royal troops to fresh demands. Their mood was hardly sweetened by the appearance of Craterus' veterans who had already been handsomely rewarded. Accordingly

[37] This delay is not explicitly attested, but it must have occurred. At the time of Craterus' death in Asia Minor Antipater was well on his way to Cilicia (Diod. 18.29.7, 33.1). After the new regents were appointed, Antipater was summoned to the kings, but when the royal party reached Triparadeisus, it was still some days before he arrived in camp (Diod. 18.39.3). The royal army had at least three times the distance to cover from Memphis. Antipater was certainly not hurrying to meet it.

[38] Strabo 16.2.19 (756). It is usually assumed that Strabo's Paradeisus is the same as Diodorus' Triparadeisus. So R. Dussaud, *Topographie historique de la Syrie antique et médiévale* 112, accepted in the new Barrington Atlas.

[39] Arr. *Succ*. F 1.31–2; Diod. 18.39.3. See further Ch. 3, p. 87.

Antipater was nearly lynched when he tried to address the mutinous troops of the royal army and was only saved by the intervention of Antigonus and Seleucus (who had commanded the Silver Shields under Alexander). What happened next is obscure. It is attested that Antipater was able to calm the unrest and intimidate Eurydice, and it is most likely that he threatened to use his army, which was comparatively fresh, against the mutineers. The tension must have recalled the crisis at Babylon when infantry and cavalry came close to open hostility. At Triparadeisus the threat was enough, and Antipater was acclaimed regent a second time by both armies. Now his powers had a legitimacy that Perdiccas could never claim, endorsed as they were by practically all the Macedonians under arms.

Like Perdiccas, Antipater supervised another distribution of satrapies. There were few surprises. Most satraps, particularly in the east, were confirmed in office. Otherwise the adherents of Craterus or murderers of Perdiccas were rewarded. The previous regents received strategic areas: Arrhidaeus succeeded Leonnatus in Hellespontine Phrygia, while Peithon was assigned to his former satrapy of Media, probably with an overriding command in the Iranian highlands.[40] Elsewhere Seleucus received Babylonia, the nucleus of his future kingdom; Craterus' admiral, Cleitus, replaced Menander in Lydia, while the king's brother, Amphimachus, was appointed to Mesopotamia.[41] The military arrangements are interesting. Antipater clearly wished to be separated from the mutineers who had threatened his life, and transferred the 3,000 Silver Shields to Susa, where they were to relocate the royal treasury to the coast. The war against the Perdiccan forces in Asia Minor was assigned to Antigonus, who, as satrap of Phrygia, was most strategically placed for the campaign, and he was given charge of the rest of the royal army, which now predominantly comprised non-Macedonian troops. The position of chiliarch was retained, and Antipater named Cassander in place of Seleucus, to command the élite cavalry

[40] Diod. 19.14.1. See Ch. 4, n. 27.
[41] Arr. *Succ.* F 1.35; Diod. 18.39.6. See Ch. 4, pp. 113–14.

squadron and be head of protocol at court.[42] The regent retained his own army, and along with the kings he accompanied Antigonus into Asia Minor. The year was now 320, and events at Triparadeisus had been fatefully protracted. The outlawed commanders in Asia Minor had been given time to consolidate and recruit local forces. There were two foci. In Pisidia Alcetas attracted a number of refugees from the east. The most important was Perdiccas' admiral and brother-in-law, Attalus, who brought his fleet from Egypt via Tyre, which he turned into a bastion against the new regime, and brought a considerable army to Pisidia to reinforce Alcetas. From Babylon Docimus, appointed satrap by Perdiccas, made his way to Asia Minor, and by the end of the year he was operating in Alcetas' camp.[43] Eumenes meanwhile had consolidated his own army, strengthening the loyalty of the Macedonians he had acquired from Neoptolemus and the formidable contingent of Cappadocian cavalry that he had levied in 322. Unfortunately for him, Alcetas and his fellow Macedonian commanders refused to co-operate, out of jealousy for his success, and the two groups fought separately against the royal armies. Even so, Eumenes was no easy target. For the latter part of 320 he held his own against Antipater and Antigonus. He began operations in Lydia, in close contact with Cleopatra, but then moved to occupy Phrygia, outmanœuvring Antipater and Antigonus, and the winter of 320/19 saw him in Antigonus' capital, Celaenae.[44] This campaign is very poorly attested and difficult to follow, but it is clear that there was some discord between Antipater and Antigonus. Antipater's military performance was dismal; during the winter Eumenes was able to plunder localities supposedly under his protection without his intervening. The troops were not impressed, and the Macedonian veterans had little stomach for fighting their old comrades serving under Eumenes. Some 3,000 of them

---

[42] Arr. *Succ.* F 1.38. The chiliarchy was renewed the following year at Antipater's deathbed (Diod. 18.48.4–5; Plut. *Phoc.* 31.1).

[43] Arr. *Succ.* F 24.3–5; Plut. *Eum.* 8.8; Diod. 18.45.3. See also the Göteborg palimpsest (Ch. 3, p. 88). Cf. Billows, *Antigonos* 382–3, no. 35.

[44] Plut. *Eum.* 8.7. I have attempted to reconstruct this campaign in my essay 'History and Artifice' 56–89.

deserted, and forced their repatriation to Macedonia.[45]
Added to that there was discord between Cassander and
Antigonus, which was resolved by Antipater's decision to
withdraw to Macedon with the kings and leave the campaign
in Asia Minor exclusively with Antigonus. For that he gave
him the bulk of the army which had crossed with him into
Asia, no less than 8,500 Macedonian infantry and half the
cavalry and elephants.

Together with the remnants of the royal army which fell
under his command at Triparadeisus, these forces gave
Antigonus an overwhelming superiority over both the enemy
camps. For all his tactical genius Eumenes was forced into
two battles early in 319, and lost most of his army by death
or desertion. By the end of spring he was undergoing siege in
the fortress of Nora, in southern Cappadocia, and capitulation was only a matter of time. The defeat of Alcetas followed,
as Antigonus stormed west into Pisidia and overwhelmed the
modest army there. Alcetas fled to Termessus, where he was
eventually killed and his body surrendered to Antigonus; his
lieutenants were for the most part taken alive and sent to close
confinement in a mountain fortress in the Taurus.

By the summer of 319 Antigonus was by far the most powerful figure east of Macedonia, with an army that comprised
most Macedonian troops who were serving in Asia. It is
hardly surprising that the sources allege he already had
designs on supremacy, for in military terms he was already
supreme.[46] Antipater had virtually abandoned Asia, now
that he was back in Pella with the kings in his power, and he
had returned weakened from the chequered campaign he had
fought. By the autumn of 319 he was dead, and before his
death he had nominated his friend Polyperchon to succeed him
as regent, passing over his own son, Cassander, who remained
chiliarch. It was a controversial decision, bitterly resented
by Cassander, and within a few months he had fled from
Macedonia, taking refuge with Antigonus, who was happy
enough to support his feud with Polyperchon. Antigonus himself deployed his massive army to expel Arrhidaeus from

[45] Polyaen. 4.6.6. See Ch. 3, p. 90.
[46] See Diod. 18.41.4–5, 47.5, 50.2; Plut. *Eum.* 12.1.

Hellespontine Phrygia and Cleitus from Lydia. This he achieved in the summer of 318. Since Caria was in the hands of his friend and ally Asander, he effectively controlled Asia Minor from the Hellespont to the Cilician Gates. He had the resources to invade Europe, and the pretext to do so in the person of Cassander. Eumenes had become an irrelevant nuisance, and Antigonus came to terms with him at Nora, releasing him from the siege in return for acknowledgement of his supremacy. As a free agent, Eumenes was open to offers of employment from early 318, and he was approached by Polyperchon to act as royal general and to take command of the Silver Shields. Three distinct theatres of war were now developing: Polyperchon was espousing the cause of democracy and attempting to remove the oligarchies in southern Greece that remained loyal to Cassander; in Asia Antigonus was occupied by land and sea in the Propontis and Lydia; and Eumenes was gathering forces in Cappadocia.

Here we may leave this outline sketch. The scene is set for the more detailed discussion in the central chapters of the book, which amount to a history of the period between 318 and 311. The epic duel between Antigonus and Eumenes is treated at length in Chapter 4, and the story is taken further in Chapter 6, which covers events between 316 and 311, when Seleucus established his regime in Babylon.

3. THE BASES OF KNOWLEDGE

The two decades after Alexander's death are comparatively rich in source material. There is a moderate scatter of documentary evidence. A number of important Greek inscriptions shed light on the relations between the city-states and the ruling dynasts; Athens supplies a rich crop, increasing in volume after the restoration of (limited) democracy in 307. From Babylonia we have a considerable number of cuneiform documents, most of them economic,[47] and the archives have

---

[47] The documents (other than the financial texts) are conveniently assembled and edited with translation and commentary by G. F. Del Monte, *Testi dalla Babilonia Ellenistica* I. See now the very useful doctoral thesis by Tom Boiy, 'Laatachaemenidisch en hellenistisch Babylon' (Katholieke Universiteit, Leuven 2000) esp. 128–38.

yet to be systematically explored. However, even in our present incomplete state of knowledge, the complex dating system under the regnal years of Philip III, Antigonus, Alexander IV, and Seleucus has recently been elucidated. Egypt has been less fruitful, with a comparative dearth of material from the early Ptolemaic period, but there is at least one document of prime importance, the so-called stele of the satrap.[48] Documentation of a different kind is provided by the coins. Increasing hoard evidence is refining our knowledge of the dating and distribution of the multifarious royal emissions.

These individual pieces of evidence shed single beams of light. They need to be set in a chronological and contextual framework, which is a feasible prospect. The sequence of rulers and regnal years is relatively well established. There are several king lists from Babylonia, which cohere with the lists compiled much later by Porphyry of Tyre and incorporated in Eusebius' Chronicle.[49] Other chronicles give year by year records of events. From the Greek side the most important is the Parian Marble, which contains a year by year account of key events, dated by the archon at Athens.[50] The stone itself is mutilated, and the notes are laconic, but it does give the main events between 323 and 302/1. It was compiled in 264/3, only half a century after the events, but its accuracy is distinctly variable, thanks in part to the difficulty of adapting the calendar and campaign year to the Athenian archon year, which began in midsummer. Events can be dated a year too late. From Babylonia comes a very different document,

[48] See Ch. 6, pp. 241–2.

[49] The principal Babylonian documents are the Uruk king list (BaM Beih. II 88 = Del Monte 207), a list from Babylon (*Iraq* 16, pl. 53 = Del Monte 208–9) and the so-called Saros Canon (*ZA* 10 66–7 = *LBAT* 1428). The relevant fragments of Porphyry are most easily consulted in *FGrH* 240 F 2 (1–2), 3 (1–9). They come from the Armenian version of Eusebius' *Chronicle* (on the text and its history see A. A. Mosshammer, *The* Chronicle *of Eusebius and Greek Chronographic Tradition* (London 1979) 41–65); Jacoby uses the German translation of Josef Karst (Mosshammer 58–60).

[50] The most convenient text is that of Jacoby, in *FGrH* 239: translations with brief annotation are to be found in M. M. Austin, *The Hellenistic World from Alexander to the Roman Conquest* (Cambridge 1981) 8–9, 39–41 and Phillip Harding, *From the End of the Peloponnesian War to the Battle of Ipsus* (Cambridge 1985) 1–6.

the so-called Chronicle of the Successors.[51] This is contained on a fragmentary cuneiform tablet now in the British Museum, and lists events between the fourth year of Philip III (320/19) and the eighth year of Alexander IV (309/8). Like the Parian Marble this is a fragmentary text, and its interpretation is extraordinarily difficult. Much of the detail concerns internal events in Babylon, for which the Chronicle provides the only evidence, and the references to events in the west are brief and enigmatic. The tablet becomes more informative on the reverse, which deals with the period between 311 and the late summer of 309. Between these dates the tablet documents a major war in Babylonia between Antigonus and Seleucus which has left practically no trace in the Greek tradition,[52] a melancholy indication of how defective our historical knowledge must be.

The contextual framework for these years is provided by the narrative histories of the period. Of these by far the most important are Books 18–20 of Diodorus Siculus. These give a continuous record of events from the death of Alexander to the eve of the Battle of Ipsus at the end of the archon year 302/1. Book 18 is unusually expansive and cohesive. It deals with the period between 323 and 318, and is devoted entirely to events in Greece and the east; there is no reference to Sicilian affairs, which only resume in book 19 with Agathocles' rise to power in Syracuse. From that point the narrative regularly switches from west to east, as is the case elsewhere in Diodorus, but in the separate theatres of action his narrative remains detailed and lucid.[53] It is universally acknowledged that these books are a high point for Diodorus. They contrast with the rhetorical, sensational treatment of Alexander's reign in Book 17, and present a wealth of detail: troop numbers and dispositions, satrapal appointments,

---

[51] BM 36313 + 34660, first published by Sidney Smith, *Babylonian Historical Texts* (London 1924) 124–49. The standard edition is at present A. K. Grayson, *Assyrian and Babylonian Chronicles* (Locust Valley, NY 1975) 115–19, no. 10. Del Monte 183–94 gives an improved text, taking account of the join made by I. L. Finkel. Cornelia Wunsch has been working on a new edition of the text, which I trust she will publish, and I have made use of some of her readings.

[52] See Ch. 6, pp. 217–18, 244–5.

[53] This is rightly emphasized by Jane Hornblower, *Hieronymus,* especially 32–9, a section entitled 'The homogeneity of Books XVIII–XX'.

political events in Athens and elsewhere. Documents are quoted, such as the text of Alexander's Exiles Decree or Polyperchon's edict of 318, authorizing a second restoration.[54] Above all there is constant discussion of the motives of the leading dynasts, and the narrative is noticeably written from a court perspective.

For the years between 323 and 319 Diodorus is supplemented by the remains of the history of the Successors written by L. Flavius Arrianus (Arrian). The author is best known for his extant History of Alexander, but he also wrote a much more expansive account of events after Alexander's death (τὰ μετὰ ᾿Αλέξανδρον) which devoted no less than ten books to the five years after Alexander. This history has survived through the precis of Photius, who gave a very patchy sketch of its contents, ranging from almost verbatim reproduction to the most extreme contraction. Some fragmentary pieces of the original have survived on papyrus and palimpsest, and the wealth of detail is staggering, the few mutilated extracts providing us with a mass of uniquely attested material.[55] This was a complex work, which, if the Alexander history is any guide, is likely to have been taken from a number of selected sources and embellished by highly rhetorical speeches as well as extensive moralizing digressions. However, it is clear that Arrian shared material with Diodorus and there is a very considerable overlap between their narratives, most clearly revealed in their accounts of the distributions at Triparadeisus which contain the same names in the same order and with much the same explanatory material.[56] Both clearly followed a common source extremely faithfully.

[54] K. Rosen, *Acta Classica* 10 (1967) 41–94, listed over seventy references to documents in these books. See also Hornblower, *Hieronymus* 37–9, 131–7.

[55] The standard edition is the Teubner text of A. G. Roos, *Flavius Arrianus II: Scripta Minora et Fragmenta* (2nd edn. rev. Gerhard Wirth: Stuttgart 1967) 253–86. It contains the Vatican palimpsest fragments (F 24–5) with Roos' personal readings, and Wirth adds a full text of the Florentine papyrus (*PSI* XII no. 1284) at pp. 323–4. Jacoby, *FGrH* 156 also prints the fragments known to 1926, but excludes many that are not explicitly attributed to Arrian. The best edition (with photographs) of the new Göteborg palimpsest is provided by B. Dreyer, *ZPE* 125 (1999) 39–66. A. Simonetti Agostinetti, *Flavio Arriano: gli eventi dopo Alessandro* provides text, translation, and brief commentary. There is an English translation with patchy commentary by Walter J. Goralski, *AncW* 19 (1989) 81–108.

[56] Arr. *Succ.* F 1.34–8; Diod. 18.39.5–7.

Alongside Photius' epitome of Arrian we have his brief digest of the four-book history of events after Alexander by P. Herennius Dexippus, which was written about a century after Arrian and (according to Photius) was largely in agreement with him. Apart from some fragments of rhetoric which seem Thucydidean pastiches we only have Photius' reproduction of his list of appointments at Babylon, which follows Arrian with some errors and variants.[57] A more extended epitome is Justin's digest of the *Philippic History* of Pompeius Trogus, which was written in the Augustan period.[58] Out of the 44 books of Trogus' work three (13–15) covered the period between the deaths of Alexander and Cassander (323–297), and they clearly contained much of value, in particular an account of the origins of the Mauryan dynasty in India. However, Justin is as capricious an epitomator as Photius and tends to be at his fullest when the material is most sensational. The greater part of Trogus is lost, and much that Justin digests is contracted to the point of unintelligibility; but when he is more expansive, as in his account of events in Babylon, he can be a valuable supplement. Finally in this category there is the so-called Heidelberg Epitome, an anonymous work in a late mediaeval manuscript, which deals with the succession of guardians after Alexander's death and gives a sketchy account of the early wars.[59] It has affinities with Diodorus, but it rarely adds anything to our knowledge.

We also possess various biographies. The most important are Plutarch's *Lives*, the *Eumenes*, *Demetrius* and *Pyrrhus*. It is the first two that concern us in this book.[60] Both give very

---

[57] The fragments can be found in Jacoby, *FGrH* 100 F 8. 31–6. Roos 253–8 prints Photius' digests of Dexippus and Arrian in parallel columns.

[58] On Trogus' life and work see now J. C. Yardley and Waldemar Heckel, *Justin. Epitome of the* Philippic History *of Pompeius Trogus* Books 11–12 1–41. A continuation dealing with Books 13–15 is forthcoming (there is already a commentary in Dutch by R. N. M. Boersma, *Justinus' boeken over de Diadochen, een historisch commentar* (Amsterdam 1979)). Yardley has published a fine translation of the whole of Justin, with introduction and explanatory notes by R. Develin (APA Classical Resources Series, no. 3: Atlanta, Ga. 1994).

[59] The text is most conveniently found in Jacoby, *FGrH* 155. For literature see Seibert, *Das Zeitalter der Diadochen* 53–4.

[60] The *Eumenes* as yet has no commentary (see, however, Bosworth, 'History and Artifice'). There are annotated editions of the *Demetrius* by E. Manni (Florence 1953) and O. Andrei (Milan 1988).

detailed pictures of their subject, richly embellished by anecdote. But they can hardly be termed works of history. They are carefully patterned to compare and contrast with their parallel Roman *Lives*: Eumenes is the counterpart of Sertorius, the strategically gifted exile who was betrayed by his own men, while Demetrius is set alongside Antony as the paradigm of brilliant promise undermined by arrogance and self-indulgence.[61] Plutarch clearly deploys a range of sources for illustrative material and has no hesitation in adapting their content to conform with his portrait. He also omits major events if he does not consider them germane to his biography; the great battle of Paraetacene is passed over altogether and Demetrius' victory at Salamis is contracted to a single sentence—it is the capture of his mistress Lamia and the assumption of the royal diadem that engages his interest.[62] However, for all the embroidery it is apparent that Plutarch operates with much of the material that is used by Diodorus. In the *Eumenes* especially, the two accounts often run parallel, and there are verbal correspondences which cannot be fortuitous.[63]

The extant historical sources display a pattern comparable to the so-called 'Alexander Vulgate'. That is a convenient label for the common material found in large segments of Diodorus 17, Curtius Rufus, Justin and Plutarch's *Alexander*, which is most plausibly ascribed to Cleitarchus of Alexander.[64] There is a similar phenomenon in the histories of the Successors. There is a good deal of material common to Diodorus, the remains of Arrian, Plutarch, Justin, and the Heidelberg Epitome, and all seem to be drawing on a common source.[65]

---

[61] See Andrei's Introduction, esp. 36–42; C. B. R. Pelling, *Plutarch Antony* 18–26.

[62] *Demetr.* 16.3 (sea battle), 16.4–7 (Lamia), 17.2–18.1 (assumption of diadem).

[63] For examples see Ch. 4, nn. 185, 196. The most famous is probably the remarkable statement about the age of the Silver Shields: not a man under 60 and many over 70 (Diod. 19.41.2; Plut. *Eum.* 16.7; cf. Hornblower, *Hieronymus* 192–3).

[64] For a short explanation of the 'Vulgate' see Bosworth in *Al. in Fact and Fiction* 6–8.

[65] On Diodorus and and the extent of his usage of Hieronymus the fundamental text is now Hornblower, *Hieronymus*, in particular 18–75, 263–79, which is indebted to (but supersedes). Felix Jacoby's classic treatment in Pauly–Wissowa (*RE* viii 1540–61 = *Griechische Historiker* (Stuttgart 1956) 245–56). See also the shorter, somewhat sceptical discussion by Paul Goukowsky in the introduction

That source is almost universally identified as Hieronymus of Cardia, the friend, fellow citizen, and possibly relative of the great Eumenes.[66] As it happens, our knowledge of Hieronymus' career is mostly known from Diodorus, who refers four times to crucial episodes in his career, and on each occasion refers to him as 'the author of the Histories'.[67] What is more, the references occur within the historical narrative, and it is difficult to evade the conclusion that Diodorus is preserving autobiographical material provided by his primary source, which he then identifies as the historian. Hieronymus, moreover, played a fairly central role in events. He negotiated with both Antipater and Antigonus to procure Eumenes' release from Nora: he was wounded and captured at the Battle of Gabiene, taken into Antigonus' entourage, and supervised the harvesting of bitumen in the Dead Sea with dubious success. Later, in 293, he served as harmost of Thebes for Demetrius, and had close relations with his son, Antigonus Gonatas. He lived, it is attested, to the grand old age of 104, retaining all his faculties and his health until the last.[68] His history may have been as long as his life; at least the sophisticated Dionysius of Halicarnassus opined that, given its inferior style, no one could bear to read it to the end.[69] It certainly covered a vast span, from (it seems) the

(pp. xx–xxiv) of his Budé edition of Diodorus 18 (Paris 1978), and K. Meister, *Die griechische Geschichtsschreibung von den Anfängen bis zum Ende des Hellenismus* 124–6.

[66] This was denied by F. Landucci Gattinoni, *Invigilata Lucernis* 3–4 (1981–2) 13–26, on the grounds that the frank treatment of the ambitions of Antigonus the One-Eyed would not have been palatable to his grandson, Gonatas, who was Hieronymus' patron at the time he published his history. On this see Hornblower, *Hieronymus* 170–1, arguing (after T. S. Brown, *American Historical Review* 52 (1947) 694–5) that Gonatas may have shared his grandfather's aspirations but disapproved of his obsessive *pleonexia*; and so 'Hieronymus censured in Monophthalmus not his objectives but his methods.'

[67] Diod. 18.42.1, 50.4; 19.44.3, 100.1–3 = *FGrH* 154 T 3–6. The model was probably Thucydides, who identified himself at Amphipolis as the author of the history (Thuc. 4.104.4: ὃς τόδε ξυνέγραψε). Landucci Gattinoni (above, n. 66) 15–17 denies that first three passages came from Hieronymus himself, on the ground that they depict him in at best an ambiguous light. He is certainly said to have taken money from Antigonus to open negotiations with Antigonus (Diod. 18.50.4), but the gifts may have been represented as a mark of Antigonus' esteem: there is no hint that Hieronymus had deserted Eumenes at this stage.

[68] [Luc.] *Macr.* 22, on the authority of Agatharchides of Cnidus (*FGrH* 86 F 4).

[69] Dion. Hal. *De comp. verb.* 4, line 112 (Usener and Radermacher) = *FGrH* 154 T 12. Hieronymus is one of a very numerous crop of historians indicted for their

death of Alexander[70] to at least the death of Pyrrhus 50 years later, in 272. This was contemporary history, written by a major actor in events who served with Eumenes until his death and then lived in the court of successive Antigonid monarchs, incurring criticism for his excessively favourable treatment of Gonatas.[71] It is by far the most likely hypothesis that he provided Diodorus with the bulk of his material for events outside Sicily and Italy in Books 18–20, and his intimate contact with the rulers of the day explains the mass of detail and the court perspective. Presumably Hieronymus, like Thucydides, collected information on events as they happened and was involved in historical activity, if not its literary shaping, throughout his adult life, and was as close to the defining events and the principal actors in them as any historian of antiquity. His work was politically and militarily informative, and it also contained a rich spectrum of digressions, geographical, antiquarian and ethnographical. It was not free from bias, and perhaps, like all great histories, it contained a subtle subtext, insinuating the author's political and moral attitudes into the primary narrative.[72]

Diodorus cannot be treated as a reflecting mirror of Hieronymus.[73] He need not be using Hieronymus exclusively. Some passages of his narrative are so complimentary to Ptolemy that it has been argued that he turned on occasion to an encomiastic writer in the Ptolemaic entourage, and there is a recent suggestion that he also drew on an encomium of Eumenes quite separate from Hieronymus.[74] Even when he

---

miserable diction and including such diverse figures as Phylarchus and his principal critic, Polybius.

[70] Richard Billows has recently argued that there was an introductory section, giving a coverage of Alexander's reign, 'no doubt fuller for the later years' (*Al. in Fact and Fiction* 300–5).

[71] Paus. 1.9.8 = *FGrH* 154 F 9: Hieronymus 'has the reputation' (ἔχει δόξαν) of hostility to other kings and of unjustly favouring Gonatas. Cf. Hornblower, *Hieronymus* 246–8.   [72] I explore this topic fully in Ch. 5.

[73] On his techniques and his personal contribution see Kenneth S. Sacks, in Simon Hornblower (ed.), *Greek Historiography* 213–32.

[74] On the hypothesized Ptolemaic source see R. Schubert, *Die Quellen zur Geschichte der Diadochenzeit* 184–7; Seibert, *Untersuchungen* 82–3; Hornblower, *Hieronymus* 50–6. A Rhodian source has also been posited: Hiller von Gaertringen, *SBBerlin* 36 (1918) 752–62; Hornblower, *Hieronymus* 56–60, 280–1. For the encomiastic biography of Eumenes see R. A. Hadley, *Historia* 50 (2001) 3–33. In

resumes Hieronymus directly, his choice of material can be capricious. His narrative may become excessively contracted, an inevitable danger when boiling down a much longer work; one need only compare the detail in the palimpsest remains of Arrian's *History of the Successors*. There are also startling omissions, almost a whole year of action, for instance, after the conference at Triparadeisus, and events may be reported out of context, like the single enigmatic sentence on the naval engagements of the Lamian War which comes in without any report of the preceding campaign and ignores the sequel.[75] None the less, when we can compare his narrative with other sources, he appears to have been conscientious in repeating the substance of what he chooses to excerpt. As a result Hieronymus has come down to us as a far more rounded figure than any other historian of the period, and we know infinitely more about his work than any other attested history of the Successors.

Historians other than Hieronymus are on record and were certainly used by some of out extant sources, but it is almost impossible to track down more than the occasional indirect citation. Duris of Samos is known to have written a universal history beginning in 370/69 with the death of Amyntas III of Macedon and continuing until the death of Lysimachus.[76] Athenaeus used him as a source of exotic detail like the personal habits of Demetrius of Phalerum or the famous Athenian ithyphallic which hymns the godhead of Demetrius.[77] Plutarch refers to him in a number of *Lives*, including the *Eumenes*,[78] but the bulk of the references come from the Alexander period.[79] There are traces in the

---

contrast, I. L. Merker, *AHB* 2 (1988) 90–3, argues that Diodorus worked directly from Hieronymus alone.

[75] Diod. 18.15.9. On this passage see my discussion in my article cited above, n. 20.

[76] Diod. 15.60.6 = *FGrH* 76 T 5. On the work of Duris see (in brief) Meister (above, n. 55) 96–100. There are monographs by R. B. Kebric, *In the Shadow of Macedon: Duris of Samos* and L. Torraca, *Duride di Samo La maschera scenica nella storiografia ellenistica*. [77] Athen. 12. 542 B–E = *FGrH* 76 F 10; Athen. 6.253 D–F.

[78] *Eum.* 1.1 (paternity of Eumenes) = *FGrH* 76 F 53. F 50–1 come from the *Phocion*.

[79] It has recently been argued that Duris along with Cleitarchus was a primary source for Diodorus 17 (L. Prandi, *Fortuna e realtà dell'opera di Clitarco* 125–6, 138–40. It has often been maintained that Duris' work, including his monograph on Agathocles (F 16–21, 56–9) was the source of much of the Sicilian history in Diodorus 19–20.

Demetrius,[80] but one can hardly prove that he was a major source for Plutarch. His use of sources is so eclectic that without a control it is impossible to track down material that is not explicitly identified. Duris, we feel, must have made an impact on the extant tradition, but we have no way of defining it. The same may be said of the Athenian historians Diyllus and Demochares. Diyllus is known to have written a general history of the period 356 to 297,[81] and the 26 books of it must have given a generous coverage of the generation after Alexander's death. As for Demochares, the nephew of Demosthenes, it is known that he wrote a general history which dealt with Demetrius' second regime at Athens (294–288) in Books 20–21.[82] Polybius attests that he was bitterly hostile to Demetrius of Phalerum, and Athenaeus details his criticism of the honours offered to Demetrius the Besieger. But that is the almost the sum of it.[83] Our knowledge of the period from Alexander's death down to Ipsus comes predominantly from Hieronymus, as digested by Diodorus. Our debt to him becomes apparent when we look at the period after 301 when we know his work only from sparse extracts. The half-light of Books 18–20 fades into almost total eclipse, and what knowledge we have is based on Plutarch, Justin, and Pausanias supplemented by considerable but capricious inscriptional evidence. If we have any sort of history of the years after Alexander (and many other periods), we owe it to Diodorus, who has arguably contributed more to our knowledge than any historian of antiquity.

---

[80] See Ch. 5, n. 132.

[81] Diod. 16.14.5, 76.6, 21.5 (*FGrH* 73 T 1–3). Only three fragments of Diyllus survive and give no hint of the character of his work. The fact that Diodorus records most of what we know of it encouraged Hammond to identify Diyllus as a major source for Diodorus' narrative of Alexander (*Three Historians of Alexander the Great*, esp. 160–5).

[82] We do not know the dimensions of the work. Not surprisingly, Demochares dealt with the death of his uncle in 322 (Plut. *Dem.* 30.4 = *FGrH* 75 F 3), and he treated the events of 291 in Book 21 (Athen. 6.253 B–D = F2). It reached at least to the death of Agathocles ([Luc.] *Macr.* 10 = F 5).

[83] There is little point pursuing even more shadowy figures such as Nymphis of Heraclea (*FGrH* 153), who is alleged to have written an extensive (22-book) history of Alexander, the Diadochi and the Epigoni ('Suda' s.v. Νύμφις = T 1). Of this only one dubious fragment survives (Ael. *NA* 17.3 = F 17), discoursing upon the mammoth vipers and tortoises in the land of the Troglodytes.

2

The Politics of the Babylon Settlement

No previous event in Macedonian history was anything like the Babylon Settlement.[1] There had been succession crises aplenty, but all had been significantly different. Reigning kings had left living sons. They may have been immature boys (like Archelaus' son, Orestes),[2] but at least they were there—as usually was a plethora of males of the Argead house. The problems had arisen from an oversupply of potential kings.[3] What is more, the succession to the throne had been played out within the boundaries of Macedon, in the traditional heartland of the kingdom. Alexander himself had come to power in the old capital of Aegae, with the entire nobility around him and the armed forces united in Macedonia. His accession may have been bloody, but the circumstances did not favour a protracted crisis. Rivals and potential rivals who were close at hand were quickly eliminated,[4] and he was able to achieve recognition in Macedon and stamp his authority on the League of Corinth within a

[1] The older bibliography is summarized in J. Seibert, *Das Zeitalter der Diadochen* 84–9. The most useful items are: R. M. Errington, *JHS* 90 (1970) 49–77; Schachermeyr, *Al. in Babylon*. Newer contributions include: Billows, *Antigonos* esp. 49–59; A. B. Bosworth, *CQ* 43 (1993) 420–7; R. M. Errington, *A History of Macedonia* 114–29; N. G. L. Hammond, *The Macedonian State* 237–43; see also *HM* iii.98–107; R. M. Martin, *AJAH* 8 (1983 [1987]) 161–90; E. M. Anson, *CPh* 87 (1992) 38–43; P. McKechnie, *Historia* 48 (1999) 44–60.

[2] Diod. 14.37.6 (παῖς ὤν); he was promptly murdered by his guardian, Aeropus.

[3] Amyntas III, for instance, left three sons by his wife Eurydice, and three more by a second wife, Gygaea. All three sons by Eurydice were to reign in their own right: one of the sons of Gygaea was executed by Philip II and the other two fled to Olynthus (Just. 8.3.10; cf. J. R. Ellis, *Historia* 22 (1973) 350–4; G. T. Griffith in *HM* ii.699–701). There were other Argeads in contention (Argaeus and Pausanias), who emerged to challenge Philip II in the tumultuous year after his accession (*HM* ii.208).

[4] These included his cousin, Amyntas son of Perdiccas, and two Lyncestian princes (cf. Arr. 1.25.1–2; Curt. 7.1.5–6; Just. 11.2.1–3). For background see Bosworth, *Conquest and Empire* 25–8: Badian, in *Al. in Fact and Fiction* 54–6.

matter of weeks. The only serious problem of distance involved the expeditionary force in Asia Minor. Alexander had to resort to the diplomacy of treachery to dispose of his chief enemy, Attalus.[5] In 323 those problems must have seemed insignificant. There was no direct issue to the deceased king. His wife was six (or eight) months pregnant.[6] There was no guarantee that the offspring would be male, still less that it would survive and thrive. An object lesson had already been given late in 326 when a son born to Rhoxane had died shortly after birth,[7] and, given the prevailing infant mortality, few people would have had any confidence that the pregnancy would result in a healthy male child. There remained Alexander's surviving son, Heracles, but he was not regarded as a legitimate heir, given that his mother, Barsine, was never more than a royal concubine.[8] The only other Argead in contention was the surviving son of Philip II, Arrhidaeus, but his attested psychiatric disorder meant that he could never rule as a king in his own right.[9]

The paucity of acceptable Argeads was exacerbated by problems of distance. When Alexander died, his court was

[5] Diod. 17.2.4–6, 5.2; Curt. 7.1.3. Alexander's agent, Hecataeus, colluded with Attalus' fellow general and father-in-law, the great Parmenion.

[6] Curt. 10.6.9 (six months); Just. 13.2.5 (eight months).

[7] *Metz Epit.* 30. This is the only source, but the information is credible enough. See Bosworth, in *Al. in Fact and Fiction* 11–12.

[8] On the status of Barsine see Plut. *Al.* 21.8–9, citing Aristobulus (*FGrH* 139 F 11); *Eum.* 1.7. At Alexander's death she and her son were in residence at Pergamum (Just. 13.2.9; Diod. 20.20.1).

[9] There is no point in attempting a diagnosis (see, most recently, Elizabeth Carney, *AHB* 15 (2001) 63–89, arguing at length that Arrhidaeus suffered 'mild' retardation, requiring intermittent support in social interaction). The ancient sources are vague: Diod. 18.2.2 speaks vaguely of incurable psychiatric disorders, and other sources are no more specific (App. *Syr.* 52.261; Porphyry, *FGrH* 260 F 3.2). The *Heidelberg Epitome* (*FGrH* 155 F 1.2) terms him 'sluggish, and furthermore epileptic'. Justin's reference at 13.2.11 to his 'valetudo maior' has also been interpreted as epilepsy since Freinsheim's day (cf. Apul. *Apol.* 50; Festus 268.14 (Lindsay); Cels. *De med.* 3.23.1)). However, the one description of him in action suggests a disturbance more complex than simple epilepsy (Plut. *Phoc.* 33.5–7), which in itself would have been unlikely to disqualify him from the kingship. Plutarch's allegation (*Al.* 77.8) that Olympias destroyed his mind with drugs falls in the same category of doubt as other anecdotes about malevolent stepmothers, but presupposes serious mental disorder. But Arrhidaeus' psychological condition became the subject of political propaganda (see below, pp. 41 ff.), and that has irredeemably polluted the source tradition. We can no more tell whether he was clinically mad or simply retarded than we can whether Alexander was poisoned.

located in Babylon along with a majority of marshals, including the seven known Bodyguards. But that was not the only
centre of power. In Macedon the regent Antipater administered the kingdom and controlled the armed forces which
remained there. Little or nothing is known of his court and
the figures of influence (other than his numerous sons), but
there must have been a coterie of powerful nobles who had
remained in Macedon throughout the reign, many of them
survivors from Philip's day, and they will have had their
views on the succession. But the most important single
group outside Babylon was based in Cilicia. This was led
by Alexander's senior general, Craterus, the most successful
commander on the staff and phenomenally popular with his
men.[10] With him were over 10,000 veterans destined for
repatriation in Macedonia, who formed the most efficient
fighting force in the empire, superior in numbers at least to
the Macedonian troops left in Babylon.[11] Craterus had
a commission to replace Antipater as regent in Macedonia
and also had written instructions to operate in Cilicia,[12]
where a vast armament was being assembled in anticipation
of Alexander's campaigns in the west; and the necessary
resources had been concentrated in the treasuries of the area,
in particular the fortress of Cyinda.[13] If, then, Craterus had
wished to fight for the kingship (and we are told that he
affected regal dress),[14] he'd got the ships, he'd got the men,
he'd got the money too, not to mention legitimation from the
dead king, if he wished to establish himself in power in
Macedon. He had his lieutenants, a mini-court which could
almost challenge the constellation at Babylon. With him

---

[10] On Craterus' career see Heckel 107–33. His popularity is strikingly attested
(Arr. *Succ.* F 19 = Suda s.v. Κρατερός; Plut. *Eum.* 6.1–3, *Demetr.* 14.2–3). After his
death in 321 his bones were carefully preserved by Eumenes (as a talisman?) and
surrendered to his wife Phila for burial in 315 (Diod. 19.59.3–6).

[11] For the figures and their implications see below, pp. 73–5.

[12] Diod. 18.4.1, 12.1. For discussion see Bosworth, *From Arrian to Alexander*
208–10.

[13] For its history and importance see J. S. Bing, *Historia* 22 (1973) 346–50. Even
after Eumenes had exploited its resources in 318 (Diod. 18.62.2; Strab. 14.5.10
(672)) some 10,000 talents remained for Antigonus in late 316 (Diod. 19.56.5).
Later still Antigonus paid his army for three months out of the money he took from
Cyinda for the campaign of Ipsus (Diod. 20.108.2).

[14] Arr. *Succ.* F 19.

was a senior cavalry commander, Cleitus the White, and at least three commanders of phalanx regiments: Polyperchon, Gorgias and Antigenes.[15] Given this dispersion of commanders, men, and resources it would be fatuous to imagine that any provision for the succession that was made in Babylon would necessarily command assent or would remain unchanged. Why for instance should arrangements brokered at Babylon by Perdiccas and the Bodyguards be thought to be binding in Macedon? They might be approved by the Macedonian forces there, at a pinch, but both Antipater and Craterus had their own Macedonians who might give vocal support to alternative arrangements presented to them. For all we know, they did so. Our evidence is limited to events in Babylon, and nothing has survived of any description of the reception of Alexander's death in either Macedon or Cilicia. As always, we have only a fragment of the jigsaw.

The situation, then, was constitutionally unique and politically complex. In that light it comes as quite a shock to read much of the traditional literature on the Settlement. It presupposes that there was something akin to statute law, with fixed positions and procedures for a regency, and deals with a single definitive settlement, which was reached at Babylon and agreed by all the diverse players in the dynastic game.[16] In fact there was constant intrigue, constant negotiation, and constant compromise. We have evidence for that process within the narrow context of Babylon, and there is every reason to assume that it continued after Perdiccas achieved predominance there. Negotiations would have continued between Perdiccas, Craterus, and Antipater, and they are fairly well attested.[17] We hear of Perdiccas' marital overtures

[15] Arr. 7.11.4; Just. 12.12.8. Justin also mentions a Polydamas, who may well have been the Polydamas responsible for the murder of Parmenion (Berve ii no. 648; Heckel 359–61). Alexander had every reason to be quit of him. There is no record of any senior command that he may have held in the last years of the reign.

[16] See Seibert's bibliography (above, n. 1). The most clear-cut recent defence of 'constitutionalism' is presented by N. G. L. Hammond, in *HM* iii.98–106 (see also *The Macedonian State* 237–43). I have studied the complex views of Fritz Schachermeyr and the development of his views on the Succession in *AJAH* 13 (1988) 57–9.

[17] One very important intermediary may have been Cassander, Antipater's eldest son. There is no record of his presence at Babylon at the time of Alexander's death,

to Antipater, designed to reconcile the regent in Macedonia to Perdiccas' *de facto* usurpation of power in Asia.[18] There will also have been a diplomatic traffic between Perdiccas and Craterus, and for this we have indirect evidence. Antigenes, a phalanx commander sent off with Craterus in 324, is later attested in the entourage of Perdiccas. He commanded the élite Silver Shields during the invasion of Egypt and was instrumental in Perdiccas' murder.[19] The name is rare,[20] and it looks as though we are dealing with a single individual. Antigenes, then, acted as an emissary of Craterus, but was tempted to remain in Babylon, assuming the command of the most prestigious infantry group in the Macedonian army.[21] This is a hypothetical reconstruction, but, if correct, it is interesting corroboration of the diplomatic contacts and the political opportunism that the crisis generated.

The Babylon Settlement, then, is a misnomer. What we are dealing with is the first stage of a complicated process of political bargaining. It is the compromise between the conflicting factional groups at Babylon which entrenched Perdiccas as the dominant figure—the dominant figure at

and if there is any truth in the highly coloured and partisan story of the Alexander Romance, he left court a little before the king's death and lingered a while around Cilicia (*Metz Epit.* 100; Ps. Call. 3.32.3). If so, he can hardly not have met Craterus, and carried messages back to Antipater in Macedon.

[18] Diod. 18.23.1; Arr. *Succ.* F 1.21; Just. 13.6.5–7. A papyrus of the Hellenistic period, purporting to represent an altercation between Demades and Deinarchus at a judicial hearing in Pella, claims that Nicaea was betrothed to Perdiccas by Alexander himself (*PBerl* 13045 = K. Kunst, *Berliner Klassikertexte* VII (Berlin 1923)).

[19] Arr. *Succ.* F 1.35, 38; Diod. 18.39.5, 59.3, 62.4–7 etc.; Plut. *Eum.* 13.3; cf. Bosworth, 'History and Artifice' 66–70; Heckel 312–16. Antigenes had briefly commanded a phalanx regiment under Alexander, and he was attached to Craterus on the return march from India (Arr. 6.17.3) and later at Opis (Just. 12.12.8).

[20] There is possibly one other Antigenes, the one-eyed Macedonian veteran who falsely listed himself as a debtor early in 324 (Plut. *Alex.* 70.3–6; cf. *Mor.* 339C, where he is conflated with Atarrhias). He was clearly not of high status, and can hardly be identified with the phalanx commander, although he may be the 'Antigenes' (the MSS read *Antigonis*) who received a minor hypaspist command in late 331 (Curt. 5.2.5 with Atkinson's commentary *ad loc.*). See also Billows, *Antigonos* 27–9, who revives Tarn's hypothesis (*Al.* ii.314) that Plutarch's story is a garbled version of a tradition relating to the most famous *monophthalmos* of the age, Antigonus himself.

[21] Heckel 312 (after *SO* 57 (1982) 57–67) argues that Antigenes was left in Cilicia as Craterus' lieutenant, and deserted to Perdiccas when he moved on Egypt.

Babylon. We have no idea how it was received by Craterus or Antipater, or even whether they accepted the authority of the officers and rank-and-file at Babylon. It is the story of Perdiccas' success, interesting enough in itself, but only part of the political mosaic. Even here we are plagued with defective evidence. Most of the sources are the briefest of epitomes. Photius' excerpts of Arrian and Dexippus are dominated by the catalogue of satrapal appointments; they are practically uninformative about the events which led to the settlement. The same can be said of Diodorus, who is at his most laconic when describing the political conflict at Babylon. Our chief authorities, at least the most expansive, are Justin and Curtius Rufus. They do give a summary of events, but they are mutually contradictory. Are they using different sources, or do they have different agendas? Justin is excerpting Trogus' *Historiae Philippicae* in a notoriously capricious and slapdash manner, whereas Curtius is explicitly looking to the present, contrasting the dissolution produced by the division of powers at Babylon with the state of felicity achieved at Rome by the uncontested elevation of the current emperor. Justin may have mutilated the sense of his original beyond reconstruction, while Curtius, to put it crudely, may be indulging in historical fiction.[22] Can we establish any firm principles of criticism, or is the truth beyond human elucidation?

I shall begin with what is arguably the best attested episode, the first meeting after Alexander's death and the acclamation of Arrhidaeus. After a gloomy description of the mourning by Persians and Macedonians alike, exacerbated by the ritual quenching of all fires overnight,[23] Curtius gives a detailed description of a gathering of senior officers in the royal palace. It is meant to be private, but it is infiltrated by rank-and-file who refuse to be excluded (10.6.1–3). As a result it turns into a strange blend of council and assembly,

[22] So, most dogmatically, McKechnie (above, n. 1), following and intensifying the arguments of Martin.

[23] Curt. 10.5.16. Some months before Alexander had ordered the quenching of fires after the death of Hephaestion, an honour exclusive to the King and seen as prophetic of his own death (Diod. 17.114.4–5; cf. Schachermeyr, *Al. in Babylon* 46–8). Curtius interprets the custom as a sign of general demoralization: 'nec quisquam lumina audebat accendere'.

consilium and *contio*. Various proposals are canvassed inconclusively, until Meleager, a senior infantry commander, objects violently to the prospect of Perdiccas as regent for Alexander's
unborn child, and bursts out of the meeting (10.6.20–4). At
that stage an unknown infantryman speaks out for Arrhidaeus,
who has not hitherto been mentioned (10.7.1–3), and
Arrhidaeus is then introduced to the meeting by Meleager
and hailed as king by the infantry (10.7.7). Justin's account is
significantly different. The initial debate is confined to the
senior commanders.[24] The infantry is excluded, and objects
to the fact;[25] it then spontaneously declares for Arrhidaeus.
Meleager only appears as a delegate sent alongside Attalus to
reconcile the rank-and-file to the decision of the marshals—
at which point he deserts his mission and sides with the
mutineers. That is essentially the story of Diodorus,[26] and it
comes from a common tradition.

By contrast, Curtius' account is a confused pot pourri, and
it has been argued that it has been carefully shaped to draw
an analogy between the proclamation of Arrhidaeus and the
accession of Claudius in January, AD 41.[27] The description of
the meeting is based on the senatorial debate during the night
after Caligula's assassination, when (so Josephus claims) a
common praetorian drew attention to the fact that they had
Claudius ready at hand, an emperor in waiting.[28] Arrhidaeus

---

[24] Just. 13.2.5–3.1: the commanders first meet and confirm Perdiccas' proposal,
They swear allegiance to the four guardians, as then do the cavalry (3.1). Only then
does the infantry enter the equation.

[25] Just. 13.3.1: 'indignati nullas sibi consiliorum partes relictas.'

[26] Diod. 18.2.2–3. His account begins with the phalanx opting for Arrhidaeus;
the preliminary council of the marshals is omitted, as it is in Photius' miserable
summary of Arrian's *History of the Successors* (F 1a.1–2).

[27] So, *in primis*, Martin (above, n. 1) 176–84. See also Atkinson, i.36–8;
H. Bödefeld, *Untersuchungen zur Datierung der Alexandergeschichte des Q. Curtius
Rufus* 21–6. For a rather different interpretation, stressing Perdiccas' dissimulation,
see Atkinson, in *Al. in Fact and Fiction* 321–3. A. M. Devine (*Phoenix* 33 (1979)
153–4) had already compared Tiberius and Alexander as masters of deception. For
a compendium of Roman echoes see Baynham, *Alexander the Great. The Unique
History of Quintus Curtius* 215.

[28] Jos.*BJ* 2.211–12. There is no counterpart in the more extensive version in *AJ*
19.248–53. In it the soldiers collectively call upon the senate to choose a ruler (249),
and there is no dramatic gesture by any individual. It seems *prima facie* likely that
Josephus' account in *BJ* is rhetorically shaped to echo the events of 323. See below,
n. 33.

as a literary echo of Claudius is an attractive idea, but I do not think it can have originated in Claudius' reign. It was too near the bone to make even an implicit comparison between a mentally defective king, a tool in the hands of his regents, and an emperor who looked grotesque and felt impelled to defend himself against allegations of stupidity.[29] Arrhidaeus' mental incapacity, it is true, is not stressed in our extant text of Curtius, but the omission is less worrying when one takes into account the dreadful state of the manuscripts. Take, for instance, the vivid scene in which Peithon the Bodyguard remonstrates with the infantry as they press for the recognition of Arrhidaeus. He begins with fulsome praise of the soldiers: Alexander was to be pitied for being denied their presence and services, for they were obsessed by the memory of their king and blind to all else (10.7.4). Then Curtius continues surprisingly: 'there was no doubt that he was hostile (?)[30] to the young man who was marked out for kingship; the insults which he had discharged brought him more resentment than they brought Arrhidaeus contempt.' Now, there is no insult explicit or implicit in the preceding speech of Peithon. He simply notes the Macedonians' overwhelming devotion to their late king, and suggests that it prevents their appreciating the current political problems. There is no hint what those problems are.[31] It will not do to argue that Curtius has deliberately suppressed material in his source

---

[29] Suet. *Claud.* 38.3: in a number of orations he claimed that his apparent *stultitia* was a front to help him survive Gaius' reign. The protestation evoked an anonymous pamphlet on the Regiment of Fools. When he was safely dead, Seneca could maliciously satirize the imperial moron (*Apocol.* 7.3, 8.3).

[30] The manuscripts read as follows: *haud ambigue iuvenem cui regnum destinabatur* † *impense probra quae obiecerat magis ipsi odium quam Arrhidaeum contemptum attulerunt.* The text has been variously emended (<*in*> *iuvenem ... infensus*, Bardon; *tum in eum ... ingessit probra.* <*at*> Hedicke; *impugnans. Sed* Damste, printed in Müller's text and the recent Mondadori edition) but nothing that has yet been suggested is palaeographically compelling. The corruption could be explained by the hypothesized lacuna (noted by Müller), beginning after *destinabatur*, in which case the text resumes with *impense*. There will have been a substantial omission. The text presumably detailed Peithon's objections to Arrhidaeus and concluded: 'for all the vehemence (*impense*) of his attack, the insults which he had discharged ...'

[31] So Martin (above, n. 1) 164: 'Curtius handles the matter of Arrhidaeus' condition with such extreme delicacy that readers ignorant of the truth would be unable even to guess what sort of alleged shortcoming was at issue.'

and omitted the insults to Arrhidaeus. If that were the case there was no point in drawing attention to the *probra* or even mentioning Peithon's intervention. But Curtius' text is here corrupt and almost certainly lacunose. I would argue that Curtius did make Peithon spell out what the soldiers were blind to: the mental condition and low birth of their intended successor to the throne. But, as he then states, the attack was counter-productive. It would seem that Curtius' text did originally place various *probra* in the mouth of Peithon, and they have been lost, thanks to the lamentable tradition of Book 10, which is positively riddled with lacunae.

We cannot, then, be sure that Curtius suppressed all references to Arrhidaeus' mental condition, and the probability is that he did not. Indeed the portrait of Arrhidaeus that we find in Curtius is not uniformly favourable. He may on occasion behave with dignity, but on the whole he is passive, responding without question to the manipulation of those closest to him. That is not the most tactful parallel to Claudius, even if Claudius is favourably contrasted with Arrhidaeus. The comparison itself is grossly unflattering.[32] In any case one may perhaps doubt the historicity of the anonymous praetorian in Josephus. He appears only in the *Jewish Wars*: there is no reference to him in the longer account in the *Antiquities*. If there is imitation, it is probably imitation by Josephus, borrowing material from Curtius' source.[33] If the peculiarities in Curtius' account can be explained in another context, that of the early Hellenistic period, there is no need

---

[32] One might draw the parallel with Nerva in the hands of the praetorians, compelled to hand over the assassins of Domitian, much as Arrhidaeus was forced to countenance the execution of the phalanx mutineers (Curt. 10.10.18–19). The accession of Trajan brought instant relief, a *princeps* who was capable of sole rule and prevented the empire being dismembered. Only a Trajan, one assumes, could have saved Alexander's empire.

[33] Martin 181 will have nothing of this, arguing that Josephus' account of Alexander's treatment of the Samaritans is different from what we find in Curtius. Perhaps so, but Curtius did not use a single source, any more than Josephus. If Curtius' account of the succession debate was, as is often argued, taken from Cleitarchus, then it was familiar to a wide Greek and Roman readership, and there is nothing surprising in Josephus taking a motif from it. He demonstrably knew Hieronymus' work (cf. *FGrH* 154 F 6), and may well have been familiar with Cleitarchus.

to posit extensive literary shaping to force Arrhidaeus into the mould of the early empire.

We can perhaps make some progress by comparing Curtius' account of the succession debate with that of Justin. The basic shape is similar. Motions are presented by individual marshals. Perdiccas proposes that the kingship ultimately be vested in the child of Alexander, if it proves to be a son,[34] and after heated exchanges that is the conclusion reached. The presumed son of Alexander is to be king, and his future protectors are to be Perdiccas, Leonnatus, Craterus and Antipater.[35] So far so good. In between Perdiccas' proposal and its ratification both Justin and Curtius record a number of interventions, and though the content is similar, the speakers are quite different. In Justin (13.2.6–8) Meleager speaks out and proposes alternatives: Heracles is a son of Alexander, Arrhidaeus a brother, and either could be king; there is no need to wait for the offspring of Rhoxane. Ptolemy is made to reply with an outright attack on Arrhidaeus, focusing on his disreputable mother and his questionable health. In place of a token king he proposes a governing junta of marshals (13.2.11–12). Within the general story there are discrepant details. Meleager apparently supports the cause of Heracles, but he then denounces the offspring of Rhoxane as a product of the conquered people—as though Heracles' mother was not herself a Persian. There is confusion here, and possibly conflation. When we turn to Curtius, the situation is partly clarified. The case for Heracles is made not by Meleager but by Nearchus,[36] who had been given a daughter of Barsine as his wife in the Susa marriages, and was the obvious person to promote the cause of Barsine's son. Curtius makes it clear that this was a minority view, strongly objectionable to the masses.[37] The next move was to rule out both Heracles and the future child of Rhoxane as Persians

---

[34] Curt. 10.6.9; Just. 13.2.5.   [35] Curt. 10.7.8–9; Just. 13.2.13–14.

[36] Curt. 10.6.10–12. For Nearchus' marriage to Barsine's daughter by Mentor of Rhodes see Arr. 7.4.6 and on its implications Errington (above, n. 1) 74; Badian, *YCS* 24 (1975) 167–9.

[37] Curt. 10.6.12: 'nulli placebat oratio'. Alexander himself may have faced some criticism of his oriental marriages shortly before his death (Bosworth, in *Transitions to Empire* 143–4).

and subjects,[38] and that is the role that Trogus apparently gave to Meleager. His epitomist has fused together Nearchus' proposal and Meleager's objections. The objections are associated with a concrete proposal, the proclamation of Arrhidaeus as king. The proposal is in its turn attacked by Ptolemy, who has his own programme of collective rule.

Trogus seems to have presented a list of proposals, each countered by the next speaker, each of whom has an idea of his own. The pattern is repeated in Curtius with significant differences. The most notable is that Arrhidaeus is excised from the debate. The attack on Heracles and the future Alexander IV follows the same lines, horror at the prospect of rule by a king of Persian extraction, but it comes not from Meleager but from Ptolemy.[39] It leads directly to a proposal for collective leadership which corresponds roughly to Ptolemy's proposal in Justin.[40] Meleager intervenes at a later stage, after Aristonous offers the kingship to Perdiccas himself, attacking the very idea of an unborn king and objecting in the strongest terms to Perdiccas as king or regent.[41] That leads directly to the intervention of the unknown phalangite and the long delayed introduction of Arrhidaeus. The two accounts have a similar framework, but they contradict each

[38] Just. 13.2.9: 'nec esse fas ut Macedonibus ex sanguine eorum quorum regna deleverint reges constituantur.'

[39] Curt. 10.6.14: 'est cur Persas vicerimus, ut stirpi eorum serviamus?'

[40] Curt. 10.6.15. Here Ptolemy envisages the chief marshals deciding policy by majority vote and meeting before the empty throne of Alexander. That is exactly the stratagem later adopted by Eumenes and the satrapal coalition (Diod. 19.15.3–5; Plut. *Eum.* 13.5–8; Nep. *Eum.* 7.2–3; Polyaen. 4.8.2: see below, pp. 101, 114), and may have been modelled upon Ptolemy's proposal at Babylon. Justin (13.2.12) makes Ptolemy suggest a choice of ruler(s) from the totality of Macedonian marshals, but it is uncertain from the wording whether Trogus envisaged a single monarch or collective government like that envisaged in Curtius.

[41] Curt. 10.6.16–22. Meleager's sentiments seem echoed in a fragment of Arrian's *Successors* (F 11 Roos = *FGrH* 156 F 129): 'for while he (sc. Alexander IV) was an immature child, they would be his guardians and under his authority (ὑπὸ τῷ ἐκείνου προσχήματι) do everything they pleased with regard to their subjects.' We do not have the context in Arrian, and there are any number of occasions when the sentiments might have been uttered; but there is (as Roos and Jacoby noted) a strong resemblance to the rhetoric that Curtius (10.6.21) places in Meleager's mouth: 'nec vero interest Roxanes filium, quandoque genitus erit, an Perdiccan regem habeatis, cum iste sub tutelae specie regnum occupaturus sit.' If the passages relate to the same context, then it is impossible to dismiss Curtius' account of the debate as his own invention.

other in the crucial matter of Arrhidaeus. In this, probability
definitely favours Justin. It is practically inconceivable that a
council of Macedonian nobles discussed the credentials of
Heracles son of Barsine but passed over a son of Philip and
half-brother of Alexander, however serious his mental disorder (it did not prevent his occupying a ceremonial role).[42]
Meleager's support for him in the debate would make even
more sense of his siding with the phalanx troops later, when
they were actively proclaiming Arrhidaeus king.[43] He had
voiced support for the last surviving son of Philip, and it
struck a chord with the infantry. They declared themselves
for Arrhidaeus, and the initiative for the declaration may
well have come from an unknown and unidentifiable ranker.
Curtius, however, has thrown the initiative forward and
transferred it to the council proper, representing Arrhidaeus
as the spontaneous choice of the troops. He may have done it
for dramatic reasons of his own—and there could conceivably be a deliberate allusion to the accession of Claudius,
written when that emperor was safely dead. But need we
posit authorial license on Curtius' part? Could the aberrant
story of Arrhidaeus' proclamation be explained in the context of the period of the Successors?

   The figure of Ptolemy bulks large in this debate. It is agreed
that he proposed a system of collective leadership, and attacked
some of the candidates for the kingship. But the targets of
the attack are different. In Justin he attacks Arrhidaeus, in
Curtius Heracles and Rhoxane's unborn child. What is more,
in Curtius there is no possibility of an attack on Arrhidaeus
until his name is introduced by the unknown soldier towards
the end of the meeting, and then the objections are voiced
not by Ptolemy but by Peithon the Bodyguard. Is there any
reason for such a distortion, if distortion it is? There was no
point in a historian of the early empire divorcing Ptolemy
from the attack on Arrhidaeus, but in the period of the
Successors there may have been a solid political motive.

---

[42] Curt. 10.7.2: 'sacrorum caerimoniarumque consors'. It is usually assumed that
Curtius envisaged some Macedonian sacral function (so, e.g., Hammond, *CQ* 30
(1980) 475; *The Macedonian State* 22–3); I once, perhaps too adventurously,
posited that the ritual was Babylonian (*Chiron* 22 (1992) 78–9).

[43] Just. 13.3.2; Diod. 18.2.2–3.

Arrhidaeus was a figure of some importance in the dynastic struggle in Macedon. When civil war erupted in 318, he and his wife broke with the regent Polyperchon and sided with Cassander.[44] It was a disastrous move; Arrhidaeus and Eurydice were deserted by their army, which refused to fight against the mother and son of Alexander.[45] Popular sympathy moved in their favour after they were barbarously done to death by Olympias. Cassander returned to Macedon to avenge them, and within a few months he had forced Olympias to capitulation and death at Pydna and become master of Macedonia. He promptly rehabilitated Arrhidaeus and Eurydice, giving them solemn burial at Aegae[46] (and, if Olga Palagia is correct, Arrhidaeus dominates the hunt fresco on Tomb II at Vergina, being represented almost as a heroic figure).[47] At the same time Alexander IV and his mother were interned at Amphipolis, secluded from politics and treated as commoners.[48] In some ways Arrhidaeus legitimized Cassander. He and his wife had disowned Cassander's enemy, Polyperchon, and appointed Cassander regent (Justin 14.5.3), and Cassander had championed him against Olympias. It was in Cassander's interest to portray Arrhidaeus as a worthy protégé, to downplay his mental incapacity and to stress his popularity with the troops. He would have thoroughly approved of Curtius' general presentation, with Arrhidaeus intervening to prevent an armed clash between cavalry and infantry and acting as the virtual broker of peace and concord (10.8.16–23). It could not be denied that he was essentially passive, but he is shown with the capacity for effective, even noble action. What is more, he is the favourite of the troops, who spontaneously present his case to the council of nobles and later endorse his attempt at mediation. This was hardly the man to be deserted by his own troops, and if it happened in 317, it was not his fault.

Curtius' picture of Arrhidaeus was well suited to the political programme of Cassander, and the role of Ptolemy also makes sense. When Cassander rebelled against the royal

---

[44] Just. 14.5.3; Diod. 19.11.1, Cf. *HM* iii.137–40; Bosworth, *Chiron* 22 (1992) 71–3.   [45] Diod. 19.11.2; Justin 14.5.10.
[46] Diod. 19.52.5; Athen. 4.155A = Diyllus, *FGrH* 73 F 1.
[47] O. Palagia, in *Al. in Fact and Fiction* 195–6.   [48] Diod. 19.52.4, 61.3.

authority vested in Polyperchon, one of his earliest backers was Ptolemy, and Ptolemy readily joined with him in the alliance against Antigonus, which was concluded early in 315 and lasted until the Peace of the Dynasts in 311. The alliance was renewed (after a period of intermittent hostility) in 303. As the ally of Cassander, Ptolemy would not have wished to emphasize the hostility towards Arrhidaeus that he had expressed at Babylon, and a historian writing in his entourage might well have glossed over it in the interest of international relations. Ptolemy himself had reason not to depreciate Arrhidaeus. He had twice received his satrapy at his hands. Perdiccas had distributed the satrapies in 323 at the behest of Arrhidaeus,[49] as probably did Antipater at Triparadeisus. Neither was particularly popular, and Perdiccas was posthumously discredited. It was hardly flattering to Ptolemy to have received Egypt as a gift from a mentally deficient ruler manipulated by unscrupulous regents. By contrast Ptolemy's great rival, Antigonus, could boast that he had received his power base in Asia Minor from Alexander the Great. It was therefore in Ptolemy's interest to insinuate that Arrhidaeus was not mentally incompetent but a serious actor in his own right. Hence it was better that the opposition to Arrhidaeus' accession came not from Ptolemy himself but from Peithon (who was safely dead by 315), and the targets of Ptolemy's invective became the future Alexander IV, who was virtually disowned by Cassander, and Heracles, who was maintained by Antigonus as a potential usurper.[50] Curtius' account of events in Babylon, then, makes sense if it derives from an author writing in the Ptolemaic camp at a time when it was imperative to maintain good relations with Cassander. In that case the only viable candidate would appear to be Cleitarchus of Alexandria, who has been the most popular

---

[49] This is explicit in Arrian (*Succ.* F 1a.5: ὡς ᾽Αρριδαίου κελεύοντος). There is nothing so clear-cut in the tradition for Triparadeisus, but it is likely enough that Antipater acted as Arrhidaeus' mouthpiece, exactly as Polyperchon was to issue his exiles' decree in the name of the kings; the regent is only named as the executive officer carrying out the royal command (Diod. 18.56.7–8: compare Alexander's earlier instructions to Antipater at Diod. 18.8.4).

[50] Heracles was resident at Pergamum at the time of Alexander's death, and he was still there when Polyperchon invited him to Macedon in 310 (Diod. 20.20.1). For the last eight years of his stay he was directly under Antigonus' control.

choice as Curtius' source and whose history has been recently dated to the years around 310.[51] If it is accepted, this reconstruction supplies independent corroboration.

The other peculiarity of Curtius' account is the role given to Aristonous, who presses for Perdiccas to assume the throne, arguing that Alexander had already designated him by the transfer of his signet ring.[52] The intervention leads in turn to Meleager's outburst against Perdiccas. This is a perplexing tradition. It is true that Aristonous was a supporter of Perdiccas. He remained with him at court until 321, when he was appointed to lead the invasion of Cyprus,[53] and he could have taken loyalty far enough to propose that the kingship devolve upon Perdiccas. On the other hand, for what it is worth, there is no trace of this radical proposal in Justin or any other source, and Aristonous was a prominent supporter of Olympias and Polyperchon in the struggle against Cassander.[54] In fact Cassander had him treacherously murdered in 316 after he surrendered Amphipolis; his distinction as a Bodyguard of Alexander was such that he could not be disposed of openly.[55] Curtius' account might reflect negative propaganda, insinuating that Aristonous was so contemptuous of the Argead heritage that he was prepared to see Perdiccas as king, the most ambitious and violent of the marshals at Babylon. It certainly shows Aristonous as the cat's-paw of Perdiccas.[56]

---

[51] See for instance Badian, *PACA* 8 (1965) 5–11; Schachermeyr, *Al. in Babylon* 211–24; Bosworth, *From Arrian to Alexander* 87–93; Prandi, *Fortuna e realtà dell'opera di Clitarco* 66–71.

[52] Curt. 10.6.16–17 ('placere igitur summam imperii ad Perdiccam deferri'). The proposal, according to Curtius, was almost successful; it was only Perdiccas' reluctance to take the ring that prevented his being hailed king there and then (10.6.18–19).

[53] Arr. *Succ.* F 24.6 (Roos). He must have made his peace with Antipater, who would have found it difficult to dispose of a Bodyguard of Alexander; he presumably returned to Macedon with Antipater's army (he would have helped in dealing with the mutinous troops) and after Antipater's death he was employed by Polyperchon, who may have been a long-time friend.

[54] Diod. 19.35.4, 50.3, 7–8, 51.1. Cf. *HM* iii.142–3; Heckel 276.

[55] Diod. 19.51.1. See below, pp. 160–2, for Antigonus' identical dilemma when disposing of Peithon, another Bodyguard of Alexander.

[56] In that case Cleitarchus can hardly be the source for Curtius' description of Aristonous' heroism at the Malli town (9.5.15, 18). Given that he explicitly discounts Cleitarchus' statement that Ptolemy was involved in the action (9.5.21), it is unlikely that he used Cleitarchus' account of the rescue of Alexander. That section (9.5.15–18) has no counterpart in Diodorus (cf. 17.99.4) and is grafted on to the vulgate tradition from another source.

Some firm conclusions have emerged from this complex discussion. Justin's outline, for all its faults, is the more reliable and coheres with the brief digest of Diodorus. It suggests that the preliminary council was indeed a closed council of senior officers which debated the various alternatives for the kingship and concluded by endorsing Perdiccas' initial proposal: the king would be the son of Alexander by Rhoxane, and his guardians (*tutores*) would be Perdiccas and Leonnatus, the senior Bodyguards at Babylon, and Craterus and Antipater in the west. This was in fact delaying decisions. It would be some months before it could be known whether a king would materialize from Rhoxane's womb, and in that time the balance of power might shift dramatically. In any case, the baby might be female or stillborn, and then the whole issue would need to be addressed again. In the meantime the main centres of power remained untouched: Antipater in Macedonia, Craterus in Cilicia and the marshals in Babylon. In Babylon the dominant figure was undoubtedly Perdiccas. Of the six known Bodyguards present in the city he had the firm backing of Aristonous, and Leonnatus was evidently prepared to support him, provided that he ultimately had a share in the regency. Then again Perdiccas was practically unique among the senior cavalry officers in that he had held a phalanx command for many years,[57] and his brother, Alcetas, and brother-in-law, Attalus, were currently infantry commanders and present in Babylon.[58] As chiliarch, commander of the élite first hipparchy and second at court to Alexander himself,[59] he enjoyed a power base and personal

---

[57] He had commanded the battalion recruited from Orestis and Lyncestis (Diod. 17.45.2) and done so from the start of the reign (Arr. 1.6.9, 14.2) until some time after Gaugamela.

[58] Alcetas had commanded Perdiccas' old battalion since 327 at latest (Arr. 4.22.1; cf. Bosworth, *HCA* ii.140; Heckel 171). Attalus' battalion command dates from the same period (*HCA* ii.112; Heckel 180). The marriage to Perdiccas' sister, Atalante, is only attested in 321 (Diod. 18.37.2–3), and Heckel 381–4 has argued that the union was contracted in 323, as the price of Attalus' acquiescence in Perdiccas' regency (see also *CQ* 28 (1978) 379–82). That may well be true; Atalante could have come to Asia as a new bride along with Antipater's daughter, Nicaea. However, that does not imply that the Attalus who allegedly sided with Meleager against Perdiccas (Justin 13.3.2, 7) was the phalanx commander. The name is common, and, once Perdiccas secured power in Babylon, any commander who had sided with Meleager was likely to have shared Meleager's fate.

[59] See below, pp. 50–1.

distinction that none of the officers at Babylon could match. He could hope to build upon it and make himself invulnerable by the time Rhoxane's child was born—and with luck it would be a girl!

The challenge came sooner than he had anticipated. The phalanx infantry was unwilling to countenance a period of uncertainty without a designated king. Curtius (10.5.13–14) states that Alexander's death immediately provoked fears of civil war, a rational enough reaction, one which the troops had already experienced when Alexander was reported dead at the Malli town.[60] They wanted a king, and, when it was denied them, they chose the only remaining member of the royal house. The movement was exploited immediately by Meleager, who saw his chance to undermine the foundations of Perdiccas' predominance. Sent initially to remonstrate with the mutineers, he embraced their cause and gained possession of the person of Arrhidaeus, acting as his champion and mouthpiece. Having gained the initiative, he could not let it slip. At his urging the infantry attacked the palace in full force, and after a brief, tense confrontation the bulk of the senior officers and cavalry vacated Babylon.[61] Significantly, Perdiccas remained behind, hoping to re-establish his influence over the infantry. With him, if we may believe Curtius (10.8.3–4), was a contingent of royal pages, the group charged with the day to day service of the king. It was a clear signal of his ambition. Meleager then attempted to have Perdiccas killed. Both Curtius and Justin agree that an execution squad was sent,[62] but Perdiccas managed to outface it by sheer bravado. That was the critical moment for Meleager. Once Perdiccas escaped, his grasp on the situation loosened.

[60] Arrian's vigorous description of the scene (6.12.1–2) stresses the threat posed by a multitude of equipollent marshals. The dark suspicions that the commanders were concealing their king's death (6.12.3) recur in the reports (from the *Ephemerides*) of Alexander's last days (Arr. 7.26.1; Plut. *Al.* 76.8). The context in Arrian is deeply influenced by Xenophon (Bosworth, *Alexander and the East* 54–6), but the suspicions of the generals have no counterpart in his literary model. They must have been mentioned by his historical source, in this case, it would seem, Nearchus.

[61] Curt. 10.7.16–20 gives the most detailed description. It is confirmed in outline by other sources (Diod. 18.2.3; Just. 13.3.4–5).

[62] Curt. 10.6.2–4; Just. 13.3.7–8. The details are similar, except that the initiative for the assassination, according to Justin, comes from Attalus (see above, n. 58) rather than Meleager. Either of the proponents of Arrhidaeus could have suggested the assassination, which was ordered in the name of the king (Curt. 10.8.2, cf. 6).

There followed a period of waiting and extreme tension. The sources again diverge. In Justin the initiative comes from Perdiccas himself, who approaches the infantry and addresses an assembly, pleading for reconciliation. He is accepted as leader, while the cavalry in turn acknowledge Arrhidaeus as king.[63] In Curtius events are more complex. The news of the planned assassination of Perdiccas is received with outrage, and the Macedonians (presumably the cavalry) vote to take reprisals by force of arms. At this point the text is interrupted by a lacuna and resumes with an assembly of the infantry at Babylon.[64] The subject is clearly responsibility for the attempt on Perdiccas' life. Arrhidaeus is asked by someone unknown whether he had ordered Perdiccas' death, and replies that he did give the order at the prompting of Meleager; Perdiccas, however, is alive, and there is no cause for disorder. One can only guess at what has been omitted, but it looks as though the news of the cavalry meeting came to the city and Meleager himself summoned a meeting to discuss responsibility. Perhaps it was Alcetas himself who posed the direct question to Arrhidaeus and gained the admission that the failed assassination was the work of Meleager. At all events Curtius (10.8.7) emphasizes that Meleager was threatened, lost the initiative and spent three days in fruitless cogitation. The next stage comes when the cavalry commandeer food supplies for the city and there is the prospect of hunger, if not starvation.[65] At this point there is another assembly, which results in an embassy being sent to the cavalry. We are not informed who made the proposal, but there is no hint that Meleager played any

Essentially passive, even in Curtius, he gave formal approval to what would have been plain murder.

[63] Just. 13.3.8–4.1.

[64] Curt. 10.8.6: 'atque ille seditione provisa *** cum regem adisset, interrogare eum coepit, an Perdiccam comprehendi ipse iussisset.' The first clause (before the lacuna) presumably refers to Meleager; he had foreseen the agitation which the botched assassination would provoke, and summoned an assembly to justify the act as a royal command. The stratagem was frustrated when his rivals induced Arrhidaeus to admit that the order was only given at Meleager's urging. There is a substantial omission, several lines at least; and the crucial account of the outmanœuvring of Meleager has been lost.

[65] Curt. 10.8.11–13. Other sources agree that the cavalry took the offensive (Diod. 18.2.4; Just. 13.3.5); the food embargo marked the opening of hostilities.

significant role. Instead it is Arrhidaeus who selects three emissaries.[66] The names are curious, and only one, Perilaus, seems to be Macedonian (it is the name of a brother of Cassander).[67] The other two are Greeks, 'Pasas' of Thessaly and 'Amissus' of Megalopolis.[68] These are hardly mercenary commanders, as some have alleged, or even naturalized officers of the phalanx.[69] Neither could expect to get a sympathetic hearing from the cavalry. They are most probably associates of Arrhidaeus, members of his entourage in Babylon (as the Thessalian origins of Pasas would suggest), who had played no role in the mutiny and were therefore qualified to serve as neutral ambassadors. They were accordingly received by the cavalry commanders, but the response they brought back was uncompromising. There would only be reconciliation if the ringleaders of the mutiny were surrendered for judgement.

At this point the rhetorical tone of Curtius' narrative rises perceptibly. At the report of the embassy the soldiers rush to arms, but are restrained by Arrhidaeus who rushes from the palace and pleads for concord (10.8.15–16). The pathos increases as he removes his diadem and offers to resign the kingship rather than shed Macedonian blood. As a result he

---

[66] Curt. 10.8.15: 'igitur a rege legatur Pasas Thessalus et Amissus Megalopolitanus et Perilaus.'

[67] Plut. *Mor.* 486 A. Berve no. 630 identifies the ambassador as the 'Perillos' mentioned by Plut. *Mor.* 179 F. There is no reason for the identification, nor any reason to exclude Cassander's brother. Indeed, if Cassander's brother had been a long-term adherent of Arrhidaeus, it would help explain Cassander's energetic involvement in his cause later, in 317.

[68] The names are generally agreed to be corrupt. No 'Amissus' is recorded in *LGPN* iiiA except for this lone Megalopolitan. He was presumably a scion of one of the distinguished Megalopolitan families which established ties of *xenia* with Philip II (cf. Dem. 18.295; Theopompus, *FGrH* 115 F 119, 230), but we cannot venture a precise identification. It is within the bounds of possibility that 'Amissus' is a corruption of 'Damis' (cf. Heckel 148 n. 148), in which case we have to do with the Damis of Megalopolis who acquired technical knowledge of elephant fighting under Alexander (Diod. 18.71.2) and had sufficient social distinction to be appointed governor of Megalopolis by Cassander (Diod. 19.64.1). As for 'Pasas', the simplest correction is Hedicke's 'Pasias', which gives us a relatively frequent name, but it is not as yet attested in Thessaly, and we have no prospect of teasing out the family background.

[69] For a list of suggestions see Schachermeyr, *Al. in Babylon* 101: functionaries of the royal chancellery (hence agents of Eumenes), colleagues of Chares (royal chamberlains), or senior members of the phalanx.

is given free rein to negotiate,[70] and he sends the same ambassadors back to demand that Meleager be recognized as *tertius dux*, presumably to share command with Perdiccas and Leonnatus. The demand is accepted and the formal agreement follows. Everything here is paradox. Arrhidaeus makes a passionate, unprompted intervention which wins the heart of the assembly. It is the only exercise of his initiative to be recorded in any source,[71] and within a few paragraphs he reverts to type, as he tamely acquiesces in the execution of the phalanx mutineers—without surrendering his diadem.[72] What is more, the demands of the second embassy are most extraordinary. They have reported a demand for the surrender of the ringleaders and respond with a counter-demand to promote the most prominent of the mutineers. To our surprise these extraordinary representations are accepted and the conflicting parties are reconciled.[73] As happens at the end of tragedies, what is expected has not been fulfilled, and the gods have found a way for the unexpected, if not the impossible.

Justin gives a valuable clue to what has happened. When Perdiccas spontaneously approaches the infantry assembly, he gives a passionate plea for concord, urging against civil war in much the same terms as Arrhidaeus,[74] and as with

---

[70] Curt. 10.8.21: 'itaque cuncti instare coeperunt, ut quae agitasset exequi vellet.' The proposals favour Meleager, but in this tradition he plays no part in their formulation. The initiative comes exclusively from Arrhidaeus.

[71] Few direct utterances are attested, even in Curtius. Arrhidaeus is wholly passive and mute during his acclamation (cf. Curt. 10.7.10, reminiscent of Plutarch's famous picture (*Alex.* 77.7) of Perdiccas dragging Arrhidaeus along as a mute extra on the stage of kingship (see now Carney (above, n. 9) 75–6)). Later he rubber-stamps the assassination of Perdiccas, lamely admitting, when forced to do so, that it was Meleager's fault and adding naively that there was no need for the troops to be upset (10.8.6). That is a far cry from the high-flown rhetoric when the embassy returned.

[72] Curt. 10.9.18–19: 'Philip neither vetoed it nor gave it his approval; and it was apparent that he would only claim an action as his own when it had been proved successful in the event.'

[73] Curt. 10.8.22: 'haud aegre id impetratum est.' The justification given is political: Meleager would not be able to stand against Perdiccas and Leonnatus in a future triumvirate. That is a shrewd enough calculation, but it hardly justifies the waiving of the demand for the surrender of the mutineers or explains why the mood of the cavalry switches overnight from recalcitrance to conciliation.

[74] Just. 13.3.9–10: the infantry is taking arms against fellow citizens, not enemies; cf. Curt. 10.8.18: 'remember that you are dealing with fellow citizens, and to

Arrhidaeus his plea is successful. He so stirs the soldiery that they approve his advice and unanimously choose him as their *dux*. We can now place the episode in context. The ambassadors did indeed return with a demand to surrender the ringleaders, and the demand did cause consternation. But they returned with Perdiccas, and he was able to calm the agitation, suggesting that the cavalry might be amenable to renewed overtures and even accept Meleager in the high command. It was the last stage of a carefully orchestrated exercise. Perdiccas' agents in the phalanx had suggested that Arrhidaeus send emissaries;[75] he ensured that the reply was designed to cause fear and alarm, which he could dissipate in person. He could then propose a compromise which both sides would accept—for the moment. In Curtius' account Perdiccas has been written out of his own scenario and replaced by Arrhidaeus. Ptolemy's enemy was denied one of his crowning moments, and the credit was given to Cassander's protégé. It is the most striking instance of propaganda in the whole episode, and the most paradoxical. Instead of Perdiccas the peacemaker we have Arrhidaeus, a model of sanity and altruistic passion.

The reconciliation, both authors agree, followed immediately. The cavalry took the critical step of recognizing Arrhidaeus as king, with the proviso that he would be joined by any son born to Rhoxane.[76] There was a formal union of hearts, Perdiccas and Meleager leading infantry and cavalry at a ceremony of reconciliation, and some definition of power took place, perhaps in the presence of Alexander's corpse.[77] At this point Photius provides us with digests of

break off hope of reconciliation precipitately is the mark of men intent on civil war'. In Curtius this is the sole theme of Arrhidaeus. In Justin Perdiccas makes much of the related theme that the vanquished would watch their victors destroy themselves.

[75] According to Plutarch (*Eum.* 3.2), Eumenes, who had remained in Babylon with the infantry, was instrumental in smoothing the tension. He will have colluded with his future patron, Perdiccas, backing him in his address to the infantry assembly and perhaps playing a role in the initial overtures to the cavalry (Schachermeyr, *Al. in Babylon* 101–2).

[76] Just. 13.4.2–3; cf. Arr. *Succ*, F 1.3; Diod. 18.2.4.

[77] Just. 13.4.4. There is every reason to accept the detail, given that the body remained untreated until the initial disturbances were over (see below, p. 55) and it would have added an impressive solemnity to the occasion. The scenario may have

Arrian and Dexippus, which give almost identical formulations.[78] In Dexippus the provisions seem anachronistically embedded in the later distribution of satrapies,[79] whereas in Arrian they come where Justin places them, at the moment of reconciliation. Much has been made of the terminology, particularly the definition of Craterus' position, and wide-ranging conclusions about Macedonian *Staatsrecht* have been drawn.[80] In actuality there is little substance behind the pretentious terminology. The agreement is essentially ratification of the *status quo*. In the case of Antipater that is evident. He is confirmed as regent in Macedonia, with powers extending over Greece, the Illyrians, and even Triballians. Alexander's recall is implicitly countermanded, and Antipater has in essence the position he enjoyed between 334 and 324. Nothing else was feasible without provoking civil war. Similarly with Perdiccas. Both Arrian and Dexippus claim that it was agreed that Perdiccas should have the chiliarchy which Hephaestion held, and Arrian adds that it meant administration of the entire kingdom.[81] Now, there is no doubt that Perdiccas was already chiliarch. He had been promoted to the position after the death of Hephaestion, taking on the command of Hephaestion's hipparchy while his own command devolved upon Eumenes.[82] As chiliarch under

been arranged by Eumenes, who was later to exploit the reconciling influence of the dead king (see below, p. 101).

[78] Phot. *Bibl.* cod. 92: 69ᵃ19–24 = Arr. *Succ.* F 1a.3; cod. 82: 64ᵇ3–9 = Dexippus, *FGrH* 100 F 8,3–4.

[79] Dexippus includes them in his list of European appointments, after Lysimachus receives Thrace. He gives the details of Antipater's command in Macedon, Greece, and the north, and describes the position of Craterus and Perdiccas. He must have added that Antipater's recall had been in effect rescinded and explained how he was to share power with Craterus and Perdiccas. Such digressions seem to have been a recurrent feature of his satrapy list.

[80] For a survey of earlier views see Seibert, *Das Zeitalter der Diadochen* 84–91, to which add Anson, *CPh* 87 (1992) 40–1. The most detailed and elaborate is that of Schachermeyr, *Al. in Babylon* 164–84, on which see Bosworth *AJAH* 13 (1988) 57–9.

[81] Arr. *Succ.* F 1a.3: Περδίκκαν δὲ χιλιαρχεῖν χιλιαρχίας ἧς ἦρχεν Ἡφαιστίων (τὸ δὲ ἦν ἐπιτροπὴ τῆς ξυμπάσης βασιλείας).

[82] It is explicit in Plutarch (*Eum.* 1.5; cf. Nep. *Eum.* 1.6): Eumenes took over Perdiccas' hipparchy when he moved to Hephaestion's position (εἰς τὴν ἐκείνου τάξιν). The contradiction in Arrian 7.14.10 is superficial: Alexander continued to name the royal guard (the cavalry chiliarchy) after Hephaestion *honoris causa*. The actual command (for the guard must have had a commander) was exercised by Perdiccas, and he presumably discharged the chiliarch's functions at court

Alexander he was in charge of court ceremonial and the senior official of the empire, and it was natural enough that he received Alexander's ring.[83] The confirmation of his position was a mark of the pre-eminence he had won over recent days, stamping his ascendancy over cavalry and infantry alike. Justin, however, has nothing about the chiliarchy, defining the position of Perdiccas and Meleager as *castrorum, exercitus et rerum cura*, oversight of the camp, the army, and the business of state. There has been a tendency to emend the text, reading *regum cura*, in other words the guardianship of the kings.[84] Unnecessary and improbable. The last thing Perdiccas would have wished was to include Meleager in the guardianship of Arrhidaeus, still less mark him out as the future guardian of Alexander's child. All that the received text implies is that Perdiccas and Meleager had control of the military resources at Babylon and transacted the business of state. It confirmed Perdiccas' position as vizier and military commander—at Babylon, and associated Meleager with him. What Perdiccas was *not* doing at this stage was assuming a regency, which would be a direct challenge to Antipater and Craterus. He was perhaps maintaining a fiction that Arrhidaeus could govern in his own right, in which case, as before, he was the chief figure at court. Meleager was associated with him, but according to Arrian he was subordinate, Perdiccas' ὕπαρχος. However it was spelled out, the position of Perdiccas and Meleager was simply the position of supremacy they had achieved at Babylon. The three separate foci of power were recognized.

We now revert to Craterus, and the famous (or infamous) definition of his position. For Arrian he is προστάτης of the

(cf. Heckel 143). Arrian's source, who here must be Ptolemy, failed to mention Perdiccas' elevation, perhaps out of malice (Errington, *CQ* 19 (1969) 239–40); he did not, however, go so far as to deny it (contra Heckel 148 n. 454).

[83] Curt. 10.5.4, 6.4–5; Just. 12.15.12; Diod. 17.117.3; 18.2.4 (cf. *Heidelberg Epit. FGrH* 155 F 1.2, which uses the same source); Nep. *Eum.* 2.1. On the historicity of the tradition (which is often denied) see Badian, in *Zu Al. d. Gr.* i.605–9 (Hammond, *AJPh* 110 (1989) 159–60=*Collected Studies* iii.181–2, reaffirms his disbelief). By the end of the 4th century the story was famous enough to be absorbed into the earliest strands of the *Alexander Romance* (*Metz Epit.* 112).

[84] Just. 13.4.5. The emendation goes back to Madvig (*Adversaria critica* ii (Copenhagen 1873) 623–5), and is printed in the text of Otto Seel's standard Teubner edition. Schachermeyr, *Al. in Babylon* 167, regards it as probable.

kingdom of Arrhidaeus. Dexippus is more expansive: Craterus was entrusted with the maintenance (κηδεμονία) and what amounted to the προστασία of Arrhidaeus' kingdom;[85] this he glosses as the highest position of honour among the Macedonians. Finally Justin (13.4.5) states baldly that Craterus' function was the safekeeping of the royal treasure ('regiae pecuniae custodia Cratero traditur'). We may perhaps begin with this last statement, which most scholars have dismissed as hopelessly garbled. Abbreviated it certainly is,[86] but not necessarily distorted. Craterus was based in Cilicia,[87] at this period perhaps the richest of the western satrapies. Harpalus had spent time at Tarsus, enjoying its palace facilities,[88] and, as we have seen, it was the centre of the great military build-up which Alexander had commissioned in his last year. The treasury of Cyinda was the principal receptacle of money, and vast sums were lodged there. As late as November 315, after six years of war in which Cilicia figured prominently, Antigonus was able to draw 10,000 talents from Cyinda alone.[89] Much more would have been there for the taking in 323. We can compare the situation in which Eumenes found himself in 318. He received a commission from the current regent, Polyperchon, urging him either to return to Macedon and share the guardianship of the kings or to stay in Asia and fight it out with Antigonus. The commission is described in general terms as care and solicitude for the royal house (τὸ δ' ὅλον ἀπεφαίνετο μάλιστα πάντων πρέπειν Εὐμενῆ τῆς βασιλικῆς οἰκίας κήδεσθαι καὶ φροντίζειν),[90] and to support the task he is given unlimited drawing rights on the monies in Cilicia, which is seen as the

---

[85] Dexippus, *FGrH* 100 F 8.4: τὴν δὲ κηδεμονίαν καὶ ὅση προστασία τῆς βασιλείας Κράτερος ἐπετράπη.

[86] As Schachermeyr, *Al. in Babylon* 125–6, pertinently observed. See too his early essay, *Klio* 16 (1920) 332–7.

[87] Diod. 18.4.1, 12.1, 16.4. For the background see Bosworth, *From Arrian to Alexander* 207–11.

[88] Theopompus, *FGrH* 115 F 254; Cleitarchus, *FGrH* 137 F 30; cf. Diod. 17.108.4.

[89] Diod. 19.56.5 (cf. Billows, *Antigonos* 107–8). Much later, in 302, Antigonus was able to pay his entire army for three months 'from the money he had brought down from Cyinda' (Diod. 20.108.2). See above, n. 13.

[90] Diod. 18.57.3–4. The protection (κήδεσθαι) of the royal house is, of course, reminiscent of Craterus' κηδεμονία of the kingdom.

financial hub of the Levant.[91] As a result Eumenes was able to raise a substantial mercenary army in a matter of months and maintain himself as royal general in Asia. The parallel with the position voted for Craterus in 323 is evident. It is a commission in the vaguest terms to promote the interests of the royal house. Eumenes can stay in Asia or return to Europe; he has free disposal of the financial and military resources of the area and bases himself in Cilicia. In 323, however, Craterus' position was infinitely stronger. He had arguably the best and most united force of Macedonian veterans and controlled Cilicia and its treasures. Hence the definition of his position at Babylon. He was given authority (or encouragement) to promote the royal house in whatever way he thought fit and to draw on the resources of the area at will. The vagueness of the formulation was deliberate. The marshals at Babylon were not sufficiently strong or united to give orders to Craterus. He was at liberty to follow whichever directives of Alexander he pleased. He might escort his veterans back to Macedonia as Alexander had intended, consolidate his position in Cilicia or even launch the programme of western expansion which Alexander had planned. The commission he received from Babylon gave him *carte blanche* to do everything, except possibly return to the east.

For the moment Perdiccas was conciliatory. He would not challenge Antipater or Craterus directly, and he had their *de facto* positions recognized by the army at Babylon. But there was already one casualty from the crisis. Leonnatus, who had been designated along with Perdiccas to be guardian of the anticipated infant king, has apparently fallen out of the inner circle. No account of the reconciliation has any reference to him, and it is only Perdiccas and Meleager who share power in Babylon. There is no *tertius dux*, as we should have expected from Curtius' narrative (10.8.22). This is the first clear sign of Perdiccas' ascendancy. His role in the reconciliation made him the favourite of the infantry. Leonnatus

[91] Diod. 18.58.1; Plut. *Eum.* 12.2. Eumenes was given 500 talents for his own use and unlimited funds for recruiting troops. The commission had general application, and was honoured as far afield as Susa, where the treasurers acknowledged that he had exclusive drawing rights (Diod. 19.15.5; see below, p. 114). In Cilicia itself Ptolemy was unable to shake Eumenes' authority to draw on the monies of Cynda.

could not match his influence—and possibly the men would not tolerate him in command.[92] Meleager was a more serious embarrassment. Though perhaps technically subordinate to Perdiccas, he had demonstrated his influence and popularity through the proclamation of Arrhidaeus and he would not hesitate undermine the chiliarch if he had the opportunity. Not surprisingly Perdiccas resorted to intrigue, the type of intrigue which had seen the downfall of Philotas seven years before. He encouraged seditious talk (so Curtius reports), ensured that Meleager was aware of it and promised that he would reveal the mutineers at a solemn lustration of the army. The plot is reminiscent of the stratagem which Xenophon claims was used by Tissaphernes to lure Clearchus and his fellow generals to their death, but there is no reason to doubt its historicity.[93] There is general agreement in the sources that a lustration took place and that it witnessed a number of executions.[94] Meleager countenanced the scenario, but was wholly taken aback when the troops selected for punishment proved to be his own supporters, the 30 (or 300) who had been instrumental in elevating Arrhidaeus.[95] Meleager himself survived for the moment, but his power was broken and

[92] Although a Bodyguard, Leonnatus never seems to have held an extended command over any unit of Macedonians, infantry or cavalry. He is attested at the head of mixed forces, combined for separate operations (Arr. 4.24.10–25.3; 6.18.3), most notably in Oreitis (Las Bela), where he crushed a native revolt (Arr. 6.22.3; 7.5.5; *Ind.* 23.5). However, unlike (say) Meleager, he had no continuous contact with any large body of troops. He may have been a relative of Eurydice, the mother of Philip II and an intimate of Alexander from boyhood ('Suda' s.v. Λεόννατος = Arr. *Succ.* F 12), but there is no evidence of any specific regional affiliation. However lofty his lineage (Curt. 10.7.8), he could not compete with Perdiccas for the loyalty of the troops.

[93] Curt. 10.9.7–9. For the parallel in Xenophon see *Anab.* 2.5.24–32. Atkinson (*Al. in Fact and Fiction* 322–4) has recently compared Perdiccas' *dissimulatio* with that of the emperor Tiberius. However, there are no grounds for concluding that Curtius is simply imposing Roman *color*. Such intrigue was rife in the early Hellenistic period, as Antigonus demonstrated when he disposed of Peithon (Diod. 19.46.1, a classic exercise in duplicity) or Cassander when he arrested and executed Nicanor (Polyaen. 4.11.2; Diod. 18.75.1; cf. Bosworth, *CQ* 44 (1994) 64–5).

[94] Curt. 10.9.12–18; Arr. *Succ.* F 1a.4; Just. 13.4.7–8; Diod. 18.4.7.

[95] Curt. 10.9.18 (around 300); Diod. 18.4.7 (30). Justin (13.4.7) alleges that Perdiccas arranged the lustration without Meleager's knowledge ('ignaro collega'); that may be a contraction of the more detailed story in Curtius, where the lustration is planned in consultation with Meleager, but Meleager remains in blissful ignorance of its intended outcome.

he was presently arraigned before the king he had created, and was killed when he attempted to escape.[96]

Some time had passed between the reconciliation and the lustration. There is no means of telling how long. Justin (13.4.7) writes vaguely of a lustration which Perdiccas declared 'for the future' (*in posterum*),[97] while it is clear from Curtius (10.9.13) that there was a lapse of some days between the decision to hold a lustration and the ceremony itself, and the decision was preceded by an indeterminate period of intrigue. There has been a tendency to curtail this period, because of Curtius' note (10.10.9) that Alexander's body had remained untreated for seven days. The note is placed after the lustration and satrapal distribution, and it has been inferred that the whole period of mutiny took no more than a week from start to finish. However, there is another tradition, not admittedly very reliable, that the body remained untreated for thirty days without a sign of decay.[98] There was clearly some dispute over the fact. In any case Curtius' note falls outside his account of the political disturbances. Having recorded the dismemberment of the empire,[99] he turns to the more sensational themes, the miraculous preservation of the body and the rumours of poisoning. The body, one may assume, was handed over to the embalmers immediately after the reconciliation, and the seven day period at most covers the initial mutiny and its resolution. The lustration came later, and it may have been significantly later, a matter of weeks rather than days.

---

[96] All sources agree that there was an interval (Diod. 18.4.7: μετὰ δὲ ταῦτα; Arr. *Succ.* F 1a.4: οὐ πολλῷ ὕστερον; Curt. 10.9.21: 'mox') between the lustration and the execution of Meleager. The distribution of satrapies came in the interval (Badian *HSCP* 72 (1967) 201–2). Errington, *JHS* 90 (1970) 57) prefers to place Meleager's death before the satrapy distribution.

[97] I take the phrase to be a general reference to the future (as in Cic. *Fam.* 12.10.3; cf. *OLD* s.v, *posterus* 1b), not the rarer contraction of 'in posterum diem', 'on the following day' (as Yardley's translation has it).

[98] Ael. *VH* 12.64, agreeing that the body was neglected while the succession crisis lasted.

[99] The distribution of satrapies ends the historical narrative of events in Babylon, and Curtius rounds it off with a moralizing peroration on the ambitions of the satraps (10.10.6–8). He then addressed the body and its fate without sketching in the chronological context.

In that time Perdiccas had strengthened his position. The lustration was proof enough of that. He was able to intimidate the phalanx and remove any pockets of opposition, and the king operated placidly as his tool.[100] He now organized the distribution of satrapies and at the same time modified his own position. That would seem to follow from the promotion of Seleucus to the hipparchy previously held by Hephaestion and by Perdiccas himself.[101] This has surely to be the chiliarchy itself, which was associated with the chief cavalry command. It could be argued (and indeed it has been) that the military functions of the chiliarchy were separated from the administration, so that Seleucus had no role other than the prestigious cavalry command.[102] There is, however, no suggestion that Seleucus held anything other than the position previously occupied by Hephaestion and Perdiccas, that is, the chiliarchy itself. Again, Diodorus states that Perdiccas took over the regency: he is termed ἐπιμελητὴς τῆς βασιλείας[103] as later are Peithon and Arrhidaeus and

---

[100] Curt. 10.9.18–19 (see above, n. 72); Arr. *Succ.* F 1a.4: ὡς ἐκ προστάξεως Ἀρριδαίου αὐτοῦ παρόντος ἀνεῖλε.

[101] Diod. 18.3.4. See above, pp. 50–1.

[102] So, for instance, Schachermeyr, *Al. in Babylon* 175; Grainger, *Seleukos Nikator* 18–20. Schachermeyr makes much of Just. 13.4.17, where it is stated that the highest command in the army ('summus castrorum tribunatus') went to Seleucus; that, Schachermeyr claims, meant only the cavalry hipparchy, not the court functions of the chiliarch. However, Justin goes on to add that *Cassander* had command of the royal attendants ('stipatoribus regis satellitibusque'). Why Schachermeyr (n. 159) restricts this to the royal Pages passes my comprehension. The expression refers generally to the entourage of the king at court, and surely in this context denotes the ceremonial role of the chiliarch (cf. Schachermeyr 32–4). Here, I suggest, we have an example of the misleading contraction which pervades the satrapy list in Justin. The original account of Trogus presumably defined the powers of the chiliarch, giving both his military and ceremonial functions, and stated that the office was given to Seleucus at Babylon and *later* passed to Cassander (cf. Diod. 18.48.4–5; Arr. *Succ.* F 1.38). There is no evidence that Cassander was even present at Babylon at the settlement (see above, n. 17). Something very similar has occurred with Justin's description of Antigonus' satrapy (13.4.14–15); he was given Greater Phrygia, while Nearchus had Lycia and Pamphylia. All this territory was given to Antigonus in the Babylon settlement, whereas Nearchus only governed Lycia and Pamphylia between late 334 and 329 (Arr. 3.6.6; 4.7.2; cf. *HCA* i.156, 284; ii.41). Justin has again split the notice of a single appointment into two.

[103] Diod. 18.2.4. The *Heidelberg Epitome*, which seems to follow the same source, gives a slightly fuller form of the title (ἐπίτροπος καὶ ἐπιμελητὴς τῶν βασιλικῶν πραγμάτων). Like Diodorus, it makes the appointment of Perdiccas follow the acclamation and renaming of Arrhidaeus, and the immediate sequel is the satrapy distribution (*FGrH* 155 F 1.2).

Antipater himself.[104] This (along with the *Heidelberg Epitome*) is the only direct attestation that Perdiccas became regent at Babylon, and the context is curiously compressed. Diodorus goes directly from the reconciliation to the distribution of satrapies, and he only alludes in passing to the lustration in a retrospective note two chapters later. He seems to have associated the proclamation of Arrhidaeus as king with Perdiccas' assumption of the regency, obscuring the fact that there was a significant interval between the two events. But it was the success of the lustration, Perdiccas' intimidation of the remaining opposition, which encouraged him to have his *de facto* supremacy recognized. The troops according to Diodorus appointed Perdiccas to the regency and voted 'that the leading Companions and Bodyguards should take over satrapies and obey the king and Perdiccas'. That was critically important; the satrapies were the gift of the king, and they were given in his name (as Arrian confirms). As regent Perdiccas could preside over the redistribution and have Arrhidaeus confirm them. As Justin observes, acutely for once, it enabled him to exercise patronage and remove rivals.[105]

Remove rivals he did. The leading Bodyguards were relocated far from Babylon: Ptolemy to Egypt, Peithon to Media, Lysimachus to Thrace, and Leonnatus to Hellespontine Phrygia. Other than Perdiccas himself, the only Bodyguard of Alexander left in the capital was Aristonous, whose loyalty was unquestioned. Alcetas and Attalus remained at headquarters with the regent, as did Seleucus, but the key figures were separated from king and court. Even Eumenes was sent away to Cappadocia and Laomedon, a boyhood friend of Alexander, to Syria. There were important and dangerous tasks to be performed and the permanent prospect of friction. Lysimachus had to cope with an Odrysian rebellion with minimal forces,[106] and he was on Antipater's doorstep.

---

[104] Diod. 18.36.7, 39.1 (Peithon and Arrhidaeus); 18.39.2 (Antipater); 18.48.4; *Heidelberg Epit., FGrH* 155 F 1.5 (Polyperchon).

[105] Just. 13.4.9. Arr. *Succ.* F 1a makes a similar observation: 'none the less he resolved to appoint the men he suspected to satrapies, on the ostensible orders of Arrhidaeus'.

[106] Diod. 18.14.3; Arr. *Succ.* F 1.10. On the background see H. S. Lund, *Lysimachus* 20–6; F. Landucci Gattinoni, *Lisimaco di Tracia* 97–104.

Victory and defeat alike would present complications. Similarly Eumenes was instructed to pacify Cappadocia with forces supplied by Leonnatus and Antigonus,[107] and the predictable clashes of authority and personality surfaced as soon as he arrived in Asia Minor. The distribution was placing ambitious and difficult men in close proximity but with insufficient forces to be a serious threat except to each other. After ten years and more in the close entourage of Alexander the satrapal commands cannot have been attractive, least of all to Leonnatus, who had the strategically placed but small satrapy of Hellespontine Phrygia,[108] not even Lydia with its great citadel and treasury at Sardes. But there was no choice. Perdiccas had control of the army at Babylon, and the other Bodyguards, singly and collectively, were impotent to resist. They could only go to their satrapies and pursue their ambitions on a regional basis, and without access to significant numbers of Macedonian troops their military potential was limited.

Perdiccas could control his rivals at Babylon. He had no hold over Antipater or Craterus, and there was no guarantee that they would accept the army at Babylon as a legitimizing body or the king it had proclaimed. Any provisions he made which affected them had to be extremely circumspect. There is some slight evidence of the diplomacy he used. In Arrian's account of the satrapal division the territorial limits of Antipater's authority are stated in detail, but the territory is assigned to Craterus as well as Antipater.[109] Something may be wrong with Photius' summary here,[110] but in general his

---

[107] Plut. *Eum.* 3.3–6; Nep. *Eum.* 2.3–5.

[108] Leonnatus' ambitions were nothing if not overt. He modelled his hairstyle and dress on Alexander, and rode in state on royal Nesaean horses, followed by an élite squadron (ἄγημα) of Companions ('Suda' s.v. Λεόννατος = Arr. *Succ.* F 12).

[109] Arr. *Succ.* F 1a.7: τὰ δὲ ἐπέκεινα τῆς Θρᾴκης... καὶ οἱ Ἕλληνες σύμπαντες Κρατέρῳ καὶ Ἀντιπάτρῳ ἐνεμήθη. Cf. Schachermeyr, *Al. in Babylon* 166 n. 136, claiming, against his earlier views, that the reference to Craterus is a slip of Photius. Contrast Errington, *JHS* 90 (1970) 57: 'Perdiccas therefore... reverted to the first proposal of the nobles' consensus, that Craterus would share command in Europe with Antipater.' So too Anson, *CPh* 87 (1992) 42–3, agreeing that Perdiccas assumed the regency at this stage ('In the aftermath of the reconciliation Perdiccas emerged as the "*prostates* of the kingdom."').

[110] One might infer that Arrian mentioned Alexander's intended replacement of Antipater by Craterus, and Photius misinterpreted the replacement as a shared

reproduction of lists is fairly reliable, if occasionally truncated.[111] In all probability Perdiccas had Arrhidaeus confirm
Antipater's position in Macedonia and at the same time rat-
ify Alexander's instructions to Craterus. If he returned to
Macedonia with his veterans, he would hold power there; but
it would be as a colleague of Antipater, and the two of them
would have to establish a *modus vivendi*. Perdiccas continued
his subtle persuasion, exploiting his predominance over the
army. The documents which he presented to the troops and
had quashed were directly relevant to Craterus. In particular
the vast project of naval construction, already under way in
Cilicia, Phoenicia, and Cyprus, was cancelled, as was the
proposed campaign against Carthage.[112] This limited the
options open to Craterus. There was to be no western expansion and hence no use for the fleet which was being built
under his supervision. In other words he should revert to
Alexander's original commission and return to Macedonia.[113]
There was, it would seem, no attempt to give Craterus direct
instructions, but political pressure was certainly brought to
bear. The grandiose plans of conquest had been rejected by
the rank-and-file at Babylon, who had decided not to carry
out any of the projects presented to them. This hardly
had any binding constitutional force, but it was a public

command. That is possible, but the obvious place for such a retrospective note
would be the initial confirmation of Antipater's regency in Europe, which Arrian
mentioned at a much earlier point (*Succ.* F 1a.4).

[111] His version of Arrian's account of the Susa marriages (Phot. *Bibl.* cod. 91:
68^{b}5–18) compares well with the original (Arr. 7.4.4–6). Photius echoes Arrian's
phraseology and represents the names accurately (except that 'Barsine', the eldest
daughter of Darius, appears as 'Arsinoe'). The list of wedded couples is trimmed by
random omissions, but what is selected is a close approximation to the original.

[112] Diod. 18.4.1–5. On the historicity and political implications of this remarkable passage see the bibliography in Seibert (above, n. 1). For the implications of
the annulment see Badian, *HSCP* 72 (1968) 201–4; Errington, *JHS* 90 (1970) 59;
Bosworth, *From Arrian to Alexander* 207–11. It hardly matters in this context
whether Alexander did in fact formulate all the projects attributed to him. The
troops at least took them to be authentic and disowned them in their totality.

[113] It is unlikely that the vote also quashed Craterus' commission to replace
Antipater, as suggested by Badian (202; endorsed by Heckel 128–9). The troops
only reject the specific proposals put to them (ἔκριναν μηδὲν τῶν εἰρημένων συντελεῖν);
it is not a blanket rejection of Alexander's *acta*. The cancellation of the Last Plans
in fact left Craterus with only one valid commission from Alexander: the return to
Macedon.

statement by the troops of Babylon that they would have nothing to with war in the west. Craterus might choose to ignore it on the grounds that the army at Babylon was not representative of the totality of Macedonians, but he would have to reckon with his own troops. The men of Opis will not have been anything other than sympathetic to the cancellation of the Last Plans. The naval preparations in Cilicia were keeping them from home, and if Craterus considered it his pious duty to embark on conquest in the west, then they would be doing the fighting. The very public decision of the army at Babylon was a clear signal to them to put pressure on Craterus to return to Europe. It could also improve Perdiccas' standing with Macedonians under arms wherever they were. He was consulting his men and acting on their recommendations, a far cry from the Alexander who had tried to force them against their will across the Hyphasis and into the Ganges plain. Pressure on Craterus there certainly was, but we have no idea how he reacted to it or how he responded to Perdiccas. He did not act upon the political suggestions from Babylon and remained in his centre of power in Cilicia for nearly a year, until the summer of 322.[114] As we have seen, there must have been diplomatic exchanges with Perdiccas, and some degree of compromise was reached.[115] At least in 322 Perdiccas took the royal army into Cappadocia to subject the area to regal authority, and there is no record of contact with Craterus. He must have moved shortly before Perdiccas arrived in Cappadocia and avoided the necessity of a meeting.

Relations with Antipater were simpler. Soon after Alexander's death Perdiccas approached him for the hand of his daughter, Nicaea, a sign according to Diodorus that he was bent on co-operation (κοινοπραγία).[116] Presumably

---

[114] For the chronology of his movements see Schmitt, *Der Lamische Krieg* 144, who follows Schwahn (*Klio* 24 (1931) 320) in dating Craterus' departure from Cilicia to June 322. That seems the latest possible.

[115] It was a conciliatory step to appoint Philotas satrap of Cilicia. He was a friend of Craterus, and was later deposed by Perdiccas for that very reason (Arr. *Succ.* F 24.2; cf. Just. 13.6.16).

[116] Diod. 18.23.2; cf. *CQ* (43 (1993) 423–4, where I retract my earlier suggestion (*CQ* 21 (1971) 134–5) that Perdiccas made his overtures before Alexander's death.

Perdiccas made it clear that he would not interfere in Macedonian affairs provided that he was given a free hand in Asia. He could not guarantee Craterus' movements, but it was not necessary for him to do so. In a matter of weeks Antipater was embroiled in the Lamian War, in which he experienced the first reverses of Macedonian arms on Greek soil since the Sacred War and was ingloriously confined to the city of Lamia. His importance as a dynastic rival declined abruptly, and Perdiccas was freed of any worries of a challenge from Macedon. By autumn the news of the outbreak of war would have reached Babylon. But then the situation had changed yet again. Rhoxane's child was at last born, in August or October. At the same time Perdiccas became aware of the serious unrest in the east of the empire, where Greek settlers in Alexander's new foundations left their domiciles and combined in a formidable army to force their way home.[117] That necessitated detaching 3,000 of his precious Macedonian troops under the command of Peithon the Bodyguard,[118] and it now appears that the expeditionary force only left for Bactria in December 323.[119] There were

Errington's suggestion (*JHS* 90 (1970) 58–9) that it came at the time of the first negotiations at Babylon is more probable. Cf. Schachermeyr, *Al. in Babylon* 178–9.

[117] Diod. 18.4.8, 7.1–2; Trogus *Prolog.* 13. On the course of the uprising see Schober, *Untersuchungen* 32–7; Holt, *Alexander and Bactria* 87–92. The movement clearly took some time to develop momentum. News of Alexander's death had to percolate through the north-eastern satrapies, and some weeks will have elapsed while the colonists reassured themselves that this time Alexander's death was accurately reported (cf. Diod. 17.99.5). At Athens the *demos* held back from open war until eye-witnesses arrived from Babylon (Diod. 18.9.4; cf. Schmitt, *Der Lamische Krieg* 53–6); and the colonists would have been prudent to wait for similar confirmations. Then they would have to co-ordinate themselves and agree on the hierarchy of leadership. It is unlikely that news of the uprising reached Perdiccas at Babylon before the autumn of 323.

[118] Diod. 18.7.3. Peithon had been given the satrapy of Media in the Babylon distribution (Heckel 277). He may well have assumed his command by the time the news of the eastern revolt broke. In that case he was recalled to Babylon, where he took command of the Macedonian foot and cavalry which had been allotted to him. He was also able to communicate with his fellow satraps from Ecbatana, to ensure that the combined expeditionary force of mercenaries and native cavalry (Diod. *loc. cit.*) was ready for him on his return.

[119] A. Sachs and H. Hunger, *Astronomical Diaries and Related Texts from Babylonia I. Diaries from 652 BC to 262 BC* 211 = Del Monte 12. This is a chronological note placed at the end of the ninth Babylonian month (Kislīm): 'he went to Bactria with his troops to combat the army of the Hani'. There is some doubt about the precise translation, but Del Monte seems to have shown that the reference is to

several dangers: if Peithon was defeated, Perdiccas' military resources were seriously depleted, but if he was victorious and added the defeated Greeks to his entourage, then he could emerge as a serious rival (as, we are told, Perdiccas feared when he made the appointment).[120] As it turned out, Peithon served Perdiccas' interests impeccably. He was victorious, but his troops massacred the returning colonists and he was unable to supplement his forces from the defeated army. Peithon, then, lacked the resources to pursue his ambitions. His victory came at much the same time as Perdiccas' invasion of Cappadocia, and Peithon returned with his Macedonians to replenish the royal army.[121] At that time events in the west were undecided. Leonnatus had fallen in battle relieving Antipater at Lamia, and Craterus had not as yet joined forces for the decisive battle. Perdiccas was in the ascendant, and it was apparently after his victory in Cappadocia that he had Alexander's child proclaimed joint king by the army.[122] The infant was nearly a year old, apparently with good prospects of survival, and he could be combined with Arrhidaeus in the monarchy. This time there was no hesitation. Perdiccas acted as regent for them both and was *de facto* king. He had profited from the comparative weakness of his rivals and established himself as the leading figure in the empire.

We should end on this note. Perdiccas had achieved a political coup which for the moment gave him control of the kings and the military resources to enforce his will. Military resources had been the key to the settlement from the beginning. Then Perdiccas lost control of the infantry for a short

---

the departure of Peithon. Not necessarily from Babylon. The crossing of the Zagros would be difficult in December, and the entry may refer to the combined army taking the field in Media.

[120] Diod. 18.7.5. If Peithon was away from Babylon when he was given his command against the colonists, it gave Perdiccas ample time to intrigue with the Macedonian phalanx officers and ensure that their troops would be primed to loot and massacre.

[121] Diod. 18.36.5. There is no indication exactly when Peithon returned, but it is unlikely that he participated in the Cappadocian campaign. He joined the army at the earliest for the later attacks on Laranda and Isaura, towards the end of 322.

[122] Arr. *Succ.* F 1a.1 attests the fact but not the time. For argument that the acclamation came in summer 322, after the Cappadocian campaign, see Bosworth, *CQ* 43 (1993) 423–6.

time, and had to win back his predominance through intrigue and personal bravado. Once he had negotiated the reconciliation and purged the infantry of its dissidents there was no serious rival to his supremacy at Babylon, and he could act as regent for Arrhidaeus, in Asia at least. But he carefully refrained from a direct challenge to Craterus and Antipater. Neither was threatened with demotion or replacement, but Perdiccas tried to manœuvre them into a position where they would have to come to terms with Alexander's orders. Whether Craterus and Antipater shared power or came into conflict, Perdiccas' interests were served. The main danger to him was the possibility of Craterus using Alexander's last plans as the base for further imperial annexation—for himself—and so he used the moral influence of the troops to end the plans for expansion. There was little or no legal basis for his actions. Not surprisingly, for the situation was unique. There was no relative from the Argead house to assume the regency. In Macedon proper there was already a viceroy who had been empowered by the defunct king. And for the first time there was an overseas empire, and Macedonians were in charge of the key satrapies. There was a multitude of commanders eager to succeed, but no predetermined hierarchy of succession. The marshals had no choice other than to compete for supremacy and appeal to the troops under their command to support them and confer a measure of legitimacy on the positions they created. They were not following a clearly defined constitutional procedure, for there was none, at least none that applied to the situation at Babylon. They made up the rules as they went, and created the precedents that would be invoked in later crises.

3
Macedonian Numbers at the Death of Alexander the Great

Few subjects are as important and contentious as the demographic effect of Alexander's conquests. It is accepted that Macedonia was far weaker by the end of the third century than had been the case under Philip and Alexander, but what caused the debilitation is intensely disputed. In 1986 I published an article which presented the argument that Alexander's demands for reinforcements, in particular the demands he made between 334 and 330, drained the military resources of Macedonia and were ultimately responsible for her decline over the next century.[1] My conclusions have been sharply challenged, by Nicholas Hammond, Ernst Badian, and Richard Billows,[2] all of whom argue that Macedonia had the resources to cope with the demands made by Alexander and that Alexander was less responsible for the decline in Macedonian armies than his immediate successors and the Gauls who invaded Macedon in 279. The problem is complex, and conjecture reigns supreme. We have no figures for the population of Macedon, no suggestion what proportion of the male population was comprised of the men actually under arms. Nor is there any reason to think that our sources have given us complete, exhaustive figures for the reinforcements and repatriation which took place during and immediately after Alexander's reign. There are obvious limits to the conclusions which can be drawn, and in the end one can only extrapolate from the army figures which have been preserved in the sources. However, it is vital to make the most of that evidence, not to read too much into it, and to

[1] A. B. Bosworth, 'Alexander the Great and the Decline of Macedon', *JHS* 106 (1986) 1–12.
[2] N. G. L. Hammond, *JHS* 109 (1989) 56–68 (see also *GRBS* 25 (1984) 51–61); E. Badian, in *Ventures into Greek History*, esp. 261–8; R. A. Billows, *Kings and Colonists*, 183–212.

interpret it within its context. These seem obvious principles, but all writers who have addressed the subject, myself
included, have offended against them all, and some of the
basic texts have been persistently misused. In this chapter I
intend to explore some of those fundamental passages and
draw some implications from what I see as their clear meaning. I also analyse the military situation between 323 and
319, when Macedonian reserves were stretched to the full,
and assess the impact of the campaigns of those years, which
were arguably more destructive—for Macedon—than the
entire reign of Alexander.

First things first. The starting point for any assessment
of the strength of Alexander's army is Diodorus' detailed
description of his army at the crossing of the Hellespont in 334
(17.17.3–5). From it most scholars have inferred that
Alexander divided the Macedonian infantry under arms into
two groups, each 12,000 strong, one of which he took with
him and the other he left as the home army of his vice-
gerent, Antipater.[3] That, I fear, is a blatant misreading of the
passage. Diodorus does indeed state that Alexander's expeditionary force comprised 12,000 Macedonians, and goes on
to list the other groups which comprised the army, first the
infantry and then the cavalry; after each detailed list he gives
the composite total of infantry and cavalry. The numbers in
the text are internally corrupt, but Diodorus' method is clear
enough; he gives first the national groups individually and
then the sum total. After that he moves to the forces left with
Antipater: οἱ μὲν οὖν μετ᾽ Ἀλεξάνδρου διαβάντες εἰς τὴν Ἀσίαν
τοσοῦτοι τὸ πλῆθος ἦσαν. οἱ δ᾽ ἐπὶ τῆς Εὐρώπης ἀπολελειμμένοι
στρατιῶται, ὧν Ἀντίπατρος εἶχε τὴν ἡγεμονίαν, πεζοὶ μὲν
ὑπῆρχον μύριοι καὶ δισχίλιοι, ἱππεῖς δὲ χίλιοι καὶ πεντακόσιοι

---

[3] This is usually assumed without comment, as in the influential little monograph of Hans Droysen, *Untersuchungen über Alexander des Grossen Heerwesen und
Kriegführung* (Freiburg in Bresgau 1885) 5, and in 1986 I more or less replicated his
formulation (*JHS* 106 (1986) 2: 'the Macedonian infantry was 12,000 strong and
another 12,000 were left behind as the home army under Antipater.' The only note
of doubt that I can find is expressed by Beloch (iii².2.325–6), who briefly discounts
the idea that the figure could include mercenaries: there was no war and no reason
to keep a large mercenary force. Quite the contrary. The position of Antipater as
head of the Corinthian League made it inevitable that he would need mercenaries
for small-scale disciplinary actions (see below, p. 66).

('this was the size of the force which crossed into Asia with Alexander; the soldiers left in Europe, who fell under the command of Antipater, amounted to 12,000 foot and 1,500 cavalry'). The two forces, those of Alexander and Antipater, are contrasted, and it is their total size that is at issue. What Diodorus does *not* say is that the infantry left with Antipater was exclusively Macedonian. He says nothing about its composition, merely giving its total. Far from balancing the troops with Alexander, Antipater's army was little more than a third of the force which crossed the Hellespont and comparable in size to the advance force sent ahead into Asia Minor in 336.[4] In that army Macedonians are unlikely to have predominated, any more than they did in Alexander's own entourage. Antipater admittedly will have had no allied troops from the Greeks of the Corinthian League, but we should expect a nucleus of Macedonians supplemented by mercenaries and contingents from the north, comparable to the Odrysians, Illyrians, and Triballians listed in Alexander's force. That was the type of army Philip had favoured. So Demosthenes informs us in a famous passage: Philip did not simply use his phalanx of heavy infantry, he had auxiliary forces of light-armed, cavalry, archers, and mercenaries, forces that gave him the flexibility to campaign all year round.[5] For garrisons in places like Phocis and Nicaea he used mercenaries, as he did when he went on rapid forays to Euboea and the Peloponnese.[6] This was exactly the sort of assignment which Antipater would have faced as acting *hegemon* of the Corinthian League. In fact Antipater needed precisely the variegated army which Philip had used. He faced the same military demands. The conclusion seems to me

---

[4] For the advance force we have a round figure of 10,000 (Polyaen. 5.44.4), not necessarily the full complement (cf. *JHS* 106 (1986) 2 n. 9). It certainly comprised both mercenaries and Macedonians, and there was a significant complement of the latter (cf. Polyaen. 5.44.5).

[5] Dem. 9.48–9: ἀκούετε δὲ Φίλιππον οὐχὶ τῷ φάλαγγ᾽ ὁπλιτῶν ἄγειν βαδίζονθ᾽ ὅποι βούλεται, ἀλλὰ τῷ ψιλούς, ἱππέας, τοξότας, ξένους, τοιοῦτον ἐξηρτῆσθαι στρατόπεδον.

[6] For Philip's use of mercenaries see Dem.6.15 (Messenia and Argos); 9.16 (Chersonese); 19.81 (Phocis); 19.295 (Megara); 9.33, 58; 19.87 (Euboea). For discussion see H. W. Parke, *Greek Mercenary Soldiers* (Oxford 1933) 159–64; G. T. Griffith, in *HM* ii.438–44; L. P. Marinovic, *Le Mercenariat grec et la crise de la polis* 98–103.

unavoidable. Antipater was left with a mixed force in which the Macedonian infantry (and cavalry) under arms comprised a minority. If the proportions were similar to those in Alexander's expeditionary force, he would have had 4–5,000 Macedonian infantrymen.

This interpretation has radical consequences. Our evidence suggests that the number of Macedonians under arms in 334 was significantly smaller than has hitherto been argued: 12,000 infantry crossed the Hellespont with Alexander; some 3,000 were probably operating there already, and a maximum of 5,000 was left in Europe under Antipater's command. The total pool is at least 7,000 less than had been previously suspected, and the Macedonian component in Antipater's army was relatively small. Any major military emergency would force him to call on whatever reserves remained in Macedon. Reserves there certainly were. Each year saw a number of Macedonian youths reach military age and increase the military resources of the state, and there were presumably many men capable of military service who had not been called up in 334. These reserves are unquantifiable, but they must be taken into account. If Alexander demanded reinforcements on a large scale, the home army could not provide the necessary troops, and the reserves would inevitably be depleted. Reinforcements were in fact demanded, and on a large scale. The army which fought at Gaugamela in October 331 comprised 40,000 foot and 7,000 horse,[7] comparable with the highest estimates of Alexander's army at the crossing. In the meantime there had been two major battles, sieges at Halicarnassus and Tyre, constant detachments of troops for satrapal armies and regional garrisons. The latter, as far as we can tell, were predominantly drawn from Alexander's mercenaries or his Greek alled troops, but the numbers were significant, particularly during the stress of the island war. Caria alone had 3,000 mercenaries assigned to it in 334,[8] and

---

[7] Arr. 3.12.9. The highest figure for Alexander's forces at the Hellespont is that of Anaximenes: 43,000 foot and 5,500 horse (Plut. *Mor.* 327 D = *FGrH* 72 F 29). It almost certainly includes the expeditionary force operating under Parmenion.

[8] Arr. 1.23.6. Cf. Arr. 1.17.8: the entire Argive contingent was assigned to the garrison at Sardes. In Lydia the satrap, Asander, was given 'what cavalry and light infantry appeared sufficient for the present needs' (Arr. 1.17.7); it was clearly a

Lydia, given the threat from the Persian counter-offensive, can hardly have had less. Presumably Alexander recruited mercenaries as he marched, but the gains will hardly have compensated for the losses, and it would seem that the proportion of Macedonians, whom Alexander used predominantly as his front-line troops, increased. That could only have happened through progressive reinforcement.

Reinforcements are reasonably attested in our sources. The first influx that we hear of was in the winter of 334/3 when Alexander sent home his newly married troops on compassionate leave and ordered their commanders 'to enlist as many cavalry and infantry from the land as they possibly could'.[9] The following spring the newly levied forces arrived in Gordium with their commanders, 3,000 infantry and 300 cavalry, all of them Macedonian (contingents from Thessaly and Elis are listed separately).[10] These are intriguing figures, but we should not extrapolate too much from them. Over a century ago Hans Droysen maintained that Arrian was referring to a maximum demand, and considered that a levy of 3,300 was much too small to make a serious impact upon the population of Macedonia, and he considered that Alexander drew upon a fraction of his resources.[11] He also assumed that the new recruits were predominantly young, drawn from the age classes reaching military age in the previous years. In this he has been enthusiastically followed by Badian, who infers that 'the number of men reaching military age at this time was conventionally put at 3,000 infantry and 250–300 cavalry'.[12] However, there is nothing in Arrian's

substantial force. Asander and the general in Caria were able to fight a serious and successful battle against the Persian Orontobates.

[9] Arr. 1.24.1: καταλέξαι ἱππέας τε καὶ πεζοὺς ἐκ τῆς χώρας ὅσους πλείστους.

[10] Arr. 1.29.4.

[11] Droysen (above, n. 3) 37–8: 'die angeführte Zahl ... die für ganz Makedonien sehr gering erscheint, verliert diese Auffallende, wenn sie sich nur auf einen Theil des Königreiches ... bezieht'. Droysen most implausibly considered the recruitment limited to the cantons of Upper Macedonia.

[12] Badian (above, n. 2) 261–3. He draws attention to the fact that the recruits of 333 numbered 3,000 foot and 300 cavalry and those of 331 (see below, p. 71) 6,000 foot and 500 cavalry. Hence the men of 331 comprise two years of new levies. No source, however, suggests that these figures represent age classes. The symmetry could be (and probably is) fortuitous. In any case, given the relative abundance of manpower that Badian's calculations produce, it is highly unlikely that entire age classes would

brief report to suggest that the levy was confined to a single group or was in any sense exhaustive. Alexander's orders were simply to enlist as many as was possible within the limited time that the newly married troops were on furlough in Macedonia.[13] In that case the composition of the group was probably varied. The incoming age group will have provided recruits, but so will the military population at large and perhaps even Antipater's home army—the regent could be expected to make up the losses from the reserve.

Other groups of reinforcements arrived in the course of the summer and autumn of 333. According to Curtius (3.1.24) Alexander received new drafts at the time when he moved east from Ancyra into Cappadocia, the first stage of his march to occupy Cilicia. It is possible that this is a doublet of Arrian's report of the arrival of the Macedonian levy at Gordium, placed at a slightly later juncture. But there is another possibility. According to Polybius Alexander's first historian, Callisthenes of Olynthus, recorded a contingent of 5,000 foot and 800 horse which arrived when Alexander was about to invade Cilicia.[14] That could be the group mentioned by Curtius. Commentators have been unwilling to combine the notices, and there has been deep suspicion of Polybius. His critique of Callisthenes is venomous and often misguided, and he could have misrepresented what he found. Hans Droysen again suggested that what was reported in Callisthenes was the arrival of the reinforcements at Gordium; Polybius added in the figure for the newly weds, not realizing that they belonged to Alexander's original expeditionary force.[15] His argument

be taken out of Macedonia. Billows, *Kings and Colonists* 205 also emphasizes the contribution of the new age classes between 333 and 331, but wisely concedes that there may also have been some mobilization of reserves.

[13] ὅσους πλείστους (Arr. 1.24.1) hardly means 'the most that Macedonia possessed'; it must be 'the most they could enlist'. Badian (above, n. 2) 262, however, considers that the phrase is 'rhetorical elaboration'. Hardly so, in one of the least rhetorical passages in Arrian's work. We can hardly accept the figure for the reinforcements as basic but reject the context as contaminated by fiction.

[14] Polyb. 12.19.1–2 = Callisthenes, *FGrH* 124 F 35. See my discussion, *JHS* 106 (1986) 6. Billows, *Kings and Colonists* 186 also accepts Callisthenes' reinforcements as an independent influx of troops, independent of the *neogamoi* and their recruits.

[15] Droysen (above, n. 3) 8, accepted with some reservations by Beloch (iii².2.332), who inferred that Arrian omitted a number of non-Macedonian contingents in his report of the reinforcements at Gordium. So Milns, *Entretiens Hardt* 22

has been widely accepted, but it rests on the assumption that Polybius was misguided—and presupposes that approximately one in six of the army at the Hellespont was newly married,[16] no less than 2,000 of the infantry and perhaps 150 horse. Arrian by contrast seems to imply that they were relatively few in number ('some[17] of the Macedonians who were fighting with Alexander had married shortly before the campaign'). It is surely better to conclude that Polybius (and Callisthenes) were recording a contingent not mentioned by Arrian, and perhaps identical to that of Curtius. But we cannot assume that the contingent was exclusively Macedonian. Polybius states that it came 'from Macedonia',[18] and in all probability it contained non-Macedonian troops, as did the later reinforcements which Amyntas brought to Mesopotamia. We cannot in that case calculate how many of the 5,000 infantry were Macedonians: 1–2,000 is likely enough, but it is only a guess. The same can be said of the reinforcements whose arrival was imminent at the time of Issus. Curtius mentions them in the context of a detailed narrative of the march from Mallus to Issus,[19] which is here far fuller than the account of Arrian with its lacunae. Once more there is every reason to accept that the report is authentic. Unfortunately no numbers are given, and we can only assume that the

(1976) 106. Others have been more whole-hearted, notably Badian (263–4), who considers that Droysen had solved the problem. He seems unaware of the reinforcements recorded by Curt. 3.1.24, but would presumably dismiss it as another doublet of the forces with the *neogamoi*. Given his assumption that the age classes were drawn upon in toto between 334 and 330, there is little room for additional levies.

[16] The weight of evidence, particularly that relating to the Silver Shields (see above, Ch. 1, n. 63), indicates that the average age of the troops at the Hellespont was relatively high.

[17] In Arrian ἔστιν οἵ denotes an indeterminate number on the small side (1.7.11, 22.4; 2.8.7, 23.6; 3.23.2–3; 4.4.4, 5.2 etc.). It is likely enough that his source gave no figure for the νεόγαμοι but it hardly suggested that their numbers were large.

[18] Rightly stressed by Hammond, *JHS* 109 (1989) 67 n. 57.

[19] Curt. 3.7.8. The notice is embedded in the debate on strategy which Curtius locates at Issus: were the Macedonians to advance to give battle or wait for new troops to arrive from Macedonia ('novi milites, quos ex Macedonia adventare constabat'). If that is imaginative fiction (Atkinson, *Commentary* 1.181), it is hard to fathom Curtius' motive for the invention. Most probably it was a detail from his source, a detail passed over by Arrian (2.6.2), who passes from Mallus to Myriandrus in a single sentence.

contingent comprised some thousands, including an unknown quantity of Macedonians. These reports are too deficient to build upon. They provide no concrete figures for the Macedonian troops. All they do is show that the reinforcements which arrived in Gordium were supplemented by at least two drafts which arrived later in the season.

The next influx of reinforcements is reported more meticulously. According to Diodorus and Curtius it was at the end of 332, immediately after the siege of Gaza, that Amyntas, a senior phalanx commander, was sent across the winter seas with instructions to enlist 'those of the youth who were suitable for campaigning'.[20] Once more there is no question of a levy confined to the maturing age groups, as has been argued. Diodorus' language is vague, almost formulaic,[21] and suggests only that Amyntas' recruiting was directed towards the younger and fitter members of the military population. That is what Curtius puts in the mouth of Amyntas at his later trial when he says that he enlisted 'many fit youths' who were being sheltered in Olympias' palace.[22] It is implied that there was widespread reluctance to serve in Asia, and that some coercion was necessary for men of military age to join the Asian adventure.[23] The enlistment presumably affected more than the incoming age groups, and the contingent put together by Amyntas will have been a cross-section of the younger Macedonian population. Once again the military reserve (if any) and the home army will not have been immune. The forces which reached Alexander in Sittacene, south of Babylon, amounted to 13,500 infantry of whom 6,000 were Macedonian and some 2,100 cavalry, including 500 Macedonians.[24] Between spring 334 and the end of 331

---

[20] Diod. 17.49.1: προστάξας τῶν νέων τοὺς εὐθέτους ἐπιλέξαι πρὸς στρατείαν. Cf. Curt. 4.6.30.

[21] For the phrase εὐθέτους πρὸς στρατείαν compare Diod. 1.18.5; 15.61.4; 20.4.8.

[22] Curt. 7.1.37: 'multos integros iuvenes in domo tuae matris abscondi'. On the episode see Berve ii nos. 232, 234, 293; Heckel 177.

[23] Curt. 7.1.40: 'quorum pars secutura non erat, si militiam detrectantibus indulgere voluissem.' Here in a formal speech we may indeed have rhetorical elaboration, to exaggerate Amyntas' services to the crown; but the story as a whole presupposes resistance to military service, particularly in high places.

[24] Diod. 17.65.1 and Curt. 5.1.40–2 supply the figures; Arr. 3.16.10 notes only the arrival of Amyntas with the reinforcements.

more than 9,000 Macedonian infantry had been taken east,
and it is likely enough that the sum total was closer to
12,000.[25]

Nothing is recorded of further injections of Macedonian
infantry. That might be sheer chance, one of the innumerable fortuitous omissions in our record of the period.
Reinforcements are recorded, but they are almost always
described as comprising mercenaries or native peoples of the
north. For instance the great convoy of troops which reached
Bactra during the winter of 329/8 included a contingent of
8,000 sent by Antipater, but these are described as *Graeci*,
not Macedonian.[26] There may have been Macedonian troops
included alongside a larger body of mercenaries from Greece
proper, but we cannot assume it. Alexander continued to feel
the need for more of his national troops, and a year later
three commanders of median status were sent 'to bring up
the army from Macedon' (τὴν στρατιὰν τὴν ἐκ Μακεδονίας αὐτῷ
ἀνάξοντας). As so often, Arrian's terminology is compressed,
and it is hard to infer just what his source recorded. The
definite articles suggest that there had already been some
definition of the army which was to be brought, a specific
contingent which Antipater had been instructed to raise
from various sources or perhaps even the home army itself,
which Antipater was then to replenish from the remaining
military population. The latter never arrived, and there is no
further record of the officers commissioned to lead the army
back to Asia.[27] A substantial body of troops did in fact arrive
late in 326. Diodorus records over 30,000 foot and just under
6,000 cavalry, and the numbers, he states, were made up of
allies and mercenaries from Greece.[28] It is conceivable that
the infantry included troops from Macedon as well as the
mercenaries and allied troops from southern Greece and
Asia. If so, they will have been a small minority within a

[25] Arrian alone attests 9,000 infantry in two contingents of reinforcements;
Curtius (with Callisthenes) records two other groups. Even if one dismisses the latter as unhistorical, they are hardly 'unattested' (Badian (above, n. 2) 263).
[26] Curt. 7.10.12. Beloch (iii².2.342) argued that some Macedonians were
included in the contingent; 'gänzlich ausgeschlossen' was Berve's dogmatic retort
(i.182 n. 1). On the historical background to these reinforcements see Bosworth,
HCA ii.39–40.   [27] Arr. 4.18.3, on which see Bosworth, *HCA* ii.124.
[28] Diod. 17.95.4: ἐκ τῆς Ἑλλάδος σύμμαχοι καὶ μισθοφόροι.

much larger contingent. The cavalry forces, according to Curtius, came predominantly from Thrace,[29] and the only specific figure for any infantry unit is 7,000 mercenaries from Harpalus in Mesopotamia. The evidence we have is consistent with a few thousand troops having been included in larger convoys from Macedon, but there is no record of large-scale native reinforcements between 330 and 323. The consistent, universal silence of the sources is surely significant.

At the end of the reign there are rough figures for the Macedonians under Alexander's command. In 324 he was able to dismiss 10,000 Macedonian infantry, who were to return home under Craterus' command.[30] This 10,000 is further subdivided into 6,000 survivors from the original expeditionary force at the Hellespont and 4,000 from the reinforcements who joined the army later.[31] The proportions are unlikely to be identical, for men from the reinforcing contingents were likely to be younger and had experienced less of the campaigning. Fewer of them will have died and more are likely to have been retained by Alexander. Their numbers in toto will have been roughly comparable to those

[29] Curt. 9.3.21: 5,000 horse out of a total, according to Diodorus, 'not far short of 6,000' came from Thrace. There can have been few, if any, Macedonian cavalry.

[30] The figure is generally agreed: Arr. 7.12.1; Diod. 17.109.1; 18.4.1, 12.1. It may comprise heavy infantry alone. Craterus had 1,500 cavalry with him when he marched to relieve Antipater (see below, p. 79), and they were probably veterans from Opis. Justin 12.12.7 gives the total figure as 11,000 ('over 10,000' in Diod. 18.12.1), and he may well have included cavalry (Billows, *Kings and Colonists* 188; Yardley and Heckel, *Justin . . . Books 11–12* 276).

[31] Diod. 18.16.4: the distinction is between the troops 'who crossed into Asia along with Alexander' and 'those who were added to the army in transit (ἐν παρόδῳ)'. I take the troops added in transit to be the reinforcements who joined Alexander's army during the passage of Asia (so Beloch iii².2.345; Brunt, *Arrian* ii.489; Billows 188 n. 9). There is, however, another interpretation, which goes back at least to Benedictus Niese (*Geschichte der griechischen und makedonischen Staaten seit der Schlacht bei Chaironeia* i.207): the troops were added by Craterus himself during his passage of Asia Minor and Macedonia (cf. Goukowsky, *Diodore xviii* 129; Hammond, *GRBS* 25 (1984) 54–6; *JHS* 109 (1989) 65 n. 49; Heckel 130). This alternative view has Craterus enlist exactly the same number of troops that he supposedly leaves in Cilicia—a remarkable coincidence. Beloch also objected (rightly, in my mind) that we should expect an accusative in Diodorus' text (τοὺς δ' ἐν παρόδῳ προσειλημμένους 'the 4,000 who were added in transit'), not the partitive genitive that we have ('4,000 of the men who were added in transit'). The text as we have it would imply that Craterus enlisted a larger number of Macedonian troops than he actually took to relieve Antipater. That is surely impossible. The distinction must be between the old campaigners at the Hellespont and the later reinforcements.

of the first expeditionary force. In other words Alexander's campaigning took some 30,000 men of military age away from Macedonia. When Alexander died 10,000 of them were on their way to repatriation . The number retained in the royal army is difficult to quantify. A problematic passage of Curtius has been taken as evidence that the troops remaining after the discharge of Craterus' veterans amounted to 13,000 infantry and 2,000 cavalry.[32] However, Curtius seems to be conflating two separate issues: the grievances of the Macedonians who were not to be repatriated with Craterus and the selection of a holding army to be kept in Asia as a permanent garrison. The latter at first seems to be the focus of the narrative. Now that the older Macedonians were to be repatriated, Alexander selected (*eligi iussit*) a force of infantry and cavalry, thinking that he could control Asia with a moderate-sized army, given the many garrisons and colonies he had established. This looks like a force quite separate from Alexander's royal army, which he would take on his Arabian expedition and ultimately into Africa. The new standing army would be left with his viceroy, and like other holding forces it would contain mostly mercenaries with a nucleus of Macedonians, who would be specially selected.[33] They would be a minority within the army, a few thousand at most out of the 13,000 infantry, but the prospect of selection exacerbated the unrest at the news of the demobilization of veterans and helped unleash the general demand for repatriation. That is the impression given in the speech which follows. Alexander claims that he has discharged more men than he is to retain,[34] and that is quite incompatible with a residual force of Macedonians 13,000

[32] Curt. 10.2.8: 'Alexander senioribus militum in patriam remissis XIII milia peditum et II milia equitum, quae in Asia retineret, eligi iussit, existimans modico exercitu continere posse Asiam.' For this interpretation, which goes back to Mützell (cited by Hans Droysen (above, n. 3) 30 n. 23) see Hammond, *JHS* 109 (1989) 64; Billows, *Kings and Colonists* 188 n. 10.

[33] So Beloch iii².2.346; Berve i.184; Brunt, *Arrian* ii.489. Milns, *Entretiens Hardt* 22 (1976) 112–13 takes the figure of 13,000 to refer to the totality of Macedonians at Opis *before* the dismissal of the veterans.

[34] Curt. 10.2.19: 'utpote cum plures dimiserim quam retenturus sum.' Atkinson's recent Mondadori edition (563) has it exactly right: 'if Alexander dismissed more Macedonian troops than he retained, then the figures provided in the text of Curtius ought to include non-Macedonians as well'.

strong. The passage, then, cannot be taken as evidence of the Macedonian army's strength after Craterus' departure. Quite the reverse. It implies that a majority of the army left with Craterus, and of the minority remaining a proportion would be selected for the distasteful task of policing the Asian empire.

One cannot place much emphasis on Curtius' somewhat confused and highly rhetorical description. It is better to analyse the figures which our sources give for the strengths of the various armies operating after Alexander's death. At first there are three discrete groups of Macedonians, the royal army with Perdiccas at Babylon, the veterans with Craterus, who had based themselves in Cilicia, and the army in Macedonia under Antipater. We may start with Antipater and Macedon proper. Our evidence begins with the outbreak of the Lamian War, when Antipater took an army south to deal with the Greek forces which had occupied Thermopylae. Diodorus here is at his most intriguing and frustrating. He claims (18.12.2) that Antipater appointed a certain Sippas[35] as his deputy in Macedonia, giving him 'sufficient forces' and instructing him to enlist as many troops as possible. We are not informed about the composition of Sippas' forces and there is no indication where he is to recruit his men. We assume that he was to conscribe Macedonians, but the verb used, στρατολογεῖν, suggests otherwise. It is predominantly used of acquisition of forces other than one's native troops, usually allies and mercenaries.[36] There is a fair probability that Sippas recuited yet more forces from the peoples of the north. The new troops will certainly not have been exclusively Macedonian.

Antipater himself went south with 13,000 Macedonians and 600 cavalry. On the surface this is an impressive total.

---

[35] So the manuscript reading. Goukowsky may well be right to emend to Sirrhas, an attested Macedonian name—the father of Eurydice, for instance.

[36] Compare for instance Diod. 16.73.2: εὐθὺς οὖν τῶν πολιτῶν κατέλεγον τοὺς ἀρίστους εἰς τὴν στρατείαν καὶ τῶν Λιβύων τοὺς εὐθέτους ἐστρατολόγουν. Of the eleven instances of the term in Diodorus six refer explicitly to allied troops (12.67.5; 14.36.1, 54.6, 79.2; 19.88.3, 106.5). Otherwise it is used explicitly of levying mercenaries (18.50.3). The closest parallel to Sippas raising native Macedonians would be Cyrus levying troops from the areas of Asia Minor under his control (Diod. 14.19.6).

Antipater seems to have as many infantry as Alexander at the Hellespont, and there are still troops left with Sippas and the potential for more to be recruited. However, Diodorus states parenthetically that Macedonia was short of 'citizen' troops because of the number of men despatched to reinforce Alexander's army (ἐσπάνιζε γὰρ ἡ Μακεδονία στρατιωτῶν πολιτικῶν διὰ τὸ πλῆθος τῶν ἀπεσταλμένων εἰς τὴν Ἀσίαν ἐπὶ διαδοχὴν τῆς στρατείας). It is an explicit statement, and the source is universally thought to have been Hieronymus of Cardia,[37] a well-informed contemporary. How then can Diodorus claim that Antipater could immediately call on 13,000 Macedonian foot and leave more to his deputy? It seems more like a glut than a shortage, and it hardly helps to claim that the comment merely elucidates the small number of horse with Antipater. The figures suggest that the home army 'had grown somewhat' since 334,[38] and the explanatory comment becomes an absurdity. In that case we should look closely at Diodorus' text. It is expressed in a somewhat unorthodox form: Antipater took up Macedonians to the tune of 13,000 and cavalry 600 in number (ἀναλαβὼν Μακεδόνας μὲν μυρίους καὶ τρισχιλίους, ἱππεῖς δὲ ἑξακοσίους). Superficially it implies that the cavalry were non-Macedonian, and Goukowsky supplied <πεζοὺς> μέν, making the contrast between infantry and cavalry explicit. He was certainly on the right track, for Diodorus makes the contrast between infantry and cavalry well over one hundred times, and in practically every case πεζοὶ μέν is juxtaposed with ἱππεῖς δέ. But there is more. When Macedonian foot are specified

---

[37] Badian (above, n. 2) 267 argues that the passage could derive from (mistaken) ancient speculation that Alexander exhausted Macedonian manpower. In that case the source was later than Hieronymus, or Hieronymus himself was misinformed.

[38] So Billows, *Kings and Colonists* 193, concluding (n. 23) that 'the Macedonians available to Antipatros were well in excess of the number originally left with him by Alexander'. Badian has a fall-back position shared by Goukowsky (*Diodore* xviii 124), which confines the misunderstanding to Diodorus: the scarcity according to his source refers to cavalry alone. In any case, according to Badian, 'Diodorus is referring to 'a shortage of forces under arms, not to the manpower reserves of Macedon'. True, but it would be strange, if Antipater had ample reserves, that he did not train new recruits to compensate for the losses incurred through the reinforcements sent to Asia. It is still a paradox to have a large reserve and a small field army.

(or infantry of any other nationality), they are balanced by other contingents. Consider the following:

Diod. 19.100.4: ἔχοντα πεζοὺς Μακεδόνας μὲν πεντακισχιλίους, μισθοφόρους δὲ μυρίους, ἱππεῖς δὲ τετρακισχιλίους

Diod. 20.110.4–5: τῷ δὲ Δημητρίῳ συνηκολούθουν ἱππεῖς μὲν χίλιοι καὶ πεντακόσιοι, πεζοὶ δὲ Μακεδόνες οὐκ ἐλάττους τῶν ὀκτακισχιλίων, μισθοφόροι δ᾽ εἰς μυρίους καὶ πεντακισχιλίους . . .[39]

It should by now be clear that Diodorus' text is defective. The number of Macedonian infantry has been lost and the figure preserved is that of a non-Macedonian force, probably mercenaries.[40] The corruption is easiest to explain if the Macedonian force was 3,000 strong—the scribe's eye then simply flicked from one figure to the next. In that case Diodorus' text should read: 'taking infantry forces comprising 3,000 Macedonians and 13,000 mercenaries and cavalry to the number of 600' (ἀναλαβὼν <πεζοὺς> Μακεδόνας μὲν <τρισχιλίους, μισθοφόρους δ᾽ εἰς> μυρίους καὶ τρισχιλίους, ἱππεῖς δὲ ἑξακοσίους). Such a reading restores sense to the passage and justifies the parenthesis. Antipater had a proportionately small force of Macedonians under arms, and it is explained by the demands for reinforcements during Alexander's reign.

Antipater's forces did not of course comprise all the manpower of Macedonia. Sippas retained some troops (how many of them Macedonian we cannot even guess), and there were reserves to draw upon. Naturally so. During the period 330–323 eight year-groups had come to maturity and swelled the military resources of the country. By 324 at least Alexander considered it feasible to replace the veterans of Opis with a comparable number of Macedonians in their prime (Arr. 7.12.4), and he at least considered that there were something like 10,000 relatively new troops available. But even in Macedonia it had not been a period of unrelieved tranquillity. One disaster at least was sustained when Zopyrion, general in

---

[39] For other examples see 17.17.3; 18.51.1; 19.69.1, 80.4. On the one apparent exception (19.68.3) see below, p. 92.

[40] In 323 there was a relative glut of mercenaries, after the demobilization of the satrapal armies in Asia. The troops with Leosthenes were a relatively small proportion of the total pool, and Antipater had the funds for large-scale recruitment (Diod. 18.12.2).

Thrace, lost an army north of the Danube;[41] there were problems in Thrace[42] and, for all we know, with the Illyrians. That would have reduced Macedonian numbers and added to the strain of reinforcing Alexander. Given the uncertainty of the sources we cannot hazard a figure of men under arms, but the standing army and reserves were certainly much smaller than they had been in 334.

The situation worsened in the Lamian War, as Antipater was defeated and subjected to siege in Lamia. Subsequently Leonnatus moved from Hellespontine Phrygia to relieve him. In Macedonia he collected as many Macedonian soldiers as he could and amassed a total force of 20,000 infantry and 1,500 cavalry.[43] This is a global figure, and there is no suggestion what proportion of the total consisted of Macedonians. It is unlikely to have been large.[44] Leonnatus came from Hellespontine Phrygia, and there is little likelihood that his rival Perdiccas equipped him with Macedonian infantry when he left Babylon. The 'great force' which he was instructed to use in support of Eumenes in Cappadocia[45] will have been levied locally and consisted predominantly of mercenaries. For all his imitation of Alexander, his Nesaean horses and his *agema* of Companions, Leonnatus had few, if any, phalanx troops, and any Macedonians whom he took to relieve Antipater will have come from Sippas in Macedonia itself. Diodorus refers to 'many Macedonians',[46] but there is no quantification. Many soldiers from Sippas' reserves

---

[41] Just. 12.2.16–17; 37.3.2; Curt.10.1.44. Cf. Berve ii no. 340; K. Ziegler, *RE* xA.763–4; Yardley and Heckel *Justin . . . Books 11–12* 196–8.

[42] Curt. 10.1.45. See below, pp. 269–71.   [43] Diod. 18.14.5.

[44] This seems agreed: cf. Billows, *Kings and Colonists* 193 n. 24; Heckel 105. The satrapal forces of Hellespontine Phrygia must have suffered when Calas (Alexander's first satrap) underwent defeat at the hands of the Bithynian dynast, Bas. Calas had been 'exceptionally well prepared for battle', but he was still defeated. Subsequently Macedonian generals learned their lesson and kept their distance (Memnon, *FGrH* 434 F 1/12.4).

[45] Plut. *Eum.* 3.3–4: ἀλλ᾽ ἔδει Λεόννατον καὶ ᾽Αντίγονον χειρὶ μεγάλῃ τὸν Εὐμενῆ καταγ<αγ>όντας ἀποδεῖξαι τῆς χώρας σατράπην. Pace Billows, *Kings and Colonists* 193 n. 24 there is no suggestion that either Leonnatus or Antigonus were given their 'great force' by Perdiccas. It had to be raised locally from their satrapal resources.

[46] Diod. 18.14.5: προσέλαβετο πολλοὺς στρατιώτας Μακεδόνας. Geer's Loeb translation reads 'he enlisted many additional Macedonian soldiers'. 'Additional' implies that Leonnatus already has Macedonians in his force. All the Greek here means is 'he took into his army many Macedonian soldiers'. The text tells us nothing about the composition of Leonnatus' force before he reached Macedonia.

might not have been many in absolute terms. It seems to me unlikely that more than a quarter of Leonnatus' were native Macedonians.

The situation changed abruptly in 322, when Craterus crossed into Europe with his veterans, comprising 10,000 foot and 1,500 horse, all Macedonians. He united his forces with those of Antipater, and fought the campaign of Crannon with a total of 40,000 heavy infantry and 5,000 cavalry.[47] Once more the proportion of Macedonians to non-Macedonians is not reported, but at a minimum there were 20,000, enough to inflict a crushing defeat on the Greek coalition with only 130 casualties on their side. This campaign united the Macedonian forces of the west, and for a time there were only two blocks of Macedonian soldiers, those with Antipater and Craterus and those under the control of Perdiccas. That brings us to a critical question. How many Macedonians were there in Perdiccas' army? Once more there is no precise figure. Arrian suggests that even after the departure of Craterus' veterans there was a substantial number of phalanx infantry. Shortly before Alexander's death some 6,700 were supposedly attributed to a mixed phalanx of Macedonians and Persians.[48] I say 'supposedly' because the numbers are not certain. Peucestas, the satrap of Persis, had brought 'up to 20,000' Persian troops, and Alexander 'enlisted them into the Macedonian *taxeis*'.[49] That ought to mean that Persians and Macedonians were integrated in the phalanx battalions,[50] and we are informed that there were four Macedonians and 12 Persians in each file. It would seem to follow that there were some 6,700 Macedonians in the mixed phalanx. However (and there is always a however), the number of Persians we are given is an approximation by Arrian or his source, and the actual figure could be significantly less than 20,000.[51] What is more, we are not told explicitly that *all* the Persian newcomers were included in the

---

[47] For Craterus' troops see above, p. 73. The numbers at Crannon are given by Diod. 18.16.5.

[48] This is a widespread assumption: cf. Schachermeyr, *Al. in Babylon* 14–15; Bosworth, *JHS* 106 (1986) 3–4; Hammond, *JHS* 109 (1989) 64.

[49] Arr. 7.23.3: κατέλεγεν αὐτοὺς ἐς τὰς Μακεδονικὰς τάξεις.

[50] That seems to be the sense of τὰς Μακεδονικὰς τάξεις compare Arr. 1.6.6; 2.5.6.

[51] So Milns, *Entretiens Hardt* 22 (1976) 122, arguing that only 12,000 Persians were used.

new formation. A chapter later Arrian reports on the authority of Aristobulus that Alexander brought into the Macedonian battalions not merely Peucestas' Persians but also levies from Caria and Lydia.[52] We have no reason to dismiss this notice as inaccurate or the result of a misunderstanding by Arrian. If it is correct, then there are two possibilities. Either these newcomers were absorbed in the central body of the new phalanx along with the Iranian infantry, or they were mercenaries or native levies who had been trained in the Macedonian style of fighting and could therefore be used to supplement the front-line Macedonian infantry. The latter seems the more likely. Troops fighting in the Macedonian style are frequently found in the armies of the Successors,[53] and there are likely to have been training programmes in the western satrapies as well as the far north-east.[54] If this inference is correct, then the troops brigaded with Peucestas' Persians comprised both Macedonians and Macedonian trained troops from Caria and Lydia. In that case the number of Macedonians attached to the composite phalanx was considerably less than 6,700. They were not the only Macedonian infantry in Perdiccas' army. The hypaspist corps, the so-called Silver Shields, seems to have maintained its corporate

---

[52] Arr. 7.24.1 = *FGrH* 139 F 58: καταλοχίζειν μὲν αὐτὸν τὴν στρατιὰν τὴν σὺν Πευκέστᾳ τε ἐκ Περσῶν καὶ ἀπὸ θαλάσσης ξὺν Φιλοξένῳ καὶ Μενάνδρῳ ἥκουσαν ἐς τὰς Μακεδονικὰς τάξεις. Arrian echoes and varies his earlier terminology. He may simply be drawing on the earlier chapter to give the context for the impressive portent which was the main reason for his citation of Aristobulus. But he had some reason to think that the levies from Asia Minor were used in the mixed phalanx, and it is most probable that Aristobulus mentioned them in the context.

[53] Diod. 19.14.5 (3,000 men of all races armed for the Macedonian ranks and serving with Peucestas in Persis); 19.27.6 (5,000 of such troops in Eumenes' army at Paraetacene); 19.40.3 (with Eumenes at Gabiene); 19.29.3 (8,000 with Antigonus at Paraetacene). The last group is particularly interesting. Many of the 8,000 will have come from survivors of Perdiccas' grand army, transferred to Antigonus' command at Triparadeisus, but they may have been supplemented by trained troops from Asia Minor. They are drawn up alongside the native Macedonians whom Antigonus inherited from Antipater, and immediately adjacent on their left are native troops from Lycia and Pamphylia, who were obviously adapted to phalanx fighting.

[54] Egypt seems to have had some such programme: Suda s.v. βασίλειοι παῖδες 6,000 Egyptians were under military training by order of Alexander. The training is not explicitly in Macedonian weaponry, but it is likely enough. At Gaza in 312 Ptolemy drew on Egyptians who were armed and useful for battle (Diod. 19.80.4); they could have been the product of the training programme (so Hammond, *Historia* 39 (1990) 281).

identity, and even after losses during the disastrous Egyptian campaign of 321 it numbered 3,000.[55] With the Macedonians in the mixed phalanx they make a modest total: certainly under 10,000, perhaps as low as 8,000.

The nucleus of Macedonians was carefully deployed during the period of the first coalition war. Shortly after Alexander's death Peithon was commissioned to crush the uprising of Greek colonists in the far east. For that he was given 3,000 Macedonians, selected by lot from the army,[56] and the satraps up country were instructed to provide 10,000 of their own troops. The figure again is compatible with Macedonian infantry numbers in the region of 8–10,000. Peithon and his men returned from their successful mission,[57] and the next significant division of forces came at the end of 322. Then Perdiccas was in Lycaonia with the royal army, where he destroyed the cities of Isaura and Laranda. He had deputed a body of Macedonians to operate in Armenia under Neoptolemus, a sizable army group which worried Eumenes sufficiently for him to recruit and train a body of Cappadocian cavalry 6,300 strong.[58] Neoptolemus' Macedonians must have numbered some thousands. So too will the army group which Perdiccas left with his brother Alcetas in Pisidia. This was a critical moment. Perdiccas was now at war with Antipater and Craterus and expected Asia Minor to be invaded by an army of Macedonians. The forces he left to deal with them would be substantial. In fact they faced a much greater threat than he did himself when he attacked Egypt, for Ptolemy's forces, however numerous they may have been,[59] cannot have matched the calibre of the royal army which was deployed against him.

---

[55] Diod. 18.58.1, 59.3. The argyraspid commander, Antigenes, was with Perdiccas in Egypt (Arr. *Succ.* F 1.35), and *a fortiori* his troops were there also (cf. Anson, *Historia* 30 (1981) 118–19; Billows, *Kings and Colonists* 192). There is a remote possibility that Photius misunderstood a prospective note in Arrian: 'Antigenes who was the first to attack Perdiccas and *was to command* the Silver Shields.'

[56] Diod. 18.7.3: ἐκλήρωσεν ἐκ τῶν Μακεδόνων. On this episode see above, pp. 61–2.

[57] Diod. 18.7.9: ἀπῆλθε μετὰ τῶν Μακεδόνων πρὸς τὸν Περδίκκαν.

[58] Plut. *Eum.* 4.2–4. On this episode see Briant, *RTP* 30–50; Bosworth, *GRBS* 19 (1978) 232–3.

[59] The only figure for the forces left in Egypt back in 331 is Curtius' 4,000 (Curt. 4.8.4). The commanders were Macedonian (Arr. 3.5.5; cf. Turner, *JEA* 60 (1974)

We are given no figures for the royal army with Perdiccas, but it has been recently argued that he took at least 9,000 Macedonians when he marched on Egypt in 321.[60] There were the Silver Shields, at least 3,000 strong, the troops under Peithon who had crushed the insurgent colonists, and a further group whom Diodorus terms 'hypaspists' and who are later attested alongside the Silver Shields as a distinct and separate unit some 3,000 strong. I cannot accept the conclusion, for it seems to me that the premises are faulty. In the first place I think it is erroneous to argue that the Silver Shields were totally distinct from Peithon's forces. What Diodorus states is that Perdiccas selected 3,000 infantry and 800 cavalry by lot 'from the Macedonians'. There is no suggestion that the Silver Shields were exempt from sortition, and it is reasonable that Peithon's force was a cross-section of the army at Babylon. The Silver Shields contributed proportionally. Next, we do not know when Peithon returned from his mission in the upper satrapies, but there is every possibility that he had rejoined the royal army by the time of the campaign in Lycaonia. His troops were therefore available to be used in Asia Minor. For instance they could have contributed to Alcetas' forces in Pisidia.[61]

Finally the hypaspists in the Egyptian campaign. Diodorus certainly mentions hypaspists in action on Perdiccas' side in 321, and he also mentions a mysterious group of hypaspists in Eumenes' armies at Paraetacene and Gabiene in 317/16.[62] Can the two groups be identified? Now, it is important to distinguish two uses of the term hypaspist by Diodorus. The most frequent by far is a non-technical usage, 'shield bearer'.

239–42), but their troops were almost certainly mercenaries, given the peaceful state of Egypt and the imminence of Alexander's final reckoning with Darius. Ptolemy reinforced these satrapal troops with mercenaries whom he recruited from the consolidated funds in the Egyptian treasury (Diod. 18.14.1). There is no suggestion that he had any Macedonians to speak of.

[60] Billows, *Kings and Colonists* 192: 'at a minimum count, more than 9,000 Macedonians taken by Perdikkas to Egypt'. Similar figures in Hammond, *JHS* 109 (1989) 64.

[61] For Alcetas' appointment to Pisidia see *GRBS* 19 (1978) 234; Heckel 173. Peithon's forces (other than Silver Shields) could have been detached to his command in the spring of 321, when he certainly had Macedonian soldiers (Plut. *Eum.* 5.3).

[62] Diod. 18.33.6, 34.2 (Egypt); 19.28.1, 40.3 (Eumenes).

In that sense it refers to the attendants of dynasts who bore shields for them, including Peucestas, who notably performed that office for Alexander.[63] Once only (17.110.1) it appears to refer to Alexander's foot guard, the hypaspists proper. The two references in the narrative of Perdiccas' invasion of Egypt are clearly non-technical in the first sense. The context is the siege of 'Camels' Fort' near the Nile. Perdiccas attacked with his elephants in the lead, followed by the 'hypaspists' and the ladder bearers and the rest of the personnel whom he was going to use to attack the walls.[64] The ladder bearers do not comprise a specific group of troops,[65] nor in all probability do the hypaspists. The attacking party consists of ladder bearers, whose function was to bring the scaling machinery to the walls, and the storming group proper which literally ascended under their shields (Diod. 18.34.2), hence the descriptive term ὑπασπισταί. There may well have been no discrete group of Perdiccas' army which was officially termed hypaspists. Eumenes' hypaspists are a different matter. At both Paraetacene and Gabiene they are placed alongside the Silver Shields,[66] and they certainly did fight as a unified body. But nothing indicates that these hypaspists were Macedonians, and the probability is that they were not. The coalition army under Eumenes' command was short on Macedonians and well supplied with troops trained in Macedonian fashion.[67] It is most likely that Eumenes grouped the best of these newly trained troops into an élite and gave them the title of hypaspists. As the royal general he had a crack division whose name recalled Alexander's own infantry guard. Perdiccas could well have have had a similar

[63] Cf. 8.12.2; 15.87.6; 17.99.4 (Peucestas); 18.45.3 (shield bearers of Alcetas, who are associated with his slaves); 20.33.6 (Agathocles).

[64] Diod. 18.33.6: ἐπακολουθούντων δὲ τῶν ὑπασπιστῶν καὶ κλιμακοφόρων καὶ τῶν ἄλλων δι' ὧν ἔμελλε τὴν τειχομαχίαν ποιεῖσθαι.

[65] Cf. Arr. 6.9.2–3, where some of the phalanx troops are carrying ladders; the storming party naturally takes shields for defence during the ascent (6.9.4).

[66] See below, pp. 132, 149.

[67] For these troops see above, n. 53. No one to my knowledge has suggested that Eumenes' hypaspists were of non-Macedonian origin. M. Launey, *Recherches sur les armées hellénistiques* i².298 comes close, when he admits that there were relatively few Macedonians in the infantry: the Silver Shields 'et peut-être tout ou partie des 3,000 hypaspistes'.

corps of non-Macedonian hypaspists, but, as we have seen, it does not follow from Diodorus' description of the Egyptian campaign. The royal army which attacked Ptolemy can confidently be said to have comprised the Silver Shields, 3,000 strong,[68] and an additional unspecified number of Macedonians. Given the detachment of Macedonian troops to the armies of Neoptolemus and Alcetas, I suspect that the total was hardly more than 5,000. An equivalent number was left in Asia Minor for the critical struggle against Craterus and Antipater.

The minutiae of the first coalition war are not important for our purposes. In brief Eumenes was deputed to co-ordinate the defence of Asia Minor against Antipater and Craterus.[69] His titular subordinates, Neoptolemus and Alcetas refused to co-operate, and he was obliged to fight against Neoptolemus to prevent his joining the invasion force. As a result of his preliminary victory he acquired Neoptolemus' army, which comprised several thousand Macedonian phalanx troops,[70] but he failed to blockade the Hellespont against Craterus and Antipater. They crossed into Asia with a powerful expeditionary force, and divided into two groups: one under Antipater headed for Cilicia while the other with Craterus remained in the west to face Eumenes. We have figures for his army: 20,000 infantry, 'of whom the majority were Macedonians celebrated for their valour', and 2,000 cavalry.[71] That gives us a total of rather

---

[68] Antigenes, their commander, was in Perdiccas' army and helped in the assassination (Arr. *Succ.* F 1.35), and the 3,000 mutinous troops whom he was given to transport the treasures of Susa (Arr. *Succ.* F 1.38) are surely identical with the 3,000 Silver Shields whom he brought to Cilicia in 319/18 at the behest of Polyperchon (Diod. 18.58.1, 59.3; Plut. *Eum.* 13.3. See further Bosworth, 'History and Artifice', 66–7).

[69] Diod. 18.29.3; Plut. *Eum.* 5.1–2; Nep. *Eum.* 3.2; Just. 13.6.14–15.

[70] The victory is documented sparsely in Diod. 18.29.4–5 and Plut. *Eum.* 5.5. A papyrus fragment of Arrian's *History of the Successors* (*PSI* xii.1284) most probably refers to this engagement (Bosworth, *GRBS* 19 (1978) 227–35; against, Wesley E. Thompson, *Chronique d'Égypte* 59 (1984) 113–20). That Neoptolemus had a substantial body of Macedonians is not, however, in doubt; Diodorus terms it a δύναμις ἀξιόλογος. See also p. 81 above.

[71] Diod. 18.30.4. Craterus' forces are explicitly contrasted with those of Eumenes, which also number 20,000 but are of miscellaneous composition (πανοδαποὺς τοῖς γένεσιν).

more than 10,000, probably closer to 15,000, and the nucleus will have been formed by the veterans of Opis, who certainly had a remarkable reputation. We are informed that he had the greater part of the expeditionary force,[72] and Antipater's function was to go ahead and occupy Cilicia 'to continue the war against Perdiccas'. That does not mean that Antipater was to fight the royal army by himself.[73] Diodorus (18.29.7) is explicit that it was only when Craterus had defeated Eumenes and rejoined Antipater that their combined forces would unite with Ptolemy against the army of Perdiccas. Antipater's brief was simply to occupy Cilicia, which was of critical strategic importance and could be held as a bastion if Perdiccas happened to crush Ptolemy. For that his army did not need to be over large or composed of crack troops. What mattered was to get there quickly. We are in the dark, but it is unlikely that Antipater had a army group more than 10,000 strong and more than half Macedonian. The principal striking force was with Craterus.

We can now pause and take stock of the Macedonian forces operating in the spring of 321. There were perhaps 5,000 infantry in Perdiccas' royal army and an equivalent number serving with Eumenes and Alcetas in Asia Minor. The forces with Craterus and Antipater will have comprised 15–20,000, most, if not all, of the troops which had fought at Crannon. That gives us a sum total of 25–30,000. There are also the troops left in Macedonia under Polyperchon and the various garrisons in Greece, not least that recently installed in Athens under Menyllus. Once again no numbers are given, even for the Athenian garrison, but it did not necessarily need a force of more than a few hundreds to defend the small harbour area of Munychia and preserve a gateway for a retaliatory force.[74] As for Polyperchon we are told that he brought a considerable force to crush an uprising in

---

[72] Plut. *Eum.* 6.4. Diod. 19.29.7 attests the division of the army into two parts, but does not imply that they were equal.

[73] As Billows, *Antigonos* 66–7 has argued.

[74] When Nicanor occupied Peiraeus in the summer of 318, he did not take action until he had secretly supplemented his Macedonians with a large force of mercenaries (Diod. 18.64.4; Plut. *Phoc.* 32.9).

Thessaly.[75] The circumstances, however, are of some interest. The rebellion was fomented by the Aetolians, who had sent an army into Thessaly, disposing of a Macedonian general and his forces en route.[76] That would have caused some Macedonian casualties, hard losses at this juncture. Once in Thessaly the Aetolians won over several cities, including Pharsalus, and mobilized an army of 25,000 foot and 1,500 horse. Polyperchon held aloof until the Aetolians withdrew their domestic army to deal with an invasion from Acarnania (their mercenaries remained in the field).[77] That weakened the opposition considerably, and Polyperchon intervened decisively. To crush the rebellion he did not need an overlarge army, nor a particularly formidable phalanx, and the fact that he delayed indicates that he was reluctant to take on the full allied army. It is a clear sign that trained Macedonian troops were in very short supply. Conceivably there were no more than 10,000 men under arms left in Macedonia and Greece; Antipater and Craterus had taken the maximum possible for the life and death struggle in Asia. There could well have been 40,000 Macedonians serving in the various armies in 321/20, and given the state of emergency the military reserves were stretched to the limit. The question now arises how many men found their way back to Macedon.

One thing is relatively clear. Despite the number of men under arms comparatively few Macedonians died in battle in the first coalition war. The battle between Eumenes and Craterus was largely decided by cavalry;[78] not surprisingly the phalanx troops never made contact, and Craterus' force was able to make its way unscathed to join Antipater. In Egypt the fighting was more intense. There was Perdiccas' unsuccessful attack on Camels' Fort and the abortive river

[75] Diod. 18.38.4 (the only source): ἦκεν εἰς τὴν Θετταλίαν μετὰ δυνάμεως ἀξιολόγου.

[76] Diod. 18.38.1–3. They were acting, it is said, in conformity with an agreement (συνθῆκαι) which they had concluded with Perdiccas. See further D. Mendels, *Historia* 33 (1984) 155–7; Hammond, *HM* iii.126–7.

[77] Diod. 18.38.4–5. Something similar had happened in the Lamian War, when the Aetolians withdrew their forces to deal with a domestic emergency (Diod. 18.13.3, 15.2: on the background see my forthcoming paper (above, Ch. 1, n. 20)).

[78] Diod. 18.30.1, 32.1–2; Plut. *Eum.* 8; Nep. *Eum.* 4.3. See also *GRBS* 19 (1978) 229–31.

crossing near Memphis which cost 2,000 casualities.[79] However, there is no indication how many of the dead were Macedonians. In later years the Silver Shields are described as unconquered,[80] and clearly, as Diodorus' account implies, there was no pitched battle, something Ptolemy was at pains to avoid. The casualties among Macedonians are unlikely to have been great, and when the royal army united with that of Antipater at Triparadeisus, the combined forces will have numbered over 20,000 Macedonians. However, there were dangers in this concentration, as Antipater found to his cost. The veterans of Perdiccas' army had already been incited to mutiny by Queen Eurydice,[81] and Antipater was faced with demands for the gratuities promised by Alexander and never honoured by Perdiccas.[82] His life was seriously threatened, and he was only rescued by the prompt intervention of Antigonus.[83] The veterans of Alexander and Perdiccas were a liability, and he clearly wanted nothing of them. Accordingly the Silver Shields were sent to duty in Susa, where they had access to the royal treasury and could expect their payment.[84] The rest of the royal forces were assigned to Antigonus for the forthcoming campaign in Asia Minor against the surviving lieutenants of Perdiccas.[85] These forces would have been predominantly non-Macedonian. The Silver Shields had already been earmarked for service elsewhere; Attalus had enlisted some of the defeated army and withdrawn with his fleet to Asia Minor.[86] Few Macedonians would have

[79] Diod. 18.33.4, 34.2, 5–7, 36.1–2.

[80] Diod. 19.28.1, cf. 30.6, 41.2; Plut. *Eum.* 16.7. Hieronymus clearly stressed their invincibility, which admittedly does not imply that they had suffered no losses. However, their terrifying performance at Gabiene (see below, p. 155) suggests that losses in battle would have been very few.

[81] Diod. 18.39.2–3; cf. Arr. *Succ.* F 1.31.

[82] Arr. *Succ.* F 1.32. The temper of Perdiccas' veterans (and the Silver Shields in particular) will not have been sweetened by the arrival of Craterus' Macedonians, who had already been so generously rewarded by Alexander (Arr. 7.12.1). See further Hammond, in *Zu Alexander dem Grossen* i.627–34.

[83] Arr. *Succ.* F 1.33; Polyaen. 4.6.4. It is clear that the troops who attacked Antipater came from Perdiccas' old army, which was encamped separately (cf. Billows, *Antigonos* 68–9).   [84] Arr. *Succ.* F 1.35, 38. See above, n. 68.

[85] Arr. *Succ.* F 1.38; Diod. 18.39.7.

[86] Diod. 18.37.3–4. According to Arr. *Succ.* F 1.39 Attalus amassed a force of 10,000 foot and 800 horse. A proportion would have been Macedonians, including

remained, and in any case it would have been imprudent to use them against their erstwhile comrades in arms, now serving with Eumenes and Alcetas. Craterus' veterans were also available for service in the empire. The assassins of Perdiccas had established their right to a reward, not merely plum satrapies but also Macedonian troops to maintain their sway. Hence Arrhidaeus, who had renounced the regency in favour of Antipater, received at least 1,000 Macedonian troops,[87] and it is highly probable that Ptolemy received a sizeable contingent in return for his spirited defence against Perdiccas. His forces of Macedonians, mercenaries and native Egyptian troops at the battle of Gaza in 312 amounted to 18,000,[88] and it is likely enough that he received several thousand Macedonian infantrymen in 321/20. It is difficult to see how he could have acquired them later, and at Triparadeisus he was in a position of strength, universally popular and the hero of the hour. The same applies to Peithon, an assassin of Perdiccas and one of the élite Bodyguard of Alexander. He could hardly be denied Macedonian troops. The process is clear enough, but once again we have no figures, and the number of Macedonians redistributed in this way must remain an unknown.

The focus now shifts to the campaign in Asia Minor over the campaigning seasons of 320 and 319. It is clear that the fighting there was more sustained and intense than is usually thought. Arrian in fact devoted an entire book of his history of events after Alexander to the earlier part of the war, down to Antipater's return to Europe,[89] and a fragment of that account, the so-called Göteborg palimpsest, gives us a number of illuminating details.[90] After his encounter with

those who joined the flight of 'the friends of Perdiccas' from the camp at Memphis (Diod. 18.39.4).

[87] Diod. 19.51.1. Arrhidaeus' army included 500 Persian archers and slingers, who were almost certainly detached from the troops intended for Alexander's mixed phalanx.

[88] Diod. 19.80.4: the relative proportions cannot be determined.

[89] Summarized at length by Photius (Arr. *Succ.* F 1.39–45).

[90] First published by Jean Noret, *AC* 52 (1983) 235–42. The most detailed study as yet, with excellent illustrations, is B. Dreyer, *ZPE* 125 (1999) 39–66. See also A. Simonetti Agostinetti, *Flavio Arriano: gli eventi dopo Alessandro*; S. Schröder, *ZPE* 71 (1988) 75–90.

Craterus Eumenes had kept his army together and after operations around Mt. Ida and Sardes he withdrew inland to defend his territory against Antipater and Antigonus.[91] They had returned from Triparadeisus to Sardes and followed Eumenes inland to fight over the winter of 320/19. For Antipater it was an inglorious campaign. He was out-generalled by Eumenes, much to the chagrin of his troops who criticized his failure to support his Phrygian allies 'despite leading forces which were far greater and more dependable for settling the war'.[92] Eumenes then negotiated with the other Perdiccan leaders, suggesting that they amalgamated their forces, which would then be comparable in numbers and calibre to the armies of Antipater and Antigonus.[93] Alcetas himself was eager to attract Eumenes' Macedonian troops who formed the strongest contingent in the Perdiccan armies.[94] This material indicates that the armies of Antipater and Antigonus were more or less equal to the combined forces of the Perdiccan leaders and that the greatest concentration of Macedonians was with Eumenes. A few months later in 319 Eumenes is said to have employed an army of 20,000 foot and 5,000 horse, while Alcetas had 16,000 foot and 900 horse.[95] Macedonians formed a small minority in both. Eumenes' men comprised a few thousand; they selected a bodyguard of 1,000 out of their number,[96] which is compatible with a total

---

[91] Plut. *Eum.* 8.5–8; Just. 14.1.6–8; Arr. *Succ.* F 1.40. On the source tradition see Bosworth, 'History and Artifice' 71–80.

[92] Göteborg palimpsest 73ᵛ3–11 (Dreyer 57–8).

[93] Göteborg palimpsest 72ᵛ3–8 (Dreyer 58): 'for their forces were, if combined, not inferior to those of the enemy'. Cf. Arr. *Succ.* F 1.41 (Photius' laconic summary).

[94] δύναμιν Μακεδονικὴν τὴν πλείστην οὖσαν ἐθέλων ἑαυτῷ προσποιῆσαι (72ʳ10–11). This can hardly mean 'wishing to win over a force which was Macedonian for the most part' (so Schröder, *ZPE* 71 (1988) 90; Simonetti Agostinetti 97; Dreyer, *ZPE* 125 (1999) 59–60 with n. 153). There were insufficient Macedonians to form a majority of Eumenes' army, and the force in question is described in the following line as τὸ ἑδραῖον τῆς ... πεζικῆς δυνάμεως ('the anchor of his infantry power'). It is clearly a fraction, a considerable fraction of the total, but not the majority.

[95] Diod. 18.40.7 (Eumenes: his forces contrast with Antigonus' infantry, half of which comprised Macedonians, 5,000 of them 'admirable for their bravery'); 18.45.1 (Alcetas).

[96] Plut. *Eum.* 8.7; cf. Just. 14.1.9–14. Billows, *Kings and Colonists* 191 n. 17 suggests that 'only a third or less' were so selected.

around 3,000. Alcetas presumably had around 2,000. Antipater and Antigonus had armies equivalent in number, that is, around 35,000 infantry, and the proportion of Macedonians was higher.

There are two important pieces of evidence concerning the Macedonians with Antigonus. The first is a detailed report in Polyaenus (4.6.6) of a group of 3,000 Macedonians who broke away from his army while he was wintering around Cappadocia. They occupied strongpoints in Lycaonia and southern Phrygia, ravaging the land and confronting Antigonus with the possibility that they might join Alcetas. This is clearly an episode from the winter of 320/19,[97] when the Macedonians under Antipater and Antigonus were resentful at the inconclusive campaign against Eumenes. One group decided to strike out for itself and deserted. Polyaenus describes the intrigue by which Antigonus lured the dissenters from their mountain bases and intimidated them into returning to Macedonia. These troops were probably veterans. They had a good deal of independent initiative, and they would have felt particularly uncomfortable confronting their old comrades in Eumenes' army. Given their unreliability, there is no wonder that Antigonus readily countenanced their return home. Antipater followed in the spring of 319. After the consistent failures of the winter, suffering defeats at the hands of both Eumenes and Alcetas,[98] he was ready to delegate the operations to Antigonus, despite some qualms about his ambitions. He therefore made over a large proportion of the force which had crossed with him from Europe: 8,500 Macedonian infantry, half his cavalry, and 70 elephants.[99]

---

[97] So Hammond, *GRBS* 25 (1984) 60; Billows, *Kings and Colonists* 195.

[98] The Göteborg palimpsest (73ᵛ3–4) is explicit that his troops had come to despise him because of his failure against Eumenes, and he lost confidence (Arr. *Succ*. F 1.41).

[99] Arr. *Succ*. F 1.43: πεζοὺς μὲν ἐπιτρέπει αὐτῷ Μακεδόνας ὀκτακισχιλίους καὶ πεντακοσίους καὶ ἱππέας τῶν ἑταίρων ἴσους, ἐλέφαντας δὲ τῶν πάντων τοὺς ἡμίσεας οʹ. This passage has caused difficulties. Hammond (*CQ* 28 (1978) 134; *GRBS* 25 (1984) 59) argues that only 8,000 Macedonian infantry are at issue and that the extra 500 refers to some other unit. As the text stands, it implies that the cavalry Companions numbered 8,500, which is certainly impossible (so Billows, *Kings and Colonists* 195 n. 28). However, Photius' text may simply be contracted: Antipater gave Antigonus cavalry equal in number <to those he retained>; the same explicitly happened with the elephants. *Pace* Hammond 139 n. 25), the fact that almost 8,000 of these Macedonians

With the rest he marched first to the Hellespont and then to Macedonia, still plagued by his discontented troops who were pressing him for money.[100] These troops were not necessarily Macedonian, or exclusively Macedonian; Antipater had presumably promised his mercenaries donatives if he were victorious, and they would have been as insistent as the Macedonian forces at Triparadeisus. Indeed there is little scope for Macedonians in Antipater's army. 3,000 veterans had already returned, and Antigonus presumably had some Macedonian troops of his own in addition to the 8,500 Antipater had given him. The great army which he and Craterus had taken from Macedon remained for the most part in Asia.

The 8,500 Macedonians left with Antigonus are an interesting group. Almost certainly these were in the main new levies with no experience of service under Alexander. Antigonus was later to take them into Mesopotamia in pursuit of Eumenes, and they fought at Paraetacene and Gabiene (Diod. 19.29.3). At that time there was a clear generation between them and the Silver Shields who abused them for taking arms against their fathers.[101] They were the natural troops to be used against Eumenes and Alcetas, as they had never experienced service with the men they were to fight. It was the proper strategy, and the campaigns of 319 were a *succès de fou*. Assisted by treachery he inflicted two defeats upon Eumenes. The second and decisive battle he fought with infantry numerically inferior but half Macedonian.[102]

---

served with Antigonus at Paraetacene actually supports the received reading of Photius. One would hardly expect the whole complement to have survived almost three years campaigning (including major battles against Eumenes in 319) and remained intact. Given the fighting in Anatolia and the calamitous campaign near Susa (see below, pp. 114–18), it is surprising that so many lived to fight in Iran.

[100] Arr. *Succ.* F 1.44–5. Photius writes that 'the army' mutinied again, pressing for its money, and he gives no indication of its composition. Antipater's stratagem of crossing the Hellespont by night and leaving the troops in Asia supports the hypothesis that his forces were largely mercenaries. They could be threatened with exclusion from the coastal cities and gradual starvation, as had happened with the 10,000 at Byzantium (Xen. *Anab.* 7.1.1–17).

[101] Diod. 19.41.1 ('you are sinning against your fathers, who conquered the world with Philip and Alexander'); Plut. *Eum.* 16.8. See below, p. 151.

[102] Diod. 18.40.7. On the source tradition see Bosworth (above, n. 68) 78–9, 87 n. 119.

Eumenes sustained 8,000 casualties out of an infantry force 20,000 strong and the survivors mostly deserted *en masse* to Antigonus, including the majority of his Macedonian veterans. By now Antigonus had infantry forces 40,000 strong and over 7,000 cavalry. After he defeated Alcetas and his colleagues the totals increased to 60,000 foot and 10,000 horse, by far the most formidable army of its day.[103] Of that grand total some 13,000 were Macedonians.[104] It was the largest such group outside Macedonia itself and was crucial in the campaigns of the next three years which left him master of Asia.

Few Macedonian troops returned with Antipater, and those who did were veterans. The men who were freshly levied in 321 stayed in Asia with Antigonus and apparently never went home. Of course there were new age groups maturing for military service. It had been two years since Antipater left, and the reserves would have been somewhat replenished. Accordingly when Polyperchon marched on Peiraeus in 318 he had a considerable army of 20,000 Macedonian infantry along with 4,000 'from the other allies', 1,000 cavalry and a number of elephants.[105] So Diodorus tells us. But once again there is an anomaly, reminiscent of the report of the numbers with Antipater in 323. No mercenaries are recorded in Polyperchon's army, which is very hard to believe. Once again,[106] it would seem, there is contraction. The figure of 20,000 could refer to mercenaries alone, in which case, the Macedonian numbers have simply disappeared, or Diodorus himself has lumped together the Macedonians and mercenaries as a single composite mass. On either hypothesis Polyperchon had a large army with him, significantly larger than the force Antipater took to

---

[103] Diod. 18.45.1 (against Alcetas); 18.50.3 (at Antipater's death).

[104] Not all were of equal value. Antigonus did not apparently use the veterans from Eumenes' and Alcetas' armies when he fought in Iran. They could not be trusted against their old comrades, especially when those comrades were as redoubtable as the Silver Shields.

[105] Diod. 18.68.3: εἶχεν δὲ μεθ᾽ ἑαυτοῦ στρατιώτας πεζοὺς μὲν Μακεδόνας δισμυρίους, τῶν δ᾽ ἄλλων συμμάχων περὶ τετρακισχιλίους, ἱππεῖς δὲ χιλίους, ἐλέφαντας δὲ ἑξήκοντα πέντε, On this reading ἄλλων must be taken as pleonastic, 'of the others, namely allies'. However, if there *is* a lacuna, it is possible that Diodorus' text named some specific allied troops and contrasted them with 4,000 'others'.

[106] As with Diod. 18.12.2; see above, pp. 76–7.

inaugurate the Lamian War. This comprised the home army Polyperchon had used in 321, the new recruits and the veterans who had returned with Antipater. In addition there was a small expeditionary force under his son, Alexander, which had been sent to assist the democratic revolution in Athens.[107] Polyperchon himself operated in Phocis. He received the rival Athenian embassies there, at a site as yet unidentified,[108] and he was still in the region when Cassander sailed into the Peiraeus.[109] It looks as though the long-delayed reprisals against the Aetolians were under way, and Polyperchon was assembling an armament comparable in size to the forces used by Craterus and Antipater in 322/1.[110] The Aetolians had proved themselves a power not to be underestimated, and Polyperchon was concentrating his military strength to knock them out before Cassander could enlist them in his cause, as Perdiccas had done in 321 (Diod. 18.38.1). However, the sudden arrival of Cassander in Peiraeus interrupted the final solution to the Aetolian problem,[111] and the army was diverted into Attica. The regent had assembled a large composite army, but there is no reliable evidence as to the proportion of Macedonians in it. All we can say is that Polyperchon considered it prudent to keep his army intact. He did not apparently risk fighting on two fronts.

---

[107] Diod. 18.65.3; Plut. *Phoc.* 33.1. Both texts attest that Alexander arrived with an army (μετὰ δυνάμεως), but give no hint of its size or composition.

[108] Plut. *Phoc.* 33.7: 'a place named Pharygae, by Mt. Acrurion, which they now call Galate'. Neither Galate nor Acrurion is attested elsewhere. A town named Pharygae is recorded in eastern Locris, close to Thronium; it was the name in Roman times (Strab. 9.4.6 (426)) of the city of Tarphe (for its conjectural location, against the favoured site of Mendenitsa, see W. K. Pritchett, *Studies in Ancient Greek Topography* iv (Berkeley 1982) 155–6, 167–8). There has been a tendency since Droysen (ii².1.221) to identify Plutarch's Pharygae with this Locrian settlement. However, Plutarch (who had local knowledge) places Pharygae explicitly in Phocis, and it seems that Locrian Pharygae was still termed Tarphe when Demetrius of Callatis wrote, at the end of the 3rd century BC (Strab. 1.3.20 (60) = *FGrH* 85 F 6). *A fortiori* that would have been the case in 318. Plutarch's Pharygae, then, lay in Phocis, at some unknown location west of Elateia.

[109] Diod. 18.68.2: ἔτυχε μὲν διατρίβων περὶ τὴν Φωκίδα.

[110] Craterus and Antipater attacked with 30,000 infantry and 1,500 cavalry (Diod. 18.24.1). The troubles they encountered underscored the need for a large invasion army.

[111] This is no exaggeration. In 322/1 the Macedonian commanders had envisaged the transplantation of the entire Aetolian population to Asia (Diod. 18.25.5).

Let us draw some conclusions. There was certainly a large efflux of men from Macedonia during the reign of Alexander. At least 27,000 and probably closer to 30,000 infantrymen served in Asia. Apart from the newly married troops who returned for the winter of 334/3 and the small group of veterans discharged at the Oxus, 900 strong at most and probably less,[112] none found their way back to Macedon during Alexander's lifetime. Few did so thereafter. Craterus' veterans returned for the campaign of Crannon, which continued into the winter of 322/1 with the invasion of Aetolia. The following spring saw the invasion of Asia Minor and the civil wars. Then came the reallocation of troops at Triparadeisus, the winter campaign against Eumenes and the Perdiccans and Antipater's return to Macedonia. At that stage, if we may believe Polyaenus, some 3,000 veterans were able to negotiate their way back home, but the vast majority remained with Antigonus, who continued to absorb troops from the conquered Perdiccan factions. For Macedonia this was a loss of something like 26,000 men, who were taken away at their prime and never returned. I was wrong to write of a dead generation. Many of the troops, unlike their leader, had married and produced children before they went on campaign, and clearly, as we have seen, Alexander did not take with him the entire military population of his kingdom. But what appears to have happened is that the demands of Alexander in Asia and the home army in Europe absorbed an increasingly large number of the Macedonian males who would not otherwise have been required for military service. The reserves dwindled, and, as Diodorus states explicitly, there was a shortage of native Macedonians in 323.

Such shortages could be remedied over time. If hostilities were avoided and procreation encouraged, then a military population could be augmented quite rapidly.[113] However,

---

[112] The figure comes from Curtius (7.5.27), who does not mention the nationality of the troops discharged. Arr. 3.29.5 states that they were the most senior of the Macedonians and those Thessalian cavalry who had volunteered to remain with the army. Curtius' total of 900 could comprise the two groups.

[113] As did in fact happen in the reign of Perseus, who substantially increased the military strength of Macedon by keeping the peace for a generation (Livy 42.51.3–11). Cf. Bosworth, *JHS* 106 (1986) 10; Billows, *Kings and Colonists* 185–6.

the period after Alexander witnessed civil war on several fronts, the military population was stretched to the limit, and few of the soldiers in the field returned to Macedon. Worse, the troops left with Antigonus in 319 were new levies, detached from young families (if indeed they had families), and their potential was lost to the country. What this meant in real terms cannot be quantified, for we have no figures for the population and there is no adequate basis for extrapolating them.[114] But the overall loss was serious. Fewer children, considerably fewer, will have been born in the period 334–319, and so the classes reaching military age 18 or so years later will also have been smaller than they were under Philip. There was always the possibility of catching up later, given a period of peace and tranquillity, but that was rarely available. After 319 Macedonia was riven by civil war within a year, and armies were raised by the many contenders for power: Polyperchon, Cassander, Olympias, and Eurydice. Our sources do not mention major battles with serious loss of life,[115] but the record of the hostilities is seriously defective; we know nothing, for instance, of Cassander's first invasion of Macedonia in 317,[116] and no troop numbers or casualty figures are given for episodes such as the siege of Pydna.[117] For all their obscurity these operations will have had more direct impact on Macedonia than any of the warfare preceding, for the homeland itself became the theatre of operations, and the civilian population was exposed to death and starvation. At the very least this was not a period when the pool of men of military age could be expected to expand.

By contrast the power of Macedonia's rivals, in particular that of Antigonus, grew significantly, as mercenaries and military colonists were attracted by the huge financial resources of the new dynasts. The situation is nicely illustrated by the

---

[114] For a valiant attempt see Billows, *Kings and Colonists* 202–4.

[115] The most decisive was the defeat of Eurydice, whose forces went over to Olympias *en masse* (Diod. 19.11.2), as later happened to Demetrius (below, p. 258).

[116] Referred to in passing by Diod. 18.75.1; 19.35.7. On this campaign see Bosworth *Chiron* 22 (1992) 63–4, 71–2.

[117] For the fate of the besieged, who had to brave the rigours of winter, see Diod. 19.49.3–4. Pella and Amphipolis were also involved in the action (Diod. 19.50.3, 6–8).

events of 302, in the prelude to Ipsus. Faced with warfare in Asia Minor and on his borders Cassander sent an expeditionary force into Asia with his general Prepelaus, and took the rest of his army to face an invasion by Demetrius. The force with Prepelaus seems to have been relatively small; it augmented the larger army of Lysimachus, who assigned him a mere 6,000 foot and 1,000 horse to operate in Aeolia and Ionia. In Macedon Cassander concentrated all his forces in the face of Demetrius' invasion, and he was able to field an army of 29,000 infantry and 2,000 cavalry. The proportion of native Macedonians in that levy we cannot guess, but since Cassander had recently lost a number of Macedonian defenders at Heracleia, they may not have constituted a majority. By contrast Demetrius had a huge army of 56,000, including 8,000 Macedonians and 15,000 mercenaries, and Cassander could thank all his gods that his adversary was summoned back to Asia by his father. Much has recently been made of the vast force which Demetrius was amassing to support his ambitions of reconquering Asia. That was in 288, while he was still king of Macedon. The numbers are indeed prodigious: Plutarch (*Demetr.* 43.3–4) alleges that he had assembled 98,000 foot, 18,000 horse, and was laying the keels for 500 warships. This is superficially impressive, but, as so often, the key figure, that of the number of Macedonians, is omitted. What is more, we are not told where this vast force was being concentrated. It might have been in southern Greece, around Athens, Corinth, and Chalcis, where Demetrius' main shipyards were located. The majority of this army was almost certainly comprised of Greek allies and mercenaries, and the Macedonians were in a small minority. There was no vast army waiting in Macedon when Pyrrhus and Lysimachus invaded from the east and west. Demetrius had to rush back from Greece to preserve his kingdom, and he was promptly deposed when his troops refused to support him. If that vast force described by Plutarch was ever assembled,[118] it was certainly not in

---

[118] In the *Pyrrhus* (10.5) he describes Demetrius' force as a project only (ἐγνωκὼς δὲ μεγάλων πραγμάτων ἀντιλαμβάνεσθαι καὶ τὴν πατρῴαν ἀρχὴν ἀνακτᾶσθαι δέκα μυριάσι στρατοῦ καὶ ναυσὶ πεντακοσίαις). Demetrius doubtless had intentions of raising such vast numbers, but they may never have materialized.

Macedon. In any case it was a composite force, and however large the intended numbers, they tell us nothing about the strength of Macedon itself, merely the forces which Demetrius was confident he could attract.

It would seem that Macedonian numbers were relatively static between 323 and 301. They had declined from their peak at the end of Philip's reign, and the threats which faced Macedonian rulers required a larger demand on Macedonian reserves. Alexander's demands for troops in Asia had stretched resources very thin, and as a result the opening of the Lamian War produced a crisis which would have been unthinkable in 336. New recruits came to maturity in the years around his death, but they were used in the civil wars and eventually went to supplement the armies of Antigonus, and the pattern continued in the following years. Macedon under Cassander seems decidedly weaker than Macedon under Philip II. We cannot tell whether the population as a whole had declined. There are no statistics, and we know too little of the internal history of the area to undertake any speculation. We have to remain with the army figures, and these definitely show a reduction of numbers after Alexander. No doubt a period of peace and tranquillity would have redressed the situation, but there was no such happy state. Macedonia in 323 was weaker in military terms than it had been in 336, and it never again enjoyed the predominance which had been achieved by Chaeroneia. That is directly attributable to the campaigns of Alexander and the ambitions of his Successors.

4

The Campaign in Iran: Turbulent Satraps and Frozen Elephants

The winter of 317/16 witnessed what is arguably the most momentous campaign in the entire post-Alexander period. Two massive coalition armies led by Eumenes and Antigonus the One-Eyed manœuvred delicately and skilfully in the desolate terrain of central Iran, and the two great battles they fought were recorded by a participant (Hieronymus of Cardia) who was an intimate both of Eumenes and the Antigonids.[1] That account was used by Diodorus, and his narrative of the campaign is one of the most detailed and colourful in his entire encyclopaedic history. And the results were decisive. Antigonus ended as master of Asia from the Hellespont to Arachosia and the borders of India, and he was accorded regal honours in the heartland of the old Persian empire.[2] Richly documented, militarily and politically of the highest significance, these events should be a focus of any serious historical investigation. In effect they have suffered the fate of the virtuous Athenian woman, to be least talked about for good or ill. General histories tend to gloss over the Iranian campaign in a few pages; even Droysen gives us no more than a paraphrase of Diodorus. Strategic analyses are few, and those that exist deal exclusively with numbers and battle tactics.[3] I know of no attempt

---

[1] Hieronymus was with Eumenes from at least the time of the siege of Nora in 319, and was wounded at Gabiene. Immediately afterwards he joined the entourage of Antigonus (Diod. 19.44.3 = *FGrH* 154F 5; cf. Hornblower, *Hieronymus* 10–12).

[2] Diod. 19.48.1. See below, pp. 162–3.

[3] The standard treatment is that of J. Kromayer and E. Kahnes, in *Antike Schlachtfelder* i.391–434 (hereafter *AS*). This is a thorough and sometimes acute analysis of the numbers, battle dispositions and tactics on the field; but there is no attempt to set the campaign in a wider context, or even to define the topography. The same applies to the two more recent articles by A. M. Devine in *AncW* 12 (1985) 75–86 (Paraetacene), 87–96 (Gabiene). Otherwise there are only the narrative descriptions in regular histories: Droysen ii².1.275–300 is the fullest, but little more than a paraphrase of Diodorus and Plutarch (so too the biographical essay by

to set the campaign in its political context, nothing that comes to grips with the formidable problems that the terrain and weather posed for the participants, nothing that addresses the complex composition of the coalition armies and the problems of command which resulted. This chapter is an attempt to redress the balance and indicate some of the critical issues which determined the strategy and outcome.

1. POLITICAL BACKGROUND

The campaign effectively began in the late summer of 318. That was the time that Eumenes received his commission as general with instructions to promote the interests of the kings. It was the direct consequence of the political turmoil in Macedonia. Polyperchon, the regent and guardian of the kings, was faced by a hostile alliance between Cassander, the disappointed aspirant to the regency, and Antigonus, the commander of the great army which had disposed of the last remnants of the Perdiccan faction in Asia Minor. The commission to Eumenes was a blatant attempt to embroil Antigonus in a local war to the east of his domains and prevent an invasion of Europe. Eumenes was apparently given the choice of crossing to Europe and sharing the guardianship of the kings,[4] but that was a deliberately unattractive alternative. He would only get an army and financial help if he stayed in Asia, and in Asia he remained.

In theory Eumenes' position was unpromising. He had only just been released from the blockade at Nora, where he had held out against Antigonid forces for nearly a year. The price had been formal submission to Antigonus,[5] and Eumenes was

August Vezin, *Eumenes von Kardia* (Münster 1907) 85–125, 142–9); the most useful in my opinion is the recent sketch by Billows, *Antigonos* 85–106.

[4] Diod. 18.57.3–4. The alternatives are clearly expressed; Eumenes can either join Polyperchon as regent in Macedonia or receive an army and fight Antigonus. The second is the only one mentioned by Plut. *Eum.* 13.2, and was clearly the option that Eumenes was expected to take. Craterus was in a similar position in 323, when the marshals at Babylon gave him every inducement to return to Macedon. See above, pp. 58–60.

[5] Diod. 18.53.6. Plut. *Eum.* 12.2–4 (so Nep. *Eum.* 5.7) claims that the formal agreement was never ratified (cf. Anson, *GRBS* 18 (1977) 251–6; Bosworth,

reduced to a precarious existence in Cappadocia with a makeshift force of associates, no more than 2,500 in all.[6] It hardly posed a challenge to the huge army of Antigonus with its nucleus of Macedonians. However, Antigonus had his own problems. He was fighting a campaign in the Propontis against the Macedonian satrap, Arrhidaeus,[7] who had backing from a fleet led by Cleitus the White, victor in the naval battles of the Lamian War.[8] As a result Antigonus was fully occupied around Byzantium until late summer, 318. Eumenes could make capital out of his difficulties and attract adherents by his own formidable military reputation. He had after all out-generalled Craterus and inflicted a defeat on a superior army of Macedonians, and held the forces of Antipater and Antigonus at bay over the winter of 320/19.

There was another factor. The name of the kings still held some charisma. Mentally deficient Philip III may have been, but he was the son of Philip and the choice of the phalanx infantry at Babylon; and, his oriental mother notwithstanding, Alexander IV was the only legitimate offspring of the conqueror. Accordingly, when Polyperchon commanded the Silver Shields to leave their billet in Susa and join with Eumenes, they were only too ready to do so, and their commanders, Antigenes and Teutamus, deferred reluctantly to Eumenes' authority.[9] They may have had reservations about

---

'History and Artifice' 65–7; Hadley, *Historia* 50 (2001) 18–20). Justin 14.2.4–5 is badly garbled, and impossible to explain satisfactorily (see n. 7, below).

[6] Diod. 18.53.7; cf. Plut. *Eum.* 12.5–6, claiming that Eumenes had slightly under 1,000 horse when he left Nora.

[7] Arrhidaeus had allegedly made moves to relieve the siege of Nora (Diod. 18.52.4). If so, they came to nothing. It has been argued that this underlies Justin's allegation (14.2.4) that Antipater sent help to Eumenes: Antipater is a slip for Arrhidaeus (H. Kallenberg, *Philologus* 36 (1877) 462; cf. Goukowsky, *Diodore xviii* 154).

[8] Diod. 18.72.2–73.1; Polyaen. 4.6.8; cf. R. Engel, *Klio* 55 (1973) 141–5; Billows, *Antigonos* 82–7; Bosworth, *CQ* 44 (1994) 63–4.

[9] Diod. 18.59.3; Plut. *Eum.* 13.3–4. The Silver Shields appear to have been attached to their commander, Antigenes, when he was assigned to Susa after Triparadeisus (Arr. *Succ.* F 1.38). It is usually assumed that they had been commissioned to bring the treasures of Susa to Cyinda in Cilicia (Droysen ii².1.144, 256, a hypothesis widely accepted; cf. Heckel 313). Arrian does state that Antigenes was ordered to remove the treasures of Susa, but there is no indication of their destination. One may indeed doubt whether Antigenes carried out his instructions, since the treasury at Susa was evidently well supplied during Eumenes' campaign there (see below, p. 114). In any case Diodorus states that they came from a considerable

serving under a Greek, and a Greek whom they had collectively condemned to death after the defeat of Perdiccas,[10] but
he had the mandate of the kings, and for that matter the
mandate had been conferred by Polyperchon, who had commanded a phalanx battalion through most of Alexander's
reign and had been instrumental in the repatriation of the
veterans of Opis.[11] His name would have carried clout among
the surviving troops of Alexander and was clearly one of the
reasons for his designation as regent in preference to
Cassander.[12] Eumenes considered it prudent to invoke the
dead Alexander, to associate the commanders of the Silver
Shields in discussions of policy before the empty throne.[13] It
was not merely the deified, unconquered king who was
invoked as the spiritual leader of the enterprise; the regalia of
kingship were on display, and implicitly endorsed Eumenes'
appointment as paramount general ($\sigma\tau\rho\alpha\tau\eta\gamma\grave{o}\varsigma$ $\alpha\mathring{v}\tau o\kappa\rho\acute{\alpha}\tau\omega\rho$) of
Asia.[14] Accordingly, when Ptolemy appeared with a fleet and
issued propaganda attacking Eumenes, he was totally unsuccessful. The Silver Shields refused to listen to his overtures,
and the treasurers of the great fortress of Cynda disbursed

distance to meet Eumenes in Cilicia. That surely excludes their having fulfilled a
commission to bring funds to the Cilician treasury. Cf. Bosworth, 'History and
Artifice' 66–7.

[10] For the condemnation (by the Macedonian forces in Egypt, which included
the Silver Shields) see Diod. 18.37.2; Plut. *Eum.* 8.3; Arr. *Succ.* F 1.30; Just.
13.8.10. Both Ptolemy and Seleucus tried to exploit the verdict to undermine
Eumenes, but had no success (Diod. 18.62.1; 19.12.2).

[11] For his career under Alexander see Heckel 188–93. He received his phalanx command after Issus (Arr. 2.12.2) and retained it for the rest of the reign. When the veterans left Opis he was Craterus' second-in-command (Arr. 7.12.4; cf. Just. 12.12.8).

[12] Diod. 18.48.4 stresses that he was 'held in honour by the people in
Macedonia'; cf. 54.2.

[13] Diod. 18.61.1–3; the central act was the burning of incense and the offer of
proskynesis to Alexander 'as a god'. See also Polyaen. 4.8.2; Plut. *Eum.* 13.5–8; Nep.
Eum. 7.2.

[14] Diod. 18.61.3. This is one of the passages which Hadley (*Historia* 50 (2001)
10–17) identifies as deriving from an encomium of Eumenes separate from the
wider history of Hieronymus. I agree that the source stresses the legitimacy of
Eumenes' command and underlines the troops' respect for royal authority, but I do
not see that there is anything that could not come from Hieronymus himself (see
above, p. 26). It was in part a justification of his own loyalty to Eumenes against his
future master, Antigonus. While the dual monarchy lasted, Eumenes could legiti-
mately be seen as its protector.

money to Eumenes in the kings' name.[15] Ptolemy, the hero of
the army after the death of Perdiccas, could make no head-
way with the troops who had feted him in 321. Antigonus
was no more successful when he sent Macedonian agents to
intrigue in Eumenes' camp. The letter in which he demanded
the arrest and execution of Eumenes was rejected, and
Eumenes himself was confirmed by his troops who apparently shared his view that Antigonus was in rebellion against
the royal house.[16]

In the summer of 318 Eumenes' position improved. He
made Cilicia his base,[17] an area easily defensible and familiar
to Macedonian veterans from the campaign of Issus. That
alone would have encouraged Eumenes' forces as they deliber-
ated in the Alexander tent in the spiritual presence of the
conqueror. The vestigial army Eumenes brought with him
from Cappadocia was immeasurably strengthened by the
arrival of the 3,000 Silver Shields from Susa, and his recruiting officers circulated in the region, enrolling mercenaries.
There was even time for volunteers to be attracted from the
cities of Greece proper, so that he had some 10,000 infantry
and 2,000 cavalry in addition to the Silver Shields.[18] This
was an army that no satrap in the area could match in
quantity or quality, and Ptolemy himself was vulnerable.
His annexation of Syria in 320 was generally regarded as
unjustifiable,[19] and Eumenes could threaten to restore the
area to royal authority. He moved into Phoenicia, where he
intended to create a navy, drawing on the resources of

[15] Diod. 18.62.2: 'but no one paid any attention to him because the kings and
their guardian Polyperchon and also Olympias had written to them that they should
serve Eumenes in every way, since he was the paramount general of the kingdom'
(ὡς ὄντι τῆς βασιλείας αὐτοκράτορι στρατηγῷ).

[16] Diod. 18.62.4–63.6. What decided matters was Eumenes' appeal to his troops
to follow the decrees of the kings and not listen to one who had become a rebel
(63.4).

[17] Diod. 18.59.1–3. Despite the modest forces with Eumenes the Antigonid
general Menander (Billows, *Antigonos* 402–3, no. 71) considered it prudent not
to advance into Cilicia. He was an experienced commander and could calculate
the risks.

[18] Diod. 18.61.4–5. Most of the recruiting took place in southern Asia Minor
(Lycia and Pisidia), northern Syria and Cyprus. The recruits would be conveyed to
Cilicia by sea, and Antigonus was in no position to interfere until his naval victory
off Byzantium.   [19] See Ch. 6, esp. nn. 17–18.

Cilicia, Phoenicia, and Cyprus, a navy which would give him the capacity to intervene in Asia Minor at will or even attack Egypt. He could certainly overrun the Syrian coast and expel Ptolemaic garrisons.[20] Eumenes had become a major power in a matter of months, and Antigonus could not overlook the threat. Intrigue and diplomacy had failed, and there was no alternative to military intervention.

Antigonus moved quickly. Once he had consolidated his victory at Byzantium, he detached a large portion of his army, 20,000 infantry and 4,000 cavalry, and marched with the minimum of baggage[21] to confront Eumenes. Faced with the possibility of a double offensive, with Ptolemy attacking from Egypt, Eumenes avoided a frontal engagement and moved eastwards towards Mesopotamia and ultimately Iran. For the moment he was outnumbered by Antigonus alone, and he needed extra forces. The eastern satrapies would provide them.

Diodorus gives us very little information at this point, as he is rounding off affairs in the east and eager to move to the stirring story of Agathocles in Sicily with which he opens Book 19. He merely states that Eumenes was eager to make contact with the so-called 'upper satrapies'.[22] The situation is to a degree clarified some chapters later, when Diodorus gives an all too brief résumé of events in the east.[23] There was a major power struggle in the satrapies which fringed the great Iranian salt desert east of the Zagros. The most powerful

[20] Diod. 18.63.6. Ptolemy had garrisoned Phoenicia in 320 (Diod. 18.43.2), but there is no hint of any opposition to Eumenes. Garrison commanders were not likely to risk a siege from such a formidable army, and did not resist the royal general. For his part Eumenes claimed to be acting in the interests of Polyperchon, providing the transports necessary for a future invasion of Asia.

[21] That I take to be the meaning of εὐζώνους at Diod. 18.73.1 (contra Goukowsky's Budé translation, 'légèrement armés', and Geer's Loeb, 'lightly equipped infantry'). Antigonus certainly did not take only light infantry, which would have been suicidal against the Silver Shields. He left behind the usual straggle of camp followers and took only the bare minimum of equipment, as the Greek coalition did at Lamia before closing with Leonnatus (Diod. 18.15.1; cf. 19.32.1, 93.2). There was no ἀποσκευή to slow down progress or provide a tactical distraction. Compare the description of the Campanian attack on Syracuse (Diod. 14.9.2): they left their baggage at Agyrrhium and ἐξώρμησαν ἐπὶ Συρακούσας εὔζωνοι.

[22] Diod. 18.73.2: σπεύδων τῶν ἄνω λεγομένων σατραπειῶν ἅψασθαι.

[23] Diod. 19.14.1–4. There is a detailed discussion by Schober, *Untersuchungen* 74–9.

player was Peithon, the former Bodyguard of Alexander, who had put down the rebellion of the Greek colonists in 322 and was instrumental in the assassination of Perdiccas. For his services he was promoted to the regency itself, which he shared with Arrhidaeus for a brief, turbulent period before resigning in favour of Antipater.[24] He was then reinstated as satrap of Media, and probably had his garrison forces strengthened by detachments from the former grand army that had attacked Egypt.[25] His rival was Peucestas in Persis to the south. Peucestas could bask in retrospective glory after saving Alexander's life at the Malli town. He also had the rich and populous heartland of the old Persian empire firmly under his control; he knew the language, dressed in Persian style and was popular with his subjects.[26] He and Peithon inevitably clashed, and the clash came soon after Triparadeisus, when Peithon was confirmed in Media with enhanced powers, nothing less, it would seem, than a supervisory command in the upper satrapies.[27]

[24] Diod. 18.36.6, 39.1–3; Arr. *Succ.* F 1.30–1. For a digest of his career see Heckel 276–9.

[25] Arrhidaeus, his colleague in the regency, seems to have had at least 1,000 Macedonians under his command when he held the satrapy of Hellespontine Phrygia (Diod. 18.51.1). It is hardly conceivable that Peithon received less (see above, p. 88).

[26] This is a consistent theme. See Arr. 6.30.2–3; 7.6.3; Diod. 19.14.5–6, 48.5 (see below, p. 163). According to Diodorus (19.14.5) the wearing of Persian dress was a unique privilege granted by Alexander; it endeared him to his Persian subjects but had infuriated the Macedonian rank and file (Arr. 7.6.3), and probably stood in the way of his attempt to attract the loyalty of the Silver Shields.

[27] Diod. 19.14.1: στρατηγὸς δὲ τῶν ἄνω σατραπειῶν ἁπασῶν γενόμενος. This command has been interpreted as a usurpation by Peithon (e.g. Schober, *Untersuchungen* 77; Heckel 278), but Diodorus reads as though it was a formal appointment, like the one Antigonus was to advertise in 316 (Diod. 19.46.1). It is in fact reminiscent of Antigonus' appointment in 321/20 as στρατηγὸς αὐτοκράτωρ of Asia for the war with the Perdiccans (Diod. 18.40.1, 50.1; cf. Arr. *Succ.* F 1.38; App. *Syr.* 53.266). Peithon may have had a similar commission to deal with troubles in the east. There is no hint of this in either of our accounts of the dispensation at Triparadeisus, but neither Diodorus nor Photius/Arrian show much interest in the east and may have omitted the *strategia*. Alternatively, and perhaps preferably, the commission may have been a later enactment by Antipater when trouble erupted in Parthyaea. Schober, *Untersuchungen* 74–8 argued that Diodorus' text should be emended: for γενόμενος read γεν<ησ>όμενος (or better, γεν<έσθαι βουλ>όμενος). In that case Diodorus would be referring to Peithon's ambitions, not to an appointment or usurpation. But the received text makes adequate sense: Peithon had been appointed satrap of Media and (later) became general of the upper satrapies. The

There had been some disturbance in the strategic province of Parthyaea, where the Persian noble Phratapherna had governed throughout the latter years of Alexander.[28] Confirmed in office at Babylon, he was replaced at Triparadeisus by a certain Philippus, who is usually identified as the Philippus attested as satrap of Bactria and Sogdiana at the death of Alexander.[29] That is a reasonable supposition. It could be that Phratapherna had allied himself to the Perdiccan faction (perhaps one of his daughters had been given to Alcetas or another senior member in Alexander's great collective wedding at Susa).[30] In that case he is likely to have been stripped of his satrapy when Perdiccas was assassinated, much as Perdiccas' own father-in-law, Atropates, seems to have lost his dominion in north-west Media. At Babylon Atropates was allowed to coexist with Peithon, but he is notably absent from the record of the satrapal distribution at Triparadeisus.[31] He was probably supplanted by Peithon, whose territories were consequently expanded to incorporate both sections of Media. Similarly, Philippus could have been transferred from Bactria to Parthyaea with instructions to remove Phratapherna.

What happened next is opaque. Phratapherna disappears from the historical record, and so does Philippus. We have only a corrupt resumptive note in Diodorus to the effect that Peithon had killed the previous general, Philotas, and

fact that the eastern satraps refused to accept his authority does not disprove the commission.

[28] For the murky evidence see Bosworth, *HCA* ii.122, 320–1.

[29] Arr. *Succ.* F 1.36; Diod. 18.39.6 (Just. 13.4.23 retrojects Philippus' appointment to the Babylon settlement: cf. Schober, *Untersuchungen* 45). The identification of Philippus with the former satrap of Bactria was proposed by Beloch (iv².2.315) and is widely accepted. However, Philippus is a very common Macedonian name, and one might argue that the satrap of Bactria was killed during the revolt of the colonists shortly after Alexander's death and has nothing to do with the satrapy of Parthyaea.

[30] That might be the context of the obscure reference to his son Sisines, who was apparently mentioned by Arrian in Book II of his History of the Successors (Arr. *Succ.* F 3 = *FGrH* 156F 4).

[31] Justin 13.4.13 appears to state that Peithon was assigned Greater Media and Atropates the father-in-law of Perdiccas Lesser Media. Diod. 18.3.1, 3 separately mentions both Peithon and Atropates as governors of Media (Arrian, Dexippus, and Curtius mention Peithon alone in connection with Media). For Perdiccas' marriage to an unnamed daughter of Atropates see Arr. 7.4.5; Just. *loc. cit.*

imposed his own brother, Eudamus.[32] There are many possible scenarios. One is that Philippus died in the campaign to extrude Phrataphernes, to be succeeded by his second-in-command, Philotas; Peithon then intervened and summarily executed Philotas for insubordination, replacing him with his own brother. Other hypothetical reconstructions are possible, but the major issue is clear enough. By 318 Peithon had occupied Parthyaea, and extended the area he directly controlled from the Caspian Gates (east of modern Tehran) to the strategic crossroads of Iran. He directly menaced Areia and Drangiana to the east and south, and could take an army north of the Kopet Dag range through Margiana to Bactria. Not surprisingly his neighbours reacted strongly, and a coalition of satraps pooled their forces and expelled him from Parthyaea, defeating him in battle. By early 317 he had left Media (still, it seems, controlled by his troops) and was soliciting support from Seleucus in Babylonia.[33]

The war was far from over. A coalition army of satraps concentrated in Persis under the leadership of Peucestas. They included the satrap of neighbouring Carmania, Stasander from Areia, and Sibyrtius from Arachosia. Contingents came from as far afield as Bactria and Parapamisadae.[34] They did not comprise the full resources of the eastern satrapies, for more troops needed to be retained in the east to defend Parthyaea against an attack from Media, but even so Peucestas commanded a formidable army of over 18,000 foot and 4,000 horse.[35] It was a force of great diversity. Peucestas

---

[32] Diod. 19.14.1. The Teubner text reads Πίθων σατράπης μὲν ἀπεδέδεικτο Μηδίας, στρατηγὸς δὲ τῶν ἄνω σατραπειῶν ἁπασῶν γενόμενος Φιλώταν μὲν τὸν προϋπάρχοντα Παρθυαίας στρατηγὸν ἀπέκτεινε, τὸν δὲ αὑτοῦ ἀδελφὸν Εὔδαμον ἀντὶ τούτου κατέστησεν (the MSS read Παρθυαῖος ὅς, transposed to follow γενόμενος; that is ungrammatical nonsense). There has been a tendency from Wesseling onwards to 'emend' Philotas to Philippus (cf. Schober, *Untersuchungen* 74–5 n. 1). But Philotas is surely the *lectio difficilior*. We may concede that a Macedonian satrap was unlikely to have a general of equal status appointed over his troops. Nothing, however, suggests that Philotas was appointed alongside Philippus. He could have been his successor. Almost three years had elapsed since Triparadeisus, and that was a long time in this period of confusion.

[33] Diod. 19.14.2–3. The satrapal coalition seems to have been centred in Persis, in easy access to Susa (Diod. 19.15.1); it seems not to have been sufficiently confident to attack Media.   [34] Listed by Diod. 19.14.5–7.

[35] The total given at Diod. 19.14.8 is 18,700 foot and 4,600 horse, but the individual contingents he lists amount 18,500 foot and 4,210 horse. The discrepancy

himself provided the majority, 10,000 Persian infantry as well as 3,000 eastern infantry trained in Macedonian style, and a cavalry contingent in which 600 Greeks and Thracians were balanced by 400 Persians. We do not have similar descriptions of the other satrapal forces, but they presumably combined native levies with mercenaries and Macedonian trained infantry.[36] They were miscellaneous collections of troops with no corporate identity—and there were few Macedonians, only the personal entourage of the satraps.[37]

On the other hand there was a huge, literally huge, asset in the 120 elephants which had recently arrived from the Indus valley. This was the largest accumulation of such beasts since Alexander had begun his march down the Hydaspes with 200 elephants in his train. The satrapal alliance had contacted King Porus and requested help,[38] and the help came in unexpected circumstances. Eudamus, the senior Macedonian official in the area, assassinated Porus.[39] The circumstances are mysterious, but it seems certain that Eudamus had Indian associates, at least one (Ceteus) of princely status,[40] and we may fairly posit a conspiracy against Porus, perhaps backed by Porus' old enemy, the ruler of Taxila. At any event Eudamus disposed of Porus, and his Indian allies were grateful enough to entrust him with what must have been the entire elephant stable of the dead ruler. It was a colossal acquisition, something

has not been satisfactorily explained, but it is likely enough that Diodorus omitted a small regional contingent; the Gedrosians and Euergetae to the south-east of Drangiana would be a possibility.

[36] At Paraetacene Eumenes deployed 5,000 infantry trained in Macedonian style (Diod. 19.27.6), and, since he had little opportunity to acquire any during his march through Mesopotamia and Babylonia, it is practically certain that something like half came from the satrapal contingents.

[37] Note Arr. 6.27.3: the satrap of Gandhara under Alexander (Philippus, son of Machatas) had two groups of troops, his mercenaries and his Macedonian body-guard. The latter were numerous enough to dispose of the mutinous mercenaries who had assassinated their commander.

[38] This follows from the controversial (unemended) text of Arr. *Ind.* 5.3. Sibyrtius' friend, Megasthenes, claimed that 'he met Sandrocottus (Chandragupta) the greatest king of the Indians, and also met Porus, who was yet greater than him'. On the implications see Bosworth, *HCA* ii.242–4; *CPh* 91 (1996) 113–27, esp. 119–20.

[39] Diod. 19.14.8. For the appointment in Alexander's reign see Arr. 6.27.2; Curt. 10.1.21 with Bernard, *Orientalia Iosephi Tucci memoriae dicata* 83–8; Heckel 333–4.

[40] Diod. 19.33.1. See Ch. 5.

that Peithon could not hope to match, and it gave the alliance a strong psychological advantage. There were also problems, the victualling and stabling of the great beasts, who could consume up to 270 kg. of green vegetation in the wild and even in periods of inactivity require some 45 kg. of hay.[41] Provisioning, watering and (in winter) heating would have been expensive and labour-intensive.

Eumenes was aware of the troubles in Iran from a relatively early date, certainly by the end of 318, and they were what drew him eastwards away from the joint threat posed by Antigonus and Ptolemy. The satrapal alliance could swell his own numbers, and he could give them what they most needed, the most effective corps of Macedonian veterans in the world. Against that combination Peithon would stand no chance of survival. But first Eumenes had to reach Iran. He spent the winter of 318/17 in Babylonia, in a location to the north of the satrapy.[42] There he contacted Seleucus and

---

[41] There is a useful compilation of material in Bernard 92–3 (above, n. 39). In India under British rule elephants in service had 6.8 kg. of cereals, 90.5 kg. of dry fodder, 217.5 kg. of green fodder and various supplements. In Perth Zoo the one adult (female) elephant is fed three times daily: at 10.30 a.m. 6 kg. pellets, 2 kg. oaten hay; at 1 p.m. 2 kg. red and green apples, 2 kg. carrots, 2 kg. sweet potatoes; at 5.15 p.m. 3 kg. apples, 3 kg. carrots, 2 kg. sweet potatoes, 1 kg. cabbage, 10 kg. hay, 1.5 kg. lucerne hay, 400 g. salt, 40 ml. linseed oil, 20 kg. fodder. In addition there is hay and fodder to browse on throughout the day. (I am grateful to Colin Walbank for this information.) Macedonian elephants on active service cannot have had such a variegated diet, still less the pellets and supplements that captive elephants enjoy in modern zoos. Aristotle (*HA* 8: 596ª3–9) seems to envisage a diet of fodder and barley groats, with an admixture of wine. The figures are expressed in Macedonian *metretae* and Persian *mareis*, and there is a *prima facie* case that the information came from Alexander's soldiers in Babylon who took over the upkeep of the Achaemenid elephant stables (cf. P. Briant, in P. Brulé and J. Oulhen (eds.), *Esclavage, guerre, économie en Grèce ancienne* 184–7, suggesting that the figures may ultimately derive from an official table of rations). Whether they are transmitted accurately is another matter. The text seems to envisage something like 320 kg. of fodder and 235 kg. of barley, whereas the rations at Vincennes Zoo, which Bernard cites, allow for only 80–100 kg. of dry fodder and 10 kg. of oats or barley and 10 kg. of fresh vegetables.

[42] Diod. 19.12.1 (παρεχείμασε μὲν τῆς Βαβυλωνίας ἐν ταῖς ὀνομαζομέναις Καρῶν κώμαις). The location of these Carian villages cannot be fixed. They were clearly distinct from Carrhae in Mesopotamia (Diod. 19.91.1: see below, p. 231) and also (*pace* Geer) from the so-called Κάραι κῶμαι which Alexander passed on his way from Susa to Bisitun and Media (Diod. 17.110.1): this latter location was east of the Tigris and relatively close to Susa (cf. Herzfeld, *The Persian Empire* 9). Eumenes crossed the Tigris in the following spring (Diod. 19.12.3) and was clearly stationed north of Babylon for the winter.

Peithon in Babylon and tried to win them over to his cause. With their combined armies he could perhaps repel Antigonus without enlisting the help of the eastern satraps. But it was a forlorn hope. Peithon would hardly entrust his forces to Eumenes and leave Media exposed to attack until Antigonus was defeated—if he could be defeated. So propaganda came to the fore yet again. Seleucus professed his loyalty to the kings, but attacked Eumenes' command as illegitimate; in his eyes he was a condemned rebel, and the sentence passed in 321 still held.[43] Eumenes' embassy returned to his headquarters with a counter-embassy which appealed directly to the Silver Shields, asking them to repudiate his command. This was no more successful than the earlier appeals by Ptolemy and Antigonus, nor was a later direct appearance by Seleucus and Peithon in person.[44] Even Seleucus' standing as a hypaspist commander under Alexander could not subvert the commission Eumenes had received from the kings. Eumenes was, for the moment, secure in his command. but there was now no strategic choice. He had to cross Babylonia into Susa, the satrapy of Antigenes and the old base of the Silver Shields. That allowed direct communications with Persis and the satrapal alliance.

2. SUMMER 317: FROM BABYLONIA TO IRAN

Crossing Babylonia was not easy.[45] The country where Eumenes had wintered was naturally exhausted, as was the land to the south, which Seleucus had stripped of provisions, much as the Persians had done in the past in the face of the Ten Thousand. Eumenes was forced to attempt a crossing of the Tigris at a point some 60 km. from Babylon,[46] in the

[43] Diod. 19.12.2–3. See above, pp. 101–2.

[44] Diod. 19.12.2–3, 13.1: this second diplomatic offensive represented Eumenes as a non-Macedonian responsible for huge Macedonian casualties; it looks ahead to the gibe of the Silver Shields, who termed him 'the plague from the Chersonese' (Plut. *Eum*. 18.2).

[45] Diod. 18.73.3 mentions a night attack by local natives in the vicinity of the Tigris. This is a prospective passage, not taken up in the fuller narrative in Book 19, and it is impossible to give it a precise setting.

[46] Diod. 19.12.3 locates the crossing point 300 stades from Babylon. Eumenes clearly never entered the capital. The view that he captured the palace

vicinity of Opis and the later foundation of Seleuceia. That
was easier said than done. The water level was rising, there as
on the Euphrates, and by April/May it would reach its
maximum level. Fording was impossible, and Eumenes
needed to gather transports for his men, some 300 flat-
bottomed vessels, which (it seems) had been constructed by
Alexander to transport his men across the Babylonian watercourses when he was in the area during 324 and 323.[47] As
the water rose, Seleucus and Peithon sailed up the Tigris
and tried one last time to persuade the Silver Shields to
renounce their allegiance.[48] When their diplomacy failed,
they took offensive action. It was the time of year that the
Pallacotta canal was opened to check the flow in the main
channel of the Euphrates, and there was a large work force
of natives already mobilized for the clearing of the canals.[49]
Consequently Seleucus was able to open up an old canal to
the north of Eumenes' position.

The new channel cut across Eumenes' line of retreat, and
left his army marooned on an island, threatened with total

(cf. Hornblower, *Hieronymus* 112–13) rests on an over-adventurous interpretation
of the Babylonian Chronicle (*ABC* 10, Obv. 15) which does indeed refer to the
palace of Babylon, in a very obscure context. In any case the entry is dated to some
time after Tašrīt in Philip's seventh year (October 317), when Eumenes and his
army were in Iran.

[47] Diod. 19.12.5, 13.3 (cf. 19.18.4) refers to them as πλοῖα κοντωτά, usually translated as 'punts'. These were light vessels, which could operate in shallow water,
propelled by poles, but they must also have had sails to traverse the deep bed of the
Tigris. In the Ptolemaic navy they counted as the lightest form of warship (App.
Prooem. 10.40) and in 306 Ptolemy himself was to use them to ferry Antigonid
deserters across the Nile (Diod. 20.75.1–3). These boats constructed by Alexander
(Diod. 19.12.5) should not be associated with his planned Arabian expedition. They
were intended primarily for transporting his army across the numerous rivers and
canals of Mesopotamia. One should note the difficulties the Ten Thousand experienced crossing the water courses in north Babylonia, even at low water (Xen.
An. 2.3.10, 13), over improvised bridges of palm trunks. Alexander could prepare
more thoroughly for his passages of Babylonia in 324 and 323, and clearly had
special craft built.   [48] See above, n. 44.

[49] Arr. 7.21.3–5; Strabo 16.1.9 (740), both based on Aristobulus (*FGrH* 139 F
55–6; on the interrelation of Arrian and Strabo see Bosworth, *From Arrian to
Alexander* 56–9). A workforce of 10,000 was apparently occupied for over two
months each year. The Pallacotta is clearly the Pallukatu Channel which figures in
Babylonian records of the Hellenistic period. In 329 it was closed at low water in
October/November. High water is recorded as peaking at Babylon in April and
May. Cf. T. Boiy and K. Verhoeven, in *Changing Watercourses in Babylonia*
147–58, locating the mouth of the canal in the vicinity of Sippar.

inundation.[50] That may have made the crossing easier, as the
volume of water in the main channel of the Tigris would have
decreased, and the bulk of the army was able to cross in a
single day. However, Eumenes had to return with at least part
of his army, to safeguard the baggage train, which contained
the material possessions of the Silver Shields (including their
families) and was in danger of being waterlogged.[51] Diodorus
claims that he was deeply anxious about the baggage, and the
anxiety was no doubt heightened by protests from his men,
who absolutely refused to be separated from their possessions—an omen of what was to come. Eumenes now received
information from local inhabitants, who showed him how to
excavate a cut to turn the canal away from the Macedonian
camp. The details in Diodorus are extraordinarily obscure,
but it is clear that Eumenes cleared, or was set to clear, the
inundation around his camp.[52] The baggage train was saved
from the flood waters, and he was in a position to transport it
across the Tigris at his leisure. At this stage Seleucus and
Peithon gave up any attempt to stop the passage and made a
truce with Eumenes.[53] His army now moved unopposed
down the east bank of the Tigris, taking three separate routes
to exploit all the scanty food reserves of the district, which

---

[50] Diod. 19.13.2. In his earlier prospective resume Diod. 18.73.3 seems to place
the episode on the Euphrates. This is not necessarily a blunder by Diodorus (so
Billows, *Antigonos* 88 n. 13; Goukowsky, *Diodore xviii* 170). The text reads
ἐπιθεμένου τοῦ Σελεύκου παρὰ τὸν Εὐφράτην; it is possible that the source described
the direction of Seleucus' attack, *along* the Euphrates (north from Babylon) and
then eastwards to the Tigris and the vicinity of Opis. On this hypothesis Diodorus
is guilty of a misleading contraction, not gross error.

[51] It was also vulnerable to attack by Seleucus' cavalry. Far outnumbered by
Eumenes' army (Diod. 19.13.3), the Seleucid forces could not prevent his crossing
or landing, but the baggage was left with, it seems, minimal protection. Eumenes
may have had wind of an attack. The locals had clearly come to cooperate with him,
at least to the extent of getting the thousands of hungry mouths out of their territory—and doing so peacefully.

[52] Diod. 19.13.4. According to the slipshod prospective account at 18.73.3
Eumenes was able to transfer his camp to a mound (χῶμα) while he diverted the
channel. That would have eased the immediate danger from the flood. In that case
he had part of his army already across the Tigris, part of it labouring to divert the
canal and the baggage train for the moment encamped on dry ground.

[53] Diod. 19.13.5. Seleucus was eager to get Eumenes' forces out of his satrapy.
Not surprisingly. He did not have the military resources to injure them, and, left to
his own devices, Eumenes could devastate the satrapy with impunity.

was totally devoid of grain,[54] and by the beginning of summer he had reached Susa.

In the meantime Antigonus had been active. When Eumenes moved east from Phoenicia, he did not follow him. The force he had brought from the west was equipped with only the basics.[55] If he was to campaign for a protracted period in the east, he needed his baggage train. There were also his elephants. Antipater had left him with 70 of the beasts in 319, and he was able to marshal 65 of them at Paraetacene.[56] He had not used them in his mobile expeditionary force against Eumenes, and now he needed to consolidate his resources. He probably occupied Cilicia in the wake of Eumenes' departure,[57] and concluded a non-aggression pact with Ptolemy. At least Ptolemy is attested in a state of 'friendship' with Antigonus in 316 (Diod. 19.56.4), and Antigonus surely made arrangements to protect his communications between Cilicia and the Euphrates.

All this took time, and the One-Eyed was not ready to follow Eumenes until the following year. The winter of 318/17 found him in Mesopotamia, and in the spring he received the invitation of Peithon and Seleucus to resist Eumenes and the satrapal coalition.[58] He was in Mesopotamia, apparently stationary, for several months. Diodorus claims that he was enlisting more soldiers, which is likely enough, given that Eumenes was openly negotiating with the eastern satraps. Seleucus might be sufficiently impressed by the royal general and the Silver Shields to throw in his lot with them and abandon Peithon to his fate. It is not surprising that Antigonus opted for caution and waited to be invited into Babylonia by its satrap. Then with troops refreshed he could march at

---

[54] Diod. 19.13.6. The area had abundant resources of rice, sesame, and dates but not, it seems, sufficient for the entire army in bulk. And unripe dates could be lethal, as the Macedonians had discovered in Gedrosia (Strab. 15.2.7 (723); Theophr. *HP* 4,4,12; Pliny, *NH* 13.50).   [55] Diod. 18.73.1. See above, n. 21.
[56] Arr. *Succ.* F 1.43; Diod. 18.50.3; 19.27.1.
[57] Eumenes had left behind a fleet, which is attested operating at Rhosus under the command of the experienced admiral, Sosigenes of Rhodes (Polyaen. 4.6.9; cf. Arr. *Succ.* F 24.6). The Phoenician crews, however, refused to fight against Antigonus' fleet, fresh from its victory off Byzantium, and left Sosigenes in the lurch (Polyaen. *loc. cit.*). The occupation of Cilicia was evidently bloodless.
[58] Diod. 19.13.5, 15.6.

speed into Susiana—and the blistering summer heat. He was, then, based in Mesopotamia for several months. What he did there (except levy troops) is not attested, but it is likely that there was some friction with the satrap of the area, Amphimachus. Now, Amphimachus is an interesting and obscure figure. His appointment to Mesopotamia is noted by Arrian, who terms him brother of the king.[59] It is a dramatic qualification, and it has been treated with some scepticism.[60] However, there is no reason to doubt the explicit statement. Philinna, the mother of Philip Arrhidaeus, could well have had an earlier marriage and produced a son before she entered the Macedonian court.[61] In that case Amphimachus was a Thessalian of distinction[62] who could boast the king as his half-brother, and he may have found the pretensions of Antigonus difficult to endure. At all events he is next attested in the camp of Eumenes, to whom he brought a modest contingent of 600 cavalry.[63] The king's general was joined by the king's brother, and Eumenes' legitimacy gained a further

[59] Arr. *Succ.* F 1.35: Ἀμφιμάχῳ τῷ τοῦ βασιλέως ἀδελφῷ cf. Diod. 18.39.6. Amphimachus is the only Macedonian of that name recorded in Tataki, *Macedonians Abroad* 239, no. 133.

[60] Beloch (iv².2.316, accepted by Roos) argued that there was some confusion between Arrhidaeus the king and Arrhidaeus the governor of Hellespontine Phrygia, and that Amphimachus was brother of the latter. Confusion we do indeed find, but only in Justin (13.4.6). There is no confusion between the two anywhere else in Photius/Arrian, and no reason to suspect it here. Berve (ii.32 no. 66) was right to take the text at face value. So now Greenwalt, *AncW* 10 (1984) 69–72; Carney, *Women and Monarchy in Macedonia* 61, 276 n. 45; Ogden, *Polygamy, Prostitutes and Death* 38 n. 156.

[61] Philinna came from the aristocracy of Larisa (Satyrus, *ap.* Athen. 13. 557 C). The hostile strand in Justin (9.8.1; 13.2.11), who terms her a dancer or prostitute (*scortum*) from Larisa might be based on the fact that Philip was not her first husband. It would be interesting to know who that was. If he had been a powerful and popular dynast, then Philip may have gained a lasting political advantage from the alliance, just as Demetrius Poliorcetes was to be materially assisted by the fact that his wife had been married to the phenomenally popular Craterus.

[62] The name is comparatively rare in Thessaly (3 listings in *LGPN*, but a 4th-century epitaph honouring an Amphimachus has been recently discovered at Atrax, to the west of Larissa (A. Tziafalias, *AD* 46 B1 (1991) 222 = *SEG* 46.623). There can hardly be a question of identity, but at least the name is attested in the right place at the right period. The Thessalian evidence contrasts with that from Macedonia, where the name is apparently unknown (above, n. 59). I am grateful to Elaine Matthews and Jean-Claude Decourt for valuable advice in this matter.

[63] Diod. 19.27.4 (he fought with Eumenes at Paraetacene).

boost. When he marched to Susa Amphimachus was with him and not with Antigonus.[64]

In summer 317 the tempo of events increased. His army refreshed and reinforced, Antigonus answered the appeal from Seleucus and Peithon and entered Babylonia. He added their satrapal forces to his army and moved south. In the meantime there had been a meeting of the coalition leaders in Susa, and the bitter rivalry between them had surfaced. Peucestas had commanded the combined army in Persis, while Susiana, the theatre of operations, was the satrapy of Antigenes, commander of the Silver Shields.[65] Eumenes, however, had the advantage that he was the only person authorized to draw money from the royal treasuries, and Xenophilus, the treasurer at Susa, was scrupulous in implementing the royal instructions.[66] That gave Eumenes the resources to pay his Macedonians for six months, and he was also able to give Eudamus the massive sum of 200 talents for the maintenance of his elephants. The sources interpret this as a bribe,[67] but it is likely enough that the expenses of keeping the beasts fit and contented were indeed prodigious. As the virtual paymaster of the army Eumenes had what amounted to overriding authority, and he was able to reconcile the conflicting ambitions of the satraps by his happy stratagem of the Alexander tent, where the satraps and senior commanders met each day to discuss policy under his chairmanship. There was no supreme commander, but Eumenes had what amounted to a moral supremacy, and the Silver Shields responded to his commands. The decisions made in the field were in fact his.

The policy adopted was strictly defensive. Susa was evacuated, except for the garrison in the citadel, and the allied forces withdrew eastwards to the Pasitigris, the modern River Karun, four days' march from the capital (about 50 km.

---

[64] Amphimachus is most likely to have joined Eumenes while he was near Mesopotamia. Otherwise he would have needed to pass through the territory of Seleucus or Peithon, both of whom were allied with Antigonus.

[65] Diod. 18.39.6, 62.7; Arr. *Succ.* 1.35. See Bosworth, 'History and Artifice' 66.

[66] Diod. 19.17.3, 18.1.

[67] Diod. 19.15.5; cf. Plut. *Eum.* 13.12, 16.3. Cf. Bosworth, 'History and Artifice' 68–9.

on the present configuration of the rivers).[68] The bridge across the smaller Ab-i Dez (Coprates), 14 km. from Susa was demolished,[69] and the coalition army patrolled the length of the Pasitigris from the mountains to the sea, its numbers supplemented by 10,000 additional Persian archers.[70] Why, given the large numbers involved and the calibre of the Silver Shields, was there not a more aggressive strategy? The answer is surely the extreme heat. The ancients regarded Susa as proverbially scorching, the place where lizards were incinerated crossing the streets at midday.[71] It deserved its reputation. In modern times the neighbouring city of Shustar is reputedly the hottest centre in Iran, where the mean maximum temperature in July is a nearly incredible 47.3°C. Add to that the humidity created by the surrounding rivers and sea and one has intolerable conditions. It was in late June, at the rising of Sirius, that Antigonus reached Susa.[72] Antigenes and his Silver Shields had had the pleasure of residing in Susiana since 320, and the call to join Eumenes in 318 must have seemed a welcome relief. They were not going to fight a

[68] Diod. 19.17.3. Diodorus wrongly locates the Pasitigris (which he terms Tigris) a mere day's march from Susa. The correct distance, four days' march for Alexander's army, is given at 17.67.1–2 (so Curt. 5.3.1). This may be Diodorus' error, as Hornblower, *Hieronymus* 109, argues, but she is wrong to take Diod. 19.18.1 as a corrective. That is a generalized statement that Antigonus' men were forced to make their jouneys by night. It comes in the context of a single overnight march, from Susa to the Coprates (see below, n. 74), and Hieronymus presumably noted that it was standard practice for armies in southern Babylonia. On the hydrography of Susiana see now D. T. Potts, 'Elamite Ula, Akkadian Ulaya and Greek Choaspes: A solution to the Eulaios problem', *Bulletin of the Asia Institute* 12.

[69] This is conjecture. The bridge across the Ab-i Dez is mentioned by Arrian (*Ind.* 42.7) and apparently by Strabo 15.3.5 (728), both drawing on Nearchus (cf. Bosworth in *Zu Alexander dem Grossen* 547–52, criticized by Atkinson, ii.73, 75). Strabo is misleadingly contracted, but it is clear from a later passage (15.3.6 (729)) that the main road went over the Coprates (Ab-i Dez) and then the Pasitigris.

[70] Diod. 19.17.4: ἀπὸ τῶν πηγῶν ἕως τῆς θαλάσσης.

[71] Strabo 15.3.10 (731), from an unnamed historian. Alexander himself was in Susa at the end of 331 and from March 324, when they will have experienced the heating process in spring. The behaviour of barley, popping automatically in the sun, is mentioned by Theophrastus (*HP* 8.11.7; *de igne* F44; Plut. *Alex.* 35.14), but the phenomenon is located in Babylonia, where the Macedonians spent the hot season of 323.

[72] Diod. 19.18.2. For temperatures at Shustar see the 12th edition of *Encyclopedia Britannica s.v.* ('Many of the stately houses of stone and brick have cellars called *shewadan* or *zir zamin* in which the inhabitants take refuge from the summer heat which may reach 128°F (53°C).')

pitched battle if they could help it, and so they took a waiting position. Antigonus' men could fight their way across the
Pasitigris in the scorching heat[73] and take the consequences.

The strategy was effective. Well before he reached Susa
Antigonus had suffered significant losses.[74] Even at night the
mean minimum temperatures in southern Iraq hover around
30°C, and under such conditions heat exhaustion would be a
chronic menace. Susa was occupied, but the citadel commander refused to accept Antigonus,[75] and Seleucus was left
to conduct a siege while Antigonus himself went on to the
Coprates, pitching camp there shortly before dawn. The
far bank was not held against him, but the current was fast
and the bed too deep to be forded.[76] That required boats, and
few were available. Even so Antigonus used them in relays,
hoping to fortify a base camp before the enemy could make
an attack. Eumenes' scouts brought the news that the
crossing had begun, but by the time he had brought a
counter-force from the Pasitigris (presumably marching
overnight) Antigonus had transported nearly 10,000 troops,
some 6,000 of them described as specialist foragers, who
were able to cross the river in scattered groups.[77] Presumably

[73] Diod. 19.17.3 claims that there was an abundance of sharks (θηρία τῶν
πελαγίων) in the river around the time of the rising of Sirius (a piece of autopsy on
Hieronymus' part?). They will not have made the crossing any more enticing.

[74] Diod. 19.18.1–2 suggests that the losses came *after* he left Susa. But the distance from Susa to the Coprates (Ab-i Dez) was a mere 60 stades (14 km.); cf. Strabo
15.3.5 (728)=Nearchus, *FGrH* 133F 25 with Bosworth, in *Zu Alexander dem
Grossen* 547–9. This march hardly required several nights' journey. Diodorus must
be clumsily reporting a restrospective statement in Hieronymus to the effect that
Antigonus had marched by night down to and beyond Susa but still lost many men.

[75] Diod. 19.17.3, 18.1. The regal authority of Eumenes prevailed.

[76] Diod. 19.18.3. The Pasitigris was even deeper, according to Diodorus
(19.17.3) matching the height of the elephants. A nice touch from Hieronymus, who
had presumably watched the beasts making their crossing (so Hornblower,
Hieronymus 120).

[77] Diod. 19.18.4: καὶ τῶν εἰωθότων σποράδην διαβαίνειν ἐπὶ τὰς προνομὰς οὐκ ἐλάττους
ἑξακισχιλίων. This suggests that there were troops practised in river crossings.
Given the paucity of transport vessels at the Copratas, they must have crossed by
other means, and the most likely method is by skin floats. Some of the Ten
Thousand had used this method, stuffing their tent covers with chaff and crossing
the Euphrates to purchase provisions at the city of Charmande. At the Oxus
Alexander's army crossed in five days using skins alone (Arr. 3.29.4; Curt.
7.5.17–18), while at the Hydaspes he used a large number of transport vessels in
addition to the inflated skins (Arr. 5.9.3, 12.4). Antigonus may well have had

they used inflated skins, as Alexander's men had done at the Oxus crossing in 329, and crossed the river on either side of the main bridgehead corps which used the flat-bottomed transports. Eumenes arrived before the Antigonids could consolidate their position. There was no fortified base camp, and the foraging parties were scattered far afield. His forces immediately routed the opposition; only the Macedonian troops who made the crossing offered resistance,[78] but they were overcome by weight of numbers. In the resulting panic the transport vessels were capsized and sunk by the press of fugitives, and the rapid current swept away most of those who tried to cross without benefit of their skin rafts. No less than 4,000 troops surrendered, unable to swim and hopelessly trapped. Diodorus' compressed narrative does not reveal many details, but it is clear that this was one of the great disasters of the post-Alexander period, comparable to the defeat Eumenes himself had suffered at Antigonus' hands two summers before in Cappadocia. The expeditionary force that Antigonus had sent across the Coprates was killed or captured, and his surviving army was in acute distress from the climate.

The options were limited. Antigonus could not force a crossing without even greater losses, and he could not stay in the vicinity of Susa without heat exhaustion taking its toll. He had to evacuate his army, and he could hardly withdraw northwards without incurring similar conditions. The most attractive alternative was to move north-east into the high country of Media, where his men could find relief from the heat and pursue Peithon's ambitions of controlling the central satrapies. Eumenes' troops would then be forced to help Peucestas and his coalition in Iran. One could well imagine that after the disaster on the Coprates Peithon was in a position to impose his demands on his ally. Antigonus

---

Alexander's night crossing of the Hydaspes in his mind, but he could not match the transport fleet which Alexander had so carefully prepared. What happened to Antigonus' men gives some impression of what could have taken place at the Hydaspes, had Porus managed to contest the landing.

[78] Diod. 19.18.5–6. Diodorus does not tell us how many were involved, but they were outnumbered by Eumenes' relatively small force of 4,000 foot and 1,500 horse.

would have to defer to his wishes more than he felt was palatable. But the first priority was to leave the area which had
proved a death trap. Antigonus directed his march to the city
of Badace on the Eulaeus river.[79] The location cannot be
exactly determined,[80] but Badace was obviously cooler than
Susa and so on higher ground. In all probability it lay in the
upper reaches of the river Karkheh, where the modern arter-
ial road branches north and east to Khorramabad. There
Antigonus rested his depleted army for some days before
marching directly north to Ecbatana. Almost certainly he
followed the modern road through the Zagros, passing
through Khorramabad, Borujerd, and Malayer. The entire
march from Dizful in the north of the plain of Susa to
Hamadan/Ecbatana amounts to some 550 km., nearly a
month's journey for Antigonus' army.[81]

The central part of the route, probably the stretch from
Khorramabad to Malayer, lay in the territory of the Cossaei,
the predatory mountain people whom Alexander had
attacked and partially subjugated in winter 324/3.[82] That
attack was directed from Ecbatana and may have been

---

[79] Diod. 19.19.1: ἐπὶ πόλεως Βαδάκης ἣ κεῖται παρὰ τὸν Εὔλαιον ποταμόν.

[80] See now the thorough discussion by D. T. Potts, *Isimu* 2 (1999) 13–28.
Diodorus' Badace is usually identified with the Elamite city which is named
Madaktu in Assyrian sources and also lay close to the R. Ulaya (Eulaeus). Cf. *ABL* 281
with Potts 15–17. There is no doubt that the Eulaeus is to be identified as the
ancient course of the modern Karkheh, and, Badace, it would seem, was located in
its upper reaches, but at present no identification is possible. Potts 20–4 sceptically
reviews the various candidates.

[81] Diod. 19.19.2 mentions two routes, a royal highway via 'Colon' which was hot
and entailed 40 days' marching and the other more directly through Cossaea. This
longer route seems to have followed the Tigris valley to the main royal road from
Babylon to Ecbatana, through what Diod. 17.110.4 calls 'the territory of the
so-called Celones' (cf. Herzfeld, *The Persian Empire* 11–12; Schmitt, *Untersuchungen
zur Geschichte Antiochos' des Grossen* 135; Potts (above, n. 80) 21–2). It followed the
river Diyala to the vicinity of modern Khanaqin, and veered eastwards via
Kermanshah and Bisitun to Ecbatana. That was the route taken by Alexander in
324, and would have involved a prodigious detour for the exhausted Antigonid
troops. From Baghdad to Hamadan, the northern sector of the trip, is some 560 km.,
and before that there was the torrid march up the Tigris through lands already
traversed by hungry armies.

[82] Arr. 7.15.2; Diod. 17.111.5–6; Plut. *Alex.* 73.4; Polyaen. 4.3.31. On Nearchus'
view of the campaign (Arr. *Ind.* 40.6–8; Strab. 11.13.6 (524) = *FGrH* 133F 1g) see
Bosworth, *Alexander and the East* 146, and for the location and ethnography of the
Cossaeans Briant, *État et pasteurs* 62–4, 67–9, 84.

confined to the tribesmen in the north between the Median capital and Bisitun. At all events the Cossaeans on Antigonus' route were totally unpacified, and if Alexander had established agrarian settlements among them,[83] they were gone by 317. Antigonus might have given the tribesmen presents in return for safe passage, as notoriously the Persian kings had done and Peithon advised him to do.[84] However, according to Diodorus (19.19.4), he considered it ignoble (ἀγεννές) to resort to persuasion or bribery. One may perhaps infer that the example of Alexander was the main stumbling block. The great conqueror had subdued the northern Cossaeans and seven years earlier had dealt abruptly and dramatically with a demand for passage money from the Uxian tribesmen to the south.[85] The latter episode influenced Antigonus' tactics: he sent ahead a select group of light infantry to occupy the high points in advance. But he had further to go than Alexander and lost the advantage of surprise.[86] His troops were anticipated at the salient positions, and the main army suffered a bombardment of boulders and arrows. Casualties were significant,[87] morale at a nadir, and Antigonus' authority

---

[83] As claimed by Nearchus (Arr. *Ind.* 40.8) and, probably, Cleitarchus (Diod. 17.111.6). Both could have been writing in the immediate aftermath of Antigonus' debacle; Nearchus at least may have been personally involved (Diod. 19.19.4–5).

[84] Diod. 19.19.8. For the royal gifts of the Achaemenids see Nearchus (cited n. 82) with Arr. 3.17.1.

[85] Arr. 3.17.2–5. On the location of this campaign and the complexities of the sources see most recently Atkinson ii.69–76, with full citation of earlier literature. In dealing with the Uxii Alexander had pretended to accede to their demands. Antigonus clearly intended to go one better; he is reminiscent of Alexander at Gaugamela, refusing to steal his victory (Arr. 3.10.2; Plut. *Alex.* 31.12; Curt. 4.13.8–9). Peithon by contrast took on the role of Parmenion.

[86] Diod. 19.19.5. For Alexander's success compare Arr. 3.17.3–5. He used similar tactics against the Cossaei. Compare Diod. 17.111.5, where προτερῶν contrasts ironically with ὑστερήσαντες at 19.19.5.

[87] Diod. 19.19.5–7. Billows, *Antigonos* 92 n. 20 argues at length that the Antigonid casualties were exaggerated for the greater glory of Eumenes. However, some of the premisses are faulty. Antigonus certainly had 65 elephants at Paraetacene, and he had lost very few during the summer of 317. However, the conditions at the Coprates probably suited the elephants more than the humans; they had adequate water and they were not used in the actual fighting. And though the rigours of the road across the Zagros caused them danger and hardship (Diod. 19.19.8) Diodorus mentions no losses. The elephants are no guide to the human casualties. As for the Macedonian troops, something under 8,000 Macedonians fought for Antigonus in Iran (Diod. 19.29.3), not much less than the 8,500 Antipater had given him in 319 (see above, pp. 18, 91). But Antigonus had supplemented

diminished: Peithon had been proved right. However, after nine days of misery the army came out into the civilized sector of Media, and Antigonus could rest his forces and regroup. It was now 40 days since he had entered Susiana, and it was late in August.[88]

Antigonus had left the western world exposed to Eumenes and his army. Seleucus could not resist him in Babylonia, and, if Eumenes went back to the Mediterranean coast with his army, or a nucleus of it, he could easily make Syria his own, as he had threatened to do in 318. According to Diodorus (19.21.1) the view of Eumenes, Antigenes, and all who had come up from the sea was that they should return to the coast. The members of the satrapal coalition were of course adamant against it, since such a move would leave them fatally exposed to Peithon, now reinforced by the army of Antigonus. But in theory Eumenes could leave with the Silver Shields and, with their assistance, carve himself an empire in the west. With Antigonus away in Media he did not need the satraps of the east to supplement his forces. But he capitulated to Peucestas and his fellow satraps (so Diodorus claims) to preserve the unity of the army. There was something more behind his actions, and the deteriorating situation in Macedonia may have been relevant. In 317 Cassander's position had strengthened. He had entrenched himself in the Peiraeus, disposed of his rival, Nicanor, and invaded Macedonia in the early summer, invited by interests hostile to Polyperchon.[89] The invasion was partially successful; Cassander did not wrest power from Polyperchon, but he was able to capture a fair

---

Antipater's men with several thousand from the defeated armies of Eumenes and Alcetas. The 8,000 at Paraetacene included Macedonians left by Antipater but there were others from other sources. It is probable that Antigonus moved from Cilicia with considerably more than 8,000 Macedonians. There is every reason to believe that there were serious losses from heat exhaustion and drowning at the Coprates. In Cossaea the advance column of light infantry was badly mauled (Diod. 19.19.5), as one would expect, but the casualties over the rest of the army were random; the Macedonians were not likely to have been seriously affected. It was the hardship and peril of the transit that mattered, and the state of the army when it reached Media must have resembled that of Alexander's men after the crossing of Gedrosia.

[88] The chronological data are given by Diod. 19.19.8–20.1.

[89] On Cassander's actions in Athens and Macedonia see Hammond, *HM* iii.137–8; Bosworth, *CQ* 44 (1994) 63–5; Habicht, *Athens from Alexander to Antony* 51–3, 60–2. For the chronology see Bosworth, *Chiron* 22 (1992) 62–4, 81.

number of the royal elephants (Diod. 19.35.7), and opened a dialogue with Queen Eurydice which led her to repudiate Polyperchon and transfer the generalship from Eumenes to Cassander.[90] The repudiation came late in 317 and cannot have affected the deliberations in Susiana. However, news of Cassander's invasion may have come through to the alliance in Susa, and Eumenes perhaps felt his position weakened. If he stayed with the satraps, he could at least play them off against each other and Peucestas could be relied upon to counter any ambitions that Antigenes may have had to seize command of the Silver Shields and head the coalition. However, if Eumenes headed west with Antigenes (and Amphimachus), he would lose his influence with the Silver Shields the moment that his commission was known to have been annulled. Numbers, disunity, and mutual animosity gave greater protection.

The coalition army now moved to Persepolis, a distance of some 550 km. which the army covered in 24 days. The first part of the march, southward to Behbehan, was torrid and devoid of provisions, but, as the road veered upwards, through the so-called Ladder, towards modern Kazerun, the terrain changed and the army went through valleys rich in forests, orchards, and cattle.[91] Peucestas ensured that they lacked nothing on the march, and when they reached Persepolis, Eumenes' men were entertained at a grandiose celebration in honour of Alexander and Philip, who had commemorative altars at the centre of the party enclosure. The Silver Shields were prominently feted, housed in a great circle next to the commanders, and associated with members of the satraps' guard who had fought with Alexander.[92] Past

---

[90] Just. 14.5.1–3; cf. Diod. 19.11.1.

[91] Diod. 19.21.2–3 gives a vivid description which must derive ultimately from the autopsy of Hieronymus. On the route, the so-called carriageway taken by Parmenion in late 331 (Arr. 3.18.1) see J. Hansman, *Iran* 10 (1972) 117–19; Atkinson, ii.83–4.

[92] Diod. 19.22.2–3; cf. Plut. *Eum.* 13.11 (highly generalized). The inspiration for the concentric arrangement was clearly Alexander's ceremonial pavilion at Susa (Athen. 12.539E–F = Phylarchus, *FGrH* 81F 41; Polyaen. 4.3.24; Ael. *VH* 9.3), a scenario that the Silver Shields had graced. The symbolism would not have been lost on them. For possible Iranian elements in the ceremonial see Wiesehöfer, *Die 'dunklen Jahrhunderte' der Persis* 53–4.

service in the name of the kings was recognized and honoured, and in that context no one would forget that Peucestas
had saved Alexander's life in India. It was a real challenge to
Eumenes, and he took the offensive. First he fabricated a
letter in Aramaic from Orontes, the satrap of Armenia and a
friend of Peucestas:[93] its message was that Cassander was
dead, Olympias was regent of Macedonia and guardian of
Alexander IV, and Polyperchon had invaded Asia and was in
the region of Cappadocia with a royal army and a contingent
of elephants.[94] Eumenes' patrons were depicted in power;
reinforcements were on their way led by the official regent of
the empire. If Diodorus (and Polyaenus) can be trusted, the
message was believed and Eumenes' authority enhanced.

The fiction could not last long, and Eumenes used his temporary pre-eminence to attack friends of Peucestas. The
satrap of Arachosia, Sibyrtius, was brought to trial and forced
to take flight to escape condemnation.[95] The charge was presumably collusion with Antigonus (who may have been an old
friend),[96] and Eumenes sent horsemen into Arachosia to seize
the satrap's baggage (including his family and dependants).
There may also have been a rehabilitation. When Diodorus
records the satraps who originally assembled at Persepolis, he
mentions that the satrap appointed to Carmania was Polemon
the Macedonian.[97] Now, the satrap of Carmania attested
under Alexander and later confirmed by Antigonus was
Tlepolemus, and his name has been traditionally substituted

---

[93] Diod. 19.23.3; Polyaen. 4.8.3. Orontes had commanded the Armenian contingent at Gaugamela (Arr. 3.8.5), and subsequently he must have spent time at
Alexander's court before being repatriated to Armenia (cf. Bosworth, *HCA*
i.315–16). Possibly he was installed as satrap by Neoptolemus in 321 and retained
his satrapy *de facto* after the fall of Perdiccas.

[94] It is clear that events in Macedon in the summer of 317 triggered international
speculation. Theophr. *Char.* 8.5 satirizes the rumour-monger who claims to have
first-hand information of the defeat and death of Cassander at the hands of
'Polyperchon and the king' (clearly the young Alexander). It is essentially the story
concocted by Eumenes.   [95] Diod. 19.23.4.

[96] See below, Section 5.

[97] Diod. 19.14.6: Πολέμων δ' ὁ Μακεδών, Καρμανίας σατράπης ἀποδεδειγμένος. The
manuscript reading is unanimous. Elsewhere on the numerous occasions that
Diodorus refers to Tlepolemus (18.3.3, 39.6; 19.28.3, 48.1) there is only one variant, at 19.48.1, where Παμπόλεμον is read in one branch of the tradition (R: F reads
Τληπόλεμον).

for that of Polemon.[98] However, the corruption is not easy to explain, and Polemon is a very respectable Macedonian name.[99] What is more, Diodorus seems to imply that 'Polemon's' appointment as satrap was relatively recent, and he is the only satrap to be qualified as Macedonian (although all were in fact Macedonians). It looks as though Diodorus has truncated an explanation of Polemon's elevation: he was a Macedonian recently appointed satrap of Carmania. In that case Peucestas will have flexed his muscles as commander of the allied forces in 318, and forced Tlepolemus out of office, replacing him by a dependant of his own. However, at the Battle of Paraetacene Tlepolemus is back as satrap of Carmania (Diod. 19.28.3) and he is stationed close to Eumenes, on the opposite wing from the other satrapal contingents. I would suggest that Eumenes did not merely remove Sibyrtius; he exerted pressure to reinstate Tlepolemus, who would now be a devoted adherent, hostile to Peucestas.

This was direct intimidation. There may also have been some extortion. Both Diodorus and Plutarch mention a number of loans totalling 400 talents which Eumenes took from prominent commanders in the hope of securing their loyalty.[100] To some degree that must be true, for Eumenes' creditors had a material interest in preserving him alive. But it is significant that he was able to extract the money. His prestige with the army, bolstered by the disinformation about Polyperchon, was such that they could not refuse, and he was in effect imposing a good behaviour bond. We know only two of the contributors, one a somewhat mysterious Phaedimus, nowhere else attested, and the other Eudamus himself, the elephant master.[101] No person was more important to Eumenes.

---

[98] See Fischer's apparatus and Schober, *Untersuchungen* 78 n. 1. On the career of Tlepolemus see Berve ii no. 757; Billows, *Antigonos* 449 no. 137.

[99] Tataki (above, n. 59) records a dozen instances from all periods. Of the three men of that name attested in our period (Berve ii nos. 644–6) the son of Andromenes was in custody in Asia Minor (Diod. 19.16.1), and two had been left in Egypt in 331 as commanders of the holding forces (Arr. 3.5.3, 5). The satrap of Carmania must remain an *ignotus*.   [100] Diod. 19.24.2–3; Plut. *Eum.* 13.12.

[101] Plut. *Eum.* 16.3. The anecdote is crafted to illustrate Plutarch's theme of the consistent threat to Eumenes (Bosworth, 'History and Artifice' 68–70), but there is no reason to contest the historicity of the detail.

If he could rely on his support or at least give him an interest in his survival, he had a very potent, if reluctant, ally. None of the competing satraps would readily alienate the man who controlled 120 elephants.

3. AUTUMN 317: THE CAMPAIGN IN PARAETACENE

This period of intrigue ended when news came of Antigonus' advance from Media. Since his passage of the Cossaean lands the One-Eyed had been assiduously refurbishing his forces. Peithon had requisitioned remounts and baggage animals from all over Media and raised 2,000 extra cavalry (Diod. 19.20.2–3). This would have required at least a month, and Antigonus was hardly ready to move until October. When he did, he had impressive numbers: 28,000 heavy infantry (and an unspecified number of light troops), 9,000 cavalry and 65 elephants.[102] This was not far short of the strength of Alexander's army at Gaugamela. It presented acute logistical problems. Media itself appears to have been relatively fertile, and by August the harvest from the spring sowing was available. But, as the army progressed southwards towards Persis, the land became more arid, and after the road came down into the plain of Isfahan it followed the edge of a salt lake, wholly desert to the east as far as the range of mountains which runs parallel to the Zagros. What cultivation there was occurred to the west, where the streams running down into the desert allowed the piedmont area to be irrigated. The richest and most extensive agricultural district appears to have been the catchment area of the Zayendeh Rud, the ancient Epardus.[103] Some dozens of mountain streams coalesced into a single substantial river which watered the plain of Isfahan before dissipating into the desert, forming the salt marsh of Gav Khuni. Here there were provisions in plenty, but the road led to the east of the

---

[102] The total at Diod. 19.27.1 gives only the 28,000 infantry who fought in the phalanx (Diod. 19.29.3) and omits the light-armed who formed the advance screen along with the elephants (Diod. 19.29.6). Similarly the cavalry total of 8,500 is 500 short of the number in the individual contingents listed at Paraetacene.

[103] Arr. 4.6.6; cf. *CHIran* i.274–5; *HCA* ii.36.

plain, and there was no time for forays into the mountain valleys. Antigonus was forced to move fast, stripping the country bare as he went. He could not return the same way without risking starvation.

The march from Media was long and arduous. We do not know where Antigonus mustered his army, but it was presumably to the south, away from Ecbatana. If the army began its journey in the vicinity of modern Arak, it was some 680 km. to Persepolis,[104] and would have required over three weeks.[105] At a relatively early stage his movements were reported to the coalition leaders in Persepolis. According to Diodorus (19.24.4) men from Media reported the army's departure, and one may well believe that there were opportunists serving with Antigonus who might change sides and ingratiate themselves with their new employers by bringing vital news.[106] The information arrived rapidly, and by the time Antigonus came over the watershed into the plain of Isfahan the satraps knew of his approach. They mobilized their forces immediately; some were no doubt left for the defence of Persis, but the army which set out with Eumenes had 35,000 foot, 6,100 horse, and 114 elephants (Diod. 19.28.4), a massive force at least the equal of the army of Antigonus. Over 70,000 men and nearly 200 elephants were to clash on the verge of the Iranian desert.

At this point a curious episode supervened. On the second day of his march from Persis Eumenes sacrificed and

---

[104] I have taken the road distances from the indispensable wartime Geographical Handbook Series, Vol. B.R. 525, *Persia* (Sept. 1945) 545.

[105] Diod. 19.46.6 claims that in 316 Antigonus brought his army from Ecbatana to Persepolis in 20 days. That was a distance of nearly 550 miles (880 km.), and the marching rate of 27.5 miles (44 km.) *per diem* seems practically impossible. In 1898 the French traveller, Pierre Loti, took 18 days to cover the slightly shorter journey (515 miles (834 km.)) from Persepolis to Tehran (nine days, 4–12 May, to Isfahan and another nine, 19–27 May, to Tehran) Cf. P. Loti, *Vers Ispahan*, ed. K. A. Kelly and K. C. Cameron (Exeter 1989: first published 1904). He made the journey on horseback with a small mounted escort. A massive army, including heavy infantry and elephants, could not hope to match that speed. I suspect that Diodorus has abridged his source and given the impression that one of the stages of the march (20 days) was its entire length. Such contraction is amply paralleled in Arrian (cf. Bosworth, *HCA* i.67–8, 199; ii.35).

[106] Desertion was frequent, and information usually accrued (Diod. 19.26.1), so much so that Eumenes paid some of his mercenaries to desert and convey disinformation (Diod. 19.26.3).

entertained the army sumptuously. After the ceremony there was an epic drinking bout, and Eumenes was enticed to drink to excess by his guests. As a result he fell ill, so Diodorus states, and delayed the march for some days.[107] There was an ominous parallel. Alexander had fallen ill directly after a sacrifice and a symposium, and according to the Royal Ephemerides which Eumenes himself is supposed to have compiled,[108] the illness led directly to his death. What is more, foul play was suspected. There was a persistent rumour that Alexander had been poisoned by his marshals, and one of the prime suspects was Peucestas, Eumenes' rival for the command.[109] Eumenes' illness would inevitably have evoked comparisons. There would be fears that he would go the same way as Alexander, and suspicions of poisoning would have been rife. But the crisis passed after a few days, and the army resumed its progress with Eumenes following the rear-guard in a litter,[110] while Peucestas and Antigenes, who hated each other even more than they hated Eumenes,[111] led the army. Eumenes may in fact have been ill, nursing one of the most uncomfortable hangovers in history, but one suspects that such an adept propagandist would have capitalized on his illness. It was physically in evidence as he went stage by stage in his litter, and the imitation of Alexander was never so blatant. He had only just escaped the fate of Alexander, so he implied.

---

[107] Diod. 19.24.5; Plut. *Eum*. 14.6.

[108] For Eumenes' authorship see Athen. 10.434B = *FGrH* 117 F 2b. and on the problems of the Ephemerides Bosworth, *From Arrian to Alexander* 157–84 (conclusions 182–4). For very different views see Hammond's essays in *Collected Studies* iii.151–82, against Badian, in *Zu Alexander dem Grossen* i.605–25.

[109] The *Liber de Morte*, a tendentious propagandist document from the period of the Successors, named Peucestas as one of the guests at Medeius' banquet, where Alexander was supposedly poisoned. He appears in the fullest list (in the Armenian version: cf. Wolohojian) and Ps.-Call. 3.31, and it is explicitly stated that he was one of those privy to the supposed plot. Cf. Heckel, *Last Days* 34, 39, and for the political context of the document Bosworth and Baynham, in *Al. in Fact and Fiction* 207–62.

[110] Diod. 19.24.6; Plut. *Eum*. 14.6. Plutarch stresses that Eumenes required quiet because of the insomnia caused by his illness (διὰ τὰς ἀγρυπνίας). Fever through the night was one of the persistent symptoms documented in the Ephemerides (cf. Arr. 7.25.4; Plut. *Alex*. 76.4), and typical of casebook studies (cf. Bosworth, *From Arrian to Alexander* 178–9). The enforced seclusion was also reminiscent of Alexander's convalescence after his wound at the Malli town (Curt. 9.6.2).

[111] Antigenes had violently resisted Peucestas' attempt to assume overall command of the allied forces (Diod. 19.15.2, cf. 17.4–5).

The demonstration was not lost on his men. There is an instructive anecdote in Plutarch (*Eum.* 14.7–11), describing the effect of the appearance of the Antigonid forces. The Silver Shields were demoralized without their general and refused to advance without him. At the report Eumenes brought up his litter rapidly and had the curtain drawn back so that he could extend his hand to the troops. At that they clashed shield against *sarisa* and acclaimed Eumenes in Macedonian. The scene strongly evokes the Macedonian behaviour when Alexander was ferried back to his camp, severely wounded at the Malli town and feared dead. He had extended his right arm in the same histrionic gesture and had received the same ecstatic reaction from his hypaspists, who now served as Eumenes' Silver Shields.[112] The parallel was surely intended. Eumenes displayed himself as a second Alexander, exposed to the same perils, and his troops responded to the charade. Whether staged or not, his illness strengthened his position as the defender of the heritage of Alexander, and there was no overt challenge to his leadership during the following campaign.

The armies eventually came within contact, and encamped for several days with a network of ravines between them. The terrain was too difficult for a pitched battle, and for four days the armies were stationary, no more than three stades apart, according to Diodorus (19.25.2). The location is opaque, to put it mildly. We have only a few scattered data. It was three days' march from Gabiene,[113] which, we are told, was a fertile area, so far untouched by the campaign and boasting a number of rivers and ravines. When Eumenes later occupied the region for his winter quarters, he spread his troops over a

---

[112] Cf. Arr. 6.13.1–3 (on this episode and its literary shaping see Bosworth, *Alexander and the East* 53–64): 'he ordered the awnings removed from the prow of his ship so that he would be visible to them all; but they were still in doubt, thinking that it was a corpse being carried, until the ship put in to the bank and he extended his hand to the throng; they shouted out, raising their hands to the heavens...'

[113] Diod. 19.26.1–2: the manuscripts (here and at 19.34.7) give the name as Γαβηνή, Polyaen. 4.6.13 as Γαβιηνή, Plut. *Eum.* 15.4 as the land of the Γαβηνοί (it appears as Γάβηνα in Ptol. *Geogr.* 6.2.13). Strab. 16.1.18 (744–5) terms the region Γαβιανή, and locates it between Susa and Media. That again is consistent with the area around Isfahan, It is probable that there was no fixed form of the name in antiquity, and I follow modern convention in referring to the area as Gabiene.

thousand stades.[114] That suggests a lengthy strip of the foothills of the Zagros, most probably the catchment area of the Zayendeh Rud to the west and south west of Isfahan. The district begins to the north of modern Shahriza, and extends northwards to the dividing range which separates Isfahan from Golpayegan. It is certainly rich in rivers and ravines; even in its modern state visitors have praised its fertility. Describing the Sasanid site by the modern road near Najafabad (30 km. west of Isfahan) a French scholar wrote rapturously of the uninterrupted succession of villages, surrounded by fields and orchards.[115] The region lay some way west of the main road south, and could have remained untouched by Antigonus' foragers as he moved quickly on Persis. The point where the two armies met was south of Shahriza; it must be closer to Persis than Media, as Antigonus had several days start, and the allied advance was delayed by Eumenes' illness. What is more, when Eumenes began his rapid march to Gabiene, he went downhill into a plain, so that his movements could be observed by Antigonus while only Antigonus' front line was visible.[116] That suggests a location just to the north of Yezd-i-Khast. There, in the nineteenth century, was one of the great sights of Iran, a village built three stories high on a quasi-island with ravines on either side.[117] To the north the road descends to Shahriza and the plain of Isfahan, and the distance from Yezd-i-Khast into the upper reaches of the Zayendeh Rud is something

[114] Plut. *Eum*. 15.4. All these data exclude J. M. Cook's hasty but widely accepted suggestion (*The Persian Empire* 235 n. 28) that Gabiene might be the area of Gav Khuni, where the Zayendeh Rud today ends in a salt marsh. Even if the area was irrigated and fertile in antiquity (which seems to the last degree unlikely), it can never have been intersected with impassable ravines or extended for 200 km. The source material indicates the piedmont district of the eastern Zagros (so Vezin (n. 3) 101–2, n. 3; 103, n. 2).

[115] M. Siroux, *Iranica Antiqua* 5 (1965) 71: 'Cette province fut la Gabiène, une des plus riches du plateau. En cette vallée du Zàyendeh-roud les villages, entourés de cultures et de vergers, se succédaient sans interruption.'

[116] Diod. 19.26.7–8, 29.1; cf. Plut. *Eum*. 15.2.

[117] Edward Glanville Browne, *A Year amongst the Persians* (Edinburgh 1893) 224: 'Right across our path lay a mighty chasm, looking like the dry bed of some giant river of the past. In the middle of this stood what I can only describe as a long narrow island, with precipitous sides...' The description of Loti (above, n. 105, 83–4) is very similar.

like 80 km., quite compatible with the three days' march in Diodorus. This is only a theoretical possibility which needs to be tested by autopsy, but at least the terrain seems to fit the source data and the battle site cannot be too distant.

Once the two armies had made contact, there was a stalemate. The terrain was too difficult for a frontal assault by either side, but on the other hand the provisions of the area were totally inadequate to sustain the huge numbers of combatants. For four days they foraged, devoid of all supplies (Diod. 19.25.2). On the fifth Antigonus made a last resort to diplomacy, sending an embassy to plead for the arrest and surrender of Eumenes; the satraps would retain their satrapies, and the Macedonians would be lavishly rewarded with lands in Asia or donatives to take back home. The prospects must have seemed good. The disaffected satraps might well have thought it better to make their peace with Antigonus than fight a murderous battle which, if he won, would only strengthen Eumenes' position. But the Silver Shields remained loyal to the general of the kings,[118] and Eumenes reinforced their mood by a colourful analogy, of the lion who gave away his teeth and claws and then was beaten to death.[119] The imagery was attractive, but hardly apposite. If Eumenes was removed, the army hardly lost its teeth and claws, but it was a useful concept for him to implant. It suggested that he was indispensable and that his removal would be the ruin of the entire cause. Antigonus' diplomacy had actually done him a favour, and made him (for the moment) unchallengeable as supreme commander.

But there was now a crisis. Both armies needed provisions, and the prize was the unplundered district of Gabiene. An elaborate game of deception and counter-deception ensued. By filtering false information into Antigonus' camp Eumenes

---

[118] Diod. 19.25.4. It is clear that the Macedonians had the decisive voice (τῶν δὲ Μακεδόνων οὐ προσεχόντων τοῖς λόγοις).

[119] Diod. 19.25.5–6. Interestingly, Plutarch does not mention the episode, although it provides a neat parallel for the graphic analogy of the horse's tail, which Sertorius used to commend his strategy to his Spanish allies (*Sert.* 16). Plutarch omitted the Battle of Paraetacene altogether, and with it went Eumenes' speech to his troops.

was able to make a start during the night. Once Antigonus
learned of the departure he went ahead with his cavalry, and
showing himself on the edge of hilly ground he gave
Eumenes the impression that his entire army was with him
(Diod. 19.26.6–9). Both sides now came to a standstill.
Antigonus kept to the higher ground, observing Eumenes in
the plain below. He had the strategic advantage in that he
could monitor and counter Eumenes' dispositions, whereas
he could keep his own battle line secret until the last
moment. We are fortunate in that Diodorus chose to give a
very detailed description of the two lines,[120] and we can infer
something of the pressures operating on both sides.

The general principles of the battle line were established
by Alexander. The phalanx occupied the middle of the formation, flanked on either side by cavalry. Light infantry could
provide an advance screen, and the wings would be reinforced by separate detachments of cavalry and light armed,
commissioned to counter attacks on the flank. But at this
battle there was something new, something hitherto
unknown in Macedonian warfare. The Macedonians had
fought against elephants in the past, notably at the Hydaspes,
and they had used elephants during the recent civil wars,
but, as far as I can ascertain, this was the first occasion on
which elephants were used on both sides and were expected
to fight each other. Neither commander can have been sure
what to expect. As for Eumenes he placed himself in
Alexander's preferred position on the right and held the
overall command.[121] But there was a problem what to do
with the remaining satraps. Whom could he trust close to or
away from his person, and who was to command the various
sectors of the line? Antigenes and Teutamus went with their
command, the Silver Shields, and had responsibility for the

---

[120] Hieronymus was in a unique position to give battle dispositions. As a member of Eumenes' staff he was a party to his friend's deliberations before both the
battles, and he subsequently fell into Antigonid hands and had access to detailed
report, verbal and documentary from the other side. No writer in the ancient world
had a more intimate experience of the actions he described.

[121] Diod. 19.28.3. Compare Alexander's position at Gaugamela, leading the
attack from the right, at the head of his own *agema* (Arr. 3.13.1–2 with Bosworth,
HCA i.304–5).

adjoining native hypaspists.[122] The left half of the phalanx was apparently in other hands, but Diodorus gives us no name. Similarly, the cavalry on the left must have had an overall commander, and from the battle narrative it would appear that it was Eudamus who was in control.[123] Eumenes clearly had more confidence in him (or his loan) than in any other of the satraps—and Eudamus may have had some personal antipathy to Antigonus or Peithon, for he was summarily executed after the Antigonid victory.[124]

The majority of the satrapal cavalry, native troops from the eastern provinces, was placed on the left wing. They remained in their national groupings, led by their satrap or his deputy, exactly as had happened (on the Persian side) at Gaugamela, and there was no attempt (on this wing) to group them into larger contingents. On the right it was different. Tlepolemus of Carmania, who may have been personally indebted to Eumenes, was the only commander of a satrapal contingent. Otherwise the cavalry was a collection of élite groups. There was a body of 900 Companions, which Eumenes had probably brought with him from Cappadocia;[125] in addition Eumenes had his headquarter squadron, 300 strong, which is termed his *agema*. An equally strong group was formed by the satrapal guards of Antigenes and Peucestas, combined as a single unit. Antigenes was detached from his cavalry and, as we have seen, was assigned to the phalanx. So too Peucestas was removed from his cavalry guard and perhaps commanded the left of the phalanx, balancing Antigenes and Teutamus on the right. In addition Eumenes' right flank was strengthened by miscellaneous detachments of horsemen selected from the entire army.[126] It looks as though Eumenes had

---

[122] Diod. 19.28.1. On these hypaspists, see above, p. 83.

[123] Diod. 19.30.3: Εὐδάμου τοῦ τὸ λαιὸν κέρας ἔχοντος (cf. 30.10).

[124] See below, p. 159.

[125] Diod. 19.28.3. This group of Companions (ἑταῖροι) is not attested elsewhere, and seems distinct from the veterans of Alexander who were entertained with the Silver Shields at Persepolis (Diod. 19.22.2). But the battle description of Diodorus has no reference to the cavalry which Eumenes brought with him into Mesopotamia, and he had 3,300 with him in Susiana (Diod. 18.73.4). It looks as though he gave some (or all) the honorific title of Companions, and selected an élite *agema*. He was the royal general and it was appropriate that his army had royal titulature.

[126] The dispositions are slightly obscure, but the flank appears to have been protected against any turning movement: an advance guard (πρόταγμα) of two small

eliminated any competition in his vicinity. He was surrounded by troops which he had raised himself or which had
been carefully selected and detached from their regular commanders. The only other named commander on the right
(Tlepolemus) was no threat, and probably owed his position
to Eumenes. The mass of the satraps were concentrated on
the left, and placed under the one man they could least afford
to alienate, the master of the elephant corps. Eumenes could
at least take the strategic initiative on the right without
risking dissent and opposition from his subordinates.

The battle line he organized was defensive, very like that
of Porus at the Hydaspes. The cavalry were divided into
two roughly equal groups, 3,400 on the left and 2,900 on the
right.[127] In the centre was the infantry phalanx: 6,000 mercenaries, 5,000 troops equipped in Macedonian style, the 3,000
Silver Shields and the same number of Eumenes' 'hypaspists'.
There is no indication of the depth of the phalanx, and no
data on the extent of the line, which must have been determined by the terrain. What is clear, however, is that the
elephants were intended to form a defensive screen for the
entire line. In front of the left wing were 35 (?) elephants,[128]
covering the entire front of the line, and angled back
at roughly 45° to protect the flank.[129] The spaces between the
elephants were filled with groups of archers and slingers,

squadrons recruited from Eumenes' personal slaves (these 100 (cf. Plut. *Eum.* 3.11)
are unlikely to have been personal Pages, as argued by Hammond, *Historia* 39
(1990) 270–2); four squadrons (*ilai*) each 200 strong, at right angles (πλαγίας) to the
line of battle; and lastly 300 carefully selected cavalrymen at his rear (κατόπιν).

[127] That is the total of the units individually listed. Diod. 19.28.4 gives a grand
total of 6,100, 200 short of the sum of the separate contingents.

[128] The text of Diod. 19.27.5 gives a figure of 45, but Diodorus adds that there
were two other groups of 40 elephants, amounting to 114 in all (19.28.4). It is possible that each of the figures for the separate groups is rounded up, but more likely
that Diodorus misread 35 as 45; Eumenes' left was the weaker (Diod. 19.29.1), and
it is improbable that it had more elephants than the right.

[129] πρὸ δὲ τούτων ἁπάντων ἔταξεν ἐλέφαντας μὲν ἐν ἐπικαμπίῳ. On the terminology
see A. M. Devine, *AncW* 12 (1985) 77, adducing the parallel of Diod. 17.57.5.
However, Devine confines the elephant screen to the flank, thanks to an unneces-
sarily restrictive interpretation of πρὸ...ἁπάντων ἔταξε (Diod. 19.27.5, 40.3). The
elephants were stationed 'in front of' the cavalry line proper' and 'in front of' the
flank guard, which faced left. The elephant screen, then, was continuous and
formed an obtuse angle at the end of the line.

mostly, it would seem, supplied by Peucestas from Persis.[130] In front of the phalanx were another 40 elephants and 40 more protected the right wing, angled back in the same way as they were on the left. In the interstices were more light infantry, probably 18,000 in all.[131] The left wing extended into the hills, into high ground that could not easily be out-flanked, while the right wing had a strong flank guard of select cavalry, reinforced by the elephant screen. This was exactly the formation adopted by Porus, and like Porus Eumenes was in a position where a defensive battle was the obvious choice. It was disadvantageous for him to attack uphill. He would wait for Antigonus to open hostilities, take advantage of any dislocation in his line and inflict the maximum of casualties once he attacked.

Antigonus' position was more clear-cut. He had none of the multiple problems of command that beset Eumenes. His only serious rival, Peithon, seems to have been reconciled to be his subordinate.[132] He could also observe Eumenes' dispositions and place his forces where they would have maximum advantage. His assets were a superiority in cavalry and phalanx infantry, but he was deficient in elephants and could not arrange a defensive screen to match that of Eumenes. Accordingly he countered Eumenes' heavy cavalry on the right with a combination of light horse: horse archers and javelin men from Parthyaea and Media, the expert skirmishers from Asia Minor known as Tarantines,[133] and local levies

---

[130] Diod. 19.27.5, 28.2. For the arrangement compare Porus at the Hydaspes (Arr. 5.15.5–7 with *HCA* ii.292–3; Diod. 17.87.5; Curt. 8.14.13; Polyaen. 4.3.22). For Peucestas' light troops see Diod. 19.17.6.

[131] This is again an inference to explain the discrepancy between Diodorus' grand total of 35,000 foot and the individual units of the phalanx (19.27.6–28.1) which amount to a mere 17,000 (see below, n. 177). Diodorus gives no specific figures for the light-armed, and it is quite likely that Eumenes deployed as many men in the advance screen as fought in the phalanx.

[132] So explicitly Diod. 19.31.4, contrasting Antigonus' firm hold on command with Eumenes' much more precarious position.

[133] Diod. 19.29.2. The troops had come with Antigonus from Syria. The connection (if any) with Tarentum in Italy remains obscure; cf. Griffith, *The Mercenaries of the Hellenistic World* 246–50; Launey, *Recherches sur les armées hellénistiques* i.601–2; Walbank, *HCP* i.529). In the tactical literature they are described as specialist javelin men, trained to keep their distance and encircle the enemy (Asclepiod. 1.3; Ael. *Tact.* 2.13; Arr. *Tact.* 4.5–6).

from Phrygia and Lydia.[134] In all this wing comprised 4,900, far outnumbering Eumenes.[135] The phalanx was far more numerous than Eumenes': 9,000 mercenaries, 3,000 Lycians and Pamphylians, over 8,000 troops trained in Macedonian style and just under 8,000 Macedonians. Antigonus, then, outstripped Eumenes by at least 10,000 phalanx infantry,[136] but he needed to match Eumenes' line and the depth of his phalanx to be correspondingly greater. The weight would be an advantage, but against the elephants and Silver Shields it would not necessarily be decisive. In fact Antigonus had a healthy respect for the Silver Shields. He ensured that they faced his mercenaries and Macedonian-trained Asiatics. His Macedonians he placed against the comparable sector of Eumenes' phalanx. He seems to have deliberately guarded against the possibility of Macedonians fighting Macedonians. They were too precious to waste, and it could not be guaranteed that they would actually fight against each other. The events at Gabiene, where the battle lines were not so visible, proved the wisdom of the policy.

Finally Antigonus concentrated the best, or rather, the heaviest of his cavalry forces against Eumenes. Mercenaries and Thracian cavalry adjoined the phalanx, then came Antigonus' own unit of Companions, 1,000 strong, under the command of his son, Demetrius. Many, if not all, of this élite body will have been Macedonians, so too Antigonus' *agema* which closed the line, along with an advance force of light cavalry (Diod. 19.29.4–5). On his right Antigonus arranged the strongest of his elephants, 30 in all, with light infantry filling the gaps between them. Of the remaining 35, the majority were deployed in front of the phalanx and a few remained for the defence of the left. That meant that

---

[134] There were also 1,500 cavalry of Peithon's guard, 400 lancers ($\xi\upsilon\sigma\tau\acute{o}\phi\rho\rho\iota$) under the command of an otherwise unknown Lysanias, a mysterious body of 800 horse comprising a group apparently termed $\dot{\alpha}\mu\phi\acute{\iota}\pi\pi\rho\iota$ as well as settlers from the upper reaches of Media (on the problems of identification see R. D. Milns, *CQ* 31 (1981) 347–54, esp. 352–4; contra N. G. L. Hammond, *CQ* 28 (1978) 128–35).

[135] I am assuming that the figure of 2,200 Tarantines at Diod. 19.29.2 is a mistake for 200. Otherwise the Tarantines become the largest single unit in Antigonus' cavalry force, and once again the grand total of cavalry (8,500) at Diod. 19.27.1 is almost exactly 2,000 less than the sum of the individual figures (10,450).

[136] For the elusive light troops, see below, n. 177.

Antigonus' left wing was relatively unprotected. It was intended to engage later and use harassing tactics against Eumenes' strongly defended right flank. The horse archers and lancers were to make rapid assaults wherever they could find an opening to the rear or the side[137]—and their greater numbers allowed them to outflank Eumenes at will. But Antigonus intended the weight of his attack to be on the right. His formation with its advance screen of elephants practically mirrored that of Eumenes, and his cavalry was more numerous and of higher calibre. According to Diodorus, he intended to settle the issue with his right wing, and adopted the same oblique formation that Alexander had used at Gaugamela.[138] Seen from above, the line resembled a guillotine blade with Antigonus' *agema* at the apex. He (like Alexander) would lead the assault when the opportunity offered itself, first penetrating the enemy line and then pressing towards the centre, creating disruption and panic. It looks as though what was intended was a re-run of Gaugamela.

Antigonus had put himself in the leading position, and the stage was set for an epic combat. He led his army carefully down the hillside, and, as they closed, the two sides exchanged the war cry and the trumpets signalled the start of the battle. All was set for Antigonus' opening charge. Nothing of the sort happened. Instead Diodorus states explicitly that the first to engage were Peithon's cavalry, who were supposed to be held back, with instructions to avoid battle.[139] This is a major paradox, and, not surprisingly, scholars have been tempted to hypothesize insubordination on Peithon's part.[140] Alternatively one might argue that the original source for the battle, Hieronymus, only recorded the fighting where he was personally engaged, around Eumenes. In that sector Peithon

[137] Diod. 19.29.1, 30.2.

[138] Diod. 19.29.7: λοξὴν ποιήσας τὴν τάξιν. For the terminology see Arr. *Tact.* 26.3, where the terminology of Diodorus is repeated: the λοξὴ φάλαγξ occurs when the general approaches the enemy with one wing only, keeping the other in reserve (τὸ δ' ἕτερον δὲ ὑποστολῆς σῴζουσα). For Alexander's use of the formation see Arr. 1.14.7 (Granicus); Diod. 17.57.6; Curt. 4.15.1; cf. Bosworth *HCA* i.121, 305; A. M. Devine, *AncW* 12 (1985) 81.

[139] Diod. 19.30.1: πρῶτοι δ' οἱ μετὰ Πείθωνος ἱππεῖς. Antigonus' plan for Peithon's wing had been φυγομαχεῖν (29.7).

[140] e.g. H. Droysen, *Heerwesen und Kriegführung der Griechen* 416; Devine, *AncW* 12 (1985) 82.

did take action first, and Hieronymus may have been misleading in focusing the narrative on the right of Eumenes' line.
There may indeed be some lack of perspective and excessive
concentration on Eumenes. However, one cannot argue that
the action on Antigonus' right, which Diodorus has identified
as the crucial sector, has been omitted. Somewhat later in the
battle, when Antigonus' forces on the left and in the centre
were in full flight, he himself was stationary, with a clear view
of what was happening (Diod. 19.30.7). He was still in his
advance position in the foothills, unengaged and able to react
to the tactical situation to his left. What is more, if there had
been a general engagement around Antigonus, elephant must
have met elephant, and there would have been losses. In fact
there were none. Antigonus still had his 65 beasts and
Eumenes his 114 at the next battle some weeks later (Diod.
19.40.1, 4). It is, then, axiomatic that there was no elephant
fighting in this first engagement. In all probability there was
a stalemate. Eumenes' left presented an unbroken barrier.
The higher ground at the end of the line excluded a flanking
movement, and there was presumably no gap in the defensive screen of cavalry and archers for Antigonus' cavalry to
exploit.[141] Eumenes, then, was able to do what Darius had
failed to do at Gaugamela, and prevent a frontal attack by the
strongest contingent of the enemy cavalry. Both sides seem
to have shied away from a full-scale conflict between the
elephants, and the result was that Antigonus' advance was
checked, and his left wing under Peithon gradually came
forward to a position where it could launch an attack.

In that case Diodorus is right that Peithon opened the
fighting. As we have seen, his tactics were to concentrate
on Eumenes' flank, and in particular the elephants on
the wing.[142] Diodorus notes that Peithon's formation was

---

[141] So *AS* i.420: Antigonus found Eumenes' position on the heights too strong
for a frontal assault, and held back in the hope that a better opportunity would
emerge in the course of the battle. That is an improvement on the hypothesis of
Köchly and Rüstow (*Geschichte des griechischen Kriegswesen* 371) that Antigonus
changed his plan in the course of his approach march and restrained his right wing,
but even so it does not take account of the novelty of the elephant fighting which
would necessarily follow engagement.

[142] Diod. 19.30.2 notes the damage caused (perhaps irritation rather than serious
wounding) when the elephants were too slow to respond to Peithon's hit-and-run
tactics.

relatively fluid and had no advance guard to speak of, and there is an implicit contrast with Antigonus' carefully ordered right wing with its elephant screen. Unlike Antigonus, Peithon had the advantage of free movement, and he exploited it. His horse archers proved a nuisance, harassing Eumenes' elephants until there was a danger of their becoming uncontrollable.[143] At this point Eumenes was able to perform a manœuvre which had fatally eluded Porus at the Hydaspes. He transferred a number of the light cavalry from his left wing, and they were able to ride from one side of the line to the other without attack from the superior Antigonid cavalry.[144] Antigonus' forces were too well screened, and the terrain, unlike the level sandy surface at the Hydaspes, did not easily permit a flanking movement. Eumenes was now able to counter the attacks by Peithon's horse archers. His *agema* and the troops of the select flank guard were reinforced by crack light cavalry. It was a relatively small formation,[145] but more than sufficient for the task. The counter-attack was not confined to cavalry. Eumenes used a combination of horse and light infantry, as Alexander had done to counter the circling tactics of the Saca nomads at the Iaxartes.[146] Presumably the archers and slingers stationed between the elephants moved forward with Eumenes' cavalry and engaged Peithon's horse archers. Their more accurate fire repelled the attackers and drove them back towards their own lines.[147] The elephants joined the advance, and Peithon's wing, now in considerable disorder, retreated to the foothills.

[143] In *AS* i.416–17 it is argued that Eumenes simultaneously launched a frontal attack. There is no suggestion of such an action in the text of Diodorus, who only describes the response to the flanking attack by the Median cavalry, and there is no explanation how Eumenes managed to ride through his elephant screen. And on this hypothesis it is Eumenes and not Peithon who begins the battle.

[144] Diod. 19.30.3–4. For Porus' manœuvre see Arr. 5.16.2–3, 17.1–2; Bosworth *HCA* ii.293–7. Fortunately for Eumenes, Antigonus was in no position to send a flanking group in pursuit, unlike Alexander, who held Coenus in reserve to do just that.

[145] So Diod. 19.30.4 seems to emphasize, stating that Eumenes 'led his small formation in a charge to the wing' (ἐξαγαγὼν δὲ ἐπὶ κέρας τήν ὀλίγην τάξιν). There is no justification for Wesseling's emendation: ὀλίγην to ὅλην. That gives the impression that the entire wing was involved (misleading *AS* i.417), whereas the text mentions only light infantry and the most manœuvrable (τοῖς ἐλαφροτάτοις) of the cavalry.

[146] Arr. 4.4.6, Compare the tactics at the Granicus (Arr. 1.14.6, 16.1).

[147] Diod. 19.30.4 (ῥᾳδίως) enphasizes that it was an easy victory.

These manœuvres took some time, and there had been a long period of harassment by the horse archers while Eumenes was sending for reinforcements from his left wing. In the meantime[148] the infantry phalanxes had been engaged. It is one of the many frustrating gaps in Diodorus that he does not tell us how this came about. There is no reference to action by the elephants, and it is hard to see how there could have been such action. The fact that identical numbers of elephants fought in both the battles of the winter campaign precludes there having been any losses, either through frontal combat, beast to beast, or from the opposing infantry. The Silver Shields, it should be noted, had grim experience disabling elephants during the Indian campaigns of Alexander.[149] Finally there is the incalculable factor of the unknown. Neither side had experience of fights between elephants (except perhaps the Indians with Eudamus), and there may have been some reluctance to make use of this ultimate weapon (an ancient example of the balance of terror). In any case the elephants in front of Antigonus' phalanx were outnumbered, and their mahouts may not have been willing to face combat. I assume that there was a tactical withdrawal, as the elephants backed through spaces which the phalanx infantry created for them, and something similar will have happened on Eumenes' side.[150] It is clear that the Silver Shields were able to attack en masse and engage directly with the enemy phalanx, unimpeded by the elephants, their own or the enemy's. They were presumably drawn up in comparatively shallow formation, to counter the superior numbers of the enemy, and it would have been easier and perhaps quicker for the elephants to pass through their ranks than through

---

[148] Diod. 19.30.5: ἅμα δὲ τούτοις πραττομένοις.

[149] Arr. 5.17.3; Curt. 8.14.29; cf. Bosworth, *Alexander and the East* 18–19.

[150] There was possibly a precedent in the Persian tactics at Gaugamela. Darius deployed 15 elephants alongside the scythed chariots in the centre of his line (Arr. 3.11.6, cf. 8.6; *Itin.* 56; *FGrH* 151F 1 (12–13)), but there is no hint in Arrian that they played any part in the battle, and they are not mentioned in the Vulgate tradition. Once the attack by the scythed chariots failed, they probably made a tactical withdrawal through their own lines (cf. Briant (above, n. 41) 188–90). It is just conceivable that there was some contact with the phalanx infantry (if the beasts advanced in the wake of the scythed chariots), but it is highly improbable that such a picturesque detail would have fallen out of the historical tradition.

the opposing phalanx. There may have been disorder on Antigonus' side, which the opposing infantry exploited. The Silver Shields, so Diodorus states, were the cutting edge of the entire force,[151] and their expertise in close fighting was unmatched. Their skill in handling the *sarisa* and their cohesion in line was irresistible, and their opponents were forced back. The *sarisae* of the Antigonid infantry would have been pushed out of alignment, and became an obstacle and a hazard for their own side. The confusion spread to the rest of Antigonus' phalanx, and it retreated in increasing chaos. And, as the disorder spread, the casualties increased; and the front ranks of Antigonus' phalanx were caught in a killing ground between the *sarisae* of the Silver Shields and the press of their own rear ranks. I do not doubt that the casualties were as disproportionate as Diodorus reports: 3,700 Antigonid dead and 4,000 wounded to 540 dead and something under 900 wounded on Eumenes' side.[152]

For most of the battle Antigonus was deadlocked, stationary and frustrated in front of Eumenes' satrapal cavalry, in an excellent position to observe the rout of his left and centre. His advisers urged him to admit defeat, cut his losses and withdraw to the mountains, but Antigonus had at last seen the gap he had been waiting for. As his phalanx was driven back, it was followed by Eumenes' infantry, which pressed its advantage and in so doing became gradually detached from its left wing.[153] This group remained stationary, keeping its

---

[151] Diod. 19.30.6: οἱονεὶ στόμωμα καθειστήκεισαν πάσης τῆς δυνάμεως. This is the only example of the analogy in Diodorus, but it seems to have been fairly standard; it is used and fully explained by the tactical authors (Ael. *Tact.* 13; Arr. *Tact.* 12.2).

[152] Diod. 19.31.5. I see no reason why Hieronymus should have falsified these figures to the greater glory of Eumenes, as has been argued (Billows, *Antigonos* 92 (see above, n. 87); cf. Devine, *AncW*12 (1985) 86). He also served the Antigonids and had no interest in exaggerating the number of Antigonid dead. Nor can the victory of the phalanx be directly attributed to Eumenes. It was the work of the Silver Shields and their commanders, Antigenes and Eumenes, the men who were to betray him. A friend of Eumenes had no inducement to make their victory any more impressive than it actually was.

[153] Diod. 19.30.8–9. Again reminiscent of Gaugamela, when a group of Persians and Indians were able to exploit a gap in the Macedonian phalanx (Arr. 3.14.5: on the complexities of the passage see Bosworth, *HCA* i.308–9). Fortunately for Alexander, these troops were considerably less numerous than Antigonus' cavalry—and tactically undirected.

advantage of terrain. It could not be outflanked, but in consequence it became progressively more detached from the victorious phalanx infantry. Antigonus seized the advantage and attacked immediately, his Companions heading directly for the gap and charging into the exposed flank of the satrapal cavalry. He routed the troops in his path with his heavy armed horsemen and drove the rest into retreat. At the same time he sent outriders to check the collapse on his centre and right, while Eumenes for his part sounded the recall.

This again was stalemate. Neither side could press home its advantage without risking defeat and annihilation elsewhere in the field. As the victorious troops pulled back the lines reformed, and dusk fell. The two sides faced each other, no more than four *plethra* (*c.* 130 m.) apart, and there developed a lateral movement into the plain and away from the foothills.[154] What exactly the movement was and how it took place is not stated, but it looks as though both sides were trying for another outflanking move, Eumenes attempting to attack the vulnerable left of Antigonus' line, where Peithon had given way before, and Peithon manœuvring to counter the threat. Inevitably both lines moved away from the battle site, probably in a north-westerly direction, their movements illuminated by a brilliant full moon. By midnight they had moved some 5 km. from the dead on the battlefield, and neither side had been able to find the opportunity to attack (Diod. 19.31.2). But by this time battle fatigue and hunger had set in, and the will to fight was sapped. The armies now separated. Eumenes' men insisted on returning to their main camp and protecting their precious baggage train, while Antigonus could ensure that his men remained on the battlefield, so that he could claim a moral victory. But moral was all the victory could be. Eumenes had coped with the attack by Peithon's light cavalry, and his phalanx troops had been brilliantly successful against much larger numbers. Antigonus

[154] Diod. 19.31.2. This sideways movement (so *AS* i.422–3) is clearly stated (τῶν δυνάμεων ἀντιπαραγουσῶν ἀλλήλαις ... ὡς δὲ παράγοντες): both armies went parallel, facing each other (for the terminology see Arr. 5.17.1 with Bosworth *HCA* ii.299). Geer's Loeb obscures the sense, gratuitously mistranslating the two phrases ('the armies were *forming* parallel to each other'; 'as they were moving *from column into line*' [my italics]). Bizière's Budé is less misleading.

could claim victory against the satraps on Eumenes' left; but he had inflicted practically no casualties, and he had come close to total disaster. On the other hand it was only the Silver Shields' insistence that denied Eumenes mastery of the field.

Antigonus exploited his advantage skilfully. By the time Eumenes sent the regular embassy to request a truce for burying the bodies, Antigonus had virtually completed his own obsequies and had sent his wounded and heavy baggage on their way to convalescent centres.[155] The night before Eumenes was to move in with his own burial parties, Antigonus moved away with the fit majority of his army, and by the time Eumenes had completed his pious duties he was clean away, beyond any possibility of Eumenes overhauling him. In effect he had admitted defeat. He could not now challenge Eumenes for possession of Gabiene; his supplies were desperately low, and he had to find a district which would support his army while he rested it and prepared it psychologically for another encounter. On the other side Eumenes had established the invincibility of his Silver Shields and showed the calibre of his leadership against Peithon, but at the same time Antigenes, Teutamus, and possibly Peucestas could claim credit for the major victory with the phalanx. The competition for command did not end with Antigonus' withdrawal.

4. MIDWINTER 317/16: THE DECISIVE BATTLE

The next phase of the campaign now began. Antigonus withdrew to an area of Media which had not as yet suffered from the war and was able to provision his army. Its name is uncertain,[156] and there is little clue to its location. Given that Antigonus had marched south from central Media, it would seem that he went eastwards from Isfahan, avoiding the districts where his foragers had previously been active. That

---

[155] Diod. 19.32.2. Antigonus deliberately detained the embassy, allegedly to conceal from Eumenes the real number of the casualties he had sustained (Polyaen. 4.6.10).

[156] Gamarga at Diod. 19.32.2, Gadamala (Tamarla F) at 19.37.1; Gadamarta at Polyaen. 4.6.11. The name occurs in no other context.

would take him to the district fringing the eastern outliers of the Zagros, around modern Nā'īn. From Yezd-i-Khast, the presumed site of the battle, via Isfahan, was a march of approximately 290 km., and, as we shall see, that general area is compatible with the source data for Antigonus' return march. He spread his troops in temporary winter quarters and planned his next move. Eumenes had not followed him, so he would return in due course, his army refreshed and invigorated.

Eumenes himself could occupy Gabiene, and he dispersed his forces over the entire area, so that some outposts were six days' march apart.[157] For Plutarch this was a mark of degeneration; Eumenes' troops wished to enjoy the maximum area for plunder.[158] In fact it was a logistical necessity. No single area of the Zagros piedmont could sustain the entire army over the winter, swelled as it was by non-combatants, the wives and children of the Silver Shields as well as the regular train of sutlers and vivandiers. It was inevitable that the forces were dispersed over a wide area. We learn later (Diod. 19.39.2) that the elephants were somewhat remote from Eumenes' headquarters. They above all would need to be where there was plentiful fodder, in particular vegetables and hay, and they would have been spread over one of the most protected and fertile of the tributaries of the Zayendeh Rud. We have no means of guessing which it was. What happened to the various commanders is not attested either. We do not know whether they were stationed with their troops or kept together as a council-of-war. Probably the latter, for when the news of Antigonus' surprise advance came through Eumenes and Peucestas were together, and there seems to have been some general discussion.[159] The Alexander tent,

---

[157] Diod. 19.37.1; this is compatible with Plutarch's statement (*Eum.* 15.4; so Polyaen. 4.6.11) that the army was distributed over 1,000 stades (cf. Devine 87).

[158] Plut. *Eum.* 15.4. Nep. *Eum.* 8.1 claims that Eumenes was forced to billet his troops in accordance with their wishes ('ut militum cogebat voluntas'). This he sees as a paradigm of the insubordination, so evident in his own day ('ut nunc veterani faciunt nostri'). For Plutarch it is an example of the troops' increasing taste for luxury, already witnessed in Persis (*Eum.* 13.10–11). The writers have different morals to draw, but it looks as though the common source had something to say about the insubordination of Eumenes' army (cf. Diod. 19.31.4).

[159] Diod. 19.38.1–3: NB 38.3 (πάντων δὲ θαυμασάντων).

then, will have continued in operation, and the commanders, as before, wrangled for supremacy. Eumenes' comparative success against Antigonus will have exacerbated their jealousies. Plutarch has a highly coloured story that the satraps intended to dispose of Eumenes the moment the next battle was fought.[160] It is dramatic and distorted for rhetorical purposes, but it is a measure of the growth of the sentiment against Eumenes, and the events of the next battle were to show both that Eumenes suspected his colleagues' good faith and that his suspicions were justified.

Antigonus had local informants, ready to report Eumenes' movements to Peithon, with whom they were familiar as satrap of Media.[161] He was evidently given accurate details of the disposition of the satrapal forces in Gabiene, and conceived the plan of a surprise attack over the salt desert. Around the time of the winter solstice he roused his army from its quarters, and demanded that his men brought iron rations for ten days. There were to be no fires overnight to compromise the secrecy of the attack (Diod. 19.37.4–5). The march lay across desert. Several sources describe the terrain in more or less rhetorical terms, but there is some general agreement. It was flat, salt and waterless, surrounded by high ground.[162] A direct march across it would take Antigonus to Gabiene in nine days, whereas taking the regular road through populated country would require 25 days and his advance would be discovered by the enemy before he completed a third of the journey. It seems clear enough that the desert here described is the khavir, or salt plain, due east of Gabiene.[163] It lies between two parallel lines of mountains

---

[160] Plut. *Eum.* 16.2–3 (Antigenes and Teutamus conspire with the rest of the generals). The passage is clearly shaped to draw a parallel with Sertorius (cf. *Sert.* 25–6; Bosworth, 'History and Artifice' 70–1), but the gist of it must have occurred in one at least of Plutarch's sources (not necessarily Hieronymus).

[161] Diod. 19.38.4. Eumenes had also had information supplied by locals in Media (Diod. 19.24.4: see above, p. 125; 37.6).

[162] Diod. 19.37.5; Polyaen. 4.6.11; Plut. *Eum.* 15.6–7; Nep. *Eum.* 8.4–5.

[163] J. M. Cook, *The Persian Empire* 186, suggests that Antigonus intended to cross the great inland salt desert, the Dasht-i Khavir. In that case Antigonus would have withdrawn as far as Parthyaea, and a direct route from, say, Hecatompylus across the desert to the plain of Isfahan would have entailed a march of at least 400 km. No one could surely envisage covering such a distance under atrocious conditions in nine days.

some 50 km. apart, beginning to the south-east of Isfahan
and continuing in a roughly southerly direction for some
hundreds of kilometres; and it is into this that the waters of
the Zayendeh Rud are discharged. In times of high water the
area around Gav Khuni becomes a broad salt marsh, but
Antigonus was travelling before the melting of the winter
snows and his line of march probably lay above Gav Khuni.
He presumably needed to cross some of the river courses, but
any water there would be impossibly saline and undrinkable.
It was in effect a waterless desert. If, then, Antigonus mustered his army in the vicinity of modern Nā'īn, he could cross
the dividing range unobtrusively, where there is a lower sad-
dle, and then strike across the desert. His route would take
him south-west for nearly 100 km., and he would reach the
main road to Persis some way above modern Shahriza, excel-
lently poised to mop up Eumenes' army in segments, before
it could be summoned from its diverse winter quarters.

The plan was to avoid lighting fires at night, and
Antigonus presumably expected to camp during the day and
do the major part of his march overnight. To some degree it
worked. His army endured five days of cold and fatigue, but
in time discipline crumbled, and fires were lit by night as
well (we are not told how the fuel was obtained). The behaviour of Antigonus' men is understable, given the climatic
conditions. At the time of the solstice the mean daily minimum temperature in the area is well below freezing ($-4°C$)
and the maximum does not rise above $10°$. Added to that, if
we may believe Plutarch (*Eum.* 15.6), bitter winds exacerbated the cold. It is hardly surprising that discipline cracked
under the strain. But it was not merely discipline. Of all the
contingents in the army the elephants were most susceptible
to the cold. They had experienced at least one cold winter in
the past, in Anatolia over 319/18, but they cannot have rel-
ished the conditions in the Iranian desert, marching day
after day in bitter cold. They will have needed their
warmth,[164] and many of the fires may have been kindled for

---

[164] In Perth, where winter temperatures are considerably higher, never dipping
below freezing, the elephants in the zoo are kept overnight in covered accommoda-
tion, with heating both below the floor and above. Even so, they frequently go to
shelter in the course of winter days. (I owe this information to Colin Walbank of the
Perth Zoo.)

their sake. The night fires were fatal to the plan. They were seen from a distance by the natives, who took to the road on racing camels and brought the news to Eumenes and Peucestas on the same day.[165]

Antigonus was now too close for Eumenes to muster his army, an operation which required at least a week. Two strategies were proposed. Peucestas advocated tactical withdrawal. The headquarters contingent was to leave its watching position on the main road by the edge of the desert and withdraw into the high country of Gabiene. The sources, which reflect Hieronymus' animosity, impute motives of cowardice very difficult to credit in the man who had displayed such signal heroism in the Malli town.[166] In fact the defensive strategy might have worked. If Eumenes' forces had remained dispersed in the upper valleys of the Zayendeh Rud, they could easily have blocked off the approaches to each of their winter billets. To clear them out one by one would have presented Antigonus with a series of Thermopylaes, and his army, already fatigued, could not stay long in the area, which had already sustained Eumenes' forces over several weeks. Eumenes, however, suggested other tactics, those in fact that Antigonus had used before the earlier battle.[167] With a small fatigue party he rode east to a vantage point which gave a view over the desert and lit a circle of fires around a perimeter large enough to suggest the encampment of a major army.[168] Eumenes presumably ensured that none of the local inhabitants could take the true story to Antigonus. The fires were accordingly seen from a distance, and the nomadic herdsmen there on the Median border brought the news to Peithon.[169] As a result Antigonus concluded that there was a substantial army blocking his route across the desert, and he could not risk an encounter with his cold, fatigued troops. He went on the defensive, and diverged westwards to the

---

[165] Diod. 19.37.6; Plut. *Eum.* 15.7; Nep. *Eum.* 9.1.

[166] Diod. 19.38.1–2. Plut. *Eum.* 15.8 describes Peucestas as 'absolutely mad with fear', a typical exaggeration (Bosworth, 'History and Artifice' 68–9), but based on a portrait which was already strongly negative.

[167] See above, p. 130.

[168] Diod. 19.38.3; Plut. *Eum.* 15.10–11; Nep. *Eum.* 9.3–5.

[169] Diod. 19.38.4, claiming that they saw the flames 'from the mountains opposite', in other words from the other side of the plain. That seems too far. The other sources state that Antigonus saw the fire himself.

more settled, cultivated area around the lower reaches of the Zayendeh Rud.[170] Here he rested and fed his army. He had lost the advantage of surprise. Eumenes now had the time to concentrate his army, and there would be a major pitched battle. In that case his own forces needed to be in optimum condition.

Eumenes' tactics had led to this situation, and he established a large fortified camp to accommodate his scattered forces as they arrived at base (Diod. 19.39.1). Its location is a matter of guesswork, but, given the topography and Antigonus' movements, a plausible site would be on what is now the main road from Isfahan, somewhere north of Shahriza. Antigonus for his part will have moved to the vicinity of Isfahan and taken the road south. This was a critical moment for Eumenes. His elephants had been the last to move from quarters, and it had clearly been a laborious business to prepare them for the march and action. They were probably stationed in the comparatively lush country west of Isfahan, and as the column of 114 beasts moved slowly down the plain, it came within range of Antigonus' forces, now approaching the main road south. Again the sympathies of the locals were with Peithon, and they informed him of the movement of the elephants. It was a critical moment. Antigonus sent a strong contingent of cavalry and light infantry to intercept the elephant column, and he was nearly successful. The beasts were overhauled and faced attack. Their cavalry escort was vastly outnumbered, and they could only form a defensive square and hope to fend off the assault.[171] It would only be a matter of time before they

---

[170] Diod. 19.38.6: 'they veered to the right, and advanced to both portions of the inhabited country'. The text is obscure. It is difficult to ascertain what Diodorus means by ἐφ' ἑκάτερα μέρη τῆς οἰκουμένης χώρας. Fischer's emendation (ἐπ' ἀκέραια, 'to the unplundered parts'), adopted in Geer's Loeb text, is paleologically unconvincing. It seems more likely that Hieronymus described the settled country (around Isfahan?) as comprising two segments, both of which were occupied by Antigonus (compare Diod. 2.19.8). That seems to be Bizière's interpretation of the passage (p. 159 Budé): 'Les troupes progressent sans doute en deux colonnes de chaque côté de la bande cultivée.' Diodorus' extreme brevity renders any geographical reconstruction mere speculation.

[171] Diod. 19.39.4. Antigonus had sent 2,000 of his fresh Median lancers, 200 Tarantines and all his light infantry. The elephant escort comprised a mere 400 cavalry, and presumably there were foot troops as well (though Diodorus gives no

became exhausted and either surrendered or panicked. In either case Eumenes would lose his greatest asset. However, Eumenes himself had sent a rescue party, again comprising cavalry and light infantry, and it was able to drive off the Antigonid attackers. But it was an inauspicious beginning. Eumenes had not lost any beasts, but they had been fatigued and some were wounded. Like Antigonus' animals they would not be in prime condition, and their tempers cannot have been too sweet.

The stage was set for the climactic battle. Eumenes' army, now united, marched north to meet Antigonus as he moved southwards from the area of Isfahan. They faced each other at a distance of around 8 km., on a salt plain with a river to Eumenes' rear (Diod. 19.43.5). As always the location is a matter of guesswork, but the road to Isfahan passes over a salt plain where a minor stream, the Linjan Rud, disappears into the desert like the Zayendeh Rud. That seems to fit the data in the sources. The circumstances were quite different from the previous battle, which was fought on a hillside and in which the terrain prevented outflanking moves by Antigonus' cavalry. This engagement was to be on level ground with no obstacle to cavalry manœuvres; the major problem was to be the choking pall of salt dust churned up by the combatants.[172] Once battle was joined it would be next to impossible to get an overall impression of what was happening.

It was also difficult to counter the enemy dispositions. At the earlier battle Antigonus had a clear view of Eumenes' battle line and arranged his forces accordingly. On this occasion the lines were drawn up some 8 km. apart.[173] Both sides would have sent scouts ahead to observe the dispositions, but the information would have been fragmentary. Diodorus reports that Eumenes was aware that Antigonus had placed himself on the right with the pick of his cavalry,[174] and he

---

indication, unless they were included in 'those who were set over the elephants': οἱ ἐπὶ τῶν ἐλεφάντων ἐφεστηκότες (39.5)). The mahouts cannot have been the only attendants other than the cavalry.

[172] Diod. 19.42.1, 42.4; Plut. *Eum.* 16.10; Polyaen. 4.6.13.

[173] Diod. 19.39.6; cf. 29.1.

[174] Diod. 19.40.2. It cannot have been a surprise. Antigonus had headed the right wing at the earlier battle (19.29.4–5), and it was the position of honour. It was

drew up his own army to have the weight of his cavalry and the majority of his elephants on the left; but there is no indication that Diodorus' source provided detailed reports of the exact disposition of the line. That in part might explain why his description of the armies' dispositions is so much briefer and uninformative than for the earlier battle.[175] It appears that Antigonus largely repeated his battle line at Paraetacene, the heavy cavalry commanded by himself and Demetrius on the right, the phalanx in the centre and the numerous light cavalry on the left. The elephants were extended over the whole front with light troops filling the gaps between them. He was outnumbered in most areas, with 65 elephants to Eumenes' 114 and only 22,000 foot to set against Eumenes' 36,700.[176] The figures may be misleading, if (as at Paraetacene) Eumenes' light troops are included in the total and Antigonus' not;[177] but, even so, Antigonus' phalanx had suffered heavy losses in the earlier battle and was less numerous than it had been—and certainly lower in morale. Antigonus' one advantage was in cavalry, where he outnumbered Eumenes (9,000 to 6,000) and had fresh riders newly levied from Media. The victory, if it was to be achieved, would be won on the wings.

Eumenes seems to have adopted different tactics. Whereas Antigonus had responded to his dispositions in the earlier battle, he now reacted to what he could learn of Antigonus' movements. He placed the pick of his cavalry on the left

notoriously the favoured position of Alexander (see above, n. 121), which almost guaranteed that his marshals would follow his example. In 321 the two commanders, Craterus and Eumenes had both led their right wings (Diod. 18.30.3, 31.1; Plut. *Eum.* 7.3). Demetrius was unorthodox when he took the left wing at Gaza (Diod. 19.82.1), but Ptolemy and Seleucus had advance information and were able to frustrate his tactics (83.1).

[175] One must also reckon with Diodorus, who may well have been reluctant to burden his narrative with a second catalogue of troops, but it is likely enough that the information available to Hieronymus was less complete. Added to that Hieronymus himself was wounded in the engagement and then taken as a prisoner of war (Diod. 19.44.3). Under those conditions it would have been difficult to establish details after the event.   [176] Diod. 19.40.1, 4.

[177] In Diodorus' account of Paraetacene (see above, p. 133) the separate units of Eumenes' phalanx (19.27.6–28.1) add up to 17,000 out of a grand total of 35,000 (28.4), whereas Antigonus' infantry numbers 28,000 (19.27.1), exactly the sum of the phalanx components (29.3).

against Antigonus, defended by no less than 60 of his best elephants, and the defensive screen was again angled backwards to protect the flank (Diod. 19.40.2–3). The weaker cavalry and elephants were placed on the right under the command of a certain Philippus, who was ordered to avoid battle until the issue was decided on the left. The phalanx had the same arrangement as it had at Paraetacene: hypaspists and Silver Shields adjoining Eumenes, then the mercenaries and Macedonian-trained orientals.[178] We have no figures for the component parts of the line, but it is clear that there had been a radical change from Paraetacene. The satraps were not stationed on the left with their troops, as they had been before. Most of them were placed on the right with Eumenes, each with an élite squadron of cavalry. It is striking too that the command of the left was assigned to Philippus, who is nowhere mentioned as a satrap or commander of satrapal forces. But a Philippus is mentioned in Eumenes' entourage during the campaign against Craterus in 321,[179] and in all probability he was (like Hieronymus himself) one of Eumenes' chief lieutenants, at his side during the siege of Nora and following him into Babylonia with the Silver Shields. Like Hieronymus he was probably taken into Antigonus' service after Eumenes' death, and emerged as one of Demetrius' advisers for the campaign of Gaza. He was chosen for that role because of his experiences under Alexander (Diod. 19.69.1), and he was obviously a man of high military expertise as well as a committed partisan of Eumenes. He could be trusted to follow orders, and was right for the defensive role that Eumenes assigned him at Gabiene. However, none of the members of the satrapal coalition were trusted with the position. They were separated from the bulk of their forces and grouped together in the vicinity of Eumenes, who, we

---

[178] Diod. 19.40.3; cf. 27.6–28.1.

[179] His name appears in the Florentine papyrus of Arrian's *Events after Alexander* (PSI xii.1284: col. 3, line 14: printed in Gerhard Wirth's second edition of A. G. Roos, *Arriani Scripta Minora* (Leipzig 1968) 324). The context is totally lost, but it is part of the narrative of Eumenes' engagement with Neoptolemus and consistent with Philippus being his lieutenant. For the identification see Wirth, *Klio* 46 (1965) 287; Hornblower, *Hieronymus* 123–4; Billows, *Antigonos* 422; Wheatley, *Limina* 3 (1997) 62.

may be sure, had his Companions and *agema* around him.[180] It looks as though he had little confidence in their ability or willingness to fight with their cavalry contingents on the left.

Eumenes' position had obviously remained under threat. We do not know what news had reached the alliance from the west, but something of the turbulent events in Macedonia may very well have reached Iran. In particular the quarrel between Polyperchon and Queen Eurydice could have had a very adverse effect on Eumenes' standing. She had disowned Polyperchon and transferred his command to Cassander,[181] and she must also have revoked Eumenes' commission in the name of her husband, Philip III. That momentous event took place late in summer 317,[182] to be followed shortly after by Olympias' invasion of Macedonia, the defection of Eurydice's army and her death and that of her husband at the hands of Olympias.[183] The death of Philip came in October 317,[184] and the news cannot have reached the satrapal coalition by the time of Gabiene. If it had, it would have strengthened Eumenes' position immensely. What is possible is that news of the earlier turmoil and Eurydice's disowning of Polyperchon had reached Iran. Eumenes and the satraps were effectively cut off from the west by Seleucus who held Babylonia and Susiana against them. But Seleucus would make sure that news which would damage the royal general found its way to Persis and Peucestas. Eumenes might protest disinformation, but such protests were hardly convincing after the episode of the forged letter. By now, after several weeks had elapsed, it must have been clear that no royal army was on its way under Polyperchon. At the very least there were disturbing counter-rumours that Eumenes' position

---

[180] Diod. 19.40.2 claims that he stationed 'the best' of his cavalry around himself. This includes the élite satrapal cavalry but must also refer to his own personal *agema*.

[181] Just. 14.5.3–4: 'Cassandro exercitum tradat, in quem regni administrationem rex transtulerit.' She allegedly sent the news to Antigonus in Asia, and Antigonus will have ensured that it was leaked to the opposition. In the climate of disinformation it is unlikely that the news was believed until there was confirmation by eyewitnesses.

[182] On the chronology see Bosworth, *Chiron* 22 (1972) 71–3, 81.

[183] Diod. 19.11; Just. 14.5.5–10; cf. Hammond, *HM* iii.139–41.

[184] This is a fixed point: Philip 'reigned' for six years and four months (Diod. 19.11.5).

had been revoked and his supporters in Macedonia had lost power. There must have been a welter of uncertainty. Eumenes could still dominate the satrapal council, and his strategy of confrontation had overruled that of Peucestas, but he could not rely on the loyalty of his allies. Accordingly he separated them from the mass of their troops and placed them together in the battle line in a position where he could supervise them in person. It was hardly a good augury for the battle.

What mattered was the phalanx victory, and the predominant role of the Silver Shields was enhanced even further by a nice stroke of psychological warfare. We do not have any record of the internal disposition of Antigonus' phalanx, and there is no direct evidence where he placed his Macedonian troops. However, his arrangement of troops in general was the same as at Paraetacene, and there is every reason to think that both commanders placed their Macedonian troops on opposite sides of their respective phalanxes, to avoid the incalculable risk of their meeting frontally. But the Silver Shields were able to capitalize on their age and reputation. Their commander, Antigenes, sent one of his Macedonian cavalry to the enemy phalanx, and he galloped to the sector where Antigonus' Macedonians were stationed and shouted (almost certainly shouted repeatedly until he was driven off): 'You are sinning against your fathers, you degenerates, the men who conquered the world with Philip and Alexander.'[185] The Silver Shields were certainly aware of the propaganda, which was both flattering and inspirational. It was also invidious to Antigonus, who had not served with Alexander after 333, and to his Macedonians, who were mostly new levies raised by Antipater and Craterus in 322/1. They were reminded in the most brutal way that the men they were facing, both troops and commanders, were the heroes of the past generation, and the propaganda provoked expressions of

---

[185] Diod. 19.41.1. Plut. *Eum.* 16.8 contracts the message, although he agrees on the phrasing of the first clause (ἐπὶ τοὺς πατέρας ἁμαρτάνετε, ὦ κακαὶ κεφαλαί). He also claims that it was a shout by the entire corps of Silver Shields. That is good rhetoric but bad history. The collective shout would have been less effective than the message at close range, delivered directly at the people most vulnerable to the propaganda.

discontent. They were being forced to fight, they said, and to fight against their kinsmen and elders.[186] This is a dramatic example of a pre-battle address, designed to undermine the morale of the enemy, while enthusing one's own side, and its essence was a short, pithy sound bite, which could be delivered in seconds, be repeated indefinitely, and have a strong, emotive impact.[187]

As the message circulated among Eumenes' troops, their spirits rose, and they shouted for action. He responded by sounding the trumpet signal for action. His troops raised the war cry and the attack began. This time the elephants engaged first. Perhaps it was difficult to stop them. The winter conditions probably made them bad-tempered and hard to handle. Diodorus contracts this phase of the battle to seven words,[188] and gives no information about the nature of the elephant fighting. Some beasts clearly engaged in single combat, as, we are later told, Eumenes' lead elephant did (Diod. 19.42.6), in which case they would fight to a standstill, the defeated beast vulnerable to a devastating sideways lunge from the tusks of his adversary which would slash into its loins and genitals.[189] Otherwise the beasts would charge the opposing line of light infantry and be subjected to a barrage of missiles which would wound them and ultimately drive them to a panic, unless they penetrated the defensive

---

[186] Diod. 19.41.3: ἐγίνοντο φωναί δυσχερεῖς, ὅτι συναναγκάζοιντο πρὸς συγγενεῖς καὶ πρεσβυτέρους διαμάχεσθαι.

[187] On pre-battle speeches see M. H. Hansen, *Historia* 42 (1993) 161–80 and *HISTOS* 2 (1998), against W. K. Pritchett, *Essays in Greek History* 27–109. This is a prime example of what Hansen would see as the origin of strategic rhetoric—a short message delivered to successive groups in the line.

[188] Diod. 19.42.1: συνῆψε δὲ τὴν μάχην πρῶτον μὲν τὰ θηρία.

[189] J. H. Williams, *Elephant Bill* (London 1955) 29: 'Elephant bulls fight head to head and seldom fight to the death, without one trying to break away. The one that breaks away frequently receives a wound which proves mortal... The deadly blow is a thrust of one tusk between the hind legs into the loins and intestines where the testicles are carried inside the body. It is a common wound to have to treat after a wild tusker has attacked a domesticated one.' This is a perfect parallel to Polybius' famous description of elephant fighting at Raphia (Polyb. 5.84.3–4): 'With their tusks firmly interlocked they shove with all their might, each trying to force the other to give ground, until the one who proves strongest forces aside the other's trunk, and then, when he has once made him turn and has him in the flank, he gores him with his tusks as a bull does with his horns.'

screen and impacted on the cavalry. While this fighting was taking place there was no chance of the cavalry engaging frontally. Any attack would have to be delivered from the flank or rear.

It was Antigonus who began the cavalry engagement, circling round Eumenes' right wing and avoiding the conflicting lines of elephants. As he began his flanking movement, the horses' hooves stirred up a cloud of salt dust, which added to the precipitation from the elephant battle must have reduced visibility practically to nothing. It was now that Antigonus gave the order which decided the entire campaign. He detached a large group of light cavalry, Medians and Tarantines, to attack the baggage camp of the satrapal forces.[190] This had been done by the Persians at Gaugamela without affecting the outcome of the battle. But the baggage camp at Gabiene was very different from the advance camp attacked at Gaugamela.[191] It contained not merely the possessions of the Silver Shields, acquired during years of campaigning, but also their wives and children[192]—an enormously potent bargaining counter, if they were to fall into Antigonus' hands. It would be of interest to know from what part of the line this cavalry came. At Paraetacene the Median cavalry and Tarantines had been stationed at the extreme right of the line, as far from Antigonus as it was possible to be.[193] If they occupied the same position at Gabiene, it follows that the order to attack the camp was prearranged. Diodorus, however, suggests that the order was given on the spur of the moment, when Antigonus realized how dense the pall of salt dust had become.[194] In that case he had strengthened his right flank with extra contingents of light infantry, who could now be detached to sequester the enemy's baggage. But, wherever the cavalry came from, they would have to ride around the fighting on Antigonus' right. The left was not yet engaged and a fortiori the visibility was greater

[190] Diod. 19.42.2–3; Plut. *Eum.* 16.9; Polyaen. 4.6.13.
[191] On this murky episode and its implications see Bosworth, *Conquest and Empire* 82–3; *HCA* i 294, 304, 308–9; Atkinson i.438–9.
[192] Diod. 19.42.3, 43.7; Polyaen. 4.6.13 Plut. *Eum.* 18.2; Just. 14.3.3.
[193] Diod. 19.29.2.
[194] Diod. 19.42.1–2: ὃ δὴ κατανοήσας Ἀντίγονος ἀπέστειλε κτλ.

there.[195] Antigonus, then, took his heavy cavalry on a circling move around Eumenes' flank, circumventing the elephant battle. Meanwhile the Medians and Tarantines rode in a wider arc, their movements protected by the dust cloud, and they successfully occupied the baggage camp, while the battle took its course in their rear, and transferred its contents, humans and bullion, to the Antigonid sector of the field.

The rest of the cavalry battle had been equally successful for Antigonus. When he swept in from the flank, Eumenes' allies deserted him. Peucestas refused to engage, and as the dust cloud approached, he withdrew with his squadron, taking with him all 1,500 of the satrapal *corps d' élite*. This was hardly an act of cowardice, as the sources represent it. Both Diodorus and Plutarch speak of panic,[196] and that must have been the version of Hieronymus. But it is most unlikely that there was a collective act of cowardice by men who had fought through Alexander's campaigns, not merely Peucestas but Stasander, Eudamus, and many others. It was more probably an act of betrayal, nicely judged and timed. Rather than risk defeat and the loss of their contingents they would retreat and leave Eumenes to be overwhelmed by Antigonus and his cavalry. They could rely on a victory by the phalanx (the dust to their right might already have shown the Silver Shields advancing), and with luck they would negotiate with Antigonus from a position of strength. Indeed there was probably no consensus in the decision to fight the pitched battle; Peucestas may have retained the view that he expressed when he heard that Antigonus was crossing the desert, that the best strategy was one of defence and conservation.[197] Whatever the satraps' motives, the withdrawal was disastrous for Eumenes. Outnumbered by the enemy cavalry, he made a desperate stand. He aimed for Antigonus himself in the hope of killing him in single combat, as he had killed Neoptolemus in 321.[198] But the numbers were against him,

[195] On Eumenes' right Philippus had been explicitly ordered to avoid battle (φυγομαχεῖν: Diod. 19.42.7).

[196] Diod. 19.42.4: Ἀντίγονος μέν ... κατεπλήξατο Πευκέστην; Plut. *Eum.* 165: τοῦ δὲ Πευκέστου παντάπασιν ἐκλελυμένως καὶ ἀγεννῶς ἀγωνισαμένου. Cf. Bosworth, 'History and Artifice' 68.   [197] See above, p. 145.

[198] Diod.19.42.5. On the famous single combat with Neoptolemus see Diod. 18.31.1–5; Plut. *Eum.* 7.7–12; Nepos, *Eum.* 4.1–2; Arr. *Succ.* F 1.27; Just. 13.8.8. Cf. Hornblower, *Hieronymus* 193–6.

and his elephants were being worsted; at least his strongest beast had been killed by its antagonist (Diod. 19.42.7), and its death clearly made a lasting impression upon Hieronymus. It may have been thought to have symbolized the outcome of the battle. It was at this point that Eumenes conceded defeat on his left, and withdrew with what cavalry remained to him, joining Philippus on the right, who still held his forces intact and aloof from the battle.

At this juncture both armies were split into separated groups. Antigonus' cavalry assault had detached him from his phalanx, which was vulnerable to the Silver Shields. Once more these irresistible veterans went ahead of their elephant screen and attacked in close formation, with the same result as at Paraetacene. They drove the opposition back in a disorganized mass, and the rest of the phalanx went with them, exploiting the growing confusion in the enemy line.[199] According to the sources 5,000 of Antigonus' infantry fell in the engagement, with 300 casualties on Eumenes' side, not a single one occurring among the Silver Shields.[200] The disproportionate figures mirror those of Paraetacene, except that the imbalance is even more marked. One can well believe it. After their earlier defeat Antigonus' phalanx men were weaker in numbers; they were fatigued after the arduous desert crossing and shaken in morale by Antigenes' adroit propaganda. They were fighting their fathers and were soundly beaten.

The phalanx troops were detached from their cavalry on both sides; Antigonus' infantry was more than decimated

---

[199] Devine 92 envisages the Silver Shields moving sideways to roll up the enemy line. That would only be possible if they attacked in advance of the rest of the phalanx. There is no suggestion that they did. They certainly routed the enemy in their central part of the line, and the hypaspists and mercenaries on either side will have exploited the confusion. I do not doubt that the Silver Shields forged ahead, but the adjoining troops will have kept up with them and pushed back the Antigonid phalangites in their sector too.

[200] I am here combining Diod. 19.43.1 and Polyaen. 4.6.13 (so too Just. 14.3.5), who agree that there were 5,000 casualties on Antigonus' side; Polyaenus adds that Eumenes suffered 300 losses, and Diodorus claims that not a single Silver Shield was killed. There is possibly some rhetorical exaggeration, as both Diodorus and Plutarch (*Eum.* 16.8) imply that the Silver Shields were solely responsible for the phalanx victory. Hieronymus certainly emphasized their contribution and may have said little or nothing about the role of the other phalanx troops, concentrating on the truly spectacular performance of the Macedonian veterans.

and practically destroyed as a fighting force, while Eumenes'
phalanx was almost untouched and in the flush of victory. By
that time the news broke that the baggage train was in
Antigonid hands. Eumenes attempted to turn it to his advantage, once again evoking Alexander. He consciously repeated
the famous dictum attributed to the king when he learned of
the attack on his baggage at Gaugamela: the victors would
not only regain their own property but acquire that of the
enemy. Whether or not Alexander had actually said that (it
was in any case a borrowing from Xenophon) is open to
debate, but it looks as though it was widely reported and was
familiar to Eumenes' men.[201] According to Diodorus (19.43.2)
Eumenes hoped to gain a victory which would not merely
regain his own baggage but capture that of the enemy. That
hope was probably voiced aloud and circulated as widely as
was possible in battle conditions. It conjured up the tense
scene at Gaugamela where Alexander refused to be panicked
by the attack on his camp and the encirclement on his left
and went on to win his crowning victory by his cavalry attack
on the right and the phalanx victory in the centre. Eumenes
was signalling that an equally conclusive victory could now
be won—and his phalanx was already victorious. The loss
of the baggage might even be viewed as an advantage, a spur
to victory.

Peucestas, however, did not intend Eumenes to assume the
mantle of Alexander. Far from resuming the attack he and
his fellow satraps withdrew even further from the field.[202]
Eumenes was left with his relatively weak cavalry wing on
the right, but it had a complete contingent of elephants to
screen it, the numbers perhaps swelled by beasts which he
had brought with him from the defeated left. If he could

---

[201] Plut. *Alex.* 32.7; Curt. 4.15.7; Polyaen. 4.3.6. For the sentiment in Xenophon
see *Anab.* 3.2.39. The tradition of Alexander's response with its strong animus
against Parmenion is usually and plausibly attributed to Callisthenes (cf. *Entretiens
Hardt* 22 (1976) 11–12).

[202] Diod. 19.43.3: Peucestas and his followers took their retreat further, ἐπί τινα
τόπον. This is a very weak expression, and Geer plausibly suggested ποταμόν for
τόπον in his Loeb text. The river is mentioned a few sentences later (43.5) with a
definite article which indicates that it figured earlier in the narrative. It was there
that the Silver Shields met Peucestas and vented their anger, and it is reasonable
enough that the river marked the end of Peucestas' retreat.

catch up with his infantry phalanx, it would be a combination that Antigonus without his own phalanx would be unable to resist. But evening was already approaching, and Antigonus had time to save the day. He had divided his cavalry into two groups: one threatened Eumenes himself, the other under Peithon was to attack the Silver Shields. There was no possibility of defeating the phalanx by cavalry alone, for the troops simply adopted a square formation,[203] and no horse would charge the unbroken fence of *sarisae*. But Peithon slowed their progress and prevented any liaison with Eumenes' remaining cavalry. As dusk fell, they joined Peucestas' cavalry well behind the lines, and the recriminations began, as Antigenes and Teutamus charged Peucestas with responsibility for the cavalry defeat. They were soon joined by Eumenes himself, who reached camp as night fell and the lamps were lit. He had the decided advantage, given that Antigonus' infantry was demoralized and virtually destroyed as a fighting force; even his losses in the cavalry battle had not been enormous. If he renewed the battle and his troops and commanders followed his orders, there was every chance of victory. In all probability Antigonus would cut his losses and retreat, as he had done after Paraetacene.

Unfortunately for Eumenes, military factors were no longer paramount. His command was totally undermined. The satraps insisted on a strategic withdrawal, to continue the struggle elsewhere (Diod. 19.43.6). Anything rather than continue under Eumenes' leadership. In all probability they hoped that the leaders of the Silver Shields would desert the royal general and throw in their lot with them. But the decisive issue was the captured baggage train. The rank-and-file was adamant that the first priority was to recover their families and property, and they were more than willing to listen to overtures from Antigonus. In fact they appear to have taken the initiative, contacting Antigonus in the night following the battle,[204] and they received assurances that their families would be returned once Eumenes was

---

[203] Diod. 19.43.5: οἱ Μακεδόνες εἰς πλινθίον ἑαυτοὺς ποιήσαντες ἀσφαλῶς ἀπεχώρησαν. On this formation see Ael. *Tact.* 37.9; Arr. *Tact.* 29.8.

[204] Diod. 19.43.8 (λάθρᾳ); Plut. *Eum.* 17.1; Just. 14.3.11 (*ignaris . . . ducibus*).

surrendered. The demand had been made many times before, but Antigonus now had hostages to enforce compliance. Not surprisingly the ties of family and property triumphed over loyalty to the royal house, and after some debate and discussion, variously reported in the sources, Eumenes was handed over to an escort of elephants and Median cavalry and taken to imprisonment and ultimately death.[205]

Our sources concentrate on the fate of Eumenes, and there is some suggestion that now his Greekness became an issue. Plutarch records the celebrated gibe that it hardly mattered if a pestilential Greek from the Chersonese suffered; it was far worse if the veterans of Philip and Alexander were deprived of the fruits of their labours.[206] There is some evidence that his non-Macedonian birth had weakened his influence in the past,[207] but Plutarch is probably giving it excessive emphasis, to point the parallel with Sertorius.[208] What is clear is that Eumenes was not the only person betrayed by the Silver Shields. They were equally indifferent to the fate of their Macedonian commander, Antigenes, and allowed him to be arrested by Antigonus (if they did not arrest him themselves)—and Antigonus had him burnt alive in the most atrocious manner.[209] Eumenes was comparatively fortunate. The Silver Shields had no effective commander once their delegation returned from Antigonus' camp, and they were not open to coercion from their own side. Even if the satrapal cavalry commanders had wished to influence them, they were

[205] Diod. 19.43.8–9 is very brief. Much fuller accounts of the arrest and death are given by Plut. *Eum.* 17–19; Just. 14.3.4–5.18; Nepos, *Eum.* 10.2–12.4. On this material see Bosworth, 'History and Artifice' 63–5, 70.

[206] Plut. *Eum.* 18.2, echoed in the parallel *Life* (*Sert.* 6.6).

[207] Diod. 18.60.1–3: ξένῳ καὶ τῆς ὁμοεθνοῦς τοῖς Μακεδόσιν ἐξουσίας κεχωρισμένῳ. Compare the propaganda of Seleucus and Peithon (Diod. 19.13.1; above, p. 109)

[208] The first sentence of the *synkrisis* stresses that both were foreigners commanding alien armies.

[209] Diod. 19.44.1. According to Plut. *Eum.* 17.1 the secret negotiations with Antigonus had been led by Teutamus. His fellow commander is not named, and was clearly absent. Teutamus probably promised to surrender him along with Eumenes. We have no idea why Antigonus cherished such animosity. If Antigenes had left Craterus for Perdiccas' camp (as suggested above, p. 33), he may well have been regarded as a traitor. But many others did the same without retribution. There were clearly other reasons (a very hypothetical suggestion in Billows, *Antigonos* 103 n. 27; see also Heckel 315–16).

in no position to offer force. In fact the majority were happy to make their own representations to Antigonus in the hope of keeping or expanding their satrapal commands. It was only Antigonus' personal enemies (Antigenes, Eudamus, a mysterious 'Celbanus',[210] and a few other unnamed individuals) who had an interest in holding out, and they were not numerous or influential enough to sway the rest. Within two days Eumenes' army had in fact deserted to Antigonus. He combined the two armies, and kept those satrapal commanders who were not executed in honourable custody. He was the absolute victor.

5. THE POLITICAL AFTERMATH

Antigonus now had a combined army which numbered some 50,000 infantry and at least 12,000 cavalry. It was impossible to keep it together en masse, and we may assume that Antigonus retained only the nucleus of Eumenes' army. Most of the satrapal forces, particularly the cavalry, could be sent home. Since he retained their commanders, they would be little danger in their native satrapies, and he was relieved of the problem of provisioning them. Antigonus kept the Silver Shields because it was perilous to do anything else and probably the best of the mercenary infantry and Macedonian-trained orientals. But his forces were still too large to keep as a concentrated whole, particularly in the vicinity of Gabiene, where resources had been exhausted by the winter campaign. Instead he sent the contingents in different directions to pass the winter; he himself went north with his headquarters corps to a palace near Ecbatana, while other units were distributed over the whole of Media, the largest group being

---

[210] Diod. 14.44.1. The Laurentianus here reads Κέβαλον which is a legitimate Macedonian name. However, there is no other individual recorded of that name, and it is fanciful to see a connection with the Cebalinus who played such a notorious role in the downfall of Philotas. Heckel (*BN* 15 (1980) 43–5; so Billows, *Antigonos* 103 n. 27) suggests an identification with Cephalon, who had assumed command of Sibyrtius' Arachosian cavalry (Diod. 19.27.4)). That is more attractive, but it is hard to see why the name should have been corrupted into an authentic Macedonian form. It is best to leave the issue open.

assigned to Rhagae, on the outskirts of modern Tehran.[211] That region had not been touched so far by the campaign, and it could support a comparatively large army group for the rest of winter. But the demands of the winter would have to be redressed the following year, and it was essential that Antigonus left the area to recuperate. The spring of 316 accordingly saw him on his way to Persepolis and the Mediterranean with a formidable army at his disposal.

In the meantime he had disposed of the only real threat to his supremacy. Peithon had as much responsibility for the victory over Eumenes as Antigonus himself. He had commanded the left wing in both battles, and the popularity he enjoyed in Media had been a material advantage. It won him vital information,[212] and the satrapy provided him with a seemingly endless supply of provisions, remounts, and riders. He could reasonably argue that Antigonus could not have won without him, and as a Bodyguard of Alexander he had a right to the eastern conquests which Antigonus could not match. Diodorus (19.46.2) stresses his prestige and influence: Alexander had promoted him for his achievements, he was satrap of Media and had courted the entire army. It was not easy to dispose of him openly. Diodorus claims that he was on the point of revolt, or rather that Antigonus heard that he was.[213] It is possible that the reports were true, but Hieronymus, who had just transferred to Antigonus' service, may have been unwilling to accuse his new master of treachery and preferred to insinuate that Peithon was treacherously intriguing against him. However, if he was conspiring, Peithon behaved with guileless naivety.

---

[211] Diod. 19.44.4. Rhagae was one of Alexander's halting points in his pursuit of Darius (Arr. 3.20.2), and immediately east beyond the Caspian Gates was the fertile district of Choarene (cf. Bosworth, *HCA* i.340). It is possible that detachments of Antigonus' army were stationed as far east as the Parthian capital, Hecatompylus (Shahr-i Qumis), where Alexander ended his pursuit of Darius.

[212] Diod. 19.38.4. See above, p. 143.

[213] Diod. 19.46.1: The focus is firmly on Antigonus, who hears (πυθόμενος) that Peithon was wooing the troops with gifts and was set on revolt. The first part of the allegation was no doubt true; Peithon was merely doing what Peucestas had done in Persis (see above, p. 121). The planned revolt was an inference from his public actions. Polyaen. 4.6.14 is more categorical, claiming that Peithon was enlisting mercenaries (ξενολογεῖν) and was planning to rebel, but again there is the qualification that this was the information that Antigonus received.

When Antigonus summoned him to Ecbatana, hinting that
he was to become general of the upper satrapies, the military
supremo of the eastern empire,[214] he left his winter quarters
in the extremities of Media and presented himself at
Antigonus' court, where he was brought before a council of
Antigonus' friends and condemned to death.[215] It looks as
though we have a case of judicial murder, a fictitious conspiracy with informants primed to come forward with allegations
of sedition and letters to prove their charges. It is deeply suspicious that Antigonus got rid of the one man who might
prove a threat to his own supremacy and did so a matter of
weeks after his victory. Media was too important to be in the
hands of a Bodyguard of Alexander, and so the Bodyguard
was removed, isolated from his troops and suddenly confronted with charges that he had no hope of disproving.
Alexander himself had given the example when he concocted
charges of treason against his namesake, Alexander the
Lyncestian,[216] and (some might argue) against Philotas, his
senior cavalry commander;[217] and Eumenes had used the
same methods a few months earlier, when he brought charges
against his enemy Sibyrtius.[218] Despite the precedents
Peithon fell into the trap unsuspectingly, and it is hard
to think that he would have done so had he actually been
intriguing against Antigonus. Peithon, then, was removed
without a struggle. Despite his evident popularity in the
satrapy his death was largely accepted; the only resistance
came from some 800 friends of his and Eumenes who tried
to raise the satrapy after Antigonus left for Persepolis.[219]
They had every reason to fear for their safety after the death
of their patron, and it is not surprising that they attempted

---

[214] Diod. 19.46.1–2. Polyaen. 4.6.14 adds that he was offered an army of 5,000
Macedonians and 1,000 Thracians. If so, it was a prize worth the having. It put
Peithon in the position he had enjoyed after Triparadeisus (see above, n. 27) with an
army which would allow him to dominate the region.

[215] Diod. 19.46.4: ῥᾳδίως κατεδίκασε καὶ παραχρῆμα ἀπέκτεινεν.

[216] The Lyncestian seems to have been totally flabbergasted by the charges laid
against him (Diod. 17.80.2 (ἀπορηθεὶς λόγων); Curt. 7.1.8–9).

[217] See now the comprehensive essay by E. Badian, in *Al. in Fact and Fiction*
50–95, esp. 56–60, 64–9.

[218] Diod. 19.23.4. See above, p. 122.

[219] Diod. 19.47.1–4. The uprising had some success, and the mounted rebels caused
widespread damage, but there is no hint of any support by the population at large.

to gain control of Media. That was retrospective 'proof' of conspiracy which Antigonus no doubt exploited.

Media was Antigonus' to dispose of, and he established a dual command, of the type favoured by Alexander in the middle years of his reign. A Median noble, Orontobates, was appointed satrap along with a Macedonian general, Hippostratus, who had a modest holding force of 3,500 mercenaries.[220] They would balance each other, and neither could entertain the ambitions of a Peithon. Once in Persis Antigonus revealed his wider plans for the eastern satrapies. He had evidently kept the coalition satraps with him after Gabiene without making any ruling on their future. When he reached Persepolis, he presided over an impressive ceremony. He had already been given royal honours by the native Persians:[221] in other words they recognized him as the Great King, the heir to the empire of the Achaemenids, and adopted the ceremonial they would render to a native king. Antigonus obviously voiced no objection and, now the acknowledged lord of Asia, he conferred with a council of his friends and redistributed the satrapies.[222] The scenario recalled, and was designed to recall, Antipater at Triparadeisus, when as guardian of the kings and victor over Perdiccas, he supervised the partition of the empire—aided by Antigonus himself. Antigonus was

[220] Diod. 19.46.5. Schober, *Untersuchungen* 85 canvasses the possibility that Hippostratus was given the wider post of general of the upper satrapies, the office fraudulently offered to Peithon and later held by Nicanor (Diod. 19.100.3). That seems unlikely. The arrangement would have left Orontobates without troops of his own and Hippostratus with a very small army for his wide ranging office. In any case the functions of satrap and general are separated, whereas Nicanor, we are specifically informed, combined the two positions (cf. Schober, *Untersuchungen* 89).

[221] Diod. 19.48.1: τιμῆς ... ἠξιώθη βασιλικῆς ὡς ἂν κύριος ὢν ὁμολογουμένως τῆς Ἀσίας. Geer's Loeb translation wrongly adds a qualification ('as if he were the acknowledged lord of Asia'); in this very frequent Diodoran usage ἂν tends to be superfluous (see the neighbouring examples at 19.45.1, 69.2). The natives of Persis presumably addressed him by the traditional titles of royalty and offered *proskynesis*. Polyaen. 4.6.13 fin. suggests that he was actually proclaimed king of Asia as Alexander seems to have been after Gaugamela (Plut. *Alex.* 34.1: for discussion and bibliography see now Ernst Fredricksmeyer in *Al. in Fact and Fiction* 136–55). That is possible, but, if so, the relationship was one-sided. Antigonus did not declare himself king, and documents of Babylonia refer to him as *rab uqi*, royal general, not king.

[222] Diod. 19.48.1. The language recalls his description of Perdiccas' distribution (18.3.1). For Antipater at Triparadeisus see Diod. 18.39.5; Arr. *Succ.* F 1.34; Heidelberg Epit., *FGrH* 155F 1(4).

advertising his newly acquired predominance in the most striking way. As for the satrapies he had no intention of interfering in the far east, and so Stasanor remained in Bactria, as did Oxyartes in Parapamisadae. Nearer to home Tlepolemus was allowed to retain Carmania. Diodorus (19.48.1) stresses his popularity with his subjects, but unlike Stasanor in Bactria Tlepolemus immediately adjoined Persis, and could not have resisted Antigonus' army, had he wished to invade. If, as I have suggested,[223] he had been at loggerheads with Peucestas and been temporarily deposed, it would have recommended him to Antigonus, who now ended Peucestas' tenure of Persis. Despite objections from the native nobility, Antigonus replaced him with an Asclepiodorus, presumably one of his friends.[224] In Areia Stasander received the same treatment, to be replaced by an acolyte of Antigonus, first Evitus and then, after Evitus' death, by Evagoras, who allegedly had a high reputation for bravery and practical intelligence.[225] It is a pity that we hear no more of him.

Another beneficiary of Antigonus was Sibyrtius, the satrap of Arachosia, who had fallen foul of Eumenes and taken flight to avoid condemnation. Interestingly, Antigonus summoned him to court, and Sibyrtius complied, despite the fate of Peithon who had so recently and catastrophically responded to a summons from Antigonus.[226] One may perhaps argue for an old established friendship with Antigonus. It had been Peithon whom Sibyrtius had opposed, and Peithon's ambitions had inspired the satrapal alliance which Sibyrtius had enthusiastically joined. There is no evidence that he had any quarrel with Antigonus, and, if there was actually friendship, it will have helped lend credibility to the charges of treason which Eumenes brought against him. As it was, in the summer of 316 he came to court, despite the

---

[223] See above, p. 123.

[224] Diod. 19.48.5 (cf. Wiesehöfer, above, n. 92, 55). Billows, *Antigonos* 376 no. 20, suggests that Asclepiodorus is to be identified with the financial superintendent of Babylonia appointed by Alexander in 331 (Arr. 3.16.4). Possibly so, but the name is too common (cf. Berve ii nos. 167–70) for certainty.

[225] Diod. 19.48.2. This Evagoras has been identified as the satrap 'Euagros' who served under Nicanor and fell in battle with Seleucus in 311 (Diod. 19.92.4; cf. Hornblower, *Hieronymus* 279 n. 20; Billows, *Antigonos* 385 no. 38). See Ch. 6 n. 104).

[226] Diod. 19.48.3. For his friendship with Peucestas see 19.23.4.

fact that he was a friend of Peucestas, who had been deposed along with other satraps, and held Arachosia, which was almost as remote as Parapamisadae. He must have had very good reason to expect favourable treatment. And favourable treatment he received. He was confirmed in his satrapy, and, most interestingly, he received reinforcements for his satrapal army, a strong detachment of the redoubtable Silver Shields. This is a curious episode. The sources lay emphasis on the irony of their fate. They were allegedly destined for destruction, far from the Hellenic sea, a fitting retribution for their betrayal of Eumenes.[227] Some of this judgemental material will no doubt come from Hieronymus.[228] He will have shed no tears over Silver Shields who died on service in Arachosia, and no doubt expressed some satisfaction.

The truth is likely to be more complex and less morally edifying than the simplistic interpretations of the sources. No one would seriously think of annihilating the Silver Shields in their totality. They were much too valuable a military resource. However, there were obvious dangers in keeping them together as a unit. Antigonus could not depend on their loyalty, and he could not trust them to any other commander. The only alternative was to break them up and distribute them over the satrapies. Sibyrtius received the largest detachment: Diodorus says that they were the most undisciplined,[229] and Polyaenus claims that there were no less than a thousand of them. Undisciplined or not, they comprised a formidable force which no other satrap in the area was likely to match. It is another indication of Antigonus' confidence in Sibyrtius. He had no worries that Sibyrtius would use his new acquisition to promote his personal ambitions and become another Peithon.

---

[227] Diod. 19.48.4; Plut. *Eum.* 19.3; Polyaen. 4.6.15. It is fulfilment of the curse of Eumenes recorded by Just. 14.4.14.

[228] Hornblower, *Hieronymus* 192: 'Hieronymus' moral indignation at the Argyraspids' betrayal of Eumenes can still be discerned in Diodorus and Plutarch.' So already Jacoby, *RE* viii. 1544.

[229] Diod. 19.48.3: τοὺς ταραχωδεστάτους. These were the troops who had threatened Antipater's life at Triparadeisus (Arr. *Succ.* F 1.38: στασιασάντων), and they were not amenable to discipline imposed by any commander.

There was probably more than friendship at issue. Sibyrtius had his hands full militarily, and he seems to have had every reason to approach Antigonus for reinforcements. Here we have a rare indication of provincial history during the period. There were evidently serious troubles in Arachosia and a demand for a strong military presence. Local insurrection is possible, but this was the time of the conquest of the Indus basin by Chandragupta and the establishment of the Mauryan dynasty.[230] The invaders probably clashed with the Indian peoples on the eastern borders of Arachosia, and there may well have been serious action around the Bolan Pass and the Kirthar Range. The Silver Shields had been in the area before, when they crushed the revolt of Sambus in summer 325,[231] and they were the most experienced troops in the world when it came to warfare against mountain fastnesses. Without a doubt they were subsequently engaged in heavy action, probably attacking several targets simultaneously, as they had done so often under Alexander. If, as is likely, the casualties were heavy, it would give the impression that their deaths were a matter of policy: they had been deliberately split up and exposed to danger. Hieronymus might even have suggested that Sibyrtius was following instructions from Antigonus. But this was only one, if the strongest, detachment of Silver Shields. The rest were dispersed among other satraps, and assigned to various settlements. Again there is the suggestion that this was a punitive measure, but the troops were too valuable to be simply left idle or thrown away for no military gain. They will have been distributed over nodal points of strategic importance, and it is unlikely that they literally disappeared, as Polyaenus states.[232] The Silver Shields had indeed gone as a military entity, but groups of them continued in service and probably survived

---

[230] In 316 Peithon, son of Agenor, left his satrapy (India west of the Indus) and joined Antigonus (Diod. 19.56.4). The satrapy was never again occupied by Macedonian commanders, and Chandragupta presumably annexed the area to his empire. On the scanty sources see Schober, *Untersuchungen* 90–3.

[231] Arr. 6.16.3–5; Diod. 17.102.6–103.8; Curt. 9.8.13–28, On this campaign see now Bosworth 'Calanus' 196–200.

[232] Polyaen. 4.6.15: διὸ ταχέως ἀφανεῖς πάντες ἐγένοντο.

for some years, to be exploited selectively by their new masters.[233]

The fate of the Silver Shields marks the end of the campaign. Appropriately so. They had dominated the fighting, and to a lesser extent the political interplay between the commanders. Their loyalty to the Argead house had given Eumenes his leading role among the coalition, and in the end it was their understandable attachment to their wives, children, and property which brought the end of hostilities. With them gone there was no possibility of resuming the war against Antigonus. They had made Eumenes' infantry invincible, and it was their sheer expertise that had done it. It is notable that Antigonus had more Macedonian troops in his army, but they were never able to make the same impression on the mercenaries and Macedonian-trained orientals that the Silver Shields did on their opponents. They attacked with an impact and cohesion that was irresistible, and they began a process of disruption and dislocation which the rest of their phalanx continued. It seems too that Eumenes and his officers were able to blend the disparate infantry groups into a corporate unit that was highly effective, and to some degree he foreshadowed the future: warfare between heterogeneous coalition armies in which Macedonians were at best a minority, and not necessarily the dominant minority. After the demise or retirement of Alexander's men, there seems to have been little to choose between Macedonians proper and men trained in Macedonian techniques.

The campaign was also notable for its use of elephants. Prodigious efforts and resources were expended to keep them fit and active under the most unfavourable climatic conditions, and they were consistently placed in front of the line of battle. But their contribution seems questionable. At Paraetacene the elephants seem to have taken practically no part, and though they engaged at Gabiene, the struggle was a stalemate, elephant against elephant. There is no evidence of the beasts attacking enemy infantry, as Porus' elephants had done at the Hydaspes. Perhaps the dangers of their being wounded in the eyes or trunk were too acute. The Silver

[233] For one possible base, at Carrhae, see Ch. 6.

Shields had experience with vicious sickle-shaped knives, which had been singularly effective at the Hydaspes, and if they had the same weaponry in Iran, they could have made the enemy elephants totally uncontrollable by slashing at their trunks.[234] Accordingly, elephants tended to be used against each other or to keep cavalry at bay. Their usefulness was limited, but they clearly had a mystique, a psychological advantage for their army.[235] However, they were arguably more of a liability than an asset, as Ptolemy and Seleucus were to demonstrate at Gaza, disabling the beasts with spikes and missiles and driving them back in panic into their own lines.[236] The elephants, then, were an expensive luxury, but like all such military luxuries they were irresistibly attractive to commanders, who spared no expense in acquiring them. So Seleucus proved beyond cavil when he made peace with Chandragupta and ceded the eastern satrapies of his empire in return for no less than 500 beasts.[237]

The constant throughout the campaign was political rivalry. Eumenes was under threat the whole time, not merely or principally because of his nationality. There was similar, even greater rivalry between the Macedonian satraps. Peithon's ambitions were seen as intolerable, and Peucestas himself clearly nurtured similar delusions of grandeur. On the other side Antigonus used Seleucus and Peithon to support his own campaign, and coldly disposed of them both once he had destroyed Eumenes. No single episode better illustrates the divisive ambitions of the major players, in particular the Bodyguards and senior staff members of Alexander. The motto of Achilles (and Alexander) to excel and prove superior

---

[234] 'If an elephant's trunk is injured the animal becomes unmanageable...if an elephant's trunk is seriously injured it will die of starvation, since everything it eats has to be torn down or pulled up and handled by the trunk' (J. H. Williams, *Elephant Bill* 22, 28).

[235] Diod. 19.84.1 (cf. 18.45.1) underlines the deterrent effect of the elephants at Gaza, as he does when describing the reputation of the elephants in Greece ('reputed to possess a fighting spirit and a momentum of body that were irresistible': 18.70.3). On both occasions the elephants failed to live up to their reputation.

[236] Diod. 19.83.2, 84.1–4; compare the tactics used against Polyperchon's elephants at Megalopolis (Diod. 18.71.3–6).

[237] Strab. 15.2.9 (724); 16.2.10 (752); Plut. *Alex.* 62.4. In defence of this figure see Schober, *Untersuchungen* 183–6.

to others was the motivating force, and to achieve that end all manner of intrigue, including forgery, perjury, and judicial murder, was acceptable, and Hieronymus' narrative took little trouble to conceal the fact. For Eumenes the aim was victory (and enrichment), fulfilling his role as royal general, and he had no alternative but loyalty to the crown. At best he would be the agent of the kings, wielding power in Asia in their name and representing his interests as theirs; and at times, notably before the first battle in Paraetacene, he came close to achieving his goal. For others there were no such inhibitions, and Antigonus in particular allowed the Persians to treat him as Great King in his own right after his victory. There was civil war in Macedon, and the writ of the kings and Polyperchon had ceased to run. Now the generals had emerged openly as contenders for kingship, and Antigonus at least hardly bothered with pretence.

5
Hieronymus' Ethnography: Indian Widows and Nabataean Nomads

The principal source for the period after Alexander was Hieronymus of Cardia. He is reputed for his supposedly dispassionate narrative of events, his factual accuracy, backed by verbatim citation of documents. Thucydides and Polybius are the parallels which come most readily to mind.[1] But there is another side. Like Polybius, Hieronymus had a penchant for digression, enlivening his narrative of men and events with picturesque descriptions of engineering and artistic monuments, the social mores of exotic peoples, the origins of famous cities.[2] His description of the funerary carriage of Alexander was a famous example of the genre of wonder writing (θαυμάσια), and Diodorus chose to excerpt it at length.[3] Another long excursus, if Diodorus is any guide, was the elaborate *mise en scène* at the beginning of Hieronymus' work, in which he reviewed the administrative structure of the Macedonian empire after the death of Alexander. This took the form of a digression on the revolt of the Greek colonists after Alexander's death. Diodorus echoes its opening, and optimistically claims that he will set forth the causes of the uprising, the geographical orientation of Asia and the dimensions and characteristics of the individual satrapies. He adds that his intention is to give his readers a vivid impression of the topography and the relative distances involved.[4] What he then gives is a pale shadow of the

---

[1] So explicitly Hornblower, *Hieronymus* 1 with citation of other literature. See, however, Jacoby, *RE* viii.1557: 'Ein Thukydides war H. nicht.'

[2] Hornblower, *Hieronymus* 137–53 gives an excellent survey, which is now the fundamental point of departure.

[3] Athen. 5.206 E = Moschion, *FGrH* 575 F 1; cf. Diod. 18.26.3–28.1.

[4] Diod. 18.5.1. The passage immediately follows the report of Peithon's commission to suppress the mutinous settlers (18.4.8), the first military event which required detailed geographical understanding. It may well be an inspiration for Tacitus' famous survey of the state of the Roman empire in AD 69 (Hornblower,

original. There is only the most vestigial causal analysis, a very sketchy reproduction of the geographical schema, and a tired, perfunctory catalogue of satrapies. There is no indication of the distances between major centres and nothing about the peculiarities of the satrapies. Diodorus has reproduced the historical objectives of Hieronymus, namely to provide a factual background which would make the detailed narrative readily comprehensible; but he has reduced the actual exposition to a generalized, simplistic epitome. Hieronymus clearly provided a lengthy description of the eastern world from Cilicia and Egypt as far as the Ganges and the eastern Ocean. On that canvas he will have related the troubles in the new settlements; he will have given the location of the separate Alexandrias, explained their geographical setting and analysed the reasons for the dissatisfaction of the colonists. In Diodorus the relevance of the digression is obscured, and we are left with a simple 'Gazetteer of Empire',[5] unrelated to any specific events in the surrounding history. Hieronymus' exposition must have been rich and informative, but in Diodorus it is reduced to a catalogue of exotic names. The deficient filter impairs our vision of the original, and it is unfortunately an omnipresent problem.

It is clear, for instance, that Hieronymus paid special attention to foundation legends. He described the prehistory of the Thessalian plain,[6] and, more interestingly, addressed the origins of Rome. It was a cursory account, but the first dedicated treatment of Roman prehistory and, as such, important.[7] But it is totally lost, and there is absolutely no basis for reconstruction.[8] Other foundation stories are

---

Hieronymus 87 n. 46). Syme for once was quite wrong when he claimed (*Tacitus* 147) that Tacitus 'appears to lack precedent or parallel in ancient historiography'.

[5] The term was coined by Tarn (*JHS* 43 (1923) 97; cf. *Al.* ii.309), and it is not altogether happy. It suggests (as Tarn insisted was the case) that there was an independent official document which listed the separate satrapies and was used by Hieronymus. This view gives Diodorus little credit for his ability to transform the richest documentation into a bland uninformative catalogue. He is reducing Hieronymus to a gazetteer; one cannot infer the opposite, that there was a documentary list which Hieronymus and then Diodorus copied out.

[6] Strab. 9.5.22 (443) = *FGrH* 154 F 17.

[7] Dion. Hal. *AR* 1.5.4 = *FGrH* 154 F 13. It is described as a 'summary epitome of extreme brevity' which skirted over (ἐπιδραμόντος) Roman prehistory.

[8] Good, though necessarily speculative, discussion in Hornblower, *Hieronymus* 140–2, 248–50.

preserved by Diodorus. He explains the origins of the name Rhagae (19.44.4–5), and since the etymological speculation comes as an adjunct to the report of Antigonus' actions after Gabiene, it looks almost certain that the information comes from Hieronymus, who spent time there convalescing after his wound.[9] The explanation itself is uninteresting: the name '*Ῥάγαι* ('clefts') commemorated a vast earthquake which swallowed an earlier complex of cities and changed the configuration of rivers and marshes. The etymology is repeated by Strabo in much the same terms. But he took the material from Poseidonius, and mentions Duris, not Hieronymus, as its ultimate source.[10] The overlap with Diodorus is startling, and it could be argued that Hieronymus included a picturesque detail from Duris which related to a place familiar to him from personal experience.[11] It was included solely for its antiquarian interest.

The sketch of the prehistory of Thebes is rather different. Here Diodorus gives us a relatively full account (Diod. 19.53.3–8), which serves as the backdrop to Cassander's refoundation of the city in 316. He stresses the antiquity of the city, which he implies predated Deucalion's flood, and presents its mythical past as a series of expulsions and resettlements:[12] first Cadmus returned from exile at the head of the Encheleis, an Illyrian people of north-western Macedonia, and displaced the population of Thebes;[13] and there followed

---

[9] See above, p. 160.

[10] Strab. 1.3.19 (60)=Poseidonius *FGrH* 87 F 87; Duris, *FGrH* 76 F 54. At 11.9.1 (514) Strabo ascribes the information to Poseidonius alone (F 87a).

[11] So J. G. Droysen (*Hermes* 11 (1876) 465, cf. Jacoby, *RE* viii.1549; R. B. Kebric, *In the Shadow of Macedon: Duris of Samos* 62; Hornblower, *Hieronymus* 60). There are of course other explanations. Diodorus could have taken the etymology from Duris, and superimposed it upon Hieronymus' campaign description (cf. Jacoby, *RE* viii.1550). Alternatively Strabo's quotation from Duris may be indirect. This is his only citation of Duris, and it occurs in a context generally derived from Poseidonius—and the etymology is later ascribed to Poseidonius himself. Poseidonius may have used Hieronymus without naming him and gave some supplementary detail from Duris. Strabo then assumed that the whole context derived from Duris.

[12] This is explicit from the start of the excursus: συμβέβηκε δὲ τὴν πόλιν ταύτην πλείσταις καὶ μεγίσταις κεχρῆσθαι μεταβολαῖς, οὐκ ὀλιγάκις ἀνάστατον γεγενημένην (19.53.3).

[13] Diod. 19.53.5. The stay among the Encheleis was mentioned by Herodotus (5.61.2; cf. 9.43.1) but dated to a later period, the time of the Epigoni. The tradition

a recurrent pattern of exile and repatriation, broken by the last return four generations after the Trojan War. After that there were nearly 800 years of continuous habitation until Alexander destroyed the city in 335. Traditional and familiar legends such as the Seven against Thebes and the return of the Epigoni are woven into the story, but the emphasis on repeated expulsion seems unique to Hieronymus. It may derive in part from the propaganda of Cassander, the author of the refoundation, who would have been glad to represent himself as the counterpart of Amphion and Zethus, laying the new foundations with the blessing and assistance of the gods. But Hieronymus had a personal interest in Thebes. He was appointed harmost and administrator when Demetrius occupied the city in 293, driving out the Spartan adventurer, Cleonymus.[14] It was not an entirely happy appointment, for the Boeotians took advantage of Demetrius' engagement in Thrace and revolted. What happened to Hieronymus is not known. He was presumably expelled, but he survived the experience and lived on in the entourage of the Antigonids.

But the uprising was abortive. The Boeotians were defeated in the field by the young Antigonus Gonatas before his father even returned from the north (Plut. *Demetr.* 39.7), and the Thebans were subjected to the mandatory siege at the hands of the Besieger. It was protracted, costly and resulted in a neck wound for Demetrius himself. None the less, once Thebes was finally taken, he showed unexpected clemency, executing 13 ringleaders, exiling some others and sparing the rest of the populace.[15] He was in a position to follow the example of Alexander, but despite the provocation he refrained and allowed the city to survive—under the watchful eye of a resident garrison. Hieronymus' account of

of Cadmus' invasion of Greece goes back to Euripides' *Bacchae* (1334–8, 1355–60), which was familiar to the Macedonians (Bosworth, in *Transitions to Empire* 142–9) and was no doubt a fertile source for mythological improvisation. For the location of the Encheleis (near Lake Lychnitis) see Hammond, *HM* i.94.

[14] Plut. *Demetr.* 39.3–4 = *FGrH* 154 T 8. On this episode see Jacoby, *RE* viii.1541; Hornblower, *Hieronymus* 13–15; Walbank, *HM* iii.219–21; Habicht, *Athens from Alexander to Antony* 91.

[15] Plut. *Demetr.* 40.6 (cf. Diod. 21.14.1–2). There is a vivid contrast between the apocalyptic forebodings of the Thebans (ὡς τὰ δεινότατα πεισομένοις) and the moderation of the actual settlement.

Theban prehistory set his actions in the most favourable
light. Demetrius might have been another Cadmus, destroy-
ing the city with the help of an army from the north, but
instead (uniquely among the conquerors of Thebes) he
spared the city. The legendary material is given an emphasis
which enhances Cassander's refoundation of Thebes, the
immediate context of the narrative, but it also looks some 25
years ahead to Demetrius' magnanimous treatment of the
rebellious city.[16] Had he in fact destroyed it, the emphasis
would have been quite different; the theme would have been
Theban Medism, and Demetrius, like Alexander, would have
been portrayed imposing the sentence passed by the Hellenic
League in 480.[17] The choice of material has political importance; it adds depth to the simple narrative of events and helps
predispose the reader to accept the historian's message.

Hieronymus' digressions, it may be argued, had a certain
sophistication. They were not written solely to break the
narrative and add exotic colour. There was on occasion an
implied message, moral or political, which the reader might
detect beneath the plain text of the excursus. We may see the
method at work in two of the lengthiest ethnographic inter-
ludes in Diodorus, episodes which certainly derive from
Hieronymus and which present complex problems of interpretation. The first concerns a deeply impressive event that
occurred after the Battle of Paraetacene. The commander of
the Indian contingent, a prince named Ceteus, had died
heroically in battle. He had fought on Eumenes' left wing
with Eudamus (Diod. 19.27.2), and presumably fell while res-
isting the cavalry charge that turned Antigonus' fortunes at
the end of the battle.[18] He was perhaps the most notable
casualty of the engagement, and his funeral was spectacular.
It gives us the first recorded instance of the Indian institution of *sati* (widow burning). The prince's two wives competed for the honour of accompanying him on the pyre, and
after an investigation by the council of generals the elder
woman was found to be pregnant and the younger wife was

---

[16] Diod. 21.14.2 underlines Demetrius' generous treatment ($\pi\rho\sigma\sigma\eta\nu\dot{\epsilon}\chi\theta\eta$ $\tau o\hat{\imath}s$
$Bo\iota\omega\tau o\hat{\imath}s$ $\mu\epsilon\gamma\alpha\lambda o\psi\dot{\nu}\chi\omega s$).

[17] Compare Arr. 1.9.6–7 with Diod. 17.14.2; Justin 11.3.9–10.

[18] Diod. 19.30.9–10: see above, pp. 139–40.

given the privilege of death by fire. Her death was witnessed by the entire army, which marched three times round the pyre before it was ignited and then viewed the event with varying emotions of admiration, pity or outrage.[19]

Diodorus gives a very detailed description of the funeral, and there can be no doubt that he is resuming the account of Hieronymus, who fought at Paraetacene and was an eyewitness of events.[20] Accordingly we have a very vivid portrait of the doomed wife, resplendent in jewelled rings and an elaborate necklace with multiple tiers of carefully matched stones. She was led to the pyre in a state of exaltation, crowned with garlands and accompanied by her relatives, who intoned hymns in praise of her excellence, and she faced the rising flames in courageous silence.[21] We may well believe that Hieronymus experienced all the emotions he ascribes to the audience as a whole. But he did not merely describe the event; he gave an explanation of the custom, and a fanciful description of its origin. In the past Indian couples had married by choice, and since the choice often proved mistaken, many Indian ladies transferred their affections to others and removed their current husbands by poison. This deplorable practice led to the institution of *sati*. Wives would either burn alongside their dead husbands or live a life dishonoured, in perpetual widowhood.[22]

---

[19] Diod. 19.34.1–6. The reactions of the audience are very similar to those recorded when Alexander's men viewed the suicide of the Brahman sage Calanus (Arr. 7.3.5; Diod. 17.107.5). In more modern times the factual description of Hieronymus/Diodorus and its emotional charge is very strikingly paralleled in an account of a *sati* witnessed in 1825 by a British surgeon, Dr. Richard Kennedy. It is conveniently analysed by P. B. Courtwright, in *Sati. The Blessing and the Curse* 43–7.

[20] Hieronymus was wounded at Gabiene, and clearly experienced the entire campaign (Diod. 19.44.3 = *FGrH* 154 T 5). Cf. Jacoby, *RE* viii.1541, 1559; Hornblower, *Hieronymus* 11.

[21] Diod. 19.34.3–7. The procession to the pyre has been a prominent part of the performance of *sati* into modern times; it was carefully described by Kennedy (above, n. 19).

[22] Diod. 19.33.3: νόμον ἔθεσαν ὅπως συγκατακαίωνται τοῖς τετελευτηκόσιν ἀνδράσιν αἱ γυναῖκες πλὴν τῶν ἐγκύων ἢ τῶν ἐχουσῶν τέκνα, τὴν δὲ μὴ βουλομένην τῷ δόγματι πειθαρχεῖν χήραν μὲν εἶναι διὰ τέλους καὶ θυσιῶν καὶ τῶν ἄλλων νομίμων εἴργεσθαι διὰ παντὸς ὡς ἀσεβοῦσαν.

This explanation is curious, and is invariably attributed to Greek speculation, influenced by Cynic views on the free choice of sexual partners.[23] Many have argued that the explanation is not Hieronymus' own, but inherited from Onesicritus, who had Cynic sympathies and expressed them in his writing.[24] The argument is based on Strabo, who devotes a section to the curious customs of the Cathaei, the autonomous people immediately east of the river Hydraotes.[25] He cites instances of their obsession with physical beauty, naming Onesicritus as the source,[26] and then mentions another custom unique to the Cathaei: free choice of spouses and widow burning. He goes on to give exactly the same explanation as we find in Diodorus: wives had transferred their affections and either deserted or poisoned their husbands.[27] It is the same explanation, but is it from Onesicritus or from Hieronymus? It is hardly Cynic propaganda, for the free choice of sexual partners is represented as totally pernicious, its result pure murder. Nor can we argue that the section on the Cathaei is a unitary extract from Onesicritus. It could well be a *pot pourri*, combining material from a number of sources.[28] A few pages later, when Strabo discusses the size of the Indus delta, he places Onesicritus alongside

---

[23] Cf. K. Karttunen, *India and the Hellenistic World* 66: 'The explanation offered by Onesicritus—that wives were thus prevented from poisoning their husbands—seems to be purely Greek speculation.'

[24] So, with caution, Brown, *Onesicritus* 52, 75 ('the passage in Strabo may not be derived from Onesicritus'). Pearson, *LHA* 106 is more categorical. Karttunen loc. cit. has no doubts. See also Jesús Lens Tuero, 'En Catai y en reino de Sopites', in *Estudios sobre Diodoro de Sicilia* (Granada 1994) 23–31.

[25] Arr. 5.22.1, 3–4. On the location see *HCA* ii.327–9.

[26] Strabo 15.1.30 (699–700) = *FGrH* 134 F 21. Onesicritus is named explicitly for the statement that the Cathaeans choose their kings on the basis of physical beauty, and the sentence continues with a reference to the exposure of infants if they fail to meet statutory physical requirements. This last custom is also mentioned by Curtius (9.1.25), who presumably took it from Cleitarchus. It may be a separate report of the practice, perhaps influenced by Onesicritus, but there is a possiblity that Strabo referred to Cleitarchus for the material on infanticide and cited Onesicritus only for the choice of ruler.

[27] κατὰ τοιαύτην αἰτίαν, ὅτι ἐρῶσαί ποτε τῶν νέων ἀφίσταιντο τῶν ἀνδρῶν ἢ φαρμακεύοιεν αὐτούς.

[28] So Jacoby, *FGrH* ii D 477. The Indian custom of dying beards, which immediately follows the note on exposure, was also mentioned by Nearchus (Arr. *Ind.* 16.4 = *FGrH* 133 F 11), and Strabo may have already turned away from Onesicritus.

Aristobulus and Nearchus,[29] and when he cites successive details from Onesicritus, he makes their provenance clear.[30] Not so here. Strabo mentions the curious Cathaean insistence on beauty, cites Onesicritus for some specific instances and then turns to another curiosity. There is no reason to think that he continues to use Onesicritus rather than some other source. The probability is that Strabo is drawing on Hieronymus. He was familiar with the historian's record of Antigonus and used the famous description of bitumen collection in the Dead Sea.[31] The description of widow burning was equally famous, and is echoed repeatedly in later literature, most famously in Propertius.[32] It is reasonable to assume that the explanation of the custom was also well known, and that Strabo used it directly. In that case we have two separate versions of Hieronymus, transmitted by Diodorus and Strabo.

Strabo adds one detail to the fuller account of Diodorus: widow burning was a custom peculiar to a specific people, the Cathaei. That is a valuable piece of information. It proves that the deceased prince came from Cathaean territory. Now, the Cathaei had offered resistance to Alexander in 326. Their capital, Sangala, had been captured with massive loss of life, and they had been added to the realm of Alexander's viceroy and former enemy, Porus.[33] Alexander had achieved what Porus had previously attempted,[34] a successful annexation of their territory, and they were placed under the sway of their old enemy. They may have acquiesced for the moment in the

---

[29] Strabo 15.1.33 (701) = *FGrH* 139 F 48, 133 F 21, 134 F 26. Aristobulus is cited first, then Nearchus, and finally Onesicritus. Pearson, *LHA* 106 is quite incorrect when he states that Onesicritus 'mentions no other authority by name before citing him again three paragraphs later' (sc. after the material on the Cathaeans).

[30] Strabo 15.1.34 (701): φησὶ δ' Ὀνησίκριτος... λέγει δὲ καί (= *FGrH* 134 F 8, 35)

[31] Strabo 16.2.42 (763–4); cf. Diod. 2.48,6–8; 19.98. There is no doubt that Diodorus drew directly upon Hieronymus, and the correspondence with Strabo is such that 'Strabo has clearly used Hieronymus' (Hornblower, *Hieronymus* 148, cf. 251). For other, named, citations of Hieronymus see *FGrH* 154 F 16–18.

[32] Nicolaus of Damascus, *FGrH* 90 F 124; Cic. *Tusc.* 5.78; Prop. 3.13.15–22; Plut. *Mor.* 499B; Val. Max. 2.6.14; Philo *de Abr.* 182; Ael. *VH* 7.18. Cf. W. Heckel and J. C. Yardley, *Philologus* 125 (1981) 305–11.

[33] Arr. 5.29.2, 6.2.1. Cf. Bosworth, *HCA* ii 310, 357–8; *Alexander and the East* 20.

[34] Before Alexander arrived in the Punjab, Porus and his ally Abisares had invaded the lands of the Cathaei and the other autonomous peoples east of the Acesines, but with very little success (Arr. 5.22.2).

Macedonian conquest, but they can have had little love for Porus. There is no record of unrest under Alexander, but it is significant that Porus did not long survive his master's death. He was assassinated in 318 at the hands of Eudamus, the Macedonian military commander, and Eudamus went west with Porus' elephants and a modest contingent of 800 Indian troops led by a Cathaean prince.[35] It looks as though Porus met his end in Cathaean territory, perhaps suppressing insurrection, and his Macedonian lieutenant made common cause with his local enemies. They presented Eudamus with the late king's elephants, and sent a small expeditionary force to fight the war against Peithon. This was an alliance of convenience. The Cathaean rulers used Eudamus to destroy a hated overlord. In return they were willing to surrender the entire elephant stable and send a token contingent to the war in the west. They were autonomous again—until Chandragupta came and imposed a new sovereignty.

For our purposes the Indian prince is less important than his wife. Her death was profoundly impressive, something new to the experience of the Greek audience, which watched with the same rapt attention that European observers in the eighteenth and nineteenth centuries gave to the spectacle of *sati*. Widow burning had not been witnessed before. The closest Alexander's men had come to it was the suicide of the Brahman sage, Calanus, which was attended by much the same ceremonial, a solemn procession to the pyre, the chanting of hymns and the formal act of farewell by the army.[36] There is no comparable record of *sati*. All that the Alexander historians could report was rumour. Aristobulus claimed to have heard that there were some peoples which allowed wives to be burned alongside their husbands and disgraced those who did not comply.[37] Cleitarchus apparently mentioned the custom. In his description of the Cathaeans in Book 17 Diodorus mentions that it was customary for wives to burn alongside their husbands, and adds that the custom began as the response to a single instance of a husband being

---

[35] Diod. 19.14.8. See above, p. 107.
[36] Arr. 7.3.2–6. For detailed analysis see Bosworth, 'Calanus' 174–9.
[37] Strabo 15.1.62 (714) = *FGrH* 139 F 42.

poisoned.[38] This has much in common with Hieronymus, the localization among the Cathaei and the murder of spouses, but there is a significant difference—Cleitarchus referred to a single murder and knew nothing about marriage for love.[39] In Hieronymus there are multiple poisonings, and a background of sexual license.[40] Hieronymus was clearly using and embroidering earlier explanations, but in what context was he operating? Was he attempting to outdo his predecessors, concocting an amusing piece of ethnography which would satirize Cynic doctrines on the free choice of one's sexual partner, or was he transmitting material derived (through interpreters) from Indian informants?

There certainly are echoes of Hieronymus in earlier literature, most clearly in Herodotus' description of the marriage practices of the Thracians.[41] In that society wives competed eagerly for the honour of dying with their husbands, and not to be chosen was the deepest of disgraces; and the friends of the deceased choose the victim. Herodotus also contrasts the Thracians' sexual freedom before marriage with the strict control exercised later.[42] Interestingly he gives no explanation of the practice. It is the external features which correspond to Hieronymus' description, the competition for the right to die, the selection of a single victim, the disgrace of being passed over.[43] We can hardly deny that the event in Paraetacene

---

[38] Diod. 17.91.3: διὰ μίαν γυναῖκα φαρμάκοις ἀνελοῦσαν τὸν ἄνδρα.

[39] Curt. 9.1.26 claims that partners were chosen for physical beauty rather than birth, but he does not connect the practice with the murder of spouses, nor does he imply that the marital partners had free choice.

[40] This rules out Hornblower's suggestion (*Hieronymus* 94 n. 71) that the explanation of *sati* is taken from Cleitarchus and grafted onto the 'more austere' history of Hieronymus. It would seem that the subject matter of Hieronymus was often far from austere, and even the historical lion, Thucydides, was known to laugh on occasion.

[41] Hdt. 5.5. The killing of a wife along with the husband is presented as a practice peculiar to the people north of the Crestonians (for the location of Crestonia, at the headwaters of the Echedorus, see Hammond, *HM* i.179–81). That would appear to designate the peoples of the Upper Strymon, the Sinti, Maedi, and even the Agrianians. This was an area of interest to all Macedonians; a polygamous king of the Agrianians could be considered a possible match for a widowed Argead princess (Arr. 1.5.4).

[42] Hdt. 5.6.1. This, however, is a characteristic of the other Thracians, those who did not practice wife sacrifice.

[43] Cf. Heckel and Yardley (above, n. 32) 306 point out the differences: burial instead of cremation and slaughter at the grave (σφαγή) rather than self-immolation.

was accurately described, and the correspondences in the description reflect correspondences in fact. The two cultures had very similar institutions. Perhaps the satrapal commanders were aware of the Thracian analogue (it was after all close to their Macedonian homeland), and took on the role of the friends of the deceased. Hieronymus may even have laid particular emphasis on the disgrace of not being selected, so as to sharpen the cultural analogy.[44] But there is nothing in Herodotus to match the fanciful explanation of the custom. Admittedly the reader of Herodotus would find a certain curiosity about marital choice. A passage which is perhaps interpolated (but interpolated at an early stage) mentions the eccentric behaviour of the Athenian aristocrat, Callias, son of Phaenippus, who gave his three daughters the most pre-eminent gift—the right to choose their husbands.[45] The note of surprise is palpable[46] and typical of Greek attitudes. What is stressed is the extreme rarity and aberrancy of the phenomenon. It would not be a natural inference that the poisonings of spouses were the result of free and indiscreet choice, but, if Indian informants mentioned the motif, Greek enquirers would seize upon it and give it prominence. We have here our first indication that the fanciful explanation of *sati* is an elaboration upon material provided by Indians.

Unfortunately the evidence from Indian literary sources is rarely datable and always difficult to assess. However, the epic tradition does contain early material which sheds some light on what could have been reported to Hieronymus, and it can be supplemented by slightly later religious and political writings. What is clear is that there is no evidence that *sati* was a regular custom. In the epics the queens of fallen kings

[44] Cf. Hdt. 5.5: αἱ δὲ ἄλλαι συμφορὴν μεγάλην ποιεῦνται. Diod. 19.34.3: καθαπερεί τινος συμφορᾶς μεγάλης προσηγγελμένης. There may be a literary echo here.

[45] Hdt. 6.122. The passage is omitted in some of the best manuscripts, and it has been universally declared spurious on the basis of the irrelevance of its detail (but this is after all a Herodotean digression), the peculiarity of its terminology and its syntactical clumsiness. All this may be conceded, but there seems no doubt about the authenticity of the information it contains. Cf. Davies, *Athenian Propertied Families* 256–7, who attempts to trace the husbands of two of the daughters (one of them the father of Aristeides the Just).

[46] 6.122.2: ἔδωκέ σφι δωρέην μεγαλοπρεπεστάτην.

tend to live on as widows and without disgrace.[47] There is
clearly no compulsion to die. But neither was there in
Alexander's day. Both Aristobulus and Hieronymus mentioned that widows might survive their husbands, but were
condemned to perpetual widowhood. That corresponds to
the prescriptions of the orthodox Brahman, Manu, who recommended life-long austerity for a widow ('let her emaciate
her body by living on pure flowers, roots and fruits').[48]
Neither he nor any other writer recommends death by fire,
but much the same can be said of suicide in general. The
type of self-immolation performed by Calanus was definitely
not the norm, though there are traces of a belief that suicide
was appropriate if one had reached perfection, and a higher
existence might be achieved by entering the fire.[49] Calanus'
death was unusual and perhaps unorthodox, but it commanded respect from Indians and Greeks alike. The same
was perhaps true of *sati*. To join one's husband on the pyre
was the acme of wifely devotion and commanded wide
respect (as similar acts have done in recent years), but it certainly was not mandatory. The alternative was widowhood
and austerity. Hieronymus appears to have represented the
custom accurately, except that he represents the rigours of a
widow's life as a penal sanction. That it certainly was not,
but Hieronymus (and Aristobulus) may well have been told
that the state of a widow was so unappealing that many
women preferred the glory of a public death in the place
of honour.[50]

[47] The classic discussion is that of P. V. Kane, *History of Dharmaśāstra*
II.1.624–36. Cf. Romila Thapar, *A History of India* i.41: 'That "*sati*" was merely
symbolic during the Vedic period seems evident from the fact that later Vedic literature refers to the remarriage of widows, generally to the husband's brother.'

[48] Manu 5.156–8. (I refer to the edition by G. Bühler, *The Laws of Manu* (Sacred
Books of the East XXV: Oxford 1886).) The negative side is expressed at 5.161: if a
woman remarries to have offspring, she incurs disgrace in this world and loses her
place beside her husband in the next.

[49] For the evidence and general discussion see Bosworth, 'Calanus' 181–3.

[50] In practice their relatives may have made the choice for them. Note the
following observation on the dark and tragic case of Roop Kanwar, who was crem-
ated alongside her husband in Rajasthan in September, 1987: 'Either she could
return to her parents' home, taking back her dowry and dwelling sorrowfully there
(because widows find it impossible to marry in the class and circles to which she
belonged), or she could opt to remain with her parents-in-law...Either way, as
time went on, her sexuality would pose problems and be perceived as a threat to the

There was an impressive precedent in Indian tradition for the suicide of Ceteus' wife. One of the highlights of the *Mahābārata* is the death of King Pandu, who was overcome by desire for his young wife Madri and died in the act of intercourse.[51] His elder consort Kunti insisted on following him to the realms of the dead, but the younger wife objected that unlike Kunti she had not appeased her appetite, and it was right for her to follow and satisfy the carnal desires of her late husband. 'The king in seeking me wishfully has gone to the region of spirits; therefore my body should be burnt with his.' Kunti acknowledged the logic of the argument and allowed her younger rival to mount the pyre of Pandu. There are obvious similarities with Hieronymus' story. In both cases the claims of the younger wife are upheld, but for very different reasons. In the *Mahābārata* Madri argues in purely carnal terms. What was unconsummated in this life should be fulfilled in the next.[52] For Ceteus' wives the deciding point was the pregnancy of the elder woman; the generals were not prepared to condone infanticide, and decided for the younger woman to preserve the unborn child.[53] We cannot contest that the pregnancy was a significant factor, but the precedent of Madri may well have been cited, and the tradition of the death of Pandu may also have been adduced to support the act of *sati*. Ceteus, like Pandu, was a reigning prince, a member of the *kṣatriyas*, the warrior caste, and it would have been represented to the Greek generals that it was appropriate to follow epic precedent and allow a wife to join him on the pyre.

honour of both families; a *sati* would convert impending shame into glory. Therefore, persuading her to commit *sati* seemed an attractive expedient and a culturally acceptable solution' (V. T. Oldenburg, in *Sati* (above, n. 19) 118).

[51] *Mahābārata* 1.125 (I use the translation by Pratap Chandra Roy (New Delhi 1972)). The parallel was drawn long ago by Christian Lassen, *Indische Alterthumskunde* i². 2.592.

[52] 'My appetite hath not been appeased.... This foremost one of the Bharata princes had approached me, desiring to have intercourse. His appetite unsatiated, shall I not follow him in the region of Yama to gratify him?'

[53] Diod. 19.34.3. There is an interesting later parallel in the policy of the Mughal emperors, who disapproved of *sati* but tolerated it under strict supervision, excluding any women who had young children. Cf. V. N. Datta, *A Historical, Social and Philosophical Enquiry into the Hindu Rite of Widow Burning* (New Delhi 1987); A. Nandy, in *Sati. The Blessing and the Curse* 139–40.

Indian tradition surfaces elsewhere in the story. The most exotic feature of Hieronymus' explanation of the origins of *sati* is is his stress on romantic love. In archaic India there was free choice of partners. The spouses came together by choice, not as the result of parental agreement. As we have seen, it was a bizarre concept from the Greek perspective. Not so for the Indians. In the epics (and later) there are eight forms of marriage attested,[54] ranging from marriage by purchase negotiated by the parents to a kind of marriage by capture. Among those forms was the type known as *Gāndharva*. This was entirely an affair of love, proceeding from mutual attraction and concluded by mutual consent with or without parental approval. In the sour words of Manu, '*Gandharva* springs from the passion of love and has intercourse as its purpose.'[55] Although he disapproved of it in principle, he recognized that it was an appropriate form of marriage for the warrior caste, the *kṣatriyas*. The custom is at the heart of the most celebrated romance in Sanskrit literature, the story of King Duśmanta and Śākuntāla, which provided the theme for the classic play by Kālindāsa. In the *Mahābārata* Duśmanta explains the situation to his intended bride: 'The *Gandharva* and the *Rakshasa* form are consistent with the practices of *kṣatriyas*. You need not entertain the least fear. There is not the least doubt that either according to any one of these last-mentioned forms, or according to a union of either of them, our wedding may take place.' This is high romance, the stuff of fantasy, but it was part of Indian legend and probably Indian practice. It is alleged to have been customary for girl of marriageable age to find her

---

[54] Neatly listed at *Mahābārata* 1.73, and substantially repeated by Manu 3.27–34. Alexander's historians commented on the forms they experienced. Nearchus (Arr. *Ind.* 17.4 = *FGrH* 133 F 11) describes the selection of husbands through athletic competition, reminiscent to a Greek of Cleisthenes' trial of the suitors of his daughter Agariste. Megasthenes (Strabo 15.1.54 (709) = *FGrH* 715 F 32) reported marriage by purchase; this was the so-called *ārśa* mode (Manu 3.29). There was a wide variation in marital practice, and Greek visitors recorded the forms they happened to meet without attempting to give a full description.

[55] Manu 3.32. On the institution see Kane (above, n. 47) II.1.517, 519: 'It proceeded entirely from free love and mutual inclination of a youth and a maiden, and was concluded with the mutual consent and agreement of the couple without consulting their relatives.'

own husband if her father did not a secure an acceptable match within three years of her reaching puberty. This is the practice of *svayamvara*, which amounted to much the same as marriage in the *Gāndharva* mode.[56] It was perhaps reflected in the technical term *patimvarā*, describing girls of mature age who were free to choose their husbands.[57] The practice was far more akin to Indian culture than Greek, far more likely to come from Indian informants in the entourage of Hieronymus than from popular Greek philosophy.

The other feature of Hieronymus' explanation of *sati* is the poisoning of unwanted husbands. Once more there are ample parallels in Indian literature. The most striking examples come in the *Arthaśāstra*, a political treatise of the third century AD which embodies a good deal of earlier tradition Poison is omnipresent, a perpetual threat to the security of Indian princes and a potent weapon against their enemies. An elaborate taxonomy of poisons is given,[58] and there are several graphic instances of kings being removed by their consorts: 'The queen killed the king of Kāśī by mixing fried grain with honey under the guise of honey; (the queen killed) Vairantya with an anklet smeared with poison...'[59] None of these murders are associated with free love and the *Gāndharva* mode of marriage, but it is certainly possible that Hieronymus' informants made the connection. If so, it enabled him to go one step beyond Cleitarchus, who attributed the institution of *sati* to a single atrocity. It was rather a failure in the social structure. Divorce was in practice impossible.[60] Isolated texts like the *Arthaśāstra* appear to envisage the dissolution of *Gāndharva* marriages, but both partners needed to be alienated. If either was unwilling, divorce could not take

---

[56] Manu 9.90. For other references and discussion see Kane (above, n. 47) II.1.522–3.

[57] Pāṇini III.2.46; cf. V. S. Agrawala, *India as Known to Pāṇini* 88.

[58] *Arthaśāstra*, 2.17.12. Elaborate tests for the detection of poison (1.21.4–11; political poisonings (5.1.19, 30–2, 34–6.

[59] *Arthaśāstra*, 1.20.16. It is recommended that the king only visit his queen after she has been cleared by old female attendants. For cross references to the epic tradition see R. P. Kangle, *The Kauṭilīya Arthaśāstra* 50.

[60] Cf. Kane (above, n. 47) II.1.619–23. Normally divorce was only possible in exceptional cases, when for instance the husband proved to be a madman or an eunuch (Manu 9.79).

place.[61] In such a social context it was easy to build a composite picture of mass poisoning by disillusioned wives, resulting in systematic, legalized widow burning.

The linkage of the motifs may well be the work of Hieronymus. He was clearly influenced by Indian tradition, relayed by Indian informants. They may have mentioned the saga of Kunti and Madri, talked of marriage by the *Gāndharva* mode, referred to sensational cases of poisoning within the royal houses. Hieronymus could have received a practical education in Indian society and tradition, which he distilled into a pretty piece of moralizing. The Indians had proved the dangers of the free choice of partners. This was not an attack on Diogenes as such. The founder of Cynicism had indeed advocated free choice of partners, but it was a kind of sexual communism, with changing liaisons based on mutual consent (τὸν πείσαντα τῇ πεισθείσῃ συνεῖναι).[62] Marriage was not the desired institution. We come closer to the Indian tradition with the famous association between the lady philosopher, Hipparchia, and her consort, Crates, one of Diogenes' earliest followers. Hipparchia did choose Crates against the violent opposition of her parents, married him in spite of his poverty and hump back, and shared his itinerant life, deeply shocking conventional moralists.[63] This was a marriage in the real sense, a marriage which according to Epictetus arose out of sexual passion and similar interests.[64] In that it differed from conventional Greek marriages, but closely resembled the Indian paradigm of Duśmanta and Śākuntāla—except that its context was itinerant poverty, not the splendour of a royal court.

----

[61] *Arthaśāstra* 3.3.15–16: 'A disaffected wife is not to be granted divorce from a husband who is unwilling, nor the husband from the wife. By mutual disaffection (alone) a divorce (shall be granted).'

[62] Diog. Laert. 6.72 (cf. 29, 54): wives and children are to be held in common; marriage was excluded (γάμον μηδὲ ὀνομάζων). Cf. J. Rist, *Stoic Philosophy* (Oxford 1969) 56–62; M. Billerbeck, in *The Cynics* (Berkeley 1996) 210.

[63] Diog. Laert. 6.96–7; Apul. *Flor.* 14; Clem. Alex. *Strom.* 4.19.121; Suda s.vv. Ἱππαρχία, Κράτης.

[64] Epictet. 3.22.76: the union is cited as a rare exception to the Cynic view that the sage should not marry—Hipparchia was another Crates. Crates himself was apparently contemptuous of marriage; according to Eratosthenes (Diog. Laert. 6.88–9 = FGrH 241 F 21) he introduced his son, Pasicles, to a brothel and declared that this was his father's type of marriage (τοῦτον αὐτῷ πατρῷον εἶναι τὸν γάμον).

Could Crates and Hipparchia have been in Hieronymus' mind when he drafted his description of *sati*? It is difficult to judge, but there seems a fair probability. The couple were notorious figures, habitués of royal courts. Hipparchia at least had a celebrated exchange with Theodorus of Cyrene, the so-called 'atheist', at a symposium hosted by Lysimachus,[65] and the pair could well have appeared in Demetrius' entourage after the liberation of Athens in 307. What was notorious about their behaviour was their propensity to have sex in public (the embarrassed Zeno rigged up a makeshift screen to preserve his master's modesty[66]), and it is interesting that their behaviour was compared with that of Indian peoples.[67] What was disgraceful in Greek eyes was not so among the less inhibited Indians. There may be an echo here of a wider comparison. Crates and Hipparchia were western exemplars of alien values, in their free choice of marital partners and their flamboyant sexual behaviour. To any who found the example attractive Hieronymus gave a sobering object lesson. The free choice of partners was dangerous. Crates and Hipparchia may have stayed together and had a son, but Indian tradition had proved such marriages dangerous. The marital partners repented at leisure and resorted to murder. As a result stringent sanctions were imposed, ushering in an age of virtue. If there is a deliberate message in the story, it was directed against the Cynics and their most notorious example of sexual license.

But there need be no direct polemic in the story. Hieronymus may simply be weaving together separate strands of Indian tradition: marriage by consent, the murder of kings by their queens, the tradition of widows embracing death by fire. As we have seen, Aristobulus and Cleitarchus

---

[65] Diog. Laert. 6.97–8. At that time Theodorus was acting as ambassador for Ptolemy (Diog. Laert. 2.102), after he left Athens under a cloud during the regime of Demetrius of Phalerum. Cf. M. Winiarczyk, *Philologus* 125 (1981) 64–94, esp. 69; L.-L. O'Sullivan, *CQ* 47 (1997) 136–52, esp. 143–6.

[66] Apul. *Flor.* 14: 'coramque uirginem inminuisset paratam pari constantia, ni Zeno procinctu palliastri circumstantis coronae obtutu<m> magistri in secreto defendisset.'

[67] Sext. Emp. *Pyr.* 3.200: καίτοι παρ' ἡμῖν αἰσχρὸν εἶναι δοκοῦν, παρά τισι τῶν Ἰνδῶν οὐκ αἰσχρὸν εἶναι· νομίζεται· μίγνυνται γοῦν ἀδιαφόρως δημοσίᾳ, καθάπερ καὶ περὶ τοῦ φιλοσόφου Κράτητος ἀκηκόαμεν.

paved the way by mentioning the practice of *sati*, and bringing in the motif of poisoning. Hieronymus represented husband murder as more prevalent, and associated it with the Indian *Gāndharva* marriages. The separate themes are Indian, but the composite story and its negative moral charge are Greek. Hieronymus and his predecessors would have listened to reports of Indian social tradition, but interpreted what they heard against their own experience and cultural values. There is another, more trivial, instance in the Greek representation of the name of the deceased prince. According to Diodorus he was named Ceteus, and it has long been recognized that this is a rendering of a Sanskrit name ending in -*ketu* ('banner'), highly appropriate for a *kṣatriya* prince.[68] But the name is adapted to a Greek form, and is a Greek proper name. Admittedly it is rare, and the rarity gives it a piquant edge. Apart from a legendary king of Arcadia[69] the only known example is a citizen of Tanagra who was commemorated by Ephorus. He was the fattest man in the city, and was therefore named after a whale (κῆτος).[70] This was a famous story, and the 'Tanagraean physique' became proverbial. It was surely known to the Greeks in Eumenes' army. If the Indian prince was built of epic proportions, a bull among men like King Pandu himself, then it would be a pleasant conceit to render his name in a form which drew attention to his impressive stature. The Indian name is roughly reproduced, but it is transmitted in a form that evokes a Greek parallel and a Greek context.[71] The same is true of the entire episode. On the one hand we have a detailed and vivid description of a spectacular event, the immolation of Ceteus' wife. There is an epic atmosphere, the Indian participants reliving the story of Kunti and Madri. The generals probably saw themselves as the counterparts of the Thracian elders, deciding on the wife who was to join her husband on

---

[68] The suggestion was made two centuries ago by A. W. von Schlegel, and adopted by Lassen, *Indische Landeskunde* iii². 1.347 n. 2. So O. Wecker, *RE* xi.362; Karttunen, *India and the Hellenistic World* 66 n. 283.

[69] Pherecydes, *FGrH* 3 F 157; Araethus ap. Hygin. *Astr.* 2.1.6; Schol. in Eur. *Or.* 1646 (i.237 Schwartz).

[70] Hesych. s.v. Ταναγραίων φυήν = Ephorus, *FGrH* 70 F 115.

[71] For a less successful adaptation, involving a gross misunderstanding of the Sanskrit, see Plut. *Al.* 65.5 with Bosworth, 'Calanus' 192–4.

the pyre. In that role (perhaps self-assumed) they were able to glean a considerable amount of detail about Indian tradition and practices. However, they could not interpret it in depth against an Indian background. The information was necessarily filtered through their own experiences and adapted to their own values. Accordingly the origins of *sati*, as Hieronymus expounded them, became an improving story which reinforced traditional Greek moral values and quite probably had a contemporary message.

This blend of factual reportage and *interpretatio Graeca* recurs in Hieronymus' most famous ethnographic digression, his account of the customs and lifestyle of the Nabataean Arabs. This is set in the context of the Antigonid operations in the Jordanian desert over the winter of 312/11 BC.[72] The episode is highly intriguing. It was in fact a chapter of disasters—at least as Hieronymus represented it. An unprovoked surprise attack by Antigonus' general, Athenaeus, resulted in the virtual annihilation of his expeditionary force. In the sequel a punitive expedition led by Demetrius was hardly more successful. The prince lost the advantage of surprise, unsuccessfully laid siege to a Nabataean stronghold and made a truce with the enemy, a truce which his father roundly criticized. The expedition at least made the Antigonids aware of the profitable trade in bitumen from the Dead Sea, and they attempted to control its collection and distribution. Hieronymus himself was put in charge of the operation, but, as he frankly admits, the local resistance was insuperable. He lost most of his men to a concerted Arab attack, and the bitumen harvesting was discontinued. This is a most remarkable document of failure, and the agents of the disaster are portrayed in vivid terms as nomads, absolutely and dogmatically opposed to settled habitation and agriculture and passionately committed to autonomy. The message is epitomized in an address to Demetrius by a Nabataean elder, to which the prince apparently has no reply. As Diodorus reports it, we have an improving story of the triumph of the free nomad over the unlimited imperial designs of the Antigonids.

[72] On the chronology, which fortunately does not affect the present discussion, see below, p. 229.

The story is usually taken at face value because of the involvement of Hieronymus in the action.[73] He was at the Antigonid court, in direct contact with Antigonus' planning, and if he did not go into the desert with Demetrius, he will have been aware of Demetrius' report of his campaign. And he supervised the commercial exploitation which followed. Hence we have a classic report by a contemporary on operations in which he participated in person. But the details as reported should evoke disquiet rather than confidence. Hieronymus reports a personal failure, and the failure is set in a wider context of misfortune and incompetence. The parallel in historiography is Thucydides' account of the loss of Amphipolis, where the reticence and sheer evasiveness of the narrative has always attracted comment. Thucydides makes a feature of his swift return from Thasos at the news of Brasidas' attack; he could not prevent the loss of Amphipolis but at least preserved the port of Eion for Athens.[74] However, there is no explanation why he was in Thasos in the first place,[75] and he tactfully omits the fact that he was subsequently exiled. That only emerges later, when he explains why he was in a position to record events from the Peloponnesian side.[76]

With Hieronymus we face a similar situation. He was an eyewitness, but also the principal agent in a significant defeat, and (in Diodorus' version at least) he provided singularly few details. His exact brief is not spelled out. He is termed simply

[73] As usual, Droysen (ii².2.55–9) did little more than paraphrase Diodorus, and the standard article of F. M. Abel, 'L' expédition des Grecs à Pétra en 312 avant J.-C.', *Rev. Bibl.* 46 (1937) 373–91, is largely devoted to a vindication of Diodorus' account (cf. 376: 'La relation de l'expédition grecque en Nabatène dérive directement ou indirectement d'un témoin oculaire qui est non pas un rhéteur mais un homme d'action vivant depuis 316 dans intimité d'Antigone . . .'). See also G. W. Bowersock, *Roman Arabia* 12–16; Billows, *Antigonos* 130–1.

[74] Thuc. 4.104.4–5, 106.3.

[75] Cf. S. Hornblower, *A Commentary on Thucydides* ii.334: 'Speculation is futile: our only evidence is what Th. himself tells us, which on this point is nothing at all.'

[76] Thuc. 5.26.5. Gomme (*A Historical Commentary on Thucydides* iii.585) exclaims (without a hint of irony) 'how characteristic of him to mention this only on a different occasion, in explaining his opportunities as a historian'. The exile was surely pertinent to the military and political situation in Athens during 424, and the historian who had noted the punishment of the generals in Sicily a few months before (4.65.3–4) might have been expected to comment on his own fate.

'superintendent' (ἐπιμελητής) of the new source of revenue.[77] Jacoby accordingly stated dogmatically that his position was non-military.[78] That is most unlikely, given that he was depriving the local population of an important source of income, and he could expect that the peoples which had formerly fought each other over the bitumen (Diod. 19.99.1) would combine against him. He must have had troops to fight off attack, and their numbers were probably substantial. Antigonus had instructed him to build ships, and ships he built. How many we are not told;[79] the scale of the operations is elusive. We are simply informed that there was an attack on makeshift reed rafts by 6,000 Arabs—a huge number, more than half the figure Hieronymus gave for the entire Nabataean population[80] and comparable to the army of 8,000 which destroyed Athenaeus' forces.[81] As a result almost all the crews engaged in the bitumen harvesting were killed. We inevitably recall the earlier story of the Nabataean night attack on Athenaeus, but this time there is no background information, no attempt to explain why Hieronymus' ships were caught at work by a large force of assailants, and were apparently taken by surprise. There are eloquent silences here, silences which we cannot ascribe simply to omission in Diodorus. Hieronymus, to put it mildly, was economical with the truth when it came to his own failure, and the wider context may also be affected.

---

[77] Diod. 19.100.1. Jos. *c. Ap.* 1.213 (*FGrH* 154 F 6) states the Hieronymus was a friend of Antigonus and 'administered Syria' (τὴν Συρίαν ἐπετρόπευεν). That suggests a regional command, not limited to a single function, but Josephus is not concerned to define Hieronymus' precise office, only to show that he should have had knowledge of the Jews, and his terminology cannot be pressed.

[78] *RE* viii.1541: 'Es war kein militärisches und offenbar ein nur vorübergehendes Kommando.' Hornblower, *Hieronymus* 12–13 more plausibly suggests that Hieronymus was designated to a permanent office, a regional military command (cf. Billows, *Antigonos* 391, who suggests that he might have been 'governor of Koile Syria (modern Palestine)'.

[79] Abel (above, n. 73) 391 writes imaginatively of 'la petite flotte grecque'. Diodorus (19.100.1–2) mentions πλοῖα with no hint of their number, great or small.

[80] Diod. 19.99.2; cf. 94.4 (total population—male of course—not much more than 10,000). The attack was probably not wholly or largely launched by the Nabataeans. Most of the assailants will have been resident on the coasts of the Dead Sea, the more settled tribes adjacent to the Syrian tributaries of the Antigonids (Diod. 19.94.10).   [81] Diod. 19.95.5.

One of the most obvious omissions is the motivation for the Antigonid operations against the Nabataeans. Diodorus states laconically that Antigonus adjudged the people 'hostile to his interests'.[82] There is no attempt to define what the Nabataean hostility was. One is tempted to infer that the Nabataeans had some sort of relations with Ptolemaic Egypt, but that is not implied by Diodorus. Indeed he implies the direct opposite: the Nabataean passion for liberty was such that they avoided relations with any outside power, and they considered that landed property was a positive inducement to aggression.[83] The Nabataean commitment to freedom is the first thing Diodorus emphasizes, and he implies that Antigonus' intention was outright conquest. Such at least is the message of the speech of the Nabataean elder: it is profitless to subjugate us, for you would gain nothing but despondent slaves who could not change their customs.[84] What the elder is envisaging is conquest and the forcible imposition of a sedentary agricultural economy, much like the settlement Alexander had imposed on the Cossaean mountaineers in winter 324/3, forcing them to be the agrarian workforce for new garrison cities. The speech is a classic defence of freedom against imperialism, and that for Hieronymus was at the basis of the clash between the Antigonids and the Nabataeans. Antigonus, as Diodorus repeatedly emphasizes, had designs of universal empire.[85] The Nabataeans gave an undesirable example of liberty, and could be represented as a standing encouragement for subjects to revolt or non-subjects to avoid submission. The Nabataean hostility, or rather incompatibility, is therefore represented as the fundamental reason for Antigonus' attack.

The antithesis between empire and liberty comes out in its strongest form in the ethnographical digression which follows the report of Antigonus' decision to attack the Nabataeans. Their nomadic way of life is described as extreme. They sow no crops, plant no trees (and avoid the temptation to cultivate vines by abjuring wine altogether); instead they eat

---

[82] Diod. 19.94.2: κρίνας ... τὸ ἔθνος τοῦτο τῶν ἑαυτοῦ πραγμάτων ἀλλότριον εἶναι Cf. 18.23.3.   [83] Diod. 19.94.3–4.

[84] Diod. 19.97.5: οὔθ' ἡμᾶς δύνασαι συναναγκάσαι βίον ζῆν ἕτερον, ἀλλά τινας αἰχμαλώτους ἕξεις δούλους ἀθύμους καὶ ζῆν οὐκ ἂν ὑπομείναντας ἐν ἄλλοις νομίμοις.

[85] Diod. 18.47.5; 19.56.2; 20.106.4.

meat, drink milk, and gather naturally growing foodstuffs like the pepper and date honey.[86] Above all they construct no permanent dwellings, and actually impose the death penalty for any infringement of custom. This is rigid, doctrinaire nomadism, its object to deny a potential invader any permanent, exploitable acquisition. Diodorus' description is vivid and categorical, but its literal truth is highly debatable.[87] Admittedly there are few archaeological remains from the early Nabataean period. It now seems likely that the Nabataeans moved from north-east Arabia between the sixth and fourth centuries BC and established themselves in what was their later heartland, the area between Aqaba and the Dead Sea, with a ceremonial centre located at Petra. Few material traces have been found of their early presence, but it does seem that there were permanent houses at Petra at the end of the fourth century, and there was imported Greek ceramic ware, the earliest a fragment of an Athenian lamp dating to the late fourth or early third century BC.[88] It is therefore unlikely that there was a stringent prohibition against permanent habitations. It is also improbable that there was an absolute prohibition on the drinking of wine. The vine was not cultivated, but the Nabataeans were wealthy enough to import wine, and according to Strabo's source later Nabataean rulers held elaborate symposia where

---

[86] This characterization of the Nabataeans is almost invariably compared with that of the biblical Rechabites (cf. Abel 378: Hornblower, *Hieronymus* 145; A. Negev, *ANRW* II.8 (1977) 528), who are alleged to have had the same prescriptive tradition: 'You shall not drink wine, neither you nor your sons for ever; you shall not build a house; you shall not sow seed; you shall not plant or have a vineyard; but you shall live in tents all your days' (Jer. 35.6–7). It is, however, fanciful to suppose that there was a primitive tradition of nomadism which both groups shared. Nothing suggests that the Rechabites were nomads (cf. F. S. Frick, in *The Anchor Bible Dictionary* (New York 1992) v. 630–2), and it is highly unlikely that the Nabataeans were influenced by customs of austerity existing in Edom before their arrival.

[87] It is largely accepted in modern literature as factually accurate. Abel (above, n. 73) 376–80 defended it at length against the critique of G. Dalman; see also Hornblower, *Hieronymus* 145–6. On the other hand D. F. Graf, *ARAM* 2 (1990) 51–3, has attacked Diodorus' account as an exaggerated, 'stylized literary description'.

[88] R. Wenning, *Die Nabatäer—Denkmäler und Geschichte* 200–1. M. Lindner, *Petra und das Königreich der Nabatäer* 47–8.

up to 11 cups could be drained at a sitting.[89] If that is true, there was hardly a strong tradition of abstinence.

There is clear exaggeration. We may concede that most of the Nabataeans would indeed have lived as nomads, without settled habitations or access to wine, and much of Hieronymus' description may be accepted. He makes it clear that they had considerable sophistication in hydrology and describes the underground cisterns which were presumably shown to Athenaeus and Demetrius during their crossing of the Negev.[90] He also notes that they were literate and could send dispatches in Aramaic (or conceivably cuneiform). The fact that the Nabataeans were nomads did not make them primitives. They amassed considerable wealth from their activities as middlemen in the incense trade between the Levant and South Arabia, and Diodorus states that they were the richest of the Arab peoples of the desert.[91] That made it all the more pressing to preserve their independence, and for Hieronymus the nomadic life was enforced in order to make conquest an impossibility. It is here that the distortion lies. The terrain of the Nabataeans had to be waterless and inaccessible. In fact the area around Petra has relatively plentiful rain, some 400 mm. each year,[92] and is potentially cultivable. Hieronymus exaggerated the desert conditions, and created an environment which was ideal for nomads and intractable for civilized invaders. In the same way the nomadic customs of the Nabataean were translated into a rigid code, enforced by the

[89] Strab. 16.4.26 (783). Bowersock (above, n. 73) 16–17 notes the apparent transformation of Nabataean society between Hieronymus and Strabo, and comments: 'It is a difficult matter to trace the course of this alteration.' The difficulty is less if the nomadic customs were less extreme and less prevalent than Diodorus' description would have us believe.

[90] Cf. A. Negev, *PEQ* 108 (1976) 128; *ANRW* II.8 (1977) 527, where it is claimed that the geomorphology of the central Negev consists of soft and hard limestone, with valleys covered by clayey loess. That is consistent with Diodorus' description of the Nabataean cisterns hollowed out of earth which is either clayey or of soft stone (19.94.7; cf. 2.48.2).

[91] Diod. 19.94.4–5. The trade route was familiar to Eratosthenes in the mid-2nd century: he gave figures for the distances between Heroonpolis in Egypt to 'Petra of the Nabataeans' and from Petra to Babylonia (Strab. 16.4.2 (767)).

[92] Cf. Negev (cited above, n. 86). According to David Kennedy (personal letter) 'much of the Nabataean area is not really desert at all—steppe and cultivable if water is harvested'.

death penalty. There were to be no exceptions; the Nabataeans represented the *ne plus ultra* of nomadic culture. And their institutions were not simply passed on unthinkingly by tradition; they had a theoretical justification, to preserve autonomy, and were enforced by law as well as custom.

Hieronymus was explicit and emphatic, and Diodorus was sufficiently impressed by his account to reuse it twice in Book II:[93] it was the classic account of Nabataean institutions, stressing that they defended their liberty effectively against successive invasions. None of the canonical series of imperial powers, Assyrians, Medes, Persians, or Macedonians, were able to subjugate them.[94] The description affected the second-century Alexandrian geographer, Agatharchides of Cnidus, who rhapsodized over the wealth of the Nabataean herds and the just lives of the early Nabataeans, who were corrupted by the Ptolemaic trade in the gulf of Aqaba, preying on shipwrecked sailors and embarking on naval piracy. This fall from grace resulted ultimately in a punitive expedition by the navy of Ptolemy II.[95] For Agatharchides the previous generations of Nabataeans had been characterized by their morality (δικαιοσύνη). They had been content to be self-sufficient, but were corrupted by the Egyptian trade in luxuries. For him it is moral uprightness, not liberty, which was the characteristic of the nomad Nabataeans. Both themes recur in earlier literature on nomadic peoples, most notably what is said about the Scyths of the north. For Herodotus the Scythians attacked by Darius of Persia were total nomads. What strikes him as most remarkable is their capacity to escape any invader. That is because they have no cities or fortifications but are completely mobile, living from their herds, not from agriculture, and living in wagons (Hdt. 4.46.2–3).

---

[93] Diod. 2.48.1–9; a shorter version is inserted into the digest of Ctesias at 2.1.5–6.

[94] Diod. 2.1.5, 48.6. The sequence of empire was a Herodotean concept (Hdt. 1.95ff.), and the progression from Assyrians to Medes, Persians, Macedonians and finally Romans became canonical and commonplace. Hieronymus, however, marks an early stage of development.

[95] Diod. 3.43.4–5; Strab. 16.4.18 (777); cf. S. M. Burstein, *Agatharchides of Cnidus on the Erythraean Sea* 151–2. On Agatharchides see in general Fraser, *Ptolemaic Alexandria* i.539–50; Burstein 12–36. For the conjectural placing of the punitive expedition in the reign of Philadelphus see Fraser ii.301, n. 350.

Here we have an exact parallel to Hieronymus' description, except that his Nabataeans live in tents, not the characteristic Scythian wagon, which had attracted the curiosity of the Greeks from at least the time of Hesiod.[96] The prohibition on wine also recalls some famous passages of Herodotus. The Ethiopians had no knowledge of it, and their king was mightily impressed by his first tasting. More strikingly still, wine was the downfall of the nomad Massagetae, who took full advantage of the elaborate banquet laid out for them by Cyrus and were subsequently mopped up in a helpless state of collective inebriation.[97] Real nomads, then, did not drink wine, but it was a standing temptation; the prohibition required the sanction of the death penalty which the Nabataeans enacted.

There was another line of speculation, found in its most developed form in Ephorus, which derived from Homer's praise of the Abii, the most just of men.[98] This people was identified with the Scythians of the north, who subsisted on milk like the neighbours of the Abii in Homer and led what was considered a particularly moral life. They were frugal, with little material wealth, and held all things in common. According to Ephorus the result was that the Scyths were invincible, since their poverty made them unattractive to aggressors.[99] The motif was exploited during Alexander's campaigns when he encountered the Saca peoples of Central Asia, who were considered akin to (and virtual neighbours of) the Scyths of northern Europe.[100] Alexander received the

[96] Hesiod F 151 (Merkelbach and West): Phineus was taken by the Harpies 'to the land of the Milk Eaters who have waggons as homes'. Cf. Aesch. *PV* 709–11.

[97] Hdt. 3.22.3–4 (Ethiopians); 1.211.2–212.2 (Cyrus and the Massagetae) On abstention from wine as a characteristic of nomads see F. Hartog, *The Mirror of Herodotus* 166–70. Interestingly the Massagetae are an analogue of the Nabataeans, in that they sow no crops, subsist on meat and fish and drink milk (Hdt. 1.216.3–4). They were invincible until they were ensnared by the demon drink, and proved the necessity to legislate against it.

[98] Strab. 7.3.9 (302–3) = Ephorus, *FGrH* 70 F 42 (the passage is also transmitted in abbreviated form by Anon. *Peripl. P. Eux.* 494 = *FGrH* 70 F 158). The Homeric line which inspired the discussion is *Il.* 14.1: Γλακτοφάγων Ἀβίων τε δικαιοτάτων ἀνθρώπων.

[99] *FGrH* 70 F 42: πρός τε τοὺς ἐκτὸς ἄμαχοί εἰσι καὶ ἀνίκητοι, οὐδὲν ἔχοντες ὑπὲρ οὗ δουλεύσουσι.

[100] The identification of Scyths and Sacae first occurs in Herodotus (7.64.2), and was transmitted by Choerilus (Strab. 7.3.9 (303)) and Ephorus (*FGrH* 70 F 158). By Alexander's time it was a commonplace (*HCA* i.289).

surrender of a people whom he identified as Homer's Abii. They lived an impoverished, nomadic existence in the salt desert west of Sogdiana, untroubled by others because of their lack of resources and giving trouble to nobody.[101] They were the eastern counterparts of Ephorus' Scythians, and they had the good sense to recognize Alexander and surrender their autonomy to him.

Other Sacan peoples were less accommodating. When Alexander was faced by the tribes massing north of the Syr-Darya, he crossed the river and routed them.[102] He identified them as European Scyths, and was no doubt determined to show that, despite what Herodotus and Ephorus had claimed, they were not insuperable—and the submission of the local king provided the proof. Whatever Alexander may have thought, his historians were familiar with earlier ethnographical writing and exploited it. The most interesting passage for our purposes is Curtius' story (7.8.8–9.2) of the Sacan embassy which attempted to deter Alexander from crossing the Syr-Darya. The senior delegate is given a long rhetorical speech, excoriating Alexander's imperial ambitions and stressing the poverty and remoteness of his own people which will give them victory. Unlike Alexander they have no baggage and have a mobility that he cannot match.[103] He also underlines his people's independence; they cannot be slaves and they have no desire to gain empire.[104] Poverty, autonomy, and morality go together and are contrasted unfavourably with Alexander's overweening imperial ambition. Under the thick veneer of Roman rhetoric the essentials of this tirade derive from Curtius' source. He claims that he is correctly transmitting material from the tradition,[105] and there is

---

[101] Arr. 4.1.1; Curt. 7.6.11; cf. Bosworth, *HCA* ii.13–15; *Alexander and the East* 151–2.

[102] Arr. 4.3.6, 4.1–5.1; Curt. 7.7.1–29, 8.1–9.19; *Metz Epit.* 8, 10–12. For commentary see Bosworth, *HCA* ii.22, 27–32.

[103] Curt. 7.8.22: 'transi modo Tanain: scies quam late pateant; nunquam consequeris Scythas. paupertas nostra velocior erit quam exercitus tuus, qui praedam tot nationum vehit...(23) at nos deserta et humano cultu vacua magis quam urbes et opulentos agros sequimur.'

[104] Curt. 7.8.16: 'nec servire ulli possumus, nec imperare desideramus.'

[105] Curt. 7.8.11: 'sed, ut possit oratio eorum sperni, tamen fides nostra non debet; quae, utcumque sunt tradita, incorrupta perferemus.' On this passage and its

every likelihood that Cleitarchus[106] mentioned an embassy
and a message of warning expressed in straightforward,
unpolished language. Curtius has dressed up the message in
a formal speech full of proverbs and rhetorical saws, but,
unless we assume that he is deliberately lying, we must conclude that his source did give some report of the content of
the Sacan envoy's address and that the themes included an
attack on unbridled imperialism and a warning of the
military advantages of poverty and mobility.

The envoy's speech (or part of it) finds a clear resonance in
Hieronymus' report of the rebuke of Demetrius by the
Nabataean elder. There is the same protest against unprovoked aggression, the same insistence on the advantages of
the terrain for the defenders, the same warning that liberty is
not negotiable. Above all there is the challenge of a senior
spokesman of the nomadic peoples, a challenge in both cases
offered frontally to a young and ambitious empire builder.
Both Alexander and Demetrius listen respectfully[107] and,
unlike Alexander, Demetrius digests the lesson and makes a
negotiated withdrawal. Some underlying political comment
may easily be traced here. There is an implicit opposition to
wars of conquest for conquest's sake, where there are no obvious profits to be made or military threats to be countered.
Both speeches warn of nemesis, the possibility of military
disaster, and underlying both is the premise that the nomadic
peoples cannot be effectively conquered. If Curtius' account
does derive ultimately from Cleitarchus, then we have a condemnation of imperialism that is virtually contemporary
with the Antigonid attacks upon the Nabataeans, and there

---

probable derivation from Cleitarchus see Baynham, *Alexander the Great. The
Unique History of Quintus Curtius* 87–9.

[106] It cannot be proved that Cleitarchus is the source, but the tradition is not
found in Arrian, who knows nothing of a Sacan embassy before the crossing, and
the interest in barbarian wisdom recalls Curtius' treatment of the Median astrologer
'Cobares', who delivers a similar address, peppered with proverbs and aphorisms.
This speech too is presented as an example of barbarian *prudentia* (7.4.13; cf.
Bosworth, *Alexander. and the East* 150). In this case the episode has its counterpart
in Diodorus (17.83.7–8, where the speaker is named Bagodares), and clearly derives
from the vulgate tradition and ultimately Cleitarchus. So Hammond, *Three
Historians of Alexander the Great* 61, who regards the story as fiction.

[107] Diod. 19.97.6; Curt. 7.9.1.

may be a strong element of propaganda. Anyone reading the warning of the Saca chieftain might well have thought of Athenaeus' fiasco in the desert,[108] and drawn the conclusion that nomadic peoples were best left to their own devices—which presumably was Ptolemaic policy. Hieronymus would have shared that viewpoint; the negative tone which suffuses Diodorus' references to Antigonus' imperial ambitions[109] suggests that he had little sympathy for conquest for its own sake. But in his case there was a strong ulterior motive to stress the failures. If he could represent the Nabataeans as unconquerable, it helped excuse his own debacle. Accordingly he described the customs of the Nabataeans—with some exaggeration—in language that recalled the classic descriptions of the Scythian nomads of Europe; their mobility and independence made them invincible. Diodorus sums it up in a pregnant sentence: 'being difficult to overcome in war, they continue to avoid slavery'.[110] No imperial power had ever subdued them, and the Antigonid invasion was doomed to failure. So, we conclude, was the attempt to exploit their resources in the Dead Sea; it was impossible to guard against the perpetual danger of a nomad attack. Hieronymus' mission was therefore doomed from the start.

Hieronymus' narrative, we have seen, presupposes that Antigonus had plans of conquest. However, what is actually reported hardly supports his interpretation. The first attack, led by Athenaeus, was clearly not intended to occupy Nabataean territory.[111] Quite the reverse. According to

---

[108] Athenaeus might be seen as the textbook example of an army emburdened by loot falling victim to a more mobile nomadic adversary (see Curt. 7.8.22, quoted above, n. 103).

[109] Diod. 18.41.4–5, 47.5, 50.1–2,5 (cf. Plut. *Eum.* 12.1–2), 54.4; 19.55.4–6, 56.2; 20.106.3–4; 21.1.1. There is an explicit condemnation of Antigonus' excessive passion for empire at Plut. *Demetr.* 28.2. One may concede with Billows, *Antigonos* 319–20, that some of these passages represent the propaganda of Antigonus' enemies or serve as an indirect eulogy of Eumenes, but it cannot be denied that Hieronymus repeatedly emphasized Antigonus' ambitions and had no sympathy for them.

[110] Diod. 2.48.4: ὄντες δυσκαταπολέμητοι, διατελοῦσιν ἀδούλωτοι (cf. 2.1.5). This is reminiscent of Ephorus (quoted above, n. 98), but Hieronymus could not claim that the Nabataeans avoided slavery because they had nothing to be enslaved for.

[111] Abel (above, n. 73) 374 argued that the expeditions were simultaneously raiding and conquest (most moderns assume that Antigonus was intending subjugation); the looting would extort a declaration of vassalage. That is what Hieronymus

Diodorus it was a carefully planned raid, based on precise information about Nabataean customs and geography. It was known that there was a festival held in the desert, which attracted a great concentration of Nabataeans. They left their wives, children, elders, and movable possessions on a rock stronghold, which was of course unwalled. The strategy was to take advantage of the festival and make a surprise attack on the rock. In other words it was a raid, not an invasion. The Antigonid high command obviously had detailed information about the Nabataeans, and Athenaeus' raid was planned as meticulously as Alexander's invasion of the Malli lands in the Punjab.[112] The exact date of the Nabataean festival was ascertained, and Athenaeus timed his march on the rock so as to arrive at midnight.[113] He must have had guides well acquainted with the topography of the Nabataean stronghold, as he overran it in the night (presumably in moonlight) and was able to make off with the Nabataean hoard of incense and bullion by the early morning.[114] Everything was evidently calculated to gain the greatest possible haul of booty without engaging the Nabataean warriors.

The details as Diodorus presents them are credible enough. The festival in the desert seems a regular Arab institution.[115] Agatharchides at least described a similar quadrennial celebration held by the peoples at the south-east tip of the Gulf of Aqaba. Tribes converged from all directions to the so-called 'Palm Grove' (near the Ras al-Qasbah) to sacrifice hecatombs

would have us believe, but there is no hint in the detailed narrative that permanent conquest was an issue.

[112] Cf. Arr. 6.6.2: Alexander traversed the Rechna Doab (the desert land between the rivers Acesines and Hydraotes), arriving at dawn from an unexpected direction at precisely the point where the largest concentration of refugees had mustered. On the campaign in general see Bosworth, *Alexander and the East* 133–41.

[113] Diod. 19.95.2: περὶ μέσας νύκτας.

[114] Whether one accepts (as I would) the manuscript reading at 95.3 (ἐνδιατρίψαν-τες δ' οὐ πλείω χρόνον φυλακῆς) or Kallenberg's emendation (φυλακῆς <ἑωθινῆς>) makes little difference: Athenaeus either remained for the period of a watch or remained no longer than the dawn watch. In either case the Nabataean possessions were looted by dawn, and Athenaeus was immediately on his way.

[115] Something similar is still observed. 'In modern times the nomads have continued to meet in what may be the equivalent (but now arriving in trucks and pickups). The well-known meeting place is deep into the real desert, near Ruwayshid far out into the panhandle' (David Kennedy, personal letter).

of camels. Interestingly, when one tribe (the Maranitae) went to the celebrations in force, their neighbours attacked the remnants of the population, slaughtered them and ambushed the celebrants on their return.[116] This was genocide; the Maranitae were wiped out. It was an obvious tactic with many parallels in Greek history,[117] and it was natural enough for the Antigonids and their native advisers to plan a hit-and-run attack which would take maximum advantage of the festival. Athenaeus came from the coast, where Antigonus was taking occupation of the cities vacated by Ptolemy, and moved rapidly through Idumaea, the district extending east of Gaza to the Dead Sea. His objective was probably Petra. This has been disputed, but Athenaeus was clearly attacking a very large rock fortress in a central position for a plenary gathering of Nabataeans. The rock proper was the central refuge of Umm el-Biyara, and the Nabataeans would have left their families and belongings around its base, down in the Wadi Mousa,[118] not on its summit, as they had no reason to suspect an attack. Hence they easily fell into Athenaeus' hands as he moved in from the north or east. The route he took was in all probability the main road from the coast, from Gaza via Elusa (south-west of Beersheba) and Oboda.[119] From the settled parts of Idumaea he took three days and nights to reach the Nabataean stronghold, which would correspond relatively well with the 120 km. between Oboda and Petra.[120]

[116] Diod. 3.43.1–2; Strab. 16.4.18 (776–7); Burstein (above, n. 95) 150. The Palm Grove is located near a promontory extending towards 'Seal Island' (Tiran) in one direction and Petra in the other (Phot. *Bibl.* 250.87, 457 a–b; Diod. 3.42.5). The promontory can only be the Ras al-Qasbah, directly opposite the tip of Sinai (Burstein 148 n. 2).

[117] Instances come readily to mind, in particular Cylon's abortive attempt to seize Athens during the Diasia (Thuc. 1.126.6–7). Aeneas Tacticus (17.1–4) specifically warns against the danger of revolution when there are mass religious ceremonies and armed processions outside the city walls. Cf. D. Whitehead, *Aineias the Tactician* 146–7, giving other examples.

[118] There are useful sketch maps in Abel 383 and I. Browning, *Petra* (Park Ridge, NJ 1973) 120–1.

[119] For the roads of the Negev see the convenient survey by D. F. Graf, in *The Anchor Bible Dictionary* (New York 1992) v. 783.

[120] There is some difficulty in that Diodorus (19.95.2) claims that the distance covered by Athenaeus in three days and nights was no less than 2,200 stades (440 km.). That is totally impossible for an infantry force 4,000 strong in desert terrain.

We have, then, a carefully executed raid, staged at the most propitious time and at first dramatically successful. Athenaeus made away with most of the Nabataean stocks of frankincense and myrrh and 500 talents of silver bullion. It was an impressive booty, one that would materially swell the Antigonid war chest. Unfortunately Athenaeus was destroyed by his own success. His men were exhausted after the forced march and the overnight looting of Petra and a march of some 40 km. back along the road to Idumaea. He established a rest camp, but his men were too weary to mount an efficient guard, and they were easily overpowered by the vengeful Nabataeans, who had now returned from their festival, and on their camels they were able to overhaul the raiders who had been forced to footslog through the desert. They took Athenaeus by surprise late in the night, and exterminated his army. According to Diodorus (19.95.5) only 50 cavalry escaped, and most of them were wounded. At this point Diodorus offers a sententious little sermon on the corrupting effect of success; it encourages slackness and over-confidence. That may well be his own contribution to the story. Hieronymus did lay emphasis on the exhaustion of the Antigonid forces and the slackness of their guards, but he also stated that they calculated that they were two or three days ahead of any pursuit.[121] They did not reckon on the remarkable speed and promptitude of the Nabataeans. It was not so much failure by Athenaeus' forces; the Nabataean counter-attack was so rapid that there was no reasonable defence against it. Once again the natural military advantages of the nomadic life are illustrated in the most vivid way.

Something is badly wrong, and I think it most likely that Diodorus has conflated two separate indicators of distance, that from the point on the Syrian coast where Athenaeus left Antigonus' camp and the three days' forced march from the borders of Idumaea (so Abel 387 n. 1, who speculates that Athenaeus moved south from Damascus). In that case he could have left Antigonus' camp in the vicinity of Tyre. If he went first to Gaza and then forged eastwards to Petra the march would have been something like 440 km., but only the last 120 km. would have been covered at speed in three days and nights.

[121] Diod. 19.95.3: Athenaeus and his men travelled 200 stades from Petra, and would have been down in the Araba by the time they pitched camp. Given that the news of their raid had to be conveyed to the celebrants at the festival before the pursuit could even begin, Athenaeus could reasonably have expected at least two clear days.

Athenaeus' defeat was undoubtedly a major blow to Antigonus. He had lost over 4,000 men and absolutely nothing had been gained. According to Diodorus (19.96.1–2) he resorted to deceit, responding to a Nabataean letter of protest written in Aramaic[122] by a disingenuous disclaimer of responsibility. It was designed to lull suspicions and pave the way for a second invasion. Now, this diplomatic exchange was given some prominence by Hieronymus. He stressed that the Nabataean communication was in Aramaic, hence inaccessible to the majority of Antigonus' staff, and stated that Antigonus made a formal reply acknowledging that the Nabataeans had justice on their side. One wonders whether there was any public record of these transactions. No doubt there was an exchange of letters between Antigonus and the Nabataean chiefs, but one may perhaps question whether Hieronymus participated in the drafting of Antigonus' reply or had any direct knowledge of its content. In fact the report of Antigonus' diplomatic deception leads up to a categorical statement that such subterfuge was necessary to overcome men who espoused a nomadic life and had the inaccessible desert as their refuge. This statement is Hieronymus' own and contains one of his very few detectable stylistic fingerprints.[123] Diodorus has preserved his emphasis on what Herodotus had termed the *aporia* suffered by would-be conquerors of nomads.[124] Their mobility meant that any straightforward invasion was impossible. There had to be some stratagem to take them off their

---

[122] Diod. 19.96.1: Συρίοις γράμμασι. This is most likely to be Aramaic, like the fake message from Orontes of Armenia (Diod. 19.23.3; see Ch. 4, p. 122), but one cannot quite exclude cuneiform; two cuneiform texts from the late Babylonian and Persian periods have been found in Nabataean territory (D. F. Graf, *Archäologische Mitteilungen aus Iran und Turan* 32(2000) 82).

[123] Diod. 19.96.2: οὐ γὰρ ῥᾴδιον ἦν ἄνευ δόλου τινός ... περιγενέσθαι. The phraseology recurs in both our resumes of Hieronymus' account of the appointments at Triparadeisus. Diodorus and Photius/Arrian comment in virtually similar terminology that it was not possible to remove the Indian Kings Porus and Taxiles without a royal army (οὐ γὰρ ἦν τούτους ... μετακινῆσαι χωρὶς βασιλικῆς δυνάμεως Diod. 18.39.6; ἐπεὶ μηδὲ ῥᾴδιον μετακινῆσαι αὐτούς κτλ. Arr. *Succ.* F 1.36). See also Diod. 19.48.1–2, on Antigonus' retention of the eastern satraps (above, Ch. 4, p. 163): οὐ γὰρ ῥᾴδιον ἦν τούτους δι' ἐπιστολῆς ἐκβαλεῖν ... οὐδὲ γὰρ τοῦτον ἦν ἐκβαλεῖν δυνατὸν ἄνευ χρόνου πολλοῦ.

[124] τῶν Σκυθέων τὴν ἀπορίην Hdt. 4.83.1; cf. 4.46.3 (ἄμαχοί τε καὶ ἄποροι προσμίσγειν). On this see Hartog (above, n. 97) 57–60, 202–4.

guard. If we take Diodorus at face value, Antigonus was recognizing the military superiority of the nomads in their own terrain, so much so that he was prepared to admit that his lieutenant was at fault.

In due course Antigonus sent out a punitive expedition under his son, Demetrius. This was a more carefully equipped force than that of Athenaeus. The 4,000 infantry were light troops, specially selected for their speed, and there was a large cavalry force of 4,000. The men were issued with cold provisions for several days, and sent out during the night (Diod. 19.96.4). They were to move rapidly, and attack the Nabataeans before they were alerted. This was more difficult than it had been for Athenaeus, since there was no festival to divert the Nabataean warriors, and despite Antigonus' assurances of good faith the high ground above the Wadi Araba was alive with Arab observers.[125] Accordingly Demetrius escaped detection as he avoided the established routes, but as he approached the Nabataean lands he was spotted from the heights and the natives were able to split up their herds and concentrate their baggage and families on a rock stronghold, which Demetrius then attacked. It is difficult to flesh out this skeletal narrative. What seems certain is that Demetrius attacked from a different route from that of Athenaeus. Athenaeus had the advantage of surprise and probably approached Petra along the main caravan route, whereas Demetrius had to face an enemy which was alert and expectant. He could not take the route of the previous expedition. Diodorus is explicit that he avoided the beaten tracks[126]— and in any case Athenaeus' men will have disposed of much of the fodder available. What is more, it seems unlikely that the rock Demetrius attacked was Petra itself. One gains the impression from Diodorus that the rock captured by Athenaeus was the same as the rock besieged by Demetrius, and Diodorus probably inferred that it was. But the description of Demetrius' rock, possessing a single artificial approach, is

---

[125] Diod. 19.96.3: σκοποὺς μὲν κατέστησαν ἐπὶ τῶν λόφων, ἀφ' ὧν ἦν ῥᾴδιον συνορᾶν πόρρωθεν τὰς εἰς τὴν Ἀραβίαν ἐμβολάς. From the high ground traversed by the Royal Road running south from Damascus to Petra there would be panoramic views across the Wadi Araba to the Scorpion Pass.

[126] Diod. 19.97.1: ἀνοδίᾳ πορευόμενος.

difficult to equate with the site of Petra in the Wadi Mousa, which can be approached from several directions and has no artificial access.[127] On the other hand there is an age-old citadel at Es-Sela, some 50 km. north of Petra, close to Buseirah (ancient Bosra). The rock itself had served as a place of refuge since the third millennium, has yielded a cuneiform inscription from the neo-Babylonian period, and has more than 25 water cisterns cut in the stone.[128] Most importantly there was a single artificial access route with gates hewn from the rock. This fortress would have been in Demetrius' path had he taken a route from Gaza through Beersheba and the later Roman fort of Mampsis and then struck across the Wadi Araba.[129] This route was somewhat north of that taken by Athenaeus and very much less beaten. It was only when Demetrius approached the mountains that he was observed, and the Nabataeans were able to take refuge at Sela and disperse their herds by the time he reached the royal road north of the citadel.

According to Diodorus what ensued was an inconclusive siege of the rock. Demetrius made several attempts to storm the place, but was beaten off each time. The following day he received the shouted message from the Nabataean elder and agreed to hear an embassy. The outcome was a truce: Demetrius received hostages and 'gifts' and withdrew from the Nabataean lands (Diod. 19.97.6). A 60 km. march to the north took him to the Dead Sea, where he examined the bitumen harvesting, and eventually returned to his father, who roundly criticized his agreement with the Nabataeans,

---

[127] It is possible that the Nabataeans evacuated all the lower area of Petra and took refuge on Umm el Biyara, which does have a single access (as Abel 389 assumed without discussion; cf. 383–4). But it is hard to see why there was no attempt to block the narrow approach routes. Demetrius did not have the advantage of surprise, and the Nabataeans had time to mount an effective defence.

[128] See the description by M. Lindner, *Petra und das Königreich der Nabatäer* 258–71 with the brief survey in Wenning (above, n. 88) 86–7. The most influential discussion is that of J. Starcky, 'Pétra et la Nabatène', *Supplément au Dictionnaire de la Bible* 7 (1966) 886–91, who proposed that Sela was the Edomite fortress captured by Amaziah (2 Kings 14:7); see, more cautiously, S. Hart, 'Sela: The Rock of Edom?', *PEQ* 118 (1986) 91–5.

[129] See the map in Starcky (above, n. 128) 889–90; the early stages to the Araba are described by Graf (above, n. 119) V.783; see also M. Harel, 'The Roman Road at Ma'aleh Aqrabim', *IEJ* 9 (1959) 175–9.

arguing that they had gained the moral advantage and would be much more aggressive as a result.[130] His words were prophetic. The immediate sequel was the appointment of Hieronymus to take over the bitumen industry and the surprise attack by 6,000 emboldened Arabs. Viewed from this perspective, Demetrius' expedition was disastrous. It had added to Arab grievances. It had shown a certain lack of military competence in that the Nabataeans were able to safeguard their livestock and successfully defend their stronghold. The prince attacked only for a single day and concluded an armistice which took him immediately out of the country without having impacted on the Nabataeans' military potential. He had hostages and gifts which are alleged to have been particularly precious (one thinks of the incense which formed the basis of Nabataean wealth), but there had been no loss of Nabataean life or livestock. It was hardly surprising that they were encouraged to attack the harvesting operations on the Dead Sea.

There is another source for these events, Plutarch's *Life of Demetrius* (7.1–2). The account of Demetrius' operations is extremely brief and blandly expressed, but it differs significantly from Diodorus. Plutarch agrees that Demetrius was sent to subjugate (ὑπαγαγέσθαι) the Nabataeans and adds that he came into danger because of the waterless terrain. However, he did not panic. His resolution overawed the barbarians, and he left the area with a great booty of livestock and 700 camels. This account clearly stressed the dangers from lack of water which Demetrius faced and overcame.[131] It suggests a rather longer campaign than is implied by Diodorus, who implies that Demetrius spent only a matter of days in Nabataean territory. But the crux is Demetrius' success. There is no reference to booty in Diodorus, who speaks only of gifts and states that the livestock was successfully dispersed in the desert. Plutarch by contrast is explicit that Demetrius acquired large numbers of sheep and goats and above all 700 camels, a truly impressive haul. If that is true,

---

[130] Diod. 19.100.1: λέγων ὅτι πολλῷ θρασυτέρους πεποίηκε τοὺς βαρβάρους ἐάσας ἀτιμωρήτους.

[131] Plut. *Demetr.* 7.1: ἐκινδύνευσε μὲν εἰς τόπους ἀνύδρους ἐμπεσών.

one has an inkling into the Antigonid strategy. In the autumn of 312 Syria down to the borders of Egypt fell into the hands of Antigonus, and his ultimate plans will have included invasion of Egypt, an invasion which finally took place in 306. For such an invasion there was necessarily a massive amount of logistical preparation, and a huge number of transport animals were needed to convey provisions for the desert march between Gaza and Pelusium. In 306 there was a virtual army of camels, which, we are told, transported no less than 130,000 *medimnoi* of grain as well as fodder for the other animals (Diod. 20.73.3). Such numbers could only be provided by the desert Arabs, and Antigonus may well have made overtures to the Nabataeans before he sent Athenaeus on his raid. It was the livestock which he was instructed to capture and which apparently he failed to do. Demetrius' raid had the same objective. It was partially punitive, to cow the Nabataeans and make them receptive to later Antigonid demands, but booty was central; the punishment of the Nabataeans meant the capture of their livestock on which their very existence depended. According to Plutarch he was successful in all objectives: the Nabataeans were subdued and he acquired a massive train of livestock. His father could hardly complain about that outcome.

Plutarch's source cannot be identified. One thinks of the ubiquitous and elusive Duris of Samos,[132] but there is no possibility of proof. What is interesting is that Plutarch chose not to use Hieronymus,[133] whom he drew on later in

---

[132] There is no named citation of Duris in the *Demetrius*, but there is one demonstrable borrowing, where Plutarch's text corresponds to an attested fragment (*Demetr.* 41.4; cf. Athen. 12.535F = *FGrH* 76 F 70); and it has been argued that the tragic picture of Demetrius corrupted by success comes from Duris (W. Sweet, 'Sources of Plutarch's Demetrius', *CW* 44 (1951) 177–8; Kebric, *In the Shadow of Macedon* 55–60). But one cannot discount Plutarch's own contribution; the tragic Demetrius balances the equally tragic Antony. Duris may have been a relatively minor influence, exploited for the occasional sensational detail.

[133] C. Wehrli, *Antigone et Démétrios* 144–5, argued that Hieronymus actually was the source for Plutarch. See also Jesús Lens Tuero, in *Estudios sobre Diodoro de Sicilia* 117–25, esp. 119–20, arguing that Diodorus has fused Hieronymus' account of the campaigns with a later ethnographical discussion, perhaps from Poseidonius. Given the close juxtaposition with the digression on the bitumen of the Dead Sea, which demonstrably derives from Hieronymus (Diod. 19.98; cf. *FGrH* 154 F 5), it is highly probable that the whole passage on the Nabataeans derives from the same

the *Life* and exploited in the *Eumenes* and *Pyrrhus*.[134] There is a real possibility that he regarded Hieronymus as discredited. Admittedly he may have opted for the alternative version because it was more flamboyant, more in keeping with his dashing picture of the young Demetrius. But, even if his choice was made on artistic grounds, the tradition he reports should be taken seriously. In place of Hieronymus' picture of unconquerable nomads, immune from attack because of their way of life, we have a story of a successful punitive raid, restoring Antigonid prestige and acquiring a huge amount of booty. It is unfortunate that so few of the details are preserved by Plutarch. We may speculate that the siege of the rock went on for longer than the single day reported by Diodorus and that the elders in the stronghold did not negotiate a truce so much as offer unconditional surrender—including the surrender of their flocks and camels; but that is a minimal scenario; Plutarch's source may have had a totally different story of the campaign. Should it be preferred to Hieronymus's account? Given the brevity of Plutarch's report we cannot attempt a detailed comparative critique, and we certainly cannot exclude the possibility that it was biased towards the Antigonid camp, elevating an inconclusive foray by Demetrius into a major triumph.[135] But Hieronymus' version, as we have seen, bears clear marks of distortion. There is a tendency to elevate the Nabataeans, to portray them as invincible in their environment, passionate upholders of liberty in the face of Antigonid expansionism. On the other hand, there is a defensiveness in his record, a determination to show that all attacks on the Nabataeans had been disastrous and counter-productive—and the attack that was his downfall on the Dead Sea was almost made inevitable by Demetrius' operations. It is certainly arguable that Demetrius was

---

source. It reads as a unitary whole, and the ethnography is an integral part of the exposition (cf. Hornblower, *Hieronymus* 144, 147–8, 246).

[134] There is an autobiographical detail preserved at *Demetr.* 39.3–7 (*FGrH* 154 F 8); direct citations in the *Pyrrhus* (*FGrH* 154 F 11–12, 14; and much detail common to Diodorus in the *Eumenes*. Cf. Hornblower, *Hieronymus* 67–72; Bosworth, 'History and Artifice', 57–8, 62–71.

[135] So Abel 390: 'On ne saurait mieux pallier l'échec du Grec devant les Barbares sous un formule amphibologique.' Earlier Droysen had conflated the two traditions, and subsituted the camels of Plutarch for the gifts of Diodorus.

longer campaigning in Nabataean territory than Diodorus (and Hieronymus) would have us believe, and was much more successful.

Hieronymus' account minimized the success of Demetrius, and implied that the treaty he made actually encouraged Nabataean aggression. He gave a full description of Athenaeus' debacle, illustrating the speed and elusiveness of the Arabs on their own terrain. As we have seen, the earlier failures mitigated Hieronymus' own defeat at the Dead Sea. He could not be expected to forestall the lightning attack of the Arabs, and there was ample precedent for the loss of an army at their hands. The responsibility for the disaster, so we might infer from Diodorus, should be ascribed to Antigonus rather than Hieronymus. He authorized the commandeering of local resources, further aggravating a population which was already smarting from the raids of Athenaeus and Demetrius, and virtually ensured reprisals which Hieronymus' forces could not possibly contain. The message is not spelled out directly, but after the narrative of the previous expeditions his reader would inevitably draw the conclusion.[136] But there is more to the episode than the historian's self-defence. The Nabataeans become the ultimate champions of freedom, having no truck with submission to any external power. Their resistance is justified by the inaccessibility of their terrain and the overwhelming difficulties faced by any invader. Antigonus' attempt to subjugate them was ultimately an act of folly, doomed to failure. Here Hieronymus was looking back at a history of catastrophe, provoked by Antigonid imperialism. The aggression of the period after the victory at Salamis in 306 cemented the coalition which broke Antigonus' power at Ipsus.[137] Less than 20 years later the massive armament Demetrius was accumulating to rebuild

[136] So Hornblower, *Hieronymus* 219, who concludes that 'Hieronymus must, then, have been inadequately protected.' That is a correct reading of the passage, precisely what the historian would have us think. She is also right, in my opinion, to detect 'personal animus in his account'.

[137] Cf. H. Rosen, *Hermes* 107 (1979) 460–76, esp. 475, arguing that for Hieronymus Antigonid policies down to Ipsus were the paradigm of expansionism (πλεονεξία); and the expedition against the Nabataeans was treated as an object lesson in politics and morality.

Antigonus' empire in Asia provoked the alliance between Pyrrhus and Lysimachus which drove him out of Macedon in 288, and it took his son, Hieronymus' patron, Gonatas, a whole decade to regain power in the north. In the darker, soberer atmosphere of the third century BC the naked imperial ambitions of Antigonus and Demetrius could be seen as ruinous and condemned as such. In Hieronymus' hands the Nabataean adventure could be presented as a moral lesson. Antigonus was attacking nomads with a passionate culture of freedom, a people whom he could not hope to subjugate. The disasters he suffered were predictable and almost self-inflicted, and were a paradigm of the dangers of unprovoked aggression. To that end Hieronymus exaggerated the rigidity of the Nabataean nomadic culture, making them the total antithesis of settled agrarian civilization and, as such, insuperable by conventional military means. Antigonus' expeditions were inevitably an appointment with disaster, and their failure should have been foreseen.

We have examined two colourful and contrasting episodes. One is an aetiology of an exotic, alien custom; the other is simultaneously a meditation upon the morality of empire and justification of a personal failure. On the surface both passages have considerable entertainment value. They grip the attention, and at the same time they refer back to earlier historical literature with subtle allusions that flatter the intelligence of the reader. But they also focus on the present. One is invited to make judgements on subjects as diverse as Cynic morality and contemporary imperialism. As far as we can tell—and we always have to allow for Diodorus' deficiencies—Hieronymus gave his judgements indirectly. He did not fulminate like Polybius, delivering his sermon three times over. It is all the more effective in that the message is built into the narrative text. The absurdity of trying to subjugate desert nomads is plain to any reader, as is the folly of basing marriage upon the free choice of partner. What emerges from this study is a more complex, sophisticated historian than we might have assumed. Hieronymus set himself to entertain, and the entertainment conveys a message. In the case of the Nabataeans the message has been swallowed by modern scholars with a suspension of their critical faculties which they would never allow themselves with the lurid fragments of Duris or Phylarchus. The sober prose, which owes much to Diodorus himself, gives us a false impression of simplicity, and we go no deeper than the surface. That is particularly misleading in the case of the digressions, which are carefully crafted to a specific purpose. They form a counterpoint to the 'historical' narrative of events, and often add a critical perspective. The historian simultaneously seizes our attention and lulls our suspicions because the material seems detached from the political and military events that are the overt object of the narrative. But there lies the danger. The moral and political bias is all the more insidious when the vehicle which contains it is ostensibly directed towards entertainment.

6

The Rise of Seleucus

Seleucus' rise to power is perhaps the most spectacular phenomenon of the period of the Successors.[1] Expelled from his satrapy by Antigonus in the summer of 316, he was able to retrieve it four years later and did so with a force which was remarkably small by any standards. Not only did he regain Babylonia, but he beat off an attack by Nicanor, the general supervising the upper satrapies, and immediately took the offensive, extending his dominions to Susiana, Media, and perhaps even further afield. All that took place within a year of his entering Babylonia, and a year later, in the summer of 310, he was coping with a full-scale invasion by Antigonus. He did not merely survive; he forced Antigonus out of his territories, never to resume the offensive, and by 305 he had penetrated to the Indus valley, placing almost all the satraps of the eastern empire under his sway.[2] The facts are clear enough, but there has been remarkably little attempt to explain Seleucus' success. What is more, the source tradition is extremely complex. There is a roughly coherent narrative of events provided by Diodorus Siculus. From the Babylonian side there are a number of documents, astronomical diaries and records of minor economic transactions, which provide dating parameters, as well as a very fragmentary and allusive chronicle dealing with events from mid-311 to 308.[3] These traditions have been combined in various ways in recent years, not with the happiest of results, and the chronologies adopted have had a procrustean effect, distorting the sequence of events in our sources. Most seriously what Diodorus

---

[1] The most recent discussions are L. Schober, *Untersuchungen zur Geschichte Babyloniens und der Oberen Satrapien von 323–303 v. Chr.* (Frankfurt 1981); A. Mehl, *Seleukos Nikator und sein Reich* (Louvain 1986); Billows, *Antigonos*, esp. 124–30, 136–42; J. D. Grainger, *Seleukos Nikator* (London 1990).

[2] App. *Syr.* 55.281–2; Justin 15.4.12, 20–1. On his subsequent pact with the Mauryan king, Chandragupta, surrendering land for elephants, see the exhaustive treatment by Schober, *Untersuchungen* 155–93.

[3] For bibliography see Ch. 1, p. 21.

describes as a brief incursion by Demetrius and presents as the last event in Asia for the archon year 312/11 has been conflated with the sustained invasion of Antigonus which the Babylonian Chronicle records as taking place over a year and more from summer 310 to late the following year. There is something seriously amiss here, and the subject urgently requires a new critical examination.

The early life of Seleucus is relatively uncontroversial. His career under Alexander is virtually unknown, but it was hardly undistinguished. By 326 at least he commanded the hypaspist élite,[4] and was necessarily involved in most of the engagements of the campaign. He must have been one of the most battle-hardened generals even on Alexander's staff. At Babylon in 323 he supported Perdiccas, and became his chiliarch,[5] acting as second-in-command until the ill-fated invasion of Egypt, when he acquiesced in the murder of the regent.[6] When the next regent, Antipater, came close to being murdered in his turn at the hands of the mutinous troops at Triparadeisus, he joined Antigonus in talking down the mutiny.[7] His reward was the satrapy of Babylonia, rich and strategically important, but far from the centres of power, now that the kings were with Antipater in Macedonia and the military focus was in Asia Minor, where Antigonus fought it out with Eumenes and the remainder of the Perdiccan faction.

Seleucus had moved from the centre to the periphery, but he followed the example of Peucestas in Persis and endeared himself to the native population, making Babylonia practically an independent principality.[8] In the years immediately after the Triparadeisus settlement there can have been very little, if any, regal authority in the area, and it is significant that when a royal general did eventually appear with an explicit

[4] Arr. 5.13.4, 16.3. Cf. *HCA* ii.280–5; Grainger, *Seleukos Nikator* 1–23; Heckel 254–6.

[5] Diod. 18.3.4; App. *Syr.* 57.292; Just. 13.4.17. For discussion see above, pp. 56–7.

[6] Nep. *Eum.* 5.1. It seems that Antigenes led the conspirators and was the first to attack Perdiccas (Arr. *Succ.* F 1.28; Diod. 18.39.6).

[7] Arr. *Succ.* F 1.33; cf. Polyaen. 4.6.4 (mentioning Antigonus alone).

[8] Diod. 19.90.1, 91.2 (claiming that Seleucus had designs on supremacy as early as his initial period in Babylon, wooing the populace and securing collaborators long in advance ἐὰν αὐτῷ δοθῇ καιρὸς ἀμφισβητεῖν ἡγεμονίας).

commission from the kings and their regent, Seleucus refused to support him and threw in his lot with Antigonus. He had some justification in that Eumenes had been condemned to death in the past,[9] but Seleucus' protestations of loyalty to the royal house did not prevent him joining the most notorious rebel against royal authority, Antigonus himself. Accordingly he supported Antigonus throughout the protracted and murderous campaign against Eumenes and the governors of the upper satrapies which was played out on the Iranian plateau over winter and spring 317/16. It was a kind of poetic justice when Antigonus had himself proclaimed king of Asia by the inhabitants of Persis, an act with obvious symbolism, which he exploited by reportioning the satrapies of the area.[10] Peucestas, who was on the scene and helpless in the face of Antigonus' army, he promptly deposed, and Seleucus himself found himself under pressure when Antigonus visited him in Babylon at the head of his victorious army. Seleucus threw open the treasury of Susa to him, but it was not enough.[11] Antigonus made an explicit demand for a formal account of the revenues of his satrapy.[12] There was a clear danger that Seleucus would be accused of embezzlement and misgovernment, and he reacted with a blank refusal. He did

---

[9] Diod. 19.12.2. Eumenes had been formally restored to his satrapy by the kings late in 319 (Diod. 18.57.3–4; cf. Plut. *Eum.* 13.1–2). The change of fortune raised some eyebrows (Diod. 18.59.4, where it is implied that the sentence was formally revoked by 'the kings and the Macedonians'), but there was no doubting the legality of Eumenes' commission (see above, pp. 100–2). In contrast Eumenes could reasonably claim that he had been condemned to death by a comparatively small section of Macedonians, those in the royal army of Perdiccas (Diod. 18.37.2; Plut. *Eum.* 8.2; Nep. *Eum.* 5.1; Just. 13.8.10), at the primary instigation of Ptolemy.

[10] See above, pp. 162–4.

[11] Diod. 19.48.6. The treasurer at Susa, Xenophilus, had previously retained his loyalty to the kings and respected Eumenes' orders to resist Antigonus (Diod. 19.17.3, 18.1). Xenophilus had received his appointment from Alexander as early as winter 331/30 (Curt. 5.2.16; cf. Bosworth, *HCA* i.319; Atkinson ii.67), and clearly had considerable clout. Seleucus imposed his authority on him, but retained him as citadel commander, while even Antigonus treated him with respect, and honoured him, ostensibly at least, among the most influential of his friends. There is no suggestion that he later lost his rank (cf. Billows, *Antigonos* 439–40).

[12] Diod. 19.55.2–3. App. *Syr.* 53.268 adds that there was some interpersonal friction: Seleucus abused one of Antigonus' commanders, and avoided the presence of the new king of Asia. He might have behaved in a conciliatory manner when Antigonus was at a distance, but the reality of his presence and pretensions was hard for him to swallow.

not merely deny Antigonus' authority; he denied any regal authority, claiming that he was not obliged to account for the administration of the territory. The Macedonians had given it to him in recognition of his services under Alexander, and it was his by right.[13] He skilfully exploited his prominence on Alexander's staff, a prominence contrasting markedly with Antigonus' almost total absence from the campaign. Satrap of Phrygia he may have been, and he certainly rendered good service before and after Issus,[14] but he could not compare with Seleucus who had gone through Asia at Alexander's side and had helped win the empire which Antigonus was now presuming to divide. Seleucus had the right of conquest, and he regarded the satrapy he received at Triparadeisus as his personal reward for service. As we shall see, his was not a unique view.

Seleucus could not indefinitely defy Antigonus. He fled his satrapy before he was arrested, taking refuge with Ptolemy. There was little choice. Media and Persis were in the hands of Antigonus' creatures. The satrap of Mesopotamia, Blitor, was friendly and did assist his escape, but he did not possess the resources to make a stand against Antigonus—and Antigonus promptly deposed him.[15] Seleucus could only go to the west and cast himself on the mercy of the satrap of Egypt who had recently attached Syria to his dominions, which like Seleucus he regarded as spear-won.[16] From Ptolemy's perspective the dispossessed satrap was a useful political acquisition. His own title to Syria was vulnerable; he had attacked it without provocation and dispossessed the incumbent satrap, Laomedon,[17] and Eumenes had denounced

---

[13] Diod. 19.55.3: οὐκ ἔφησεν ὀφείλειν ὑπὲρ ταύτης τῆς χώρας ὑπέχειν εὐθύνας, ἣν Μακεδόνες αὐτῷ δεδώκασι διὰ τὰς γεγενημένας ἐξ αὐτοῦ χρείας Ἀλεξάνδρου ζῶντος.

[14] Antigonus left the campaign in spring 333, when he was appointed to Greater Phrygia (Arr. 1.29.3). His previous command, over the allied troops, cannot have involved him in much serious fighting. For his achievements in Asia Minor see Briant, *Antigone le Borgne*, 45–95; Billows, *Antigonos* 41–6.

[15] App. *Syr.* 53.269. Nothing is known of Blitor, except that he was appointed either by Seleucus or Antigonus after the previous satrap joined Eumenes (above, p. 113). It is probable that he was Seleucus' man, and his appointment was part of the price Antigonus had to pay for Seleucus' support during the campaign in Iran.

[16] Diod. 18.39.5, 43.1; 20.76.7; cf. Arr. *Succ.* F 1.34.

[17] Diod. 18.43.1–2 (the invasion is described as a pre-emptive strike, to forestall any attack on Egypt from Coele Syria); App. *Syr.* 52.264 (adding that Syria was

the annexation as soon as he became royal general in Asia.[18] Ptolemy could expect pressure from Antigonus. Seleucus brought no resources other than his military expertise, but he was a valuable focus of propaganda. As one of the architects of empire, consistently in the fighting line, he was deprived of what was properly his. Accordingly when Antigonus returned to Cilicia in November 316, he was confronted by envoys from Ptolemy Lysimachus and Cassander, who demanded territory and treasure as their share of the victory over Eumenes.[19] That was specious. None of the three dynasts had given Antigonus anything other than moral support during the protracted campaign against Eumenes,[20] and what they were asking for was either territory acquired by Antigonus during the campaigns of 320 and 319 (Hellespontine Phrygia, Lycia, and Cappadocia) or illegally annexed. The only strong moral card was the treatment of Seleucus. He had resisted Eumenes in Babylonia and joined forces with Antigonus, keeping Mesopotamia as a secure base of supply for the Antigonid forces. He genuinely deserved a share in the spoils of victory, but instead he had been expelled from his satrapy. His treatment gave the coalition against Antigonus a moral justification which was otherwise totally lacking, and it figured prominently in Ptolemy's propaganda. When he made representations to Demetrius after the Battle of Gaza in 312, he focused explicitly on the

seen as a base for operations against Cyprus); Parian Marble, *FGrH* 239 B12 (wrongly dated to 319/18: see now P. V. Wheatley, *CQ* 45 (1995) 433–40).

[18] Diod. 18.73.2. When he returned to the west in winter 316/15 Antigonus' first action was to occupy northern Syria (Diod. 19.57.1).

[19] Diod. 19.57.1. The problematic item in these representations is Cassander's claim to Cappadocia and Lycia, both of which are territorially remote from Macedon. As ambit claims these are explicable. Antigonus could hardly be denied his base satrapy of Greater Phrygia, nor could his relative, Asander, be threatened in Caria. Cassander was laying claim to the territories on the periphery of Antigonus' holdings in Asia Minor, and Cappadocia at least was of doubtful status, restored to Eumenes by Polyperchon and the kings in late 319 (Diod. 18.57.3; Plut. *Eum.* 13.2), and it could be represented as one of the legitimate spoils of war. For a review of the problem see Seibert, *Das Zeitalter der Diadochen* 115–16, and most recently R. Descat, *REA* 100 (1998) 175–9.

[20] Lysimachus is particularly problematic. His one attested action during the war was the execution of Cleitus the White, the admiral of Polyperchon (Diod. 18.72.9), and there is no hint of any formal pact with Antigonus. Nor for that matter is there any evidence that he helped Cassander during his invasion of Macedonia in 317/16.

injustice done to Seleucus, which ranks alongside the denial of territory to the members of the coalition.[21] Seleucus became very active and visible in the struggle against Antigonus. At the time of the siege of Tyre in 315 he appeared at the head of 100 ships, provided by Ptolemy and equipped in royal splendour.[22] He sailed past Antigonus' encampment, deliberately emphasizing the Antigonid vulnerability to naval assault and underlining the consequences of his dispossession. The naval intervention was spectacularly successful. Seleucus led the Ptolemaic forces in Cyprus and brought practically the whole island over.[23] In 314 he was active in the Aegean, and though he was unable to prevent the Antigonid occupation of Caria, it is evident that none of the rival naval forces was willing to face him.[24] He drops out of sight during the campaign year 313, but the silence of the sources is no proof of inactivity. He and Ptolemy are described as colleagues and exercised joint control over policy and strategy.[25] Any friction between them was minimized by Seleucus' absences with his fleet,[26] and they had a mutual interest in expelling the Antigonid forces from Syria: Ptolemy would reoccupy what he regarded as his own while Seleucus

---

[21] Diod. 19.85.3. The complaint concerns the spear-won land acquired during the wars against Perdiccas and Eumenes, which were waged in common but the spoils were not divided. That may have been a slight embarrassment for Seleucus who, initially at least, fought with Perdiccas against Ptolemy, but it was more than compensated by his loss of Babylonia παρὰ πάντα τὰ δίκαια.

[22] Diod. 19.58.5 μετὰ νεῶν ἑκατὸν κεκοσμημένων βασιλικῶς. He showed his mobility by striking at Ionia later in the year, but failed to capture Erythrae when Antigonus' nephew Polemaeus came to relieve it with a substantial army (Diod. 19.60.4).

[23] Diod. 19.62.4–6. Seleucus shared command with Ptolemy's brother, Menelaus, but the successes of the campaign are ascribed to him alone.

[24] Diod. 19.68.3–4: unsuccessful attempt to coerce Lemnos away from Antigonus (cf. Hauben, *AncSoc* 9 (1978) 47–54; Billows, *Antigonos* 118–19; L. L. O'Sullivan, 'The Rule of Demetrius of Phalerum in Athens' (Diss. Western Australia 1999) 136–46) but the Antigonid admiral, Dioscurides was careful not to relieve the island until Seleucus had withdrawn to Cos.

[25] They are represented as joint commanders at Gaza (Diod. 19.81.5, 83.1, 4, 85.3), and Ptolemy is said to have launched the campaign at Seleucus' urging (Diod. 19.80.3). A little earlier Asander, Antigonus' disaffected satrap in Caria, had sent embassies to Ptolemy and Seleucus jointly (Diod. 19.75.2).

[26] Ptolemy apparently acted on his own when he dramatically intervened in Cyprus in 313 (Diod, 19.79.4–5; for the dating see Wheatley, *Phoenix* 52 (1998) 267–8, n. 58). There is no hint where Seleucus was operating.

would regain access to Babylonia. In 313 the situation became more promising as Antigonus withdrew to Celaenae in Phrygia with the majority of his army, leaving his son Demetrius in charge of the defence of Syria with three veteran advisers and a modest force of 12,900 foot (2,000 of them Macedonian), 5,000 horse, and 43 elephants.[27] The Antigonid position was much weaker, and Ptolemy and Seleucus exploited their advantage. Naval assaults on the coast of Syria and Cilicia accrued considerable loot to sweeten the tempers and preserve the loyalty of their troops, while Demetrius failed signally to beat off the attacks, and ruined his best horses in a futile attempt to save the rich Cilician city of Mallus.[28] The ground was laid for a full invasion of Syria. Ptolemy and Seleucus brought a large army from Egypt, outnumbering and outgeneralling Demetrius. The decisive battle at Gaza resulted in a crushing defeat for the Antigonids. Casualties were relatively light (500 dead), but in the aftermath of the battle more than 8,000 prisoners came into the hands of Ptolemy and Seleucus—nearly two-thirds of Demetrius' army.[29]

Demetrius now had few choices: he concentrated the garrison forces from Cilicia and Northern Syria, first at Tripolis in Phoenicia, but then falling back to Cilicia.[30] That area he could hold with a relatively depleted force if he blocked the few points of access while he recruited mercenaries and built up a respectable army.[31] In the meantime Ptolemy (and Seleucus) occupied Phoenicia, and Syria was wide open.[32] So

[27] Diod. 19.69.1–2. Antigonus crossed the Taurus (at the second attempt) in winter 314/13.

[28] Diod. 19.79.6–80.2. Mallus was taken by storm and the inhabitants enslaved, hardly a promising augury for the freedom of the Greeks, which Ptolemy was to champion.

[29] Diod. 19.85.3, Plut. *Demetr.* 5.3 claims that the dead numbered 5,000, a clear exaggeration. On the battle itself see Seibert, *Untersuchungen* 164–75; Devine, *Acta Classica* 27 (1984) 31–40; Billows, *Antigonos* 124–8.

[30] Diod.19.85.5 (Demetrius concentrates his remaining forces at Tripolis). Later Diodorus (19.93.1) notes that Demetrius returned from Cilicia to Upper Syria, and he had clearly withdrawn to Cilicia to rebuild and regroup his forces.

[31] Eumenes had given the example in 318 when with Cilicia and the resources of Cyinda in his hands he recruited some 12,000 mercenaries in a matter of months (Diod. 18.59.3, 61.4–5, 73.2). See above, pp. 102–3.

[32] The process took some little time. Ptolemy was forced to lay siege to some of the Phoenician cities, notably Tyre, where the Antigonid commander refused to surrender and held out until his soldiers mutinied (Diod. 19.85.4, 86.1–2).

was the main road to Babylon, and at some time after the Battle of Gaza Seleucus moved to the Euphrates to take occupation of his old satrapy, Babylonia.[33] One of the declared objectives of the coalition war was now to be achieved.

So far I have deliberately avoided questions of chronology, but they must now be faced. The crucial issue is the length of time that elapsed between Seleucus' occupation of Babylonia and the great invasion which Antigonus unleashed in the summer of 310. From the Babylonian side there are certain fixed pointers. Antigonus' invasion of Babylonia is firmly dated. The Chronicle is explicit that in the seventh year of Alexander IV 'Antigonus did battle with the army of Seleucus'. He did so around the month of Ab (July/August 310), and the fighting continued for some time.[34] The same information appears on a recently published astronomical tablet, dealing with observations of the year 310, which is explicitly defined as the seventh year of Alexander IV, and among the annotations for the month of Ab is a note that 'the troops of Antigonus fought in [...]'.[35] There is a clear correspondence, and it seems undeniable that there was a major invasion of Babylon in the second half of 310. The invasion is documented in the Chronicle and lasted until at least August 309, involving widespread devastation and a number of pitched battles between the two armies of Seleucus and Antigonus.[36] In the course of the fighting Antigonus was able to occupy much of Babylonia. A lease contract from Larsa is dated 22 Ab of his ninth year, in other words, late August 309.[37] In Larsa at least he was acknowledged

---

[33] Gaza is the universally accepted *terminus post quem* (cf. Diod. 19.90.1; App. *Syr.* 54.272–3; Porphyry, *FGrH* 260 F 32.4).

[34] The first item in the year (rev. 15) appears to be Antigonus doing battle with Seleucus. The next line is a chronological pointer ('[from] the month Ab till the month [...]'), and the following line refers to armies battling against each other. There must have been prolonged hostilities during the summer and autumn of 310.

[35] A. Sachs and H. Hunger, *Astronomical Diaries and Related Texts from Babylonia, i: Diaries from 652 BC to 262 BC* no. 309, line 14; Del Monte, 21–2.

[36] The extant text breaks off towards the end of Ab in the eighth year of Alexander (Sept. 309), and the war is still in progress; there is a reference to 'battle in front of the troops of Seleucus'.

[37] BM 105211: Antigonus' name appears without any title, in contrast with the earlier records down to 312/11, where he is regularly termed *rab uqi*, commander. There is also a fragmentary ration list (*TBER* 88), dated to the eighth year of a

(temporarily) as the *de facto* ruler. It seems that he was strong enough to impose a counter-satrap of his own by the spring of 309,[38] and there is no doubt that Seleucus was very hard-pressed.

Nothing of this is recorded in the Greek and Latin sources for the period. Instead we hear of a formal peace between Antigonus, Ptolemy, Cassander, and Lysimachus. Diodorus records it under the archon year 311/10, roughly a year before Antigonus' invasion.[39] Before that he documents the rise of Seleucus in a number of episodes which are occasionally and fitfully attested in Appian and Plutarch's *Life of Demetrius*. Seleucus marched on Babylonia by way of Mesopotamia, rapidly occupied the satrapy and its capital and took the palace by storm. He then repelled an invasion by Nicanor, Antigonus' general in the upper satrapies, who had raised forces from Media and neighbouring areas, ambushing the invading army and annexing the survivors to his service. Next Seleucus took the offensive outside Babylon, occupying Susiana and Media and continuing deep into the eastern satrapies. During his absence Demetrius made a lightning attack on Babylonia. He penetrated as far as Babylon, which was evacuated in the face of his advance; he took and occupied one of the capital's citadels and left a garrison force to lay siege to the other. Demetrius then withdrew to Syria before the return of Seleucus. The Peace of the Dynasts followed.

These events took a fair time, inevitably so because of the distances to be covered. From Thapsacus, the crossing point on the Euphrates, to Babylon was some 700 km,[40] and in the

dynast whose name begins *An* [. . .], and there is a strong likelihood that this is again Antigonus (see the concise exposition by Boiy, 'Laatachaemenidisch en hellenistisch Babylon' 129 n. 283); if so, it comes from territory occupied by Antigonus towards the beginning of his campaign in 310.

[38] *ABC* 10, rev. 30: 'Ariskilamu to the office of satrap [of Akkad(?) *he appointed*. . .]' This Ariskilamu may (as van der Spek has suggested) be the Archelaus whom Demetrius left as commander of the citadel in Babylon which he had occupied (Diod. 19.100.7). If so, Archelaus had secured his repatriation to Antigonid territory after Seleucus' return to Mesopotamia.

[39] Diod. 19.105.1; see below pp. 239–44.

[40] For a useful review of routes and distances see E. W. Marsden, *The Campaign of Gaugamela* 18–23. There is considerable uncertainty about the exact location of Thapsacus (cf. M. Gawlikowski, *Iraq* 58 (1996) 123–33, arguing that Thapsacus is identical to Hellenistic and Roman Zeugma; but see D. L. Kennedy, *The Twin*

period we are dealing with, the distance was covered once by Seleucus and twice by Demetrius. In the prelude to Gaugamela, Alexander had taken six weeks to march from Thapsacus to the Tigris north of Mosul,[41] and though the armies we are dealing with were much smaller and more mobile, we must allow a minimum of a month for the transit between Syria and Babylonia. Nicanor raised forces from Media, Persis, and probably some of the eastern satrapies,[42] a vast area, and we must reckon with the time required to summon and assemble the dispersed forces and then march through the Zagros into Babylonia. There must be something like an interval of two months between the news of Seleucus' entry reaching Nicanor and the defeat of his army. Lastly Seleucus' first invasion of the upper satrapies necessarily occupied several months.

Can we be more precise? There are various pieces of evidence to be considered. First is the notorious fact that the Seleucid era began in October 312 in the Macedonian reckoning or April 311 according to the Babylonian calendar. That is the beginning of the first full year of Seleucus' unbroken regime in Babylonia. One could argue either that Seleucus occupied Babylon during that year and regarded the entire year as his first or that he entered the city late the previous year and did not begin the era until the first new year of his regime. Various local documents have been thought to settle the issue. The first extant dating by the reign of Alexander IV and Seleucus comes in May 311.[43] Before that there are

---

Towns of Zeugma on the Euphrates 237: 'There is no evidence of significant settlement at Zeugma before the Macedonian towns were founded'), but the rough distance to Babylon cannot be far wrong.

[41] Arr. 3.7.1 dates Alexander's arrival at Thapsacus to the Attic month of Hecatombaeon (10 July to 9 August), and on the evening of 20 September Alexander witnessed an eclipse of the sun after crossing the Tigris to the north of Gaugamela (cf. Bosworth, *HCA* 1.285–7).

[42] According to Diodorus (19.92.1) Nicanor amassed troops from Media, Persis, and the neighbouring lands (τῶν σύνεγγυς τόπων). Since he was based in Media, it would seem that the neighbouring lands are Parthyaea to the east (so Schober, *Untersuchungen* 98) and possibly Areia. It is also possible that he drew on auxiliaries from the shores of the Caspian, the Cadusians and Albanians for instance, who had fought with the Median contingent at Gaugamela (Arr. 3.8.4, 11.3–4; Curt. 4.12.12).

[43] BM 22022, dated to 10 Ajjar. I am grateful to Cornelia Wunsch who collated the tablet and brought it to my attention. The document does not mention

various documents dated by years of Antigonus, some by his sixth year, as late as December 312[44] and one apparently from his seventh year, dated to 12 Ajjar (13 May 311), two days after the first document of Alexander IV.[45] Del Monte, who was not apparently aware of the prior document, argued that the earliest Seleucus could have occupied Babylon was the second half of May 311. In that case one would need to posit a period of uncertainty with dates oscillating between Seleucus and Antigonus. But the tablet in question is not an unequivocal statement. It is a record of payment from the archive of the brewers of Borsippa, dealing with the receipt of a small amount of silver from the accounts of year 6 of Antigonus, dated 'Ajjar 12, year 7', whose year 7 is not stated.[46] Now, we seem to be dealing with a retrospective payment authorized in year 6 of Antigonus (312/11) but not paid out until some subsequent date. It could conceivably be an otherwise unattested year 7 of Antigonus,[47] but it is possible that the payment was ultimately made in year 7 of *Alexander* (i.e. in 310/9). Another document in the same archive refers to an amount of 1440 litres of dates from year 6 of Antigonus which were made over in year 6 of Alexander IV.[48] Here the name of the king is specified to differentiate the two regnal years. If, however, year 7 of Antigonus was not formally recognized at Babylon (and the Babylonian king lists give him six years), then there was no need to add explicitly

Seleucus, but it resumes the dating by the regnal years of Alexander IV, which had lapsed since 315.

[44] BM 67398 = *CT* 49 46 (6 Kislīm).

[45] BM 40882 = *CT* 49 50 (Del Monte 216): 'Marduk-erība, son of Bulluṭu-Bēl, has received 1/8 (of a šiqlu) of silver from the accounts of the brewers of year 6 of Antigonus. Ajjar 12, year 7.' The latest tablet as yet to appear from year 6 of Antigonus is BM 67398 = *CT* 49 46, dated to the month Kislīm (December 312). Tom Boiy has suggested to me that *CT* 49 57 and 59, which are dated to Šabāṭ of year 6 of an unnamed ruler, should be ascribed to Antigonus (so Del Monte 218). If so, the documents belong to February 311.

[46] The year number is uncertain; it is obscured by a seal impression, and year 6 could possibly be read. If so, it would remove the difficulty.

[47] It would be the only tablet dated to year 7, whereas there are nine from year 6 and eleven from year 5.

[48] BM 40464 = *CT* 49 22 (Del Monte 220): '1440 litres of dates from the (store of) dates of the brewers of year 6 of Antigonus. ... Ab 15, year 6 of king Alexander, son of Alexander (i.e. late August 311, before Antigonus' invasion).'

that the year was that of Alexander. That would be highly unusual, in that the regnal name almost always appears in Babylonian documents, even when there is no possible doubt about the ruler's identity. If we are faced with a genuine reference to a seventh year of Antigonus, then there was real uncertainty in Babylonia during the spring of 311; documents could be dated either by Antigonus or Alexander IV. The situation could reflect the tense period when Seleucus was away in the Iranian highlands and Babylonia was exposed to Demetrius' invasion.

Documents unequivocally dated by Antigonus continue at least to Kislīm of his year 6 (December 312).[49] Does that mean that Seleucus was not yet in Babylon? Hardly so. There were delicate questions of legitimacy at issue. What ruler would Seleucus represent in Babylon? Alexander IV was the prisoner of his ally, Cassander, and his bitter enemy, Antigonus, was defending the rights of the young king. We can see an echo of this earlier in 315. Documents in Babylonia were dated by the defunct Philip III until at least October 316.[50] Seleucus and Antigonus had been at war with Eumenes, the general who fought in the interests of Polyperchon, Olympias, and Alexander, and it is not surprising that they were reluctant to have documents dated in the name of the king whose representative they were fighting.[51] In late 316, however, the situation changed. Cassander joined the alliance against Antigonus, and Alexander became a cause to champion. Not surprisingly, Babylonian documents of the first half of 315 date by the first and second years of Alexander,[52] before Antigonus' increasingly autocratic pretensions led him to have documents dated in his own name, not as king but royal general.[53] That situation obtained until Seleucus returned to

---

[49] BM 67398 and 40881 = *CT* 49 46 and 49.

[50] BM 78948 = *AION* 53, A2–5 (18 Tašrīt). Another tablet dates to 13 August (*TCL* 13 259).

[51] If one adopts the 'low' chronology, as most Assyriologists do, then it was Seleucus who introduced the dating by the regnal years of Alexander IV, immediately after the defeat of Eumenes.

[52] For the evidence see Boiy, 'Laatachaemenidisch en hellenistisch Babylon' 127–8 and in NABU 1998/134.

[53] The earliest surviving tablet from Babylon (BM 33718 = *CT* 49 34) dates to Kislīm of year 3, that is, December 315. Antigonus clearly considered his rule to

Babylon. He was not prepared to invoke the name of the king imprisoned by Cassander, nor would he date in his own name as Antigonus had done. Galling as it presumably was to Seleucus, the existing system remained in force, a welcome bonus for private concerns like the brewers of Borsippa. For the moment they could avoid the awkwardness and ambiguity of changing ruler and regnal year. The situation changed when Cassander opened diplomatic overtures to end hostilities with Antigonus.[54] Seleucus could now embrace the name of Alexander, who had—by proxy—given him his satrapy years before at Triparadeisus. Early in the Babylonian year 311/10 he formally inaugurated dating by Alexander IV and by himself as satrap, and Nisan 311 naturally became the starting point of the Seleucid era.[55] This is admittedly a wholly speculative construction, but it helps explain the wayward Babylonian evidence. It is certainly not axiomatic that Babylonia was in Antigonus' hands until May 311.

We may now revert to the Chronicle. In the fragmentary passage which precedes the seventh year of Alexander IV there is an entry for the month of Ab, which has Seleucus in the process of capturing the palace at Babylon. The circumstances are mysterious, since the reading of the Chronicle is uncertain. On the most recent interpretation someone (possibly Archelaus) 'took flight, and did not dam the Euphrates'.[56] We are in late autumn, at the time of low water, when the drainage canals, in particular the great Pallukatu channel, would normally be blocked, sustaining the water level in the

---

have begun in the Babylonian year 317/16, when Philip Arrhidaeus was killed and Eumenes was defeated at Gabiene. By his third year he was master of Syria, Tyre excepted, and his *de facto* sway extended from Media and Persis to Hellespontine Phrygia. He still maintained the fiction that he was general of the king (*rab uqi*), but had documents dated in his own name, not by the pitiful, imprisoned Alexander IV.

[54] See below, pp. 239–44.

[55] That seems to be the most probable explanation of the problematic lines that begin the reverse of the Babylonian chronicle: 'The seventh year of Antig[onus as the 6th year of king Alexander the son of Alexander,] Seleucus (being) general, they count.'

[56] So M. J. Geller (*BSAOS* 53 (1990) 2 n. 11), reading ṣabābu ('he flew', 'took flight'), rather than Grayson's <zabābu ('was in a frenzy'). There is no reason to assume (with most commentators) that Seleucus is the subject of the sentence.

Euphrates.[57] It is a sign of disorder that the damming did not take place; the drama in Babylon dislocated the normal administrative arrangements. Whatever the reading, the palace fell into Seleucus' hands, and he left Babylon for a location on the Tigris. Then, in the month of Arahsamnu (October/ November), there is a reference to a treaty of friendship.

There has been a tendency to equate the capture of the palace with Seleucus' first arrival in Babylon, so that the subsequent action on the Tigris can be associated with Nicanor's invasion from Media.[58] But then one has the absence of Seleucus in the upper satrapies to account for, as well as Demetrius' invasion of Babylonia. That presents the most intractable difficulties, and there are two ways to go, both unacceptable. The first is extreme compression, such as we find in the recent construction by J. K. Winnicki. Here Seleucus captures the palace in July/August 311, and the Peace of the Dynasts duly takes place later in the year. Accordingly we have the victory over Nicanor and Demetrius' invasion of Babylonia placed in the single month of August.[59] That is a patent absurdity, but if we stretch these operations to a plausible duration, we find ourselves in 310 with Demetrius' invasion overlapping the major invasion of his father, Antigonus.

At this point another possibility obtrudes. Might not the invasion of Demetrius as described by Diodorus and Plutarch be identical with the invasion of Antigonus documented in the Chronicle? In that case we have two perspectives, the contemporary Babylonian record and a distorted Greek reflection of it. That is the most popular approach,

[57] Tom Boiy and Kris Verhoeven, in *Changing Watercourses in Babylonia* (*MHEM* 5/1: Ghent 1998) 147–58, esp. 152–4.

[58] See Schober, *Untersuchungen* 111, 116 for the two schemata, the first equating the events of rev. 6–8 with Seleucus' initial capture of the palace, the second with his return from Media and expulsion of Demetrius' garrison.

[59] See the summary (*AncSoc* 20 (1989) 66–7), which has Antigonus occupy Syria in May, while Athenaeus' and Demetrius' invasions of Nabataea take place in June and July. This is compressed indeed. Grainger, *Seleukos Nikator* 76–85 has a slacker chronology, with Seleucus invading Babylonia immediately after Gaza, in late 312 and the peace of the dynasts concluded in late summer 311. That is more acceptable, but he does not give an itemized timetable of events, observing that 'It all took time' (82).

adopted by Richard Billows and by most Assyriologists.[60] But the consequences are extremely unpalatable. Diodorus' account is totally incompatible with the Chronicle. The expedition is led by Demetrius not Antigonus. It is deliberately restricted in scope within a time limit set by Antigonus, whereas in the Chronicle there are hostilities over a period of more than a year. There are no pitched battles and Seleucus is not present in Babylonia,[61] whereas the Chronicle repeatedly mentions clashes between the armies of Antigonus and Seleucus. Finally Diodorus claims that the only serious fighting in Demetrius' invasion was over the citadels of Babylon, but in the (admittedly fragmentary) Babylonian account of the events of 310/9 there is no reference to the central fortresses. It is no solution to invoke incompetence on Diodorus' part, for Plutarch has essentially the same story of Demetrius' invasion—a brief incursion with limited objectives.[62] If there is distortion, the culprit is the common source, Hieronymus of Cardia, a contemporary who served with Antigonus and Demetrius in Syria,[63] and if his account is so sensationally wrong over the Antigonid invasion of Babylonia with which he was closely associated, then there is

---

[60] Billows, *Antigonos* 136–40. On the Babylonian side the most extreme position is that of Geller (*BSAOS* 53 (1990) 3–5), who, if I understand him aright, dates Seleucus' acquisition of power after the peace of 311, and refers Diod. 19.100 (Demetrius' invasion) to the events of 310–308 BC and Diod. 19.91–2 (Seleucus' capture of Babylon) to events in 308/7 after Antigonus' invasions. This presupposes not merely extreme temporal dislocation in Diodorus but also total garbling of the order of events.

[61] Diod. 19.100.5–7 and Plut. *Demetr.* 7.2–4 have exactly the same story. Seleucus was absent in Media. His general in Babylonia, Patrocles, avoided battle and wrote urging his master to return. Demetrius marched directly on Babylon, captured one of its citadels and left a substantial garrison.

[62] Billows, *Antigonos* 142 makes much of Plut. *Demetr.* 7.5, which places Demetrius' relief of Halicarnassus in 309, immediately after his retreat from Babylon. This is hardly a 'synchronism', rather a contrast. Plutarch regards the invasion of Babylonia as a somewhat discreditable affair, marred by the ravaging of Babylonia. But (μέντοι is emphatic) he retrieved his reputation by the relief of Halicarnassus, and was inspired to liberate Greece. To achieve that objective he sailed on Athens. The action at Halicarnassus forms a narrative bridge between the events of 311 and 307, and it is not synchronized with either.

[63] Hieronymus would not have accompanied Demetrius to Babylon. He was busy with his disastrous commission to exploit the bitumen of the Dead Sea (see Ch. 5), but he would have had first-hand reports of Demetrius' expedition and will have known precisely when it occurred.

practically nothing we can believe. We have lost the whole early history of the Successors.

There is only one acceptable conclusion. Seleucus' occupation of Babylon, the counter-offensive of Nicanor and Demetrius' invasion all came in the missing part of the Chronicle. The reverse of the tablet begins in the record of the sixth year of Alexander (311/10), and the first events concern Seleucus' return to Babylonia after his campaign in the upper satrapies. Then one of his first objectives will have been to recapture the citadel occupied by the garrison of Demetrius, and the entry for Ab (July/August) 311 must deal with the operations to recover it. In that case the invasion of Demetrius came roughly between April and June of 311, and during that period Seleucus was absent in the upper satrapies. The abortive attack by Nicanor took place towards the end of 312, and Seleucus will have entered Babylon for the first time around autumn 312. That allows a comparatively leisurely schedule. Seleucus established himself quickly in Babylon by September or October, beat off Nicanor's attack by the end of December, began his own offensive early in 311, occupying Susiana, Media, and satrapies further east. In the spring Demetrius exploited his absence to stage a brief incursion into Babylonia; it was over by midsummer, and Seleucus regained control of Babylon by August. The Peace of the Dynasts followed later in 311, and Antigonus, free of entanglements elsewhere, devoted his formidable resources to the invasion of Babylonia. The Greek and Babylonian sources do not conflict; they simply cover different stretches of time, and there is practically no overlap.

This chronological reconstruction has a direct impact on the dating of the Battle of Gaza. The received opinion is now that it took place in the autumn of 312, shortly before the onset of winter.[64] That allegedly is where the chronographic sources place it. If my programme for Seleucus' movements is accepted, such a late date is impossible; the battle must have taken place earlier in the year. Now, the chronographic sources are not as unequivocal as has been

---

[64] See for instance H. Hauben, *AJP* 94 (1973) 257–65; Errington, *Hermes* 105 (1977) 499; Winnicki 59–60; Billows, *Antigonos* 125–7; Wheatley, *Phoenix* 52 (1998) 258–61.

supposed. Diodorus is unhelpful, since he runs together the archon years 313/12 and 312/11; and he gives no indication where he supposed the second year to begin. That leaves us with the Parian Marble, which does date the battle to the archon year 312/11, and the late Hellenistic chronographer, Castor of Rhodes (quoted by Josephus), who placed the battle in the first year of the 117th Olympiad.[65] The Parian Marble is not the most reliable chronological guide. There are cases where it has postdated events to the subsequent archon year,[66] and the Battle of Gaza may fall in this category. An event in spring or early summer might easily be transferred to the following year.[67] In any case the previous entry, the first for 312/11, involves a notorious misdating; it records an eclipse of the sun which occurred two years later, in August 310/9.[68] This is very dubious company. The same might be said of Castor of Rhodes. Josephus quotes him as beginning the Olympiad with his record of the Battle of Gaza.[69] That seems clear enough. There is, however, a note of confusion. Josephus implies that another source placed the event in the eleventh year after Alexander's death (i.e. 313/12 at latest).[70] This other source is almost certainly Hecataeus of Abdera, whom Josephus wishes to date. The crucial point is that Hecataeus mentioned the Battle of Gaza,

---

[65] *FGrH* 239 B16 (Parian Marble); 250 F 12 (Castor). Malcolm Errington, *Hermes* 105 (1977) 499, also cites Porphyry, *FGrH* 260 F 32.4, where the first year of Olympiad 117 also appears, but what is at issue there is the start of the Seleucid era, not the Battle of Gaza.

[66] Clear cases are the dating of the Granicus to the archon year 334/3 instead of 335/4 (*FGrH* 239 B3: for good measure Issus is brought forward a year) and the return of Cassander to Macedon, which is placed in the archon year 316/15 instead of 317/16 (B 14)—he actually returned when he heard of the murder of Philip Arrhidaeus in autumn 317 (Diod. 19.35.1; cf. Bosworth, *Chiron* 22 (1992) 61–2, 81). The installation of Demetrius of Phalerum at Athens (B 14), which took place early in 317, is also postdated to the next archon year.

[67] It is associated with Seleucus' return to Babylon ('Ptolemy defeated Demetrius at Gaza and dispatched Seleucus to Babylon'). The two events are run into one, and the anchor point seems to be the beginning of the Seleucid era.

[68] The eclipse, total when Agathocles crossed from Sicily to Carthage, is correctly dated by Diodorus (20.5.5; cf. Justin 22.6.1).

[69] Jos. *c. Ap.* 1.185 = *FGrH* 250 F 12; 264 T 7a: προθεὶς γὰρ ταύτην τὴν ὀλυμπιάδα φησίν· ἐπὶ ταύτης Πτολεμαῖος ὁ Λάγου ἐνίκα κατὰ Γάζαν.

[70] *c. Ap.* 1.184: αὕτη δὲ γέγονεν ἐνδεκάτῳ μὲν ἔτει τῆς Ἀλεξάνδρου τελευτῆς, ἐπὶ δὲ ὀλυμπιάδος ἑβδόμης καὶ δεκάτης καὶ ἑκατοστῆς, ὡς ἱστορεῖ Κάστωρ.

and Josephus adds that it was fought in the eleventh year after Alexander. He then turns to Castor, and cites his Olympic dating as rough confirmation.[71] He is only concerned with an approximate date for Hecataeus, and the trivial variation is of little moment for him. But a variant there was, and Josephus underlines the fact, contrasting the death of Alexander which all agree (πάντες ὁμολογοῦσιν) took place in the 114th Olympiad.[72] It would seem that Hecataeus and Castor placed the battle in different years, in which case Hecataeus as the contemporary source should be preferred. Castor seems to have recorded the event several months too late. In any case he begins his record of the Olympiad with the battle, and that indicates summer rather than autumn.

Diodorus adds more controversy. When Ptolemy and Seleucus broke out of Egypt with their army, Demetrius had taken up position at Gaza with the nucleus of his forces. The rest were in winter quarters, and he had to summon them from all directions (Diod. 19.80.5). We are, then, close to winter, but is it the winter of 313/12 or that of 312/11? If the latter, we should assume that Demetrius had sent his troops away prematurely for the winter and had to recall them when news broke of the Ptolemaic invasion. That is certainly a possibility, but it restricts an already tight chronology. We should have to date the battle towards December, to allow the troops time to disperse and regroup,[73] and in that case Seleucus can hardly have reached Babylon before the early months of 311. If, however, the Ptolemaic army left Egypt at the beginning of 312, Demetrius' troops were still dispersed in their winter billets, and he would have required some weeks before his army was united and ready for action. The

---

[71] There is clearly a variant: Josephus juxtaposes and contrasts the dating by years (ἐνδεκάτῳ μὲν ἔτει) with the Olympic version of Castor (ἐπὶ δὲ ὀλυμπιάδος). Castor is only associated with the dating by Olympiads, whereas the dating by years after Alexander's death immediately follows the statement that Hecataeus mentioned the victory at Gaza. Hecataeus could well have noted that it took place in the eleventh year after Alexander's death. [72] Jos. *c. Ap.* 1.185.
[73] When he returned to Cilicia in late 316, Antigonus sent his army into winter quarters after the setting of Orion, in November (Diod. 19.56.5). He had recently arrived from Babylonia, and might have divided his forces somewhat earlier had he been consistently on the Levantine coast.

battle proper could have taken place in April,[74] close enough to the middle of the Julian year to be absorbed into the next Athenian or Olympic year, especially if the chronicler were primarily concerned with the occupation of Syria which followed the battle.

If, then, Gaza was fought in spring 312, we can let events move at an even pace. In the next months Ptolemy occupied Phoenicia, overcoming resistance at Tyre, where the Antigonid governor held out against him for an indefinite period.[75] He presumably moved up the coast, forcing Demetrius back to Cilicia, where he regrouped and retrained his army.[76] All this will have taken some months, into the summer of 312. There was a period of stalemate; the Ptolemaic commanders were unwilling to force their way into Cilicia, where Alexander had given an object lesson in the strategic deployment of numbers, and Demetrius was too weak to challenge the occupation of Syria. The tables were turned militarily when Demetrius moved back into Northern Syria with his new army, and defeated Cilles, the general whom Ptolemy sent to crush him.[77] That is most conveniently dated around August 312. The news of the victory was relayed to Antigonus at his capital at Celaenae in Phrygia, and his response was to take an army to reinforce Demetrius, while his son took up a defensive position awaiting his arrival. Antigonus had to march through Anatolia, down through the Cilician Gates, across Cilicia and into Northern Syria. It would have been at least a

---

[74] For what it is worth (and the context is not impressive) Paus. 1.6.5 alleges that Antigonus heard of his son's defeat when he was at the Hellespont, and the news forced him to withdraw. Now, Antigonus had operated in the Propontis at the advent of winter 313/12, and distributed his army among the cities there (Diod. 19.77.7). When spring came, he presumably continued the delicate strategy of the previous year, hoping that the successes of his general, Polemaeus, in Central Greece would distract Cassander from the defence of Macedon. The massive defeat at Gaza put an end for the moment to his hopes of invading Europe, and he withdrew to his capital at Celaenae. There he received the news that Demetrius had retrieved the situation by his defeat of Cilles.

[75] Diod. 19.86.1–2. The length of the siege is not stated, but there was an interval between Andronicus' defiance of Ptolemy and the 'later' (ὕστερον) mutiny of his garrison troops.

[76] Demetrius needed to recruit, to replace the massive losses he had suffered at Gaza (see above, p. 216). That will have taken some months, as will Ptolemy's occupation of Syria.   [77] Diod. 19.93.1–2; Plut. *Demetr.* 6.2–5.

Table 1 A Chronology 312–309

Battle of Gaza April 312		
Occupation of Phoenicia by Ptolemy and retreat of Demetrius summer 312		
Seleucus leaves for Babylon	August (?) 312	Debacle of Cilles August 312
Seleucus occupies Babylon	September/ October 312	Return of Antigonus September 312 Antigonid reoccupation of Syria autumn 312
Defeat of Nicanor	December 312	Nabataean campaigns winter 312/11
Seleucus in the upper satrapies	March–June 311	Demetrius' invasion of Babylonia April–June 311
Peace of the Dynasts autumn 311		
Antigonus' invasion of Babylonia August 310 to late 309		

month before he joined forces with his son.[78] Now the Antigonid forces were predominant, 'many times greater', according to Diodorus (19.93.6), and Ptolemy wisely withdrew to fortress Egypt, devastating the coastal cities of Palestine as he went and transporting the booty with him. Antigonus followed and re-established his control. This would have taken the autumn of 312.[79] The complex dealings with the Nabataean Arabs then took place over winter 312/11, and Demetrius was ready to invade Babylonia in the spring of 311. Table 1 will summarize this convoluted discussion.

[78] Diod. 19.93.3 claims that Antigonus joined forces with him 'in a few days' (ὀλίγαις ἡμέραις). That hardly refers to the entire march from Celaenae but rather its final stage after crossing the Taurus.

[79] The coinage of Sidon adds a slight complication. As is well known, the royal mint there struck imperial tetradrachms in the names of Alexander and Philip III. We have a continuous series, beginning in 333/2, and each year is numbered (E. T. Newell, *The Dated Alexander Coinage of Sidon and Ake* (New Haven 1916); the results are lucidly summarized by O. Mørkholm, *Chiron* 8 (1978) 136–42; see also Price 435–44). Now, in year 22 (312/11) the regular tetradrachm duly bears the date *X* (year 22) with the city monogram *ΣI* beneath the throne of Zeus (Price nos. 3511–12). To the same year belongs a distinctively Ptolemaic issue (obv.: head of Alexander with ram's horns and elephant scalp; rev.: Athena with spear and shield); it also bears the Sidonian monogram and is dated to year 22. There can be no doubt that Ptolemy used the mint of Sidon for his emissions during part of 312/11 along with the regular coinage (I. L. Merker, *ANSMN* 11 (1964) 13–20; Mørkholm

The weight of evidence suggests that Seleucus left Syria in the late summer of 312, and that Diodorus is roughly correct in placing his departure after Ptolemy's annexation of Phoenicia and before Demetrius defeated Cilles. In that case we can draw some conclusions. What mattered was the Ptolemaic occupation of Syria—all Syria. If Seleucus was to be reasonably safe in Babylonia, it was essential to cut off access by Antigonid armies. In that case the area of the Amik plain, the heartland of the future Seleucid Tetrapolis, was vital. The plain commanded the direct route to the Euphrates, and while it was in Antigonid hands, an army could quickly be sent into Babylonia. Seleucus' security depended on a firm alliance with Ptolemy and upon Ptolemy holding Northern Syria against Antigonus. Ptolemy then became the front line of defence, forcing Antigonus either to fight for Syria or to retrace the footsteps of the Ten Thousand through Armenia and Kurdistan to the Upper Tigris, hardly an enticing prospect for a large, variegated army. Now, the Battle of Gaza did not immediately secure the whole of Syria. Demetrius' first intention was to hold the line at Tripolis in Northern Phoenicia. That left the road to the Euphrates, if not in his control, at least vulnerable to attack. The position became untenable as first Sidon and then Tyre fell into Ptolemy's hands, and Demetrius was finally confined to Cilicia. It was

137–8; Price 435; Wheatley, *Phoenix* 52 (1998) 258–61). But what part of 312/11? As Mørkholm frankly admits, we have no evidence for the start of the year at Sidon. It is mere assumption that it correlated with the Macedonian calendar and began in autumn. If the minting year began in spring, then Ptolemy's emissions can easily be fitted into the summer and autumn of 312, after he occupied Sidon. If, however, Newell was right and the year began in autumn, we should conclude that Ptolemy had his coins struck on the eve of evacuating Syria. If nothing else, having them in circulation would embarrass the Antigonids when they moved into the area. [Newell 33 based his arguments on the emissions in the name of Philip Arrhidaeus which were minted in four successive years, from year 13 (321/20) to year 16 (318/17). The only known issue of 317/16 is in the name of Alexander. Now, Philip was killed in mid-October, 317, and Newell inferred that the news reached Sidon before dies with his name began operation. That is not compelling. The news that interrupted minting in the name of Philip may have been the schism in the ruling house between Eurydice and Cassander (who acted in the name of Philip) and the 'guardian of the kings', Polyperchon. The troubles began early in 317, and the Sidonian mint may not have struck in Philip's name until the crisis was resolved— and it was only resolved by Philip's death.

there that he regrouped his forces and prepared for a new offensive, and it was the news that he had left Cilicia for Northern Syria that resulted in Cilles' disastrous campaign against him (Diod. 19.93.1). For some months he had vacated Syria altogether, and it was in those months that Seleucus began his expedition to Babylonia. The road was open to him, and there was no immediate threat from the Antigonid forces in the west. He could reoccupy his old satrapy without interference. That was one of the declared objectives of the coalition war, and after four years of hostilities it was achieved.

Seleucus set off with a minuscule force, 'no more than 800 foot and around 200 horse',[80] and Diodorus comments on its size. It pointed up Seleucus' high morale; his hopes were so elevated that he would have taken the road east with his friends and slaves even if he had had no army whatsoever (Diod. 19.90.1). Modern scholars have often noted the small numbers of the force Ptolemy provided, and some surprising conclusions have been drawn. Most recently Winnicki has argued that Seleucus left Syria only after the defeat of Cilles; the confusion it caused would have concealed his departure and maximized secrecy.[81] Furthermore Seleucus did not take the northerly route, but (so Winnicki argues) he struck across the desert, taking a route from the Egyptian border directly to Susiana, and the locality named Κάραι, where Seleucus recruited Macedonian colonists, was not Carrhae (Harran) in Mesopotamia, as is usually assumed, but the villages in Babylonia (Καρῶν κῶμαι) where Eumenes had wintered in 318/17.[82] In that case small numbers were imperative, and Winnicki makes much of the famous passage

[80] So Diod. 19.90.1; App. *Syr.* 54.273 rounds up the figures to 1,000 foot and 300 horse.

[81] Winnicki, *AncSoc* 20 (1989) 76–84; esp. 78, where the expedition is dated to the second half of March 311, when Demetrius had occupied Syria with an army 'which must have been much larger than his earlier one'.

[82] Diod. 19.12.1, often identified with the Κάραι κῶμαι of Diod. 17.110.3. In the latter passage the area is visited by Alexander on his way from Susa to Opis, and it seems to have been located west of the Tigris on the south side of Sittacene. On the location of Eumenes' Carian villages, again west of the Tigris but apparently further to the north see above, p. 108 n. 42. Seleucus would have reached Babylon before impacting upon either area.

of Arrian's *Indike* which describes the journey made by a contingent of troops which Ptolemy sent to Seleucus across Arabia.[83] It took eight days, and the men travelled at night by camel, taking water with them. If Seleucus took the same route, then it necessarily required a small force which could carry its own water supplies and could move rapidly across the desert. Hence the numbers were small because they had to be; in fact Ptolemy supplied the maximum which could make the desert crossing.

For all its ingenuity I find this reconstruction totally unacceptable. In the first place there is a telling argument from silence. Arrian's account of the desert crossing is designed to highlight the difficulties traversing Arabia.[84] No one has succeeded in exploring the entire coastline despite the fact that the Red Sea and Persian Gulf allow circumnavigation. By land even the northern 'isthmus' is so torrid that it was crossed only by survivors from Cambyses' army[85] and by the small contingent sent by Ptolemy.[86] If Seleucus had taken the same route in 312, one would have expected Arrian's source (here surely Eratosthenes) to have enlarged on the fact. In any case Ptolemy's force was highly mobile, mounted on fast camels, and could cross the desert in just over a week, consuming a limited amount of water. By contrast Seleucus had infantry and cavalry, who would have taken much longer than camels to cross the desert, and the water and provisions to supply them would have required a prodigious number of transport animals. Finally there seems no possibility that the

---

[83] Arr. *Ind.* 43.4–5. The circumstances are mysterious. There have been various attempts to provide a context for the episode, but there are too many possibilities (e.g. a request for help on the eve of the Antigonid invasion of Egypt in late 306), and no basis for speculation.

[84] See the analysis in Bosworth, *From Arrian to Alexander* 193–4.

[85] There is no other evidence for this episode. It is possible that Cambyses was represented sending a force into the eastern desert (against Petra?), just as Herodotus depicts him sending an army to Siwah (Hdt. 3.25–6). The Siwah contingent disappeared in the desert without trace, so Herodotus reported, and an expedition to the east might have suffered a similar fate with only a few survivors limping in to Susa.

[86] There is a comparable episode earlier in the century: the deposed Egyptian King Tachos, eager to make his peace with the Great King, made his way through Arabia (Diod. 15.92.5). That again would have involved a small contingent, in all probability travelling on camels.

Macedonian settlers at Κάραι were domiciled in Babylonia. Diodorus explicitly locates them in Mesopotamia. He is certainly not here making a general reference to the lands between the rivers, as Winnicki supposes. When Diodorus refers to Mesopotamia, he tends to refer to the satrapy, invariably so in the books which deal with the Successors.[87] In any case Diodorus states that Seleucus first entered Mesopotamia, took on the settlers at Κάραι, and then invaded Babylonia.[88] That makes it clear that the settlement was *not* in Babylonia and that Mesopotamia *is* indeed the satrapy of that name.

Seleucus, then, took the regular route to the Euphrates, and did so after Ptolemy occupied Northern Syria. That explains the small numbers with Seleucus. From this point the main responsibility for keeping the Antigonid armies in Asia Minor was Ptolemy's. He would need to contain and suppress any break out from Cilicia and prevent Syria falling into enemy hands. For that he needed all the troops he could muster, and they would provide the forward defence for Babylonia. Seleucus had to be content with a relatively small force. There would be no obstruction before he crossed the Euphrates, and the garrison forces of Babylon were denuded. Peithon, son of Agenor, the satrap imposed by Antigonus, had come west in 314/13 and fought with Demetrius at Gaza.[89] No doubt he had brought mercenary forces with him, many of whom will have died with him; the rest were either with Ptolemy or with Demetrius in Cilicia. Babylonia was comparatively vulnerable to a small force of high calibre. And Seleucus' contingent included veterans of Alexander's

---

[87] Diod. 18.3.4, 6.3, 39.6; 19.13.5, 15.6, 27.4, 100.5.

[88] Diod. 19.91.1: κατήντησεν εἰς Μεσοποταμίαν, τῶν ἐν Κάραις κατῳκισμένων Μακεδόνων οὓς μὲν ἔπεισεν...ὡς δ' εἰς τὴν Βαβυλωνίαν ἐνέβαλεν.

[89] Diod. 19.69.1, 80.1 (deputy of Demetrius in Coele Syria) 82.1 (reputation for service under Alexander), 85.2 (death at Gaza). In effect Seleucus encoutered minimal resistance in Babylonia, the only opposition coming from Diphilus in the citadel of Babylon. Mehl, *Seleukos Nikator und sein Reich* 89–90 draws attention to the relatively defenceless state of Babylonia (contra Winnicki, *AncSoc* 20 (1989) 77). Diodorus (19.90.2) claims that Seleucus' companions were demoralized by their small numbers in relation to the forces they would face, but this fits into the wider context of Seleucus' regal ambitions, which extended beyond Babylonia into the eastern satrapies, whose combined armies were genuinely formidable. It was not the recapture of Babylon but its sequel that was the deterrent.

expedition; his address to his friends at least represents them as having campaigned with the conqueror and received promotion because of their excellence.[90] Such a force could have an impact far beyond its numerical strength—as the Perdiccan prisoners in Asia Minor had shown when they overcame their gaolers, and some 50 of them held at bay an army of 4,000 for 16 months.[91]

Seleucus could also expect to supplement his army, and his intervention at Carrhae is an interesting case in point. By persuasion and force he recruited all the Macedonians resident there.[92] Commentators have been surprisingly incurious about this group of military settlers.[93] How were they established, and who were they? It is certain that they cannot have been a contingent settled by Alexander, for he passed through Mesopotamia at a time when he needed every last Macedonian, and that was long before the network of military colonies evolved in the eastern satrapies. There is no record of his sending discharged soldiers out as colonists when he was in Babylonia and Media in the last years of his reign, and in all cases where he established Macedonians in his new Alexandrias they were a small minority among the European settlers. The Macedonians in Carrhae were a substantial group, and they can hardly have been installed by Alexander himself. The colony, then, was established after 323. Hardly by Perdiccas,[94] who needed all the Macedonians he could muster for the invasions of Cappadocia and Egypt; and once the grand army left Babylonia there would have been few, if any Macedonians available for settlement. The first, and possibly the only occasion was in 316, after

---

[90] Diod. 19.90.3; τοὺς Ἀλεξάνδρῳ συνεστρατευκότας καὶ δι' ἀρετὴν ὑπ' ἐκείνου προηγμένους.

[91] Diod. 19.16.1–5. Cf. Hornblower, *Hieronymus* 125–6; Heckel 183–4; Bosworth, *Alexander and the East* 27–8.

[92] Diod. 19.91.1: τῶν ἐν Κάραις κατῳκισμένων Μακεδόνων οὓς μὲν ἔπεισεν οὓς δ' ἐβιάσατο συστρατεύειν αὐτῷ.

[93] Berve i.296 assumed without discussion that it was a foundation of Alexander.

[94] Eusebius' Chronicle records a settlement of Macedonians at Samaria both by Alexander (after the death of Andromachus) and by Perdiccas (Euseb. *Chron.*, ed. Schoene II p. 114, 118; cf. Schürer, *History of the Jewish People* ii.160–2). Curtius (4.8.9–11), however, reports the Samaritan revolt of 332/1 but says nothing of any foundation at Samaria. The basis for the reports may be that both Alexander and Perdiccas imposed garrisons of western troops in the native city.

Antigonus received the surrender of Eumenes' army. One particular group was demobilized and dispersed. That was the famous corps of Silver Shields. Three thousand strong at the Battle of Gabiene and hardly touched in the fighting, the troops were reallocated by Antigonus after their surrender. The largest group, 1,000 strong, went to Sibyrtius in Arachosia; the rest were distributed as garrison troops in outlying areas.[95] Carrhae was just such a place, at the edge of the desert to the south-east of Edessa,[96] under the watchful eye of Antigonus' friend, Peithon the new satrap of Babylonia. If, then, the men recruited by Seleucus were ex-Silver Shields, then he had very formidable allies. As former hypaspists of Alexander they had served under him or close to him, and it is not surprising that he was able to persuade many of them to join him. They were also arguably the most expert and experienced fighting men in the contemporary world, schooled in every branch of infantry warfare. We have no idea how many of them Seleucus enlisted to his cause, probably no more than a few hundred, but their expertise was invaluable, and it comes as no surprise to find Seleucus taking the citadel of Babylon by storm as he entered the city.[97] His men had captured innumerable hill forts in Sogdiana and Gandhara and progressed down the Indus siege by siege. No soldiers were more experienced in poliorcetics.

Seleucus' progress through Babylonia had been virtually unopposed. Perhaps the demands of Antigonus' war effort had made the previous regime appear a golden age. At all events the native population flocked to greet him.[98] An Antigonid official, Polyarchus, also surrendered; he was operating with 1,000 (mercenary) soldiers, no match for Seleucus' hardened troops, and he joined the invading army. Babylon lay open to him, and he was able to take the citadel, the old royal palace, by storm. But he could not rest on his

---

[95] Polyaen. 4.6.15; cf. Diod. 19.48.3; Plut. *Eum.* 19.3. See above, pp. 164–6 ff.

[96] Carrhae (modern Harran) is not as remote as the text of Polyaenus would have us believe were the places selected for the operations of the Silver Shields. However, the tradition is patently affected by contemporary moralizing—the Silver Shields were to pay for their betrayal of Eumenes (above, p. 164), and the unpleasantness of their assignments is overstressed.

[97] Diod. 19.91.4: κατὰ κράτος ἑλών.

[98] Diod. 19.91.1–2 (cf. 90.1); App. *Syr.* 54.274.

laurels. The grand strategy had already failed in the west. Cilles had been defeated soon after he left for Babylon, and Demetrius was entrenched in Upper Syria. That was not an irretrievable disaster.[99] Ptolemy might have renewed the offensive and crushed Demetrius before his father came to join and reinforce him. He did nothing of the kind. He left Demetrius strictly alone, and when Antigonus entered Syria with his army, he vacated Coele Syria on the advice of his friends and retired to Egypt.[100] Seleucus was now vulnerable to attack from the west. The attack would not come until Antigonus had secured Syria and taken measures to prevent a counter-offensive by Ptolemy, but in the future Seleucus could count on an Antigonid army crossing the Euphrates. He needed to increase his military resources, to be in a position to counter the invasion when it came.

The defeat of Nicanor gave him a golden opportunity. Not only did it save Babylonia from invasion; Nicanor's army promptly went over to Seleucus. They were in enemy territory and vulnerable, and there was every military reason for their surrender. However, Diodorus adds that they were alienated by Antigonus' policies.[101] The comment concerns the rank-and-file, not the commanders, and it suggests that there was widespread dissatisfaction with Antigonus' imperial ambitions among the garrison forces of Asia. It was disaffection that Seleucus could profitably exploit, all the more since his own forces were now enlarged to a total of more than 10,000 foot. There was also a massive influx of cavalry; Nicanor had apparently brought 7,000 with him, and most stayed to serve Seleucus, who previously had only a few hundreds. What is more, Nicanor's recruiting had drained the military reserves of the upper satrapies, and they were now vulnerable to an attack from Babylonia. Seleucus exploited the weakness and first annexed Susiana, which was open to attack and cannot have had the resources to counter his army. Then he moved

---

[99] Demetrius is said to have captured Cilles' entire army (Diod. 19.93.2), allegedly 7,000 strong (Plut. *Demetr.* 6.2). It was a significant loss for Ptolemy, but Demetrius was not confident enough to take the offensive. He buried himself in a fortified camp and waited for his father's army.

[100] Diod. 19.93.6–7; Plut. *Demetr.* 6.3.

[101] Diod. 19.92.4: προσκόπτοντες τοῖς ὑπ' Ἀντιγόνου πραττομένοις.

into the Iranian plateau for some of the most important actions of his career.

Here our sources are infuriatingly reticent. According to Diodorus he occupied Susiana, Media, 'and some of the neighbouring areas'.[102] What those neighbouring areas were he does not specify. We should perhaps assume that Persis was one of them; a substantial body of native Persians were now fighting with Seleucus, and Asclepiodorus, the satrap Antigonus imposed in 316, had not been a popular appointment.[103] Seleucus' newly acquired troops could have led him through the Persian Gates, and the populace would have welcomed him as the heir to the heritage of Peucestas. After Persis Media was open to him, as Nicanor was left without a viable army, and he could forge eastwards, towards Parthyaea and Areia, whose satrap, Evagoras,[104] had fallen during Nicanor's disastrous expedition. How far east he went is conjectural. Plutarch claims that he intended 'to win the nations bordering on the Indians and the provinces around the Caucasus';[105] taken literally that should mean that Seleucus' intention was to go as far as Arachosia and Parapamisadae, the satrapies bordering on India and the Hindu Kush. The language is rhetorical but for all that precise,[106] and one may

---

[102] Diod.19.92.5: προσηγάγετο τήν τε Σουσιανὴν καὶ Μηδίαν καί τινας τῶν σύνεγγυς τόπων.

[103] There was considerable native resistance to the deposition of Peucestas (Diod. 19.48.5), and Asclepiodorus was clearly unwelcome. He may have had experience as financial supervisor of Babylon under Alexander (Arr, 3.16.4; cf. Berve ii no. 109; Billows, *Antigonos* 376), but that is unlikely to have endeared him to the natives. Mehl, *Seleukos Nikator und sein Reich* 110 infers from Diodorus' silence that Persis was not occupied by Seleucus. That is improbable. It is more likely that Diodorus has vaguely summarized a longer list of territorial acquisitions, including Persis and other satrapies.

[104] I follow the orthodoxy that the 'Euagros' who is described as the satrap in command of the Persians in Nicanor's army (Diod, 19.92.4) is identical with the 'Euagoras' placed over Areia in 316 (Diod. 19.48.2).

[105] Plut. *Demetr.* 7.2: τὰ συνοροῦντα τοῖς Ἰνδοῖς ἔθνη καὶ τὰς περὶ Καύκασον ἐπαρχίας προσαξόμενος.

[106] On Arachosia as a satrapy bordering on India see Arr. 3.8.4, 28.1; for the connection of Parapamisadae and the Caucasus see Arr. 5.3.3 with Bosworth, *HCA* ii.213–17. Plutarch speaks of a plurality of provinces 'around the Caucasus', and he presumably includes Bactria (cf. Arr. 5.5.3). It is certainly possible that Seleucus sent diplomatic feelers to the far north-east; his wife Apame was the daughter of the most famous Sogdian noble of Alexander's day, and she will have helped win him the support of the natives there.

assume that Plutarch to some degree expresses what he found in his source. It would not be surprising if Seleucus made diplomatic overtures to the major satrapies of the east and contacted Sibyrtius in Arachosia and Oxyartes, if he still held sway in Parapamisadae. If so, the results of the campaign were impressive. Seleucus occupied Susiana, Media, and probably Persis and Areia, and imposed satraps of his own choosing, He may well have also obtained promises of support from most of the satraps of the east. They will have judged it imprudent to offer opposition and face Seleucus' now formidable army; it was better to acquiesce in his territorial gains and hope that he and Antigonus would destroy each other, leaving them, as before, *de facto* monarchs of their satrapies. In the meantime Seleucus had made himself a dynast to be reckoned with. According to Diodorus (19.92.5) he now had royal stature and a reputation worthy of hegemony, a rival of Antigonus himself.

Antigonus received dispatches from Nicanor, informing him of Seleucus' penetration of the upper satrapies, and he sent a retaliatory expedition under his son, Demetrius, with orders to recover Babylonia in Seleucus' absence and then return to the sea. Two features of the commission are noteworthy: first, Demetrius' force, though sizeable, was by no means the full complement of the Antigonid forces in Syria and, second, he was working in a strict time frame imposed by his father; there was a date fixed in advance for his return.[107] It comes as no surprise that Antigonus did not send his full army. If Syria was drained of the Antigonid occupying forces, it lay wide open to Ptolemy, who would gladly regain possession. But the size of Demetrius' force would have presented a risk; however large the Antigonid army, the detachment of 5,000 Macedonians, 10,000 mercenaries, and 4,000 cavalry would have been a significant diminution,[108] and Antigonus had vivid memories of what had happened the previous year

[107] Diod. 19.100.7; cf. 100.4 (καταβαίνειν συντόμως)—speed was obviously of the essence.

[108] Diod. 19.100.4. We do not know the number of troops with Antigonus in Syria, but he had brought an army with him from Celaenae (Diod. 19.93.6) and joined the forces of Demetrius, which comprised the survivors of Gaza (around 10,000, infantry and cavalry combined), the forces he had recruited in Cilicia and the prisoners from Cilles' army, an additional 7,000 (Plut. *Demetr.* 6.3). The total

when Demetrius' moderate holding army encountered Ptolemy and Seleucus at Gaza. When he gave Demetrius his commission, he must have had reason to think that Ptolemy would not attack in force, and the reason is probably connected with the diplomatic negotiations which were proceeding at the time.

During the coalition war there had been a number of overtures and meetings designed to end hostilities. In late 315 Antigonus had conferred with Ptolemy at the borders of Egypt (Diod. 19.64.8), but nothing had come of it. Similarly in 313 he had negotiated with Cassander but failed to reach agreement (Diod. 19.75.6). By 311 a general fatigue had set in. In the west Lysimachus and Cassander were eager to conclude a treaty which would prevent any Antigonid crossing into Europe, while the defection of Telesphorus (Antigonus' nephew and admiral in Greece) made Antigonus more receptive to peace with the European dynasts.[109] In the boastful circular letter he sent to the Greek cities of Asia (a copy of which was directed to the little town of Scepsis) he claims that he had devoted time and expense to the cause of the freedom of the Greeks and made concessions in their interests, and there was a protracted period of negotiation. The dynasts themselves did not meet. The business was transacted by ambassadors. In the case of Cassander and Lysimachus they were represented by Cassander's general and confidant, Prepelaus, while Aristodemus of Miletus acted in the Antigonid interest.[110] There were obviously several exchanges before agreement was reached, and finally Prepelaus arrived in Syria with an essential agreement; he had full powers to

army is said to have been many times stronger than the forces at Ptolemy's disposal (Diod. 19.93.6); Demetrius' expedition would have called on no more than half, but the numbers were still very significant, almost exactly the size of the army he had commanded at Gaza.

[109] On the defection of Telesphorus see Diod. 19.87.1–3. How serious it was is hard to tell. Telesphorus remained on speaking terms with his cousin and rival Polemaeus (87.3) and was back in Demetrius' entourage by 307/6 (Diog. Laert. 5.79; cf. Billows, *Antigonos* 435–6). But in 312 his rebellion was more or less synchronous with Demetrius' defeat at Gaza and must have shaken Antigonus' confidence.

[110] Welles *RC* 1, lines 11, 28, 47–8. On the prosopography see H. Hauben, *EA* 9 (1987) 29–36.

make minor amendments, which indicates that there was unity on the essential matters.

At this point, so Antigonus' letter asserts, ambassadors arrived from Ptolemy requesting his inclusion in the agreement. Antigonus was apparently reluctant, but he claims that he conceded in the interests of general peace.[111] There followed an exchange of envoys and eventually Ptolemy was included in the agreement. Behind the bland, self-satisfied terminology of the letter we can sense something of the ruthless diplomatic cut and thrust. When Ptolemy realized that peace was imminent between Antigonus and the European dynasts, he appreciated the risks of isolation; if there was no danger of a counter-offensive across the Hellespont, Antigonus could transfer forces *en masse* to the Syrian front and launch an invasion of Egypt. It was best to come to terms, join his allies in making peace and so pre-empt the attack. The negotiations clearly took some time before agreement was reached, and they could well have taken place over the spring of 311. During that period Antigonus could detach a large segment of his army without risk of Ptolemy exploiting their absence. On the other hand he needed his forces together after the negotiations in case they proved abortive and Ptolemy made a lightning attack. There was time for an incursion into Babylonia, which, if successful, would regain the satrapy for the Antigonids and deny Seleucus access to the lowlands of Mesopotamia.

As it transpired, the time limit was too restrictive. Demetrius occupied Babylon, which Seleucus had left almost empty of troops, but he was able to spend no more than a few days there.[112] He captured one of its citadels and left a garrison besieging the second, but then retraced his steps to the coast. Seleucus could return and re-establish his authority in the capital. This he did by August 311. Babylonia was back securely in his hands, and his influence now extended far east into the Iranian plateau, with some satraps appointed by him, others prepared to co-operate. He needed all the support he could get, for now Ptolemy was negotiating with Antigonus and in due course he became one

---

[111] *RC* i, lines 29–37.   [112] Diod. 19.100.7.

of the signatories of the Peace of the Dynasts. That peace is recorded by Diodorus as the first event of the archon year 311/10,[113] and, if my reconstruction is correct, it took place in summer or late autumn, 311. There is no doubt that the peace was concluded between four dynasts: Antigonus, Ptolemy, Cassander, and Lysimachus. Those are the names explicitly attested in Diodorus and in Antigonus' letter, and there can have been no other party. The provisions of course affected other dynasts, but they were not signatories in their own right. Now, the main feature of the peace, other than the guarantee of freedom and autonomy to Greek cities, was the formal ratification of the current territorial division. Until Alexander IV came of age and assumed the kingship Cassander was to continue as viceroy in Europe; Lysimachus was to retain Thrace, Ptolemy Egypt with its annexes of Cyrenaica and Arabia. In his turn Antigonus was to have command over all Asia.[114] The terminology is brief but pregnant. Antigonus' authority was confirmed throughout Asia, and his former adversaries renounced the demands they had made in 316/15. They now allowed him free scope to make and terminate satrapal appointments from the Hellespont to the far east, exactly as he had done in 316.

What of Seleucus? Had he simply been deserted by his allies and left to Antigonus' disposal? One can well believe that his meteoric success in 312/11 caused resentment. His previous associates had not been so successful. If we examine the famous Stele of the Satrap, inscribed in Egypt after the inundation in the seventh year of Alexander IV (the summer of 311), the position becomes very clear.[115] Ptolemy is described in the most fulsome terms, his conquests extolled. But despite the hyperbole the conquests seem somewhat restricted. Apart from a punitive expedition against an

<hr/>

[113] Diod. 19.105.1. For a thorough review of modern discussions see Seibert, *Das Zeitalter der Diadochen* 123–7 (see particularly R. H. Simpson, *JHS* 74 (1954) 25–31), to which add Billows, *Antigonos* 132–6; Grainger, *Seleukos Nikator* 85–7; Lund, *Lysimachus* 60–2.

[114] Diod. 19.105.1: Ἀντίγονον δὲ ἀφηγεῖσθαι τῆς Ἀσίας πάσης.

[115] For bibliography see Seibert 225. The most accessible English translation is in E. Bevan, *A History of Egypt under the Ptolemaic Dynasty* 29–32. For commentary and directed discussion see H. Goedicke, *BES* 6 (1984) 33–54; Winnicki, *AncSoc* 22 (1991) 164–85.

African desert people[116] there is only the conquest of Syria. With tactful reticence the stele omits any reference to the defeat of Cilles and the subsequent retreat from Syria, but it does specify how Ptolemy deprived the Syrians of their princes, their cavalry, their ships, their works of art, all of which he carried off to Egypt.[117] Here Ptolemy was behaving in true Pharaonic style. However, the action which so enriched Egypt was his looting of the coastal cities of Palestine when he vacated Syria in the face of Antigonus' invasion.[118] In terms of Egyptian propaganda this could be represented as a triumph. But there were other perspectives. According to Plutarch (*Demetr.* 7.4), when Demetrius looted Babylon, he helped cement Seleucus' right to it, for by plundering the land, he demonstrated that he did not regard it as his. Spear-won land one did not devastate, and devastation was a kind of renunciation.[119] So by pillaging the cities of southern Syria Ptolemy was symbolically accepting the Antigonid claims to it. It could be argued too that he had acquired Syria through the advice and talents of Seleucus and lost it by his own unaided efforts. The letters Seleucus sent from the upper satrapies boasting of his successes cannot have helped matters. Ptolemy may well have felt that his protégé had been a good deal too successful, and could well be cut down to size. Reaffirming the suzerainty of Antigonus was one way to apply pressure and to neutralize Seleucus' newly won dominance in the east.

---

[116] For the various suggestions made see Winnicki, *AncSoc* 22 (1991) 170–1, 175–85.

[117] 'He had assembled numerous Hau-Nebu (Greeks) with their horses and countless ships with their crews. Then he went with his soldiers to the land of the Chor-people (Phoenicians). They fought with him, and he pressed into them, his heart strong, like that of a falcon among little birds. He grasped them all together and he brought their great ones and their horses and their ships and all their precious articles to Baket (Egypt).'

[118] Diod. 19.93.7. Ptolemy is said to have destroyed Acre, Joppa, Samaria, and Gaza, and returned to Egypt with all the booty it was possible to take.

[119] The cast of thought was prevalent in the Achaemenid era. In 334 Atizyes indignantly rejected the proposal to ravage his satrapy (Hellespontine Phrygia) to impede Alexander's advance (Arr. 1.12.9–10), and, though Bessus adopted a strategy of destruction in Bactria (Arr. 3.28.8), he was half hearted in its implementation and Alexander was not incommoded. Earlier Darius had considered ravaging the upper satrapies (Arr. 3.19.1), but the policy was not put into effect.

But Seleucus could not simply be abandoned. After all his restitution to Babylon had been one of the allied demands in 315, and he could hardly be deprived of the satrapy which he and his supporters had argued was his by right. Although he was not technically a signatory to the peace, it is more than likely that there was some reference to him. The peace was the result of a long process of negotiation, and there was surely a mass of individual detailed provisions which affected the individual interests of the contracting parties. One of them we learn of indirectly through Antigonus' letter. Among the reasons why he agreed to admitting Ptolemy to the peace (so he states) was 'to deal more quickly with the matter of Polyperchon, with no one sharing oaths with him'.[120] The background to this aside is difficult to elucidate, but it must have something to do with Polyperchon's position as Antigonus' general in the Peloponnese. This position he had held since 315, and though his son shortly after deserted the Antigonid cause and was assassinated, he himself seems to have remained allied to Antigonus.[121] The agreement with Cassander must have entailed some definition of his position. Antigonus perhaps offered to withdraw his commission if Cassander agreed not to attack Polyperchon and guaranteed his safety in the Peloponnese. If Ptolemy participated in the peace, it prevented him backing Polyperchon with his fleet and using him in his own interest against either Cassander or Antigonus.

Seleucus was in the same category as Polyperchon. He was not party to the peace, but there was an obligation—and political interest—to protect his position in Babylonia. In that case there was probably some clause which asserted Seleucus' right to be satrap of Babylonia under the direction of Antigonus. His acquisitions in the upper satrapies could

---

[120] Welles, *RC* 1, lines 37–41.

[121] On Polyperchon's chequered history in the period 315–311 see Heckel 201–3. The appointment as general in the Peloponnese is attested by Diod. 19.60.1. The relationship may have come under some strain when Antigonus sent his nephews Polemaeus and Telesphorus into the Peloponnese, but they avoided confrontation and left Polyperchon undisturbed in Corinth and Sicyon, where his daughter-in-law held the reins of power (Diod. 19.74.2; cf. 20.37.1). Relations with Antigonus were not severed by the peace; Antigonus was prepared to let Heracles leave Pergamum to advance the political fortunes of Polyperchon (Diod. 20.20.1).

be tacitly passed over, and Antigonus would then have the option of asserting his authority there. If Seleucus contested possession, his erstwhile allies would be dispensed from any obligation to support him. Such a settlement would have saved face all round. Seleucus was not abandoned; he had what he claimed was rightfully his, but it was under the overall authority of Antigonus. That allowed either side to provoke a confrontation, and conflict was practically inevitable if Antigonus attempted to exercise power over the upper satrapies. In effect Seleucus' former coalition allies were wiping their hands of him. If he attempted to preserve his territorial acquisitions in the face of Antigonus, that was his affair, and he could not expect assistance.

The conflict predictably came. What sparked it off we cannot say, but the Babylonian texts are unequivocal that there was a major invasion of Babylonia in summer 310. From the fragmentary and disjointed notes in the Chronicle it would appear that there was fighting for some time at the frontiers between August and October 310.[122] By February 309 Antigonus was in Babylon, where he systematically pillaged the area around the capital and the city of Cuthah. The fighting continued until the late summer of 309, when the Chronicle breaks off with a note that there was a battle against the army of Seleucus.[123] The misery of the populace at large is reflected in the repeated notes that there was weeping and mourning in the land, and Babylonia was clearly the arena for a clash between large armies. Seleucus, we may assume, kept his grip on the upper satrapies and used them to supply troops for the campaign for Babylonia. And he was ultimately successful.[124] We have no idea how Antigonus'

---

[122] rev.15–17: hostilities took place over several months from Ab 310. Fighting and plundering around Babylon is attested in the month Šabāṭ (rev. 23–5), and the action around Cuthah took place early in a subsequent month (rev.26–7).

[123] rev. 43: '[...] on the 25th(?) of Ab [...] battle in front of the troops of Seleucus [...]'. Earlier in the summer there had been renewed weeping and mourning, as city and country were plundered (rev. 37–8).

[124] Polyaen. 4.9.1 records a decisive victory by Seleucus over Antigonus. If the story is authentic (and it records possibly the oldest and most repeated stratagem in Greek military history—remaining in formation overnight to catch the enemy unarmed and out of line), it presumably refers to the final phase of the campaign, after the record of the Babylonian Chronicle breaks off. Cf. Schober, *Untersuchungen* 129–31.

invasion ended, or what, if any, treaty was concluded, but it remains fact that Antigonus failed to occupy Babylonia.[125] From 308 his attention was focused on the west, and much of his time he spent at his new capital of Antigoneia in Northern Syria. Babylonia and the territories east he relinquished to Seleucus. What had clearly preserved Seleucus was his control of the upper satrapies. They gave him a supply of trained troops, some of them veterans from Alexander's colonies, others native Iranians, and in sufficient numbers to counter the forces of Antigonus, who had the whole of Asia Minor and Syria to draw upon. What ensured his dominance in the east was the botched invasion of Nicanor, which simultaneously augmented his own army and depleted resistance east of the Zagros. He was able to deploy his small army to its greatest effect, and the single victory opened up the eastern lands. But it was the continuing conflict in the west which ultimately preserved him. While Antigonus was simultaneously at war with Ptolemy and Cassander, he could not invade Babylonia in force and keep a significant military presence there. To invade effectively he required a stable peace, and the peace took a year to achieve. In that time Seleucus had occupied Babylon and established his dominance in eastern Iran. He was now a dynast alongside the other four, and the Antigonid invasion of 310/9 was to leave him their equal.

---

[125] The opening of Ptolemy's campaign in Lycia and Caria, and the dramatic early successes before the winter of 309/8 probably influenced Antigonus' decision to leave Babylonia well alone.

7
Hellenistic Monarchy: Success and Legitimation

The Hellenistic period could be said to have been born in a big bang. In 306 BC, four years after the sordid death of the last Argead king, Antigonus the One-Eyed declared himself and his son Demetrius kings, and assumed the diadem as the regalia of royalty. His example was followed almost immediately by Ptolemy, Seleucus, Lysimachus, and Cassander, not to mention Agathocles in Sicily. There was now a plethora of Macedonian kings who (with the exception of Cassander) held sway outside Macedon. Traditional scholarship has concentrated on the supposed contrast between Antigonus and the other kings; Antigonus was attempting to recreate the universal monarchy of Alexander, while the other dynasts had strictly regional bases of power.[1] This supposed contrast was always in doubt. Antigonus certainly did aim for universal monarchy,[2] but no dynast will have rejected the territorial empire of Alexander if it came his way. In fact Seleucus for a brief moment after Corupedion did have his writ run from eastern Afghanistan into Europe, and it could hardly be said that Ptolemy's ambitions were ever limited to Egypt. A more attractive view is that propounded more recently by Eric Gruen and others,[3] that there was indeed no difference

---

[1] The fullest discussion with extensive citation of earlier scholarship is O. Müller, *Antigonos Monophthalmos und 'Das Jahr der Könige'* (Saarbrücker Beiträge zur Altertumskunde 11: Bonn 1973). For a bibliographical *mise au point* see J. Seibert, *Das Zeitalter der Diadochen* 136–40.

[2] There are explicit statements in all sources: Diod. 18.47.5, 50.2 accredits Antigonus with absolutist ambitions as early as 319 (so Plut. *Eum.* 12.1), and there is a strong attestation in the new Cologne papyrus (*PKöln* no. 247, col. I lines 18–26: cf. G. A. Lehmann, 'Das neue Kölner Historiker-fragment', *ZPE* 72 (1988) 1–17): '[Antigonus] entitled himself king, convinced that he would easily remove all the people in positions of distinction and would himself have leadership of the entire world and acquire control of affairs just like Alexander.'

[3] E. Gruen, 'The Coronation of the Diadochoi', in *The Craft of the Ancient Historian* 253–71, accepted and developed by Billows, *Antigonos* 155–60, 351–2.

between Antigonus and his rival kings; their claim to kingship rested on their achievements and their children—demonstrated ability to maintain and transmit power. From this perspective kingship is the reward of success: Demetrius' naval victory at Salamis or Ptolemy's defence of Egypt against the Antigonid invasion. Indeed success has been seen as a necessary condition of kingship. In an influential article Michel Austin has emphasized the importance of war and plunder to all Hellenistic monarchies and takes the view that kings were seen as successful predators, and their legitimacy derived in great part from their success in campaigning and their ability to enrich themselves and their subjects at the expense of rival dynasties.[4] No one would deny that there is a large measure of truth in this picture, but it is not the whole truth. Not all kings were equally successful. Some could be said to be downright unsuccessful, and still retained the loyalty of their friends and soldiers on whom their power ultimately depended. Others were relatively successful and still came to grief, notably Demetrius Poliorcetes, who was literally expelled from his kingdom by his subjects. These apparent aberrations deserve closer investigation and may sharpen our views of the nature of Hellenistic monarchy and the mutual expectations of ruler and subject.

In 300 BC Demetrius the Besieger was on the bottom rung of the wheel of fortune. Disastrously defeated at the Battle of Ipsus, he barely retained anything of the great empire his father had created. He had been rejected by the Athenians, who adopted a position of strict neutrality, and his garrisons elsewhere in Greece were expelled, except perhaps for the nerve centre at Corinth.[5] At this point he took the offensive, attacking the Chersonese, the heartland of the territory of his enemy, Lysimachus. Plutarch tells us very little about this

---

For an antithetical, strongly legalistic view see N.G.L. Hammond, in *HM* iii.192–3; *The Macedonian State* 271–2. See also Lund, *Lysimachus* 156–61; S. Sherwin-White and A. Kuhrt, *From Samarkand to Sardis* 118–20.

[4] M. M. Austin, 'Hellenistic Kings, War and the Economy', *CQ* 36 (1986) 450–66.

[5] Plut. *Demetr.* 31.2; *Pyrrh.* 4.5. The young Pyrrhus was left in charge of affairs in Greece, and presumably based himself at Corinth, where there was a strong Antigonid garrison installed, allegedly at the citizens' request (Diod. 20.103.3; cf. Walbank, in *HM* iii.176, 202).

campaign, stating that he simultaneously injured Lysimachus and enriched and held together his own forces, which were now beginning to recover from the disaster of Ipsus.[6] This is a mysterious episode, and we know of only one incident in the campaign, an incident recorded by Polyaenus and almost universally attributed to the wrong historical context by modern scholars.[7] Demetrius and Lysimachus were locked in battle around Lampsacus (opposite the Chersonese).[8] That can hardly be accommodated in the campaign of Ipsus. Lampsacus had surrendered to Lysimachus early in 302, and Demetrius had recovered it later in the year.[9] But by that time Lysimachus was long gone. He had penetrated Greater Phrygia, held Antigonus at bay at Dorylaeum, and, when Demetrius attacked Lampsacus, he was retreating with his forces to winter quarters in the plain of Salonia, south of Heracleia Pontica.[10] Demetrius and Lysimachus did not meet at Lampsacus in 302, and Polyaenus' story presupposes that they did. It concerns 5,000 Illyrian troops[11] whose baggage Demetrius had captured 'in the battle around Lampsacus'. They had lost everything, and Lysimachus was seriously worried that they would mutiny. He therefore took

---

[6] Plut. *Demetr.* 31.2–3: καὶ κακῶσᾶμα ποιῶν Λυσίμαχον, ὠφέλει καὶ συνεῖχε τὴν περὶ αὐτὸν δύναμιν, ἀρχομένην ἀναλαμβάνειν καὶ γίνεσθαι πάλιν οὐκ εὐκαταφρόνητον. See below, pp. 259–60.

[7] Polyaen. 4.12.1. The tendency is to associate the episode with the desertion of the 2,000 Autariatae from Lysimachus' winter camp (Diod. 20.113.3). The massacre is either seen as an act of retaliation (Billows, *Antigonos* 180 with n. 30: the Illyrians are supposed to have left their baggage at Lampsacus; cf. G. Saitta, *Kokalos* 1 (1955) 78 n. 49), an authentic episode in the siege of Lampsacus in 302 (F. Landucci Gattinoni, *Lisimaco di Tracia* 146 n.95: in this case Lysimachus cannot have perpetrated the massacre in person), or a garbled echo of the desertion recorded by Diodorus (Lund, *Lysimachus* 11; at 77 she flirts with all three explanations). On the other hand Claude Wehrli (*Antigone et Démétrios* 157) makes the connection with the campaign of 300 but still conflates the two episodes, arguing that Demetrius was able to attract the Illyrians into his service. Kostas Buraselis includes Polyaen. 4.12.1 without discussion in a footnote on Demetrius' campaign in 300 (*Das hellenistische Makedonien und die Ägäis* 58 n.76); so too Walbank, in *HM* iii.202 n. 5.

[8] Polyaen. *loc. cit.*: Λυσίμαχος ... ἐν τῇ πρὸς Δημήτριον μάχῃ περὶ Λάμψακον.

[9] Diod. 20.107.2 (surrender); 20.111.3 (recapture).

[10] Diod. 20.109.6. On the location see Strabo 12.4.7 (565).

[11] They came from the tribe of the Autariatae, whom Cassander had transplanted to the foothills of Mt. Orbelus (Diod. 20.19.1; Just. 15.2.1). They were obviously a useful source of mercenaries for Lysimachus.

preventive action, withdrew them from the front on the pretext of issuing their rations and killed them down to the last man. Lysimachus and Demetrius were both present at Lampsacus, and the campaign of 300 is the only possible context for the clash.

According to Polyaenus, Lysimachus massacred his own men in cold blood. He was well advised to do so. He might well have remembered the fate of Eumenes, betrayed to the enemy by his Silver Shields after their baggage (which included their concubines and children) had fallen into Antigonus' hands.[12] The Illyrians moreover had not been reliable auxiliaries in the recent past. During the winter of 302/1,[13] 2,000 of them had defected to Antigonus and Lysimachus clearly felt that with the inducement of recovering their baggage his men would transfer their allegiance to Demetrius without any scruple. From Demetrius' perspective it was all clear profit. He had acquired the property of the Illyrians, and Lysimachus' army was reduced in numbers and morale. This was a classic use of plunder to strengthen one's own position and weaken that of one's adversary. Again Eumenes provides us with a parallel. During the winter of 320/19 he was fighting a campaign on the borders of Cappadocia against the royal army of Antipater and Antigonus.[14] Hard pressed by superior forces, he organized a number of simultaneous sorties on the territory controlled by his enemies. No concerted defence was possible, and Eumenes was able to sell or ransom what he had captured, realizing a handsome profit for his men. Not surprisingly, Eumenes' was popular with his own troops, but according to Arrian even the enemy forces 'were astounded at the speed and unexpectedness of the sortie and had even more admiration for Eumenes generalship and his intelligent direction of forces, and were induced to despise Antipater, who commanded much larger forces, more reliable to secure the issue

[12] Diod. 19.43.7–9; Plut. *Eum.* 17–18; Just. 14.3.3–4.18. On the source tradition of this episode see Bosworth, 'History and Artifice' 60–5.

[13] Diod. 20.113.3. They were welcomed by Antigonus with full pay and a generous gratuity.

[14] For the source tradition of this campaign see Bosworth, 'History and Artifice' 71–9.

of the war, and was encamped near to the enemy, yet was unable to give any assistance to his allies.'[15] This was a solid gain for Eumenes, entrenching his authority and his moral superiority against Antipater, whose authority was undermined among his own Macedonians.[16] The same was true for Demetrius in 300. He was rebuilding his power through military success, which gave him resources and prestige, while weakening one of his most serious enemies.

This campaign is an illustration of Austin's view of the Hellenistic kings as predators, their power ultimately rooted in military success, which provided the financial and moral support for the armies on which in the last analysis their regimes depended. Demetrius would hardly quarrel with that. According to Plutarch he found that his troops became disruptive if they were inactive at home, and in 289 he deliberately led them on a campaign against Aetolia and Epirus, ravaging both regions.[17] The text reads as though Demetrius' motive was caprice: he needed to occupy his army and at the same time he could add the loot to his coffers.[18] But the picture is far more complex. Demetrius was retaliating against Pyrrhus of Epirus who had overrun Thessaly shortly before, while he was engaged in the siege of Thebes,[19] and, as for the Aetolians, he was engaged in a Sacred War, to liberate Delphi from their control. In 290 he had ceremonially held the Pythian Games at Athens, denying the legitimacy of the Aetolian occupation,[20] and a campaign into Aetolia was the

[15] This comes from the new Göteborg palimpsest (Greek MS 2.72^{r}16–73^{v}8), which gives the full version of the portion briefly summarised by Photius (Arr. *Succ.* F 1.41 (Roos)). See now B. Dreyer, *ZPE* 125 (1999) 39–60.

[16] Antipater's unpopularity with the troops is a constant feature of the tradition. See n. 116 below for the unfavourable contrast between him and Craterus. After the winter campaign against Eumenes he literally did a moonlight flit across the Hellespont to avoid the contumacious demands of his men (Arr. *Succ.* F 1.44–5 (Roos)).

[17] Plut. *Demetr.* 41.1, 3; cf. *Pyrrh.* 7.4 with P. Lévêque, *Pyrrhos* 142–51.

[18] Plut. *Demetr.* 41.1: καὶ μήτ᾽ αὐτὸς ἄγειν ἡσυχίαν πεφυκὼς τους τ᾽ ἄλλους ὁρῶν ἐν ταῖς στρατείαις μᾶλλον αὐτῷ προσέχοντας, οἴκοι δὲ ταραχώδεις καὶ πολυπράγμονας ὄντας, ἐστράτευσεν ἐπ᾽ Αἰτωλούς.

[19] Plut. *Demetr.* 40.1–2; Plut. *Pyrrh.* 7.3.

[20] Plut. *Demetr.* 40.7–8. Shortly before that the Athenians had, in Plutarch's eyes, plumbed the depths of flattery in sending a sacred envoy to Demetrius, requesting an oracle sanctioning the restoration of the shields of Marathon, which had been dedicated at Delphi (Plut. *Demetr.* 13.2, as interpreted by C. Habicht,

natural sequel. The war would necessarily involve ravaging the land over a long term, as had happened late in 322 when Craterus and Antipater invaded Aetolia and forced the defenders into the mountains to suffer the privations of winter,[21] and Demetrius duly left his lieutenant Pantauchus to continue the campaign. And, given the poverty of the region, the campaign would almost certainly make a loss; the profit from the ravaging would hardly pay an army over a prolonged period of fighting. Here the financial motive was certainly subsidiary. What mattered was to follow in the footsteps of Philip II: Demetrius intended to win a Sacred War and parade himself as the liberator of Delphi. The ravaging was of course a means to the end, but not an end in itself.

Nor was military success in itself a necessary condition of kingship. Demetrius again provides an instructive example. When he took control of Macedonia in 294, he made a formal defence of his action before a Macedonian assembly. Both Plutarch and Justin agree that he made a speech, and Justin gives a digest of it.[22] Here there is no commemoration of his own successes, rather a denunciation of the previous regime which he had supplanted and a catalogue of his father's services to Philip and Alexander and his commission (voted by the Macedonians at Triparadeisus) to hunt down the remnants of the Perdiccan faction. It is the connection with and the services to the Argead dynasty which still matter. Plutarch adds that Demetrius was materially assisted by his marriage to Phila, Antipater's daughter, who was popular

Untersuchungen zur politischen Geschichte Athens im 3.Jahrhundert v. Chr. 34–44). Here Demetrius does duty for Apollo, whose shrine at Delphi is inaccessible to the Athenians, and his intention to liberate the sanctuary must have been public. It is also recognized in the notorious Athenian Ithyphallic which calls upon Demetrius to punish the Aetolians, the new Sphinx which menaces all of Hellas.

[21] Diod. 18.24.2–25.2.

[22] Plut. *Demetr.* 37.2–4; Just. 16.1.10–18. On this see Walbank, in *HM* iii.217–18, arguing that the speech in Justin is 'a rhetorical exercise.' But there is no justification for concluding that Demetrius did not address a Macedonian assembly. Plutarch merely states that there was no *need* (οὐ … ἐδέησεν) for long speeches, not that speeches were not made. There may be two traditions here, since Justin (14) makes Demetrius attack the memory of Antipater, whereas Plutarch stresses that Antipater was remembered for his moderation. But the texts are not incompatible. Demetrius may have spoken against Antipater and still profited from the popularity of his wife and her father.

in her own right and had born him his adult son, Antigonus Gonatas.[23] Nothing is said of Demetrius' successes, the victory at Salamis or the double occupation of Athens. More important was the disillusionment with the previous regime. The Macedonians wanted a change, and Demetrius could at least boast a marriage attachment to Alexander's regent.

In terms of military and territorial expansion Demetrius' six-year rule in Macedon should be judged a considerable success. He soon regained the dominance in southern Greece that he had enjoyed in 302, annexing Thessaly and crushing two successive revolts in Boeotia.[24] He took advantage of Lysimachus' disastrous war beyond the Danube to invade Thrace, and, though he was recalled by the Boeotian rebellion, he forced his rival to cede the eastern part of Macedonia to him.[25] He was also effective in curbing the territorial ambitions of Pyrrhus. In 291 he chased him out of Thessaly without a battle; in 289 he invaded and ravaged Epirus while Pyrrhus was occupied in Aetolia. In the aftermath, when Demetrius was seriously ill at Pella and Pyrrhus drove into Upper Macedonia as far as Edessa, he rose from his sick bed

---

[23] Plut. *Demetr.* 37.4. On Phila's general popularity (some of it derived from her earlier marriage to Craterus) see Diod. 19.59.3–4; Hornblower, *Hieronymus* 226–7.

[24] Plut. *Demetr.* 39.1–40.6. This information presumably derives from Hieronymus of Cardia, who was Demetrius' harmost in Thebes, and failed to prevent its second revolt (*FGrH* 154 T 8). See above, Ch. 5.

[25] So Just. 16.1.19. This is not attested elsewhere, and in particular Plut. *Demetr.* 39.6–7 reports only the liberation of Lysimachus by his Getic captor and Demetrius' return to Boeotia. But the history of these years is so ill attested that little weight can be placed on any argument from silence. It is quite possible that in 294 Lysimachus obtained part of Macedonia which had been under the control of his son-in-law Antipater, and Demetrius considered it prudent not to challenge him for it. Then, two years later, he took advantage of Lysimachus' difficulties and made him cede the disputed territory. The general tendency (cf. Walbank, in *HM* iii.215; Lund, *Lysimachus* 95; Landucci Gattinoni, *Lisimaco di Tracia* 177–8) is to date the peace with Lysimachus to 294, basing the argument on Plutarch (*Pyrrh.* 6.7). But all that Plutarch states is that Lysimachus was fully occupied when Pyrrhus attacked Macedon in 294 (ἦν ἐν ἀσχολίαις). He gives no indication where he was occupied, still less that he was involved in action against the Getae. He could have been out of Europe altogether. There may also have been an earlier defeat of Lysimachus, close to Amphipolis (Paus.1.10.2), when he came close to losing Thrace but was saved by Pyrrhus' intervention (cf. Landucci Gattinoni 178 against the general tendency to place this battle in 287). Whatever were the facts behind this sadly defective source tradition, there can be little doubt that Demetrius consistently had the upper hand in his dealings with Lysimachus.

and routed him. The Eagle of Epirus turned tail and lost a considerable part of his army under the Macedonian attack. He was forced to come to terms with Demetrius.[26] By this stage the Besieger had virtually achieved the eminence that Philip II had enjoyed after Chaeronea. Southern Greece was under his domination; Macedonia was united under his rule, and he could turn his attentions to external conquest. There is no doubt that he was preparing a vast armament to rival Alexander's last plans. He was building a fleet of some 500 warships, and had amassed a coalition army over 100,000 strong.[27] Those are Plutarch's figures, perhaps exaggerated, but even with exaggeration they dwarf the army Alexander led into Asia.

It was precisely at this apex of power and success that Demetrius lost his kingship, when his Macedonian troops deserted him in favour of Pyrrhus. This was superficially a paradox. Pyrrhus had no army that could match Demetrius' forces, and he had never seriously engaged Demetrius in pitched battle. For all his interest in stressing Pyrrhus' military brilliance, Plutarch cannot hide the fact that Pyrrhus twice withdrew precipitately rather than fight it out with the Besieger, and was forced to conclude peace. The Aetolian campaign of 289 will have temporarily enhanced his prestige. Then he had launched a counter-invasion of Aetolia, and defeated Demetrius' lieutenant, Pantauchus. More importantly he responded to a challenge by the enemy leader and worsted him in a single combat, which Plutarch describes in

---

[26] Plut. *Demetr.* 43.1; *Pyrrh.* 10.5. At this time Demetrius seems to have concluded a five year pact of peace and friendship with the Aetolians, which among other things guaranteed all Greeks access to Delphi and placed its administration once more in the hands of the Amphicyons (F. Lefèvre, *BCH* 122 (1998) 109–41, esp. 136–9). The Aetolians had not been defeated decisively, but at least Demetrius had achieved the main object of the campaign. In that case it was probably now that the Athenians restored the shields of Marathon (see above, n. 20). Pausanias (10.19.4) witnessed them *in situ*, and when the Aetolians themselves came to dedicate the Gallic shields that they captured in 278, they placed them in the Athenian treasury on its south and west sides (Habicht (above, n. 20) 42). The Athenian dedication already had its pride of place.

[27] Plut. *Demetr.* 43.3–4: the army comprised 98,000 foot and 12,000 horse. This is rounded down to 100,000 at *Pyrrh.* 10.5. Most commentators accept that it was in Demetrius' power to raise a force of this magnitude (Wehrli, *Antigone et Démétrios* 182; Walbank *HM* iii.226–7 (adducing numismatic evidence)).

Homeric terms.[28] The result was that the Epirote army defeated the Macedonian phalanx and captured some 5,000 of them. This was undoubtedly a significant achievement, even though it was short-lived. Pyrrhus was soon forced to make peace with Demetrius, as in their turn did the Aetolians.

Pyrrhus' behaviour significantly recalled that of Alexander. Exposure of one's person was expected of the royal commanders, and the defeat of one's adversary in single combat was the ultimate proof of prowess. Ptolemy made sure that his readers did not miss an engagement in Bajaur when he personally killed the leader of the opposing force of Indians and stripped his body.[29] It was something that Alexander himself never achieved, for all his desperation to capture Darius, and it was one of the few facets of his career that could be surpassed. According to Plutarch Pyrrhus' exploit favourably impressed the Macedonians of Demetrius, who allegedly saw in him a reflection of Alexander in action, whereas other dynasts imitated Alexander only in their regalia and outward mannerisms.[30] The main contrast is with Demetrius, who is represented as Pyrrhus' polar opposite, the triumph of show over substance. There is undoubtedly some distortion here. Plutarch is, as always, conscious of the parallel with Antony, who was prone to masquerade and owed his victories mostly to his subordinates, and he makes the most of the pomp and circumstance that surrounded Demetrius. But Demetrius shared most of the characteristics of Pyrrhus. On Plutarch's own account he led from the front during his numerous sieges, and suffered two serious wounds from the enemy artillery.[31] In battle he was as unsparing of his person as Pyrrhus. Diodorus gives a memorable picture of his actions at the Battle of Salamis, when he fought a single combat on

---

[28] Plut. *Demetr.* 41.3–4; *Pyrrh.* 7.6–9 (first an exchange of spears (δορατισμός), then hand-to-hand combat with swords in which Pyrrhus received one wound and inflicted two).

[29] Arr. 4.24.3–5=*FGrH* 139 F 18. On this episode and Arrian's literary treatment of it see Bosworth, *Alexander and the East* 45–7.

[30] Expressed with similar wording in *Demetr.* 41.4–5 and *Pyrrh.* 8.1–2. On the motif of display in both the *Lives* see Andrei's edition of the *Demetrius* 78–82 and Pelling, *Plutarch: Life of Antony* 21–2.

[31] Plut. *Demetr.* 33.4 (siege of Messene in 295); 40.5 (second siege of Thebes).

the stern of his flagship against a massed onset of enemy boarders; his three shield-bearers were killed or wounded, but he continued the fight at close range.[32] This evokes Alexander at the Malli town or Ptolemy at the Camels' Fort,[33] the commander giving a moral example at the epicentre of the fighting. The same had occurred at Gaza, when like Ptolemy and Seleucus he had exposed himself at the front of the fighting and fought until there was practically no one with him.[34] It happened at Ipsus too, when his pursuit of his counterpart, Antiochus, led to disaster.[35] Significantly this is the feat of arms that Plutarch chooses to describe, since it fits the negative picture of Demetrius; the more responsible behaviour at Gaza and Salamis is passed over.

Plutarch also makes much of Demetrius' regal pomp, and the resentment aroused by his luxury and exhibitionism. Some of this is probably exaggerated to draw the parallel with Antony, whose extravagance and ostentation is repeatedly stressed. Indeed a degree of stateliness ($\sigma\epsilon\mu\nu\acute{o}\tau\eta s$) was expected in a king. Alexander had given an unforgettable display of regal glory in his last years. At the mass marriage at Susa he had held court on a golden throne at the centre of a huge tent with 100 couches and 50 golden pillars, his Bodyguards on couches around him, then, in concentric circles a detachment of his Silver Shields, followed by Persian archers and melophoroi.[36] Outside the tent was the elephant division along with literally thousands of Macedonian and Persian infantry. The massive, colourful spectacle was repeated day after day, and it gave an overwhelming impression of power and majesty. Few objected to it, and seven years later

---

[32] Diod. 20.52.1–2. No doubt the picture was given heroic colouring by Hieronymus, but one cannot seriously doubt that Demetrius was active at the centre of the fighting.

[33] See particularly Arr. 6.9.5 with its strong Homeric echoes. On Ptolemy at Camels' Fort see Diod. 18.34.1–2.

[34] Diod. 19.84.5–6. At 83.5 he notes that the personal example of the commanders, exposing themselves to danger at the head of their troops, was an inspiration to the lower ranks. Note also the dictum of Antigonus, cited by Polyaenus (4.6.5).

[35] Plut. *Demetr.* 29.4–5; *Pyrrh.* 4.4; cf. Billows, *Antigonos* 183–4.

[36] The fullest description comes from Phylarchus (Athen. 12.539D–540A=*FGrH* 81 F 41). See also Ael. *VH* 9.3; Polyaen. 4.3.24. A darker picture of Alexander's court is provided by Ephippus, but it has the same emphasis on Alexander's regal pomp (Athen. 12.537E–538A = *FGrH* 126 F 5).

Peucestas staged a similar spectacle in an attempt to gain the loyalty of Eumenes' Silver Shields. The coalition commanders occupied the centre of the great feast, followed by the Silver Shields and cavalry who had fought under Alexander, then the rest of the allied forces.[37] The display was outstanding, but the common soldiers participated in it, and the veterans of Alexander were singled out. The expense was justified in that it was not monopolized by the commanders. Some of it trickled down to the army at large. This was important, and the example was given by Alexander in the elaborate festivities that marked his last days in Babylon. The court revelled for days and drank the nights away, but wine and sacrificial meat were distributed to the army by companies, and the feasting was universal.[38] His men were the beneficiaries of empire. They might have become embarrassingly indebted by the time they returned to the west, but Alexander discharged what they owed. And when he dismissed his veterans from Opis, they left with full pay and a talent a man paid as gratuity.[39] That was a truly colossal bonus, the ultimate example of royal benefaction, and it was long remembered. Not surprisingly the veterans who remained with the royal army were impatient for the same rewards, and Antipater's life was threatened at Triparadeisus when he protested that he had no ready cash.[40] The new regent was defaulting on his primary obligation.

This is relevant to Demetrius' position in Macedon. He occupied a long-established monarchy, as Pyrrhus did in Epirus, and there were clear expectations of kingship. In Epirus there was something approaching a social contract. At the sanctuary of Passaron, north of Dodona, there was a solemn exchange of oaths at each accession; the king swore

---

[37] Diod. 19.22.2; briefly mentioned by Plut. *Eum.* 14.5. See above, Ch. 4, p. 121.

[38] Arr. 7.24.4; cf. Plut. *Alex.* 75.3–4. The arduous naval training on the Euphrates was sweetened by formal races with prizes for the victors (Arr. 7.23.5).

[39] Arr. 7. 12.1–2; cf. Just. 12.12.10. On the cancellation of debts see Arr. 7.5.1–4; Curt. 10.2.9–11; Just. 12.11.1–3; Plut. *Alex.* 70.3. Plutarch and Curtius agree that Alexander disbursed 9,870 talents in debt relief; Arrian and Justin give a figure of 20,000. Whatever the reality, it was a vast sum.

[40] Arr. *Succ.* F 1.32–3 (Roos); cf. Polyaen. 4.6.4. For the repetition of the demands in 319 see Arr. *Succ.* F 1.44–5 (Roos) with Hammond, in W. Will (ed.), *Zu Alexander dem Grossen* (Amsterdam 1988) i.627–34.

that he would rule according to the laws, and representatives of his subjects pledged themselves to preserve the kingship according to the laws.[41] In Macedon nothing so formal is attested,[42] but the king was clearly expected to respect custom. In a famous passage Arrian represents Callisthenes stating that Macedonian kings traditionally ruled by law (or custom) rather than force.[43] That is a rhetorical truism to be sure, but a truism which reflects a reality, that kings should fulfil the expectations of their subjects. Now, from the anecdotal evidence, which is all that we have, there is a contrast between the attested behaviour of Alexander and Demetrius. For instance, when Alexander approached Babylon in 323, he was accosted by a multitude of embassies from as far afield as south Italy and Spain.[44] Despite the sheer volume of business he is alleged to have heard them all and (with the exception of the Greeks contesting the Exiles' Decree) he acceded to their requests.[45] The world conqueror graciously received the homage of his subjects and in return assumed the role of universal benefactor.

In contrast, Demetrius is said to have been harsh and inaccessible; he would give no time for a hearing—and he is said to have kept an Athenian embassy waiting for two years—or,

---

[41] Plut. *Pyrrh.* 5.5. Aristotle (*Pol.* 5.1313ᵃ20–24) considers that the Molossian kingdom owed its long survival to its moderation and the restrictions upon its use of power. A few lines before he identifies the volition of the subjects as the difference between kingship and tyranny.

[42] The oaths which are attested as sworn by Macedonians occurred at uncharacteristic crises. At Babylon the marshals swore to be subjects of any son born to Alexander (Curt. 10.8.9; Just. 13.2.14 states that it was an oath of allegiance to the four prospective guardians). There is, however, no record in any source of an oath to Philip Arrhidaeus. Similarly when Sosthenes usurped power, he rejected the royal title but had the army swear loyalty to him as *dux* (Just. 24.5.14). This evidence does not sustain the hypothesis that there were regular oaths of loyalty by subject to king, let alone king to subject (contra Aymard, *Études d'histoire ancienne* 154; Hammond, *The Macedonian State* 65–6). Curt. 7.1.29 suggests that some Macedonians at least swore to have the same friends and enemies as Alexander, but it is part of a rhetorical argument (we swore to have the same friends and enemies as you; Philotas was your friend; therefore we cannot be blamed for courting his friendship), and it *may* reflect Roman rather than Macedonian institutions (cf. Atkinson ii.253–4 and E. J. Baynham, *Alexander the Great: The Unique History of Quintus Curtius* 52, 182).

[43] Arr. 4.11.6; cf. Bosworth, *HCA* ii.84.

[44] On the source tradition see Bosworth, *From Arrian to Alexander* 83–93.

[45] Diod. 17.113.4; cf. Arr. 7.14.6, 19.1.

if he did condescend to give an interview, he was aloof and abrupt.[46] This cavalier attitude extended to his Macedonian subjects, if there is any truth in the famous story that he received written petitions while on a progress through Pella and then emptied them into the river Axios in full view of his petitioners.[47] If the king defaulted on his side of the implicit contract, his subjects might well do the same. Accordingly when Demetrius faced a twofold invasion at the hands of Pyrrhus and Lysimachus, he found his troops insubordinate. They began to desert to Lysimachus, so he withdrew to meet Pyrrhus, who was a non-Macedonian and had never previously held his ground against Demetrius. The result was more desertion, in increasingly larger numbers, until Demetrius was totally abandoned. According to Plutarch he was told to take himself elsewhere, because the Macedonians had had enough of war fought simply to support his own luxury.[48] The disillusion was profound. Unlike Alexander Demetrius had monopolized the spoils of his campaigns—or so his subjects thought. The planned invasion of Asia, for all the size of the armament, would not bring any ultimate return to the fighting men even if Demetrius managed to restore his father's empire. This may have been a false perception, but it was certainly the prevailing view in Macedon, and Demetrius was deserted by his troops *en masse*. It cost him the kingdom of Macedonia, although he continued to act and be recognized as king, even without any territory to speak of.

Demetrius had been brutally reminded of a necessary condition of kingship, the imperative for some semblance of reciprocity in dealings with one's subjects. However

---

[46] Plut. *Demetr.* 42.1–2. For earlier resentment of Antipater's inaccessibility see Arr. *Succ.* F 19: Τῷ ἀπροσμείκτῳ καὶ ἀνημέρῳ corresponds exactly to Demetrius' δυσόμιλον καὶ δυσπρόσοδον.

[47] Plut. *Demetr.* 42.4–6. The incident is not reported elsewhere, and the following anecdote, that of the old woman who told him not to rule if he had no time for her, is reported in several other contexts with respect to other rulers (Plut. *Mor.* 179C: Philip II; Stob. 3.13.48: Antipater; Dio 69.6.3: Hadrian).

[48] Plut. *Demetr.* 44.8: ἀπειρηκέναι γὰρ ἤδη Μακεδόνας ὑπὲρ τῆς ἐκείνου τρυφῆς πολεμοῦντας. In the *Pyrrhus* (11.9) he emphasizes the positive effect of agents sent by Pyrrhus into Demetrius' camp, but it is clear that the Macedonians were already alienated, and urged Demetrius to remove himself (11.12). Cf. Lévêque (above, n. 17) 154–8.

outwardly successful one's foreign policy, the men who comprised the armies and did the fighting needed to have a feeling of involvement. They should be able to identify with the highly charged rhetoric that Arrian placed in the mouth of Alexander: 'you are the satraps, you the generals, you the commanders. What remains to me from all these labours except the purple regalia I wear and this diadem? I possess nothing in my own right.' This is, of course, Arrian's own formulation, elaborating and transforming motifs in Xenophon.[49] It is preposterous and overstated, but none the less it emphatically underscores a basic truth. Demetrius' men felt that their king had not only the regalia and the diadem but everything else as well.

The Besieger shows us how to lose a kingdom. His rise from the abyss of Ipsus is also instructive. After the great defeat he was left practically without territory. He retained Cyprus and a number of important maritime cities, notably Tyre, Sidon, Ephesus, Miletus, and Corinth.[50] They were garrisoned, and he could move from one to the other and control them with his fleet. He had lost the army which fought at Ipsus except for the 9,000 infantry and cavalry which was all he had salvaged from the disaster. He secured Ephesus and sailed to Cilicia, where he evacuated his family from Cilicia and transferred them with his war chest to Cypriot Salamis.[51] Now the gibe of nesiarch which he had thrown at Agathocles[52] could properly be directed at him.

---

[49] Arr. 7.9.8–9 (cf. Xen. *Anab.* 3.9.7 with Bosworth, *From Arrian to Alexander* 103–5).

[50] Erythrae and Clazomenae had been strengthened by garrisons in late 302 (Diod. 20.107.5), as had Abydus, Lampsacus and Parium (Diod. 20.107. 3, 111.3). Whether they all remained loyal to Demetrius is an open question. Cf. Wehrli, *Antigone et Démétrios* 152–3.

[51] Plut. *Demetr.* 30.2 alleges that Demetrius fled from the battle to Ephesus (so too Eusebius: cf. *FGrH* 260 F 32 (2); Syncellus 230.24–5), and sailed directly to Athens, whereas Diod. 21.1.4b has him transfer his family to Cyprus after the battle, where they remained until 295 (Plut. *Demetr.* 35.5). I assume that Plutarch was eager to move from Ipsus to the next dramatic episode, Athens' rejection of Demetrius, and expressed himself with misleading brevity, merely stating that Demetrius sailed from Ephesus to Greece and omitting the long detour to Cilicia and Cyprus. Plutarch can be very casual and skip over years without alerting his readers (at *Demetr.* 7.5 he moves directly from Demetrius' invasion of Babylonia in 311 to the relief of Halicarnassus in late 309). See Wehrli, *Antigone et Démétrios* 153–4; Walbank, in *HM* iii.201.   [52] See below, p. 272.

But the island and the Phoenician cities gave him the most powerful fleet in the Mediterranean, and that was to prove his salvation. It gave him the advantage of mobility, as he proved when he sailed in rapid succession to Ephesus, Cilicia, Cyprus, back to Athens and the Isthmus, and then to the Chersonese. It was also a potent bargaining counter, as the alliance which had defeated him at Ipsus disintegrated.

The first signs of the new dispensation manifest themselves in Demetrius' campaign in the Chersonese. As we have seen, it gave him the opportunity to acquire funds and raise the morale of his troops. He was also given a free hand to do so. Plutarch claims that Lysimachus was disregarded by his fellow kings because he was thought to be as imperious as Demetrius and more of a threat because he had more power.[53] Seleucus was far away, confronting Ptolemy in Syria, but Cassander was close at hand in Macedonia, and he gave no support, even though he and Lysimachus had co-operated consistently down to 301.[54] The bitterness of the division of spoils after Ipsus was having its effect. Lysimachus had acquired the whole of Asia Minor north of the Taurus, whereas Cassander, who had provided the lion's share of his forces and confronted Demetrius in Greece, had to be content with the small area of Cilicia which his brother, Pleistarchus, had received in return for his rather chequered contribution to the campaign.[55] Lysimachus could well have given himself airs, and paraded his laurels as Bodyguard of Alexander and victor of Ipsus, and Cassander would have had some satisfaction witnessing his humiliation at the hands of Demetrius.

---

[53] Plut. *Demetr.* 31.4: ὁ δὲ Λυσίμαχος ὑπὸ τῶν ἄλλων βασιλέων ἠμελεῖτο, μηδὲν ἐπιεικέστερος ἐκείνου δοκῶν εἶναι, τῷ δὲ μᾶλλον ἰσχύειν καὶ φοβερώτερος. For ἐπιείκεια as a regal virtue, implying accessibility and cordiality, see Arr. *Succ.* F 1.19 (Roos).

[54] Diod. 20.106.3. Cf. Lund, *Lysimachus* 68–70; Landucci Gattinoni, *Lisimaco di Tracia* 142–3.

[55] Plut. *Demetr.* 31.6. On the vexed problem of the extent of Pleistarchus' territories see most recently A. P. Gregory, *Historia* 44 (1995) 11–28, esp. 20–6. There is some measure of agreement (following L. Robert, *Le Sanctuaire de Sinuri près de Mylasa* I 55–62, no. 44) that his epigraphically attested regime in western Caria was given him after his expulsion from Cilicia. See, however, Buraselis, *Das hellenistische Makedonien und die Ägäis* 27–33, arguing that Pleistarchus received a kind of 'protectorate of Cassander' in Asia Minor.

The Chersonese helped Demetrius resuscitate his fortunes, but the decisive event was the marriage alliance with
Seleucus which immediately followed. Plutarch fails to give
the background; Seleucus, he claims, needed the marriage
because Ptolemy was offering his daughters to Lysimachus
and his son.[56] He ignores the political quarrel that had
broken out between Ptolemy and Seleucus. During the
winter of 302/1 the ruler of Egypt had invaded Coele Syria
and occupied the region as far as Sidon. A particularly clever
piece of disinformation tricked him into believing that
Antigonus had won the war, and he withdrew to Egypt.[57] His
garrisons, however, remained, and after Ipsus he refused to
recognize Seleucus' claims to Coele Syria. There was a frank
and heated exchange which ended with Seleucus practically
renouncing his friendship with Ptolemy.[58] He did not go to
war, and part of the reason was undoubtedly that he did not
have a fleet which could match the naval resources of Egypt.
But relations were extremely cool, and Ptolemy clearly felt
the need to woo Lysimachus. That, as Plutarch observes,
practically drove Seleucus into the arms of Demetrius—or
rather, Demetrius' daughter. As the granddaughter of Antipater and niece of Cassander she was a prime dynastic catch
in her own right, and she brought with her Demetrius' navy.
Demetrius left the Chersonese, and sailed to Syria with his
entire fleet (ταῖς ναυσὶ πάσαις).[59] As he travelled along the
south coast of Asia he necessarily made landings to refresh
his rowers and replenish supplies—to the detriment of the
local communities. In Cilicia Pleistarchus was outraged by
the damage to his land and protested vocally to Seleucus,

---

[56] Plut. *Demetr.* 31.5. On these marital negotiations see J. Seibert, *Historische
Beiträge zu den dynastischen Verbindungen in Hellenistischer Zeit* 74, 95.

[57] Diod. 20.113.1–2.

[58] Diod. 21.1.5–6 (ὕστερον δὲ βουλεύσεσθαι πῶς χρηστέον ἐστὶν τῶν φίλων τοῖς
βουλομένοις πλεονεκτεῖν). The rights and wrongs of it were still debated 80 years later:
the Seleucids stressed the decision of the allies at Ipsus to place Coele Syria in
Seleucus' hands, while the Ptolemies maintained that Seleucus had promised the
area to Ptolemy when he joined the coalition (Polyb. 5.67.6–10). The bad blood
it caused cannot be minimized, and Just. 15.4.23–4 is perfectly justified in maintaining that the quarrels over the spoils split the dynasts into two *factiones*, Seleucus
and Demetrius against Ptolemy and Lysimachus.

[59] Plut. *Demetr.* 31.6 (the only source for these events).

criticizing him for his reconciliation with the common enemy. It was a cardinal error. Demetrius retaliated by raiding the great treasury of Cyinda and removing the 1,200 talents which remained from its vast hoard.[60] It is hard to see how he could have done so without some reassurance from Seleucus, and it certainly did not take the warmth out of his reception. His wife Phila had sailed over from Cyprus to meet him[61] and the pair crossed the gulf of Issus to meet Seleucus, who had brought his army to the coastal city of Rhosus. The reception was open and relaxed, and Plutarch stresses that it was royal.[62] What is more, there was a strong propagandist element to it. Seleucus first entertained his father-in-law to be in his camp, and received reciprocal hospitality in Demetrius' great flagship. The union of land and sea forces could not be more blatantly proclaimed. Nor could the newly found friendship of the kings; the dynasts who had recently clashed in mortal combat now spent whole days together without guards or weapons. In the aftermath their diplomat, Nicagoras of Rhodes, visited Ephesus and other Greek cities to announce the marriage alliance and protest their lasting goodwill to the Hellenes.[63] The shift in the balance of power was formally advertised, and no one would have missed its military implications.

The sequel was predictable. Seleucus escorted his bride to Antioch, and Demetrius immediately occupied Cilicia. The indispensable Phila took her diplomacy to Macedon, and countered the complaints of her dispossessed brother Pleistarchus.[64] She would have forcibly represented the dan-

---

[60] Plut. *Demetr.* 32.1. On the question of Seleucus' connivance see A. Mastrocinque, *La Caria e la Ionia meridionale in epoca ellenistica. 323–188 a.C.*37–8; Gregory, *Historia* 44 (1995) 20.

[61] That is an inference from Plut. *Demetr.* 32.2, where Plutarch notes that 'Phila was now present with him' (παρούσης ἤδη Φίλας). Previously (31.6) he mentioned Demetrius taking his daughter, but not his wife, and Phila presumably joined him later. It is most likely that she crossed from Cypriot Salamis to meet her husband in Cilicia.

[62] Plut. *Demetr.* 32.2: καί τὴν ἔντευξιν εὐθὺς ἄδολον καὶ ἀνύποπτον καὶ βασιλικὴν ἐποιοῦντο.

[63] *OGIS* 10. The Ephesians predictably reacted to the news by voting Nicagoras citizenship and the other honours conferred upon public benefactors. How could they have done otherwise, with a garrison at hand to defend their liberty?

[64] Plut. *Demetr.* 32.4. Diplomacy may have been unnecessary. By the time she reached Macedon Cassander could well have been in the grip of the prolonged and

gers of challenging the formidable new military coalition, especially when Cassander's niece was married to its senior partner. As for Demetrius, his naval power was augmented. He already had a huge fleet at his disposal, and the cedars of the Amanus range were an unlimited source of ships' timber. It is no surprise that when he attacked Athens in 295 he was able to lose one large fleet in a storm off the Attic coast and raise another in short order from Cyprus and the Peloponnese. This new fleet, no less than 300 strong, routed a squadron half its strength which had been sent by Ptolemy.[65] It was a nice illustration of the disparity of naval power. That would have been clear to Ptolemy while Demetrius held sway in Cilicia. The combination of Seleucus' land forces and Demetrius' navy were ominously reminiscent of the Antigonid invasion of 306 which had nearly cost him his kingdom. He therefore made his peace with the new coalition. It was Seleucus, we are told, who brokered a pact of friendship, based on Demetrius' betrothal to a daughter of Ptolemy.[66] He had presumably repaired relations between himself and Ptolemy, and Ptolemy as the weaker party may well have made some concessions—stopping far short of the surrender of Coele Syria.

Seleucus had some reason for a rapprochement with Ptolemy, and one may well believe that it was deeply uncomfortable to have his father-in-law in such close proximity for so long. For Demetrius clearly spent some years in Cilicia. He arrived not long after Ipsus, hardly later than the spring of 299, and he left the area for the siege of Athens, which

painful illness which killed him in the spring of 297. He was certainly in no position to intervene in Cilicia.

[65] Plut. *Demetr.* 33.2 (loss of first fleet); 33.7–8 (discomfiture of Ptolemy).

[66] Plut. *Demetr.* 32.6. The date of the betrothal is conjectural, but it was clearly close to Demetrius' forced exit from Cilicia. The commonly accepted date of 299/8 (Lévêque, *Pyrrhos* 106–7; Wehrli, *Antigone et Démétrios* 159–60; Seibert, above, n.56, 30–2) seems much too early. As part of the agreement Pyrrhus, Demetrius' lieutenant in Greece, went as a hostage to the Ptolemaic court (Plut. *Pyrrh.* 4.5), hardly a serious constraint upon Demetrius' actions. Pyrrhus was at the Ptolemaic court for some time, and married Antigone, Ptolemy's daughter by Berenice. He then established himself in Epirus with help from Ptolemy and was in a position to exploit the Macedonian dynastic troubles in 294. Cf. Lévêque, *Pyrrhos* 107–16, who dates the pact to 299/8 (so Dreyer, *Historia* 49 (2000) 62–3); nothing excludes a date as late as 297.

ended in the spring of 295. He was presumably based in
Cilicia for something like three years.[67] No events during that
period are directly recorded, and, as so often, there is a yawning
gap in our knowledge. What is clear is that the stay in Cilicia
ended in animosity and open hostility. Seleucus requested the
return of Cilicia and offered money for it. Not surprisingly
Demetrius refused, and his now estranged son-in-law
demanded Tyre and Sidon. Here Plutarch adds the interesting
comment that Seleucus was thought to be violent and totally
in the wrong[68] in harassing his kinsman when he was at a low
ebb and demanding a couple of cities when he was master of
all the land between India and the Mediterranean. It is
dressed up with all the rhetoric Plutarch can command, but
the sentiment surely comes from his source, which claimed it
was bad form to deny Demetrius what little territory he had.
It is a curious inversion of a standard modern view of kingship, that dynasts became kings through the acquisition of
territory. Here Demetrius is said to need territory because he
is a king, and Seleucus, who had territory in superabundance
should not deprive him of what little he had. What is more,
it is said to be the prevailing opinion (ἐδόκει). This may be
primarily the opinion of Hieronymus, the courtier of
Demetrius, but he cannot have expressed a view which was
totally ridiculous. There must have been some international
sympathy for Demetrius and a feeling that he was being
meanly treated. He should be given the resources to keep
himself in the regal style to which he had been accustomed.

Right or wrong, Seleucus was intent on depriving
Demetrius of some of the bases for his naval supremacy. He
may have been worried about the extension of Demetrius'
power. The Besieger had been able to strike deep into

---

[67] For the chronology see Habicht, *Athens* 89–94 with n. 58, reluctantly relinquishing his earlier argument (above, n. 20, 2–8) that Athens fell in the spring of
294. For the purposes of the present argument it hardly matters which date is
accepted. Demetrius has either three or four years in Cilicia. See now Dreyer,
Historia 49 (2000) 54–66, arguing that Demetrius intervened inconclusively in
Greece in 299/8. The evidence is very nebulous (primarily the fragmentary
and problematic final entry in the Parium Marble (*FGrH* 239 B27)), and far from
compelling.

[68] *Demetr.* 32.7: ἐδόκει βίαιος εἶναι καὶ δεινὰ ποιεῖν. The language is remarkably
strong.

Ptolemaic territory, and captured the city of Samaria which Perdiccas had established as a military colony. He had the capacity to operate inland away from his fleet, and carried out one of his celebrated acts of poliorcetics. Seleucus was well advised to be suspicious of his growing power, and come to terms with Ptolemy. The capture of Samaria is dated to 296,[69] which may be a trifle late,[70] but it certainly occurred towards the end of Demetrius' occupation of Cilicia. It was probably the catalyst for Seleucus' demands first for Cilicia and then Tyre and Sidon. The situation deteriorated, it seems, into war. The evidence is an undated anecdote in Plutarch, illustrating the universal curiosity about Demetrius' grandiose feats of military engineering. His bitterest enemy, Lysimachus had forces deployed against him when he was laying siege to the Cilician port of Soli, and asked for a demonstration of his siege engines and his ships at sea.[71] There are very few occasions when Demetrius and Lysimachus could have confronted each other at Soli. Possibly in the aftermath of Ipsus, when Demetrius was evacuating his family and war chest to Cyprus, but in that fraught time he was unlikely to be laying siege to a recalcitrant city, certainly not in the face of his conqueror.[72] The most popular suggestion is that it is Lysimachus' reaction to the expulsion of Pleistarchus, who came to take refuge with him.[73] The attack, I agree, must have taken place while Demetrius was in

---

[69] In all versions of Eusebius' chronicle (ed. Schoene II, pp. 118–19) under Ol. 121.1. The texts are conveniently listed in Schürer ii.161, n.404. See also A. Ovadiah, in *Ancient Macedonia* iii.189–91.

[70] G. Corradi, *Studi ellenistici* 40 n. 3, proposed redating the siege to 298; so Wehrli *Antigone et Démétrios* 160; J. Grainger, *Seleukos Nikator* 133, 233. The precise date in Eusebius cannot inspire confidence. He is consistently inaccurate in the dating of events after Alexander: the expulsion of Demetrius of Phalerum from Athens is entered under 305/4 (Ol. 118.4) while Ptolemy's occupation of Cyprus comes seven years too late, in 304/3 (Ol. 119.1).

[71] Plut. *Demetr.* 20.8: Λυσίμαχος μὲν γάρ, ἔχθιστος ὢν Δημητρίῳ τῶν βασιλέων καὶ πολιορκοῦντι Σόλους τοὺς Κιλικίους ἀντιτεταγμένος, ἔπεμψε παρακαλῶν ἐπιδεῖξαι τὰς μηχανὰς αὐτῷ καὶ τὰς ναῦς πλεούσας· ἐπιδείξαντος δὲ θαυμάσας ἀπῆλθε.

[72] Diod. 21.1.4. In any case the person one would have thought most likely to intervene in Cilicia in 301/0 was Seleucus, who was on his way to take possession of Coele Syria (Diod. 21.1.5).

[73] See, for instance, Wehrli *Antigone et Démétrios* 159; Lund, *Lysimachus* 89; Landucci Gattinoni, *Lisimaco di Tracia*166–7; Gregory, *Historia* 44 (1995) 24 n. 58 (undecided).

Cilicia, but it is unlikely to have been launched while relations between Seleucus and Demetrius were cordial. It presumably came after Seleucus made his demand for Cilicia. Lysimachus was duly encouraged (perhaps on Seleucus' initiative) to invade Cilicia and put direct military pressure on Demetrius—it was sweet retaliation for the ravaging of the Chersonese three years before. One may well believe that there was internal disaffection in Cilicia, with Soli declaring itself against Demetrius. The Besieger reacted in characteristic fashion and laid siege to the city by land and sea. While he was so engaged, Lysimachus presumably came down through the Cilician Gates.[74] He hardly came along the coast of Rough Cilicia, otherwise he would not have needed to ask for a demonstration of Demetrius' fleet at sea. It was a land invasion, and he came upon Demetrius while the siege was in full cry. There was no battle, it seems. Demetrius was presumably content to display his formidable armament, and withdrew with his laurels intact. At this point he probably agreed to vacate Cilicia, perhaps retaining some of the harbours where he could leave garrisons,[75] and sailed to his base in Cyprus. In the summer of 296 he reappeared in the Greek world and began operations against Athens.

The past four years had witnessed a complex power play. The constant factor was the mutual suspicion of the leading dynasts. Ipsus had created even more tensions than it resolved. Antigonus' empire was divided on the battlefield and the victors, Lysimachus and Seleucus, practically annexed it all for themselves. As a result Coele Syria immediately became a bone of contention between Ptolemy and Seleucus, while Cassander clearly resented the meagre

---

[74] It was presuably at this time that he established Pleistarchus in his little territory based around Heracleia. This was comparable to Perdiccas establishing Cleopatra as satrap of Lydia with a territorial base around Sardes (Arr. *Succ.* F 25.2 (Roos)), or Alexander's offer of a choice of Asian cities to Phocion (Plut. *Phoc.* 18.7–8; Ael. *VH* 1.25), reminiscent in its turn of the Achaemenids' treatment of Themistocles. It boosted Lysimachus' prestige to have the brother of a rival dynast beholden to and dependent upon himself. He would not have insisted that Pleistarchus won his territory by the spear (contra Buraselis *Das hellenistische Makedonien und die Ägäis* 29).

[75] One thinks of Magarsus, the port of Mallus, the inveterate enemy of Soli. If Soli had rejected Demetrius, it would be grounds for Mallus to remain loyal.

dispensation to his brother. As a result there was little inducement to track down and destroy Demetrius. Lysimachus' former allies watched complacently as Demetrius ravaged his
territory, and Seleucus was ready and willing to take his
daughter to wife so that he could exploit Demetrius' naval
power. However, there were dangers in this policy.
Demetrius' occupation of Cilicia put him in an ideal position
to increase his military strength. It recalls Eumenes in 318,
who was able to recruit mercenaries throughout the north-
eastern Mediterranean from his base in Cilicia, using the
resources of the royal treasuries there. Within a few months
he had recruited some 12,000, both infantry and cavalry, and
was poised to challenge Ptolemy for control of Phoenicia.[76]
Demetrius already had garrisons in the leading cities of
Phoenicia when he took over Cilicia; he had much longer
than Eumenes to recruit mercenaries, and he had the naval
capacity to transport them to his base. It is hardly surprising
that Seleucus and Ptolemy eventually felt him to be too
dangerous to remain in the region and allowed Lysimachus
to invade Cilicia. Seleucus may even have assisted him
militarily, for it was he, not Lysimachus, who took control of
the area.[77] It was a recurrent pattern. In 302 Antigonus'
explicit threat to Macedon had brought about the quadruple
alliance which engineered his defeat at Ipsus, and in 288/7
Demetrius' grandiose preparations for war in Asia were to
bring together yet again Seleucus, Ptolemy, and Lysimachus.
The growth of Demetrius' power in Cilicia had precisely the
same effect. Seleucus had created a monster on his own
doorstep and needed the collaboration of his fellow dynasts
to displace him.

As we have seen, even at the lowest ebb of his fortunes no
one denied Demetrius the regal title his father bestowed on
him. The closest thing attested is the protest of the affronted
Pleistarchus, who contrasted Seleucus and the other kings

[76] Diod. 18.61.4–5, 73.2.
[77] Plut. *Demetr*. 47.2. It is usually assumed that Seleucus occupied Cilicia in 295,
while Demetrius was engaged in Greece (cf. Grainger, *Seleukos Nikator* 143), but
the passage cited in support (Plut. *Demetr*. 35.5) mentions only Lysimachus' gains
in western Asia Minor and Ptolemy's recapture of Cyprus. There is nothing relevant to Seleucus and Cilicia, and it is best to conclude that he took over the area as
Demetrius vacated it.

with Demetrius the common enemy.[78] On the other hand the Athenians took care to address him as king and gave his wife Deidameia regal honours as they dispatched her to Megara.[79] As soon as Seleucus courted his daughter, he necessarily treated Demetrius as an equal, and Demetrius is mentioned before him in the Ephesian decree in honour of Nicagoras of Rhodes. Ephesus was admittedly garrisoned by Demetrius, but it is still interesting that he is presented as the senior partner.[80] His power rested on his naval forces, almost exclusively, and after Ipsus he lacked the resources to keep them in the field. Hence the need to loot and plunder in the Chersonese. It was only the occupation of Cilicia which gave him the revenue to expand his military power and become a serious threat to Ptolemy and to Seleucus himself. But even when he lacked any revenues, he still commanded loyalty. His garrisons may have been expelled from cities in mainland Greece, but Corinth itself stood firm, and there is no record of any garrison renouncing its loyalty and negotiating with the victors. That loyalty was certainly not based on Demetrius' capacity to guarantee financial reward; it was a bleak and uncertain prospect.

'A king was assumed to be wealthy, and to be a giver as well as a receiver of wealth: a poor king or a stingy king was felt to be a contradiction in terms.' So Michel Austin.[81] This is an attractive formulation, but the career of Demetrius injects an element of doubt. He was occasionally poor, and his comparative poverty did not prevent his commanding the loyalty of his supporters. And Demetrius is not unique. There are other cases which do not conform with the model. Perhaps the most paradoxical figure for orthodox theories of kingship is Lysimachus. Before 301 his territory was limited to Thrace,

---

[78] Plut. *Demetr.* 31.7: μέμψασθαι βουλόμενος τὸν Σέλευκον, ὅτι τῷ κοινῷ διαλλάττεται πολεμίῳ δίχα τῶν ἄλλων βασιλέων.

[79] Plut. *Demetr.* 30.4. Demetrius was included among the kings whom they had voted not to receive in the city. The Athenian embassy met him in the Cyclades, perhaps at Delos, where an inscription of 301 BC attests his passage (and the dung he left behind in the shrine), and refers to him simply as ὁ βασιλεύς (*IG* xi.2.146A, line 76, dated to the archonship of Lysixenus). Cf. Buraselis, *Das hellenistische Makedonien und die Ägäis* 58 n.74.

[80] *OGIS* 10.2–3: ἀποσταλεὶς παρὰ τῶν βασιλέων Δημητρίου καὶ Σελεύκου.

[81] *CQ* 36 (1986) 459. citing Claire Préaux, *Le monde hellénistique* i.208–10.

and not all of Thrace at that; and his military success was open to question. Yet he followed the Antigonid precedent and assumed the diadem in 305.[82] His territorial base was limited, his resources relatively small, his successes (as far as we can tell from the very sparse evidence) modest; yet he assumed the title and regalia of kingship and was accepted as an ally and equal by his fellow kings. We should examine his career a little more closely to see how the paradox may be resolved.

Lysimachus was given a formidable assignment when he received Thrace in the Babylon settlement. The territory was in chaos, under the control of the Odrysian ruler, Seuthes, who had rebelled against Macedonian rule in Alexander's last years, and according to Curtius almost all of Thrace was lost.[83] In 323 Lysimachus entered his territory with a small army of 4,000 foot and 2,000 horse and fought an indecisive battle, in which he lost a considerable part of his small army and had a doubtful claim to victory.[84] At this point Diodorus breaks off, stating that both sides withdrew to prepare for the decisive encounter, but he gives no indication what occurred at the supposedly decisive battle or even whether it took place. Seuthes certainly lived on and prospered. He is termed king of the Odrysians by Diodorus, both in 323 and in his next appearance in 314. We know that he had his own capital, near modern Kazanluk in the Tundzha valley, which he named Seuthopolis after himself, in clear emulation of Philippopolis, just to the south in the Hebrus valley.[85] There he struck a prolific coinage, which continued well into the third century.[86] A famous inscription, long known but only

---

[82] Diod. 20.53.4; Plut. *Demetr.* 18.3; Just. 15.2.12; *Heidelberg Epitome, FGrH* 155 F 1.7.

[83] Curt. 10.1.45 'amissa propemodum Thracia'. The revolt is described as the consequence of Zopyrion's fateful expedition against the Getae, which allegedly witnessed 30,000 casualties (Just. 12.2.16; 37.3.2). The number is probably exaggerated, and Macedonians will have comprised a small proportion of the army; but there can have been little resistance to Seuthes in western Thrace.

[84] Diod. 18.14.3: ἀμφίδοξον ἔχων τὴν νίκην. Cf. Arr. *Succ.* F 1.10 (Roos).

[85] For brief description and bibliography see G. M. Cohen, *The Hellenistic Settlements in Europe, the Islands and Asia Minor* 97–8; cf. also William M. Calder III, in *Transitions to Empire* 168–9.

[86] Y. Youroukova, *Coins of the Ancient Thracians* (22–5, 76–81; D. P. Dimitrov and K. Dimitrov, in *Actes du IIe congrès international de Thracologie* ii.165–9; Lund, *Lysimachus* 30–1.

recently published in its entirety,[87] attests the family still flourishing around 300 BC. Seuthes is apparently dead,[88] and his (Macedonian) wife Berenice holds sway with four sons, ratifying an arrangement made by Seuthes with Spartocus, the dynast of Cabyle, some 100 km. to the east.[89] There is no reference to Lysimachus, and one would never guess that these two apparently autonomous dynasts were part of the territory of a paramount king of Thrace.

Lysimachus may have pursued a policy of tolerance, allowing the native dynasts some degree of independence, as Alexander for instance had done with princes like Taxiles and Abisares in India. But in Alexander's case the limited autonomy came after the princes had formally surrendered.[90] Seuthes' position is at best ambiguous. By 313 BC Lysimachus had come to some agreement with him; at least he is described as 'defecting' to Antigonus,[91] and that presupposes some recognition of Lysimachus' authority. But the whole episode is informative. Seuthes had intervened at a moment of crisis. Lysimachus was operating on the Black Sea coast, dealing with rebellions in the Greek cities of Odessus, Istria, and Callatis, which had taken advantage of Antigonus' return to Asia Minor and expelled Lysimachus' garrisons. Lysimachus was immediately successful, forcing Odessus and Istria to capitulate and routing the Scythian warriors who had come to aid Callatis.[92] He was busy with the siege of this last remaining rebel city when news came that Antigonus had sent

---

[87] Calder (above, n. 85)170–2 (full text and translation). Calder (167–8) outlines the lamentable history of the stone (partially published as *IGBR* 1731) since its discovery in 1953.

[88] The inscription refers to dispositions made by Seuthes 'when in good health' (ὑγιαίνων), implying that he is no longer so. He is more likely to be dead (Klaffenbach) than insane (Calder).

[89] The city had been occupied by Philip II (Dem. 8.44, 10.15) and colonized (Strab. 7.6.2 (320)). It had evidently failed to thrive; and if the colonists actually were, as Strabo states, the dregs of society, they may have taken the earliest opportunity to vacate it in favour of the local Thracians.

[90] Arr. 4.22.6; 5.8.2, 29.4–5; cf. Bosworth, *HCA* ii *ad locc.*

[91] Diod. 19.73.8: Σεύθην τὸν βασιλέα τῶν Θρᾳκῶν ἀφεστηκότα πρὸς Ἀντίγονον. On his actions during this campaign see Lund, *Lysimachus* 40–3; Landucci Gattinoni, *Lisimaco di Tracia* 113–18.

[92] Diod. 19.73.1–4. The Callatians were also helped by neighbouring Thracians; they may well have been Odrysians under Seuthes' rule. His capital was some 200 km. south-west of Callatis.

two invasion forces against him, one by sea to Callatis, the other by land. Lysimachus left a holding army at Callatis and withdrew south to meet Antigonus' land force. It was now that he found the Haemus passes held against him by Seuthes, who had defected at the critical moment, and it took a major battle with a good many casualties before he forced the Odrysians from their positions.[93] He was then able to catch the Antigonid land force by surprise and forced it to surrender. This was a happy outcome, but it had been seriously jeopardized by Seuthes' defection, and Seuthes should have expected reprisals from his affronted master. But, if there were reprisals, they were remarkably ineffective. Seuthes' capital was untouched, and he continued minting throughout Lysimachus' reign, to die in his bed.

The action against Callatis seems to have been equally ineffectual. Antigonus' fleet had sailed into the Pontus, apparently unhindered by Lysimachus' forces in the Chersonese, and it was able to relieve Callatis. Antigonus later resumed his pressure, and Callatis was again under siege around 309, when the new ruler of the Cimmerian Bosporus settled a thousand starving Callatians in his domains.[94] The city was under pressure, but there is no hint that it surrendered. In winter 302/1, when Pleistarchus was transporting troops across the Black Sea to Heracleia, he was chronically short of ships and had to send his forces in relays from Odessus.[95] Callatis would have supplied him with another base and more transport vessels, but it is pointedly excluded from the operation. It may well have maintained its independence from Lysimachus.

---

[93] Diod. 19.73.8–9. There is no prospect of locating the pass that Lysimachus forced.

[94] Diod. 20.25.1. The transplantation took place early in the reign of Eumelus, an act of euergetism to compensate for the brutality of his accession. Diodorus (20.22.1–2, 100.7; cf. 16.52.10) dates his reign between 310 and 304. During that time he extended his benefactions to Byzantium, Sinope, and 'the other Greeks who live around the Pontus' (Diod. 20.25.1). Given that he had a war fleet sufficient to repress piracy by the Heniochi on the coast of the Caucasus (Diod. 20.25.2; cf. Strab. 11.2.12 (495–6)), he could have been a serious obstacle to Lysimachus' control of the Pontic cities.

[95] Diod. 20.112.2. Pleistarchus diverged from the mouth of the Bosporus to Odessus, apparently ignoring Mesembria, which lay close to Lysimachus' treasury at Tirizis. The city almost certainly boasted a war fleet at this period (Lund, *Lysimachus* 35), and would have made a useful base for shipping troops. Perhaps here also Lysimachus' control was not too secure.

The dynast's control of the Black Sea littoral was clearly limited, as was his suzerainty over the Thracians of the interior. The consequence was that he had a territorially restricted base and relatively few resources. He could not be described as militarily successful or wealthy. He was not a rich king, and there is some indication that he was sparing with the wealth he had.[96] The main evidence is the smart crack allegedly made by Demetrius' courtiers shortly before Ipsus. According to Phylarchus[97] they alleged that only Demetrius and his father were real kings; the rest were partial rulers, and they were given appropriately derisive epithets, all of them very pertinent to the current political context. Seleucus the elephantarch had traded the eastern provinces of his realm, the provinces so hard won by Alexander, for his elephant stable; Ptolemy the nauarch had lost his ships at Salamis; Agathocles the nesiarch had signally failed in his ambition to expand his rule beyond Sicily and conquer Carthage.[98] The gibe directed against Lysimachus must have been equally appropriate. *Gazophylax*, as has often been observed, has the implication that he was tightly retentive of his treasure, and there must be some truth behind it.

---

[96] An apophthegm in Plutarch (*Mor.* 233C) presupposes that he underpaid his mercenaries, but hardly at the starvation rate of four obols a day. It indicates rather that he paid in characteristic four obol coins which was the only denomination that he minted at Lysimacheia before 301 (Margaret Thompson, in *Essays in Greek Coinage presented to Stanley Robinson*, 165, 168). Another anecdote in Athenaeus (6.246D) presupposes his stinginess. See in general Stanley M. Burstein, in *Ancient Coins of the Graeco-Roman World* 57–68.

[97] Athen. 6.261 B = *FGrH* 81 F 31. Plutarch (*Demetr.* 25.7–8; cf. *Mor.* 823C–D) places the anecdote in the context of the Isthmian celebrations in 302 in a timeless discussion of Demetrius' contempt for other rulers. However, the context is surely the period before Ipsus. Hans Hauben, *AncSoc* 5 (1974) 105–17, argued the case plausibly, observing that no flatterer after Ipsus would have made such a feature of the elephants which had crushed the Antigonid army. This dating has been generally accepted (cf. Burstein (above, n. 96) 59; Lund, *Lysimachus* 129–30), but there is a counter-suggestion by Gruen (above, n. 3) 260–1 that the gibes belong to the period after 294, when Demetrius was king of Macedonia. That I find less compelling. Cassander is omitted from the list of inferior 'kings', it is true, but, if the anecdote is assigned to the later date, so is Demetrius' young rival in Epirus. Whatever the date, we certainly do not have an exhaustive list of rival rulers. Quite possibly Cassander's career did not suggest a suitably derisive epithet.

[98] By the late 290s he had acquired a considerable territory in South Italy (see, briefly, K. Meister in *CAH* vii².406–7), and the gibe of nesiarch would be less appropriate.

But it was not the imputation of meanness that touched Lysimachus to the quick. According to Plutarch he took the gibe as a slur on his manhood, since treasurers were generally eunuchs. There is real venom here. The implication is that Lysimachus' children were not his and his wife was of doubtful virtue. That has a bearing on another anecdote, again deriving from Phylarchus.[99] Demetrius had amused himself by comparing Lysimachus' court to a comic stage, not inappropriately, given that one of Lysimachus' chief courtiers was the Athenian comic playwright Philippides. Its luminaries were reminiscent of barbarian slaves with disyllabic names[100]—his own courtiers had much weightier, polysyllabic names, like Peucestas and Oxythemis, more in keeping with the dignified genre of tragedy. Lysimachus replied that he had never seen a prostitute on the tragic stage, a pointed reference to Demetrius' mistress, Lamia, at which Demetrius closed the exchange with the crushing remark that his prostitute lived more chastely than Lysimachus' Penelope. This anecdote has been dated to a later period, after Lysimachus' second marriage to Arsinoe,[101] but it clearly belongs to the time of Lamia's notoriety, when she was active in Athens before Demetrius left for the campaign of Ipsus.[102] In other words Lysimachus' Penelope was his first wife, Nicaea, to whom he had been married for nearly 20 years, and who was the daughter of Antipater and erstwhile bride of Perdiccas. Demetrius was accusing her of sexual

[99] Athen. 14.614E = *FGrH* 81 F 12. The latter part of the exchange recurs in Plut. *Demetr.* 25.9.

[100] The two specifically mentioned are Paris (otherwise unknown) and the celebrated favourite, Bithys, son of Cleon (on whom see S. M. Burstein, *CA* 12 (1980) 39–50; Lund, *Lysimachus* 181).

[101] So, for instance, Andrei's edition of the *Demetrius* (186 n. 173).

[102] She came into Demetrius' hands after the Battle of Salamis (Plut. *Demetr.* 16.5–6), and she is almost exclusively attested with Demetrius during his period in Athens before 302. It was then that Lysimachus' court poet, the Athenian Philippides, claimed that he turned the Acropolis into a brothel (Plut. *Demetr.* 26.5; cf. *PCG* 7.347 F 25; Habicht, *Athens from Alexander to Antony* 78–9), and the exchange of royal insults must surely belong to the same period. At this time the Athenians seem to have identified Lamia with Aphrodite and established cults for Oxythemis, Adeimantus and Burichus, Demetrius' senior courtiers (Demochares, *FGrH* 75 F 1; cf. Habicht, *Gottmenschentum und griechische Städte*² (Munich 1970) 55–8).

licence, and the additional gibe against Lysimachus, suggesting that he was sterile or impotent, had the additional implication that the couple's children, including Agathocles, the heir apparent, were conceived on the wrong side of the blanket.

One can easily understand Lysimachus' resentment. It was an attempt to undermine the dynastic succession, which was so important in the age of the Diadochoi. As early as 337 the contracting parties in the Corinthian League swore solemnly to preserve the kingdom of Philip and his descendants, and when the League was re-established in 301 the contracting parties vowed to do the same for Antigonus and Demetrius.[103] The same provision recurs in the oaths sworn in 309/8 between Ptolemy and the people of Iasus.[104] At that time Ptolemy had not formally assumed the diadem or the regal title,[105] but the Iasians conceived themselves as entering a formal relationship with a dynastic power which was expected to continue into and beyond the next generation. Insinuations of illegitimacy could be damaging, as Philip Arrhidaeus found when allegations were made against his mother, Philinna. She was said to have been a prostitute in Larisa,[106] and Arrhidaeus was unlikely to be an Argead by blood. On the other hand Demetrius could make a feature of his own marriage to Phila and the fact that he had an adult son by her; it was instrumental in securing his acceptance as king of Macedon.[107] We are not informed what Lysimachus had to say on the matter!

Lysimachus, then, was subjected to some very wounding propaganda at the time of the grand coalition against Demetrius. It was implied that he kept his treasure to himself

---

[103] IG ii² 236 (Philip); *ISE* no. 44.10, 142, 147 (Antigonus and Demetrius). The new Dephic inscription, which perhaps preserves the end of Adeimantus' letter to Demetrius, also refers to his descendants (Lefèvre (above, n. 26) 112 (line 10), 117).

[104] *Inschr. Iasos* 2. 31: συ[μμάχους] ἔσεσθαι Πτολεμαίωι καὶ τοῖς ἐγγόνοις αὐτοῦ ἐ[ὶς] τὸν ἀεὶ χρόνον.

[105] On his ambitions at this time see now Bosworth, in *Al. in Fact and Fiction* 228–41.

[106] She is described as a dancer and Philip's mistress rather than wife (Ptolemy, son of Agesarchus, in Athen. 13.578A; Just. 9.3.2)). At Babylon Ptolemy is said to have dismissed her contemptuously as a whore from Larisa ('Larisaeum scortum'; Just. 13.2.11).   [107] Plut. *Demetr.* 37.4. See above, pp. 251–2.

and that his heirs were of dubious legitimacy. Added to that, he had a chequered career as ruler of Thrace with little military glory to boast of. That in part explains his assumption of the kingship. He had no choice but to follow the example of his contemporaries, Ptolemy, Seleucus, and, not least, Cassander in Macedon. Otherwise he would lose credibility with his own court and army. Yet, once he assumed the diadem, he was accepted as an equal. Even the gibe of Demetrius sets him alongside the other kings whom Demetrius and his courtiers chose to denigrate. He declared himself king before the grand alliance against the Antigonids,[108] and so his acceptance cannot be explained by military necessity. What, then, lay behind his regal claims?

One very significant factor must be his past career as a Bodyguard of Alexander. He had held that position since 328 at the latest, and had taken a leading role at the Hydaspes.[109] He could certainly claim to have conquered Asia with Alexander and was entitled to some of the material rewards. What is more, he could fairly claim to have saved Alexander's life when he intervened in a lion hunt near Samarkand and placed himself between the king and the lion.[110] He was repulsed rather churlishly, but the army had been seriously worried by the incident, sufficiently so to recommend that the king should not hunt alone or on foot.[111] Lysimachus' intervention was clearly regarded as significant, and it enhanced the reputation he had made when he killed a large

---

[108] The alliance was formed in early 302, after Antigonus demanded Cassander's unconditional surrender (Diod. 20.106.2–4; Plut. *Demetr.* 28.2; Just. 15.2.15–17; cf. Billows, *Antigonos* 173–4).

[109] Curt. 8.1.45–6 (328); Arr. 5.13.1 (Hydaspes); cf. 24.5 (Sangala). Cf. Heckel, *Marshals* 272–3; Bosworth, *HCA* ii.59, 280, 334. His surprisingly low profile in the extant sources may be due to Ptolemy's unwillingness to highlight the exploits of a rival.

[110] Curt. 8.1.14. It is usually assumed that Alexander killed the lion after pushing Lysimachus aside (Berve ii.240; Heckel, 268), but the Latin is quite consistent with Lysimachus having diverted the lion out of range for Alexander—hence his chagrin.

[111] Curt. 8.1.18. The vote of the army looks ahead to the similar vote a little later, justifying the murder of Cleitus (Curt. 8.2.12). It may have been (and probably was) suggested by the senior officers, worried by the perpetual danger to Alexander. Compare the later intervention after the wound at the Malli town (the source tradition analysed by Bosworth, *Alexander and the East* 53–61).

lion with his own hands in a game reserve in Syria and was seriously mauled on his left shoulder. Years later he is said to have
shown the scars to ambassadors from Demetrius. The source
for that incident is anecdotal and late,[112] but there is more reliable evidence that Lysimachus' exploits while lion hunting
were very seriously regarded by his contemporaries. Just
before he left Macedonia for the war against Perdiccas Craterus
commissioned a grandiose monument at Delphi. The sculptors
were the greatest of their day, Lysippus and Leochares, and its
scale was huge; the niche which accommodated it measures
over 15 metres by 6.[113] It depicted Craterus coming to the aid
of Alexander, who was at grips with a lion, and the dedicatory
inscription by Craterus' son states that it was Craterus who
killed the lion and did so 'in the confines of Syria'.[114] That was
where Lysimachus' famous single-handed kill took place,
and Craterus was clearly emulating the achievement, not to
mention his later intervention in Sogdiana.

The killing of the lion was the mark of royalty, as a Spartan
ambassador is alleged to have remarked to Alexander,[115] and
Craterus certainly had regal pretensions when he returned to
Macedonia in 322. He dressed exactly like Alexander except
for the diadem, and his army paid court to him 'like a king'
(οἷα βασιλέα).[116] When he received the Greek envoys after
Crannon, he did so in royal state, seated on a golden couch
and dressed in a purple cloak.[117] The dedication at Delphi

---

[112] Plut. *Demetr.* 27.6. It contains the romantic story that Alexander had caged
Lysimachus with the lion (see Curt. 8.1.17 ; Just. 15.3.7–9; Paus. 1.9.5; Sen. *de ira*
3.17.2; Pliny, *NH* 8.54; Val. Max. 9.3 *ext.* 1). That is clearly fiction, but it is quite
likely that Lysimachus did display his scars to Demetrius' envoys.

[113] Plut, *Alex.* 40.5; Pliny, *NH* 34.64. For descriptions of the monument see
A. Stewart, *Faces of Power* (Berkeley 1993) 270–7; O. Palagia, in *Al. in Fact and
Fiction* 183–5, 203–6.

[114] *ISE* no. 73.9–10: καὶ εἰς χέρας ἀντιάσαντα ! ἔκτανεν οἰονόμων ἐν περάτεσσι Σύρων.
Plutarch states that the actual monument showed the moment before the kill, with
Craterus rushing to Alexander's side. That left it open for the dedicatory inscrip-
tion to claim credit for Craterus.

[115] Plut. *Alex.* 40.4: καλῶς . . . πρὸς τὸν λέοντα ἠγώνισαι περὶ τῆς βασιλείας. On the
royal connotations of the lion hunt see particularly Palagia (above, n. 113) 181–200.

[116] Suda *s.v.* Κράτερος=Arr. *Succ.* F 19 (the attribution to Arrian is certain on
linguistic grounds). The passage makes an interesting contrast between the combination of openness and majesty which Craterus displayed in his public appearances
and Antipater's inaccessibility and ugliness; as a result the troops treated Craterus
as a king and totally disregarded Antipater.

[117] Demetr. *Eloc.* 289. The description comes from an eyewitness, Demetrius of
Phalerum.

reinforced the regal image, and broke any monopoly Lysimachus may have claimed. The monument was not of course completed in Craterus' lifetime. His young son finally dedicated it at Delphi, probably in the regency of Polyperchon, Craterus' friend and lieutenant.[118] This played into Lysimachus' hands. Now one of the great sights of the most frequented international centres was a representation of a lion hunt in which the honorand, clearly portrayed as the familiar and equal of Alexander, did precisely what Lysimachus himself had done in Sogdiana. It elevated the prestige of the royal hunt and also of the most famous hunter of his time. Craterus was dead before his monument was dedicated and no longer a rival. Lysimachus could therefore bask in his reflected glory. His coins proclaimed the message. When he struck issues in his own name, he regularly included his characteristic device of a rearing lion, and after 297 he issued coins with what are universally agreed to be the most impressive of all the portraits of Alexander.[119] He underlined his association with the conqueror in the most dramatic way. The deified Alexander dominated and virtually authorized the coinage of King Lysimachus.

Viewed as a predator Lysimachus was not a success, at least not before 301. There are no wholly decisive victories attested, no dramatic accrual of territory, no great haul of treasure. Instead he maintained a loose control over a comparatively poor region, allowing the great Thracian dynasts a virtual autonomy. None the less his spectacular achievements under Alexander and his rank of Bodyguard gave him formidable prestige; as late as 287 Demetrius avoided meeting him in battle because of the popularity he had achieved through Alexander.[120] He also had the promise of dynastic succession

---

[118] *ISE* no. 73. The epigram was probably composed for Craterus himself, and the two lines identifying the dedicant as his son were added later (so Stewart (above, n. 113) 271). The younger Craterus states that his father 'left (him) as a child' (καὶ λίπε παῖδα); this should allude to his age at the dedication, rather than his age when his father actually died. In that case it fits in well with the regency of Polyperchon, between 319 and 316. The alternative, favoured by Moretti and others, is that the younger Craterus made the dedication after 300, when he was an adult. That is hardly consistent with the statue group being the work of Lysippus and Leochares. Both would have been at least octogenarians.

[119] Cf. Thompson (above, n. 96) 165, 168–82.

[120] Plut. *Demetr.* 44.6; *Pyrrh.* 11.7.

through his son Agathocles—which is why he resented so bitterly the slurs cast against his paternity. He needed a territory and an army of course: so did every satrap, let alone king. In his case the territory and army were of modest size when compared with the resources commanded by Ptolemy, Seleucus, and Cassander. It was first and foremost the heroic ethos that mattered. He had proved his capacity for achievement under Alexander, and that capacity enabled him to retain the loyalty of his forces and the respect of his fellow dynasts (if not their liking), who accepted him as their equal. In contrast Demetrius in 301 could hardly boast service under Alexander or territory won by his own efforts. But he had consciously cultivated a regal persona. As early as the campaign of Gaza in 312 he had been paraded in royal armour, physically striking and with a certain gentleness which was considered fitting for a young king.[121] His daring at Gaza, Salamis, and Ipsus would have reinforced the image, so that when his father was killed and his empire fell with him, he retained the loyalty of his garrisons over the Mediterranean. That in turn preserved the fleet which tempted Seleucus into the marriage alliance that restored his fortune. Demetrius may not have accompanied Alexander, but he behaved like him, even in the notorious dissipation of his private life. All this exemplifies Erich Gruen's dictum that a king's legitimacy depended on 'personal achievement and dynastic promise'. That is true, but there is another side. The regal mystique had to be balanced by continued euergetism. The services of one's subjects, great and small, had to be recognized and rewarded materially and morally. The obligation may not have been formalized, but it was a reality, as Demetrius discovered to his cost in 287.

---

[121] Diod. 19.81.4. The combination of royal pomp and gentle temperament was just the combination that Craterus had displayed. If Diodorus is reflecting Hieronymus with reasonable accuracy (Hornblower, *Hieronymus* 227–8), then Demetrius was treated as a king, the successor to his father's βασιλεία, at least six years before he officially assumed the diadem.

APPENDIX

Chronology of Events between 323 and 311 BC

This chronological table is intended to serve as a reference guide. It presents the principal events of the period in sequence and correlates the significant happenings in Asia and the Greco-Macedonian world. With some modifications it embodies the framework developed by Bosworth, *Chiron* 22 (1992) 80–1 and Wheatley, *Phoenix* 52 (1998) 279–81. I adhere to the so-called 'high' chronology, placing Perdiccas' invasion of Egypt in 321. The 'low' chronology, on which much recent work is based, dates the invasion to 320 and presupposes that an entire year elapsed between the surrender of Athens late in 322 and Antipater's winter campaign in Aetolia.[1] My own reconstruction opens out a gap between Perdiccas' death and Antipater's return to Europe in the spring of 319, and also entails a reinterpretation of the Babylonian Chronicle of the Successors which I hope to include in a full commentary on the document. However, the intricacies of dating do not significantly impact on the historical analysis contained in this book.[2]

---

[1] This chronology was advocated by Eugenio Manni (*RAL* (Serie 8) 4 (1949) 53–85) and developed by his pupil, M. J. Fontana in her monograph, *Le lotte per la successione di Alessandro Magno dal 323 al 315*. The most influential exposition is to be found in two articles by R. M. Errington (*JHS* 90 (1970) 75–7; *Hermes* 105 (1977) 478–504), refined and expanded by B. Gullath and L. Schober, in *Studien zu Alten Geschichte. Siegfried Lauffer zum 70. Geburtstag...dargebracht* i.331–78.

[2] The one exception is the discussion of Seleucus' rise to power, in Ch. 6.

Date	Events in Asia	Events in Europe
10 June 323	Death of Alexander the Great	
late June? 323	First settlement in Babylon (Philip III declared King)	
late July? 323	Lustration of army. Perdiccas regent. Satrapy distributions	Outbreak of Lamian War
autumn 323	Peithon appointed to deal with returning colonists	Defeat of Antipater in Thessaly. Siege of Lamia. Death of Leosthenes
spring 322	Peithon's defeat of the colonists. Perdiccas' campaign against Ariarathes	Leonnatus raises siege of Lamia. Antipater withdraws to Macedonia. Sea battles off Acarnania
summer 322	Ptolemy annexes Cyrenaica. Alexander IV proclaimed joint King. Destruction of Isaura and Laranda	Craterus returns to Europe. Macedonian victories at Crannon (July) and (by sea) at Amorgos
autumn 322	Perdiccas' marital intrigues and attack on Antigonus. Eumenes consolidates in Cappadocia, Neoptolemus in Armenia	Oligarchic constitution imposed in Athens (September)
winter 322/1	Eumenes takes Perdiccas' marriage proposal to Cleopatra	Craterus and Antipater in Aetolia. Antigonus sets them on a war footing against Perdiccas
spring 321	Ptolemy intercepts Alexander's cortège. Eumenes given command of Perdiccas' forces in Asia Minor	Craterus and Antipater cross the Hellespont to attack Perdiccas
summer 321	Eumenes defeats Neoptolemus and Craterus.	Aetolian invasion of Locris and Thessaly winter 321/0

Date	Events in Asia	Events in Europe
	Perdiccas invades Egypt, and is assassinated (late summer)	
autumn 321	Arrhidaeus and Peithon voted regents at Memphis, Antipater in Cilicia	
winter 321/0	Conference at Triparadeisus. Antipater becomes regent and satrapies are reallocated	
spring 320	Antipater returns to Asia Minor. Convergence of outlawed Perdiccans in Pisidia	
summer 320	Ptolemy annexes Syria. Early operations against Eumenes	
winter 320/19	Winter campaign in Phrygia. Return of Macedonian veterans	
spring 319	Antipater returns to Macedon with the Kings. Antigonus comprehensively defeats Eumenes and begins siege of Nora	
late summer 319	Antigonus defeats Alcetas and the Perdiccans in Pisidia	Death of Antipater; Polyperchon becomes regent and Cassander chiliarch
winter 319/18	Antigonus invades Hellespontine Phrygia after Arrhidaeus attacks Cyzicus	Cassander escapes from Macedon; Polyperchon issues his 'exiles' decree'. Nicanor occupies Peiraeus
spring 318	Eumenes vacates Nora. Antigonus invades Lydia	Democratic revolution in Athens; death of Phocion (May). Arrival of Cassander in Peiraeus

Date	Events in Asia	Events in Europe
summer 318	Eumenes accepts the royal generalship; meets Silver Shields in Cilicia. Antigonus intervenes at Byzantium	Polyperchon in the Peloponnese; siege of Megalopolis. Cleitus and Nicanor at the Hellespont
autumn 318	Eumenes moves from Cilicia to Babylonia, retreating from Antigonus	Polyperchon returns to Macedon
winter 318/17	Eumenes in winter quarters in Babylonia, Antigonus in Mesopotamia	Athens capitulates to Cassander: regime of Demetrius begins (after November)
summer 317	Battle of the Coprates (July). Antigonus takes his army to Media	Cassander's first invasion of Macedon. Eurydice declares herself against Polyperchon
autumn 317	Eumenes in Persis with the satrapal coalition	Olympias' return to Macedon; defeat and death of Philip III and Eurydice (October)
winter 317/16	Battle of Paraetacene (November?) Battle of Gabiene (January). Surrender and death of Eumenes. Antigonus ends the winter near Ecbatana	Cassander's second invasion of Macedon. Siege of Pydna
spring 316	Execution of Peithon in Media; Antigonus moves to Persepolis	Capitulation and execution of Olympias. Cassander takes control in Macedon
summer/ autumn 316	Deposition of Peucestas and Seleucus. Antigonus returns to Cilicia (November). Ultimatum to Antigonus from Ptolemy, Lysimachus and Cassander	Cassander's restoration of Thebes

Date	Events in Asia	Events in Europe
spring/ summer 315	Antigonus' siege of Tyre begins. Seleucus' operations in Cyprus. Asander of Caria allies himself with Ptolemy	Cassander in the Peloponnese; presides over Nemean Games
summer 314	End of siege of Tyre. Seleucus in the Aegean	Cassander active in the west. Cassander sends forces to Caria
winter 314/13	Antigonus crosses the Taurus and returns to Celaenae. Polemaeus defeats Cassander's troops in Caria	Asander visits Athens (January 313)
summer 313	Antigonus overruns Caria	Cassander intervenes in Epirus and Euboea. Polemaeus begins operations in Greece
autumn/ winter 313/12	Ptolemy attacks Cilicia; Demetrius fails to relieve Mallus. Antigonus winters at the Hellespont	Cassander returns to Macedon Polemaeus successful in Euboea and Boeotia
spring 312	Battle of Gaza; defeat of Demetrius	Polemaeus in Phocis and eastern Locris
summer 312	Demetrius regrouping in Cilicia. Seleucus invades Babylonia. Demetrius defeats Cilles	Telesphorus defects from Antigonus; war with Polemaeus. Cassander's operations in Epirus
autumn 312	Antigonus returns to Syria. Seleucus occupies Babylon	Cassander unsuccessful at Epidamnus; returns to Macedonia for winter
winter 312/11	Antigonid campaigns against the Nabataeans. Seleucus defeats Nicanor	

Date	Events in Asia	Events in Europe
spring 311	Seleucus' invasion of the upper satrapies. Demetrius' attack on Babylonia	Cassander and Lysimachus open negotiations with Antigonus
summer/ autumn 311	Ptolemy sues for inclusion in peace negotiations. *Peace of the Dynasts*	*Peace of the Dynasts*

Bibliography

The following list gives full publication details of all significant modern works which are cited in the body of the book. A survey of the ancient sources is provided in Chapter 1. A full bibliography (to 1983) of the period of the Successors is to be found in J. Seibert, *Das Zeitalter der Diadochen*, and may be supplemented by the recent works of R. A. Billows (*Antigonos the One-Eyed*), W. Heckel (*The Marshals of Alexander's Empire*), and C. Habicht (*Athens from Alexander to Antony*).

ABEL, F. M., 'L' expédition des Grecs à Pétra en 312 avant J.-C.', *Rev. Bibl.* 46 (1937) 373–91.

AGRAWALA, V. S., *India as Known to Pāṇini* (Lucknow 1958).

ANSON, E. M., 'The Siege of Nora: A Source Conflict', *GRBS* 18 (1977) 251–6.

——'Alexander's Hypaspists and the Argyraspids', *Historia* 30 (1981) 117–20.

——'Craterus and the *prostasia*', *CPh* 87 (1992) 38–43.

ATKINSON, J. E., *A Commentary on Q. Curtius Rufus' Historiae Alexandri Magni, Books 3 and 4* (Amsterdam 1980).

——*A Commentary on Q. Curtius Rufus' Historiae Alexandri Magni. Books 5 to 7, 2* (Amsterdam 1994).

——'Originality and its Limits in the Alexander Sources of the Early Empire', in A. B. Bosworth and E. J. Baynham (eds.), *Alexander the Great in Fact and Fiction* (Oxford 2000) 307–25.

AUSTIN, M. M., 'Hellenistic Kings, War and the Economy', *CQ* 36 (1986) 450–66.

AYMARD, A., *Études d'histoire ancienne* (Paris 1967).

BADIAN, E., 'The Date of Clitarchus', *PACA* 8 (1965) 5–11.

——'A King's Notebooks', *HSCP* 72 (1967) 183–204.

——'Nearchus the Cretan', *YCS* 24 (1975) 147–70.

——'The Ring and the Book', in W. Will (ed.), *Zu Alexander dem Grossen* (Amsterdam 1988) i.605–25.

——'Two Postscripts on the Marriage of Phila and Balacrus', *ZPE* 72 (1988) 116–18.

——'Agis III: Revisions and Reflections', in I. Worthington (ed.), *Ventures into Greek History* (Oxford 1994) 258–92.

BADIAN, E., 'Conspiracies', in A. B. Bosworth and E. J. Baynham (eds.), *Alexander the Great in Fact and Fiction* (Oxford 2000) 50–95.

BAYNHAM, E. J., *Alexander the Great. The Unique History of Quintus Curtius* (Ann Arbor, Mich. 1988).

—— A Baleful Birth in Babylon', in A. B. Bosworth and E. J. Baynham (eds.), *Alexander the Great in Fact and Fiction* (Oxford 2000) 242–62.

BELOCH, K. J., *Griechische Geschichte*, 2nd edn., 4 vols. (Strassburg, Berlin, Leipzig 1922–7).

BERNARD, P., 'Le monnayage d'Eudamos, satrape grec du Pandjab et maître des éléphants', in G. Gnoli and L. Lanciotti, *Orientalia Iosephi Tucci memoriae dicata* (Rome 1985) 65–94.

BERVE, H., *Das Alexanderreich auf prosopographischer Grundlage*, 2 vols. (Munich 1926).

BEVAN, E., *A History of Egypt under the Ptolemaic Dynasty* (London 1927).

BILLERBECK, M., 'The Ideal Cynic from Epictetus to Julian', in R. B. Branham and M.-O. Goulet-Cazé (eds.), *The Cynics. The Cynic Movement in Antiquity and its Legacy* (Berkeley, Calif. 1996) 205–21.

BILLOWS, R. A., *Antigonos the One-Eyed and the Creation of the Hellenistic State* (Berkeley 1990).

—— *Kings and Colonists* (Leiden 1995).

—— 'Polybius and Alexander Historiography', in A. B. Bosworth and E. J. Baynham (eds.), *Alexander the Great in Fact and Fiction* (Oxford 2000) 286–306.

BING, J. S., 'A Further Note on Cyinda/Kundi', *Historia* 22 (1973) 346–50.

BÖDEFELD, H., *Untersuchungen zur Datierung der Alexandergeschichte des Q. Curtius Rufus* (Düsseldorf 1982).

BOIY, T., 'Laatachaemenidisch en hellenistisch Babylon' (Katholieke Universiteit, Leuven 2000).

BOIY, T. and VERHOEVEN, K., 'Arrian, *Anabasis* vii 21.1–4 and the Pallukatu Channel', in *Changing Watercourses in Babylonia. Towards a Reconstruction of the Ancient Environment in Lower Mesopotamia* 1 (MHEM 5/1: 1998) 147–58.

BOSWORTH, A. B., 'The Death of Alexander the Great: Rumour and Propaganda', *CQ* 21 (1971) 112–36.

—— 'Eumenes, Neoptolemus and *PSI* XII 1284', *GRBS* 19 (1978) 227–37.

—— *A Historical Commentary on Arrian's History of Alexander* i– (Oxford 1980– –).

—— 'The Indian Satrapies under Alexander the Great', *Antichthon* 17 (1983) 39–45.

Bibliography 287

—— 'Alexander the Great and the Decline of Macedon', *JHS* 106 (1986) 1–12.

—— *Conquest and Empire. The Reign of Alexander the Great* (Cambridge 1988).

—— *From Arrian to Alexander. Studies in Historical Interpretation* (Oxford 1988).

—— 'Nearchus in Susiana', in W. Will (ed.), *Zu Alexander dem Grossen* (Amsterdam 1988) i. 541–66.

—— 'History and Artifice in Plutarch's *Eumenes*', in P. A. Stadter (ed.), *Plutarch and the Historical Tradition* (London 1992) 56–89.

—— 'Philip III Arrhidaeus and the Chronology of the Successors', *Chiron* 22 (1992) 56–81.

—— 'Perdiccas and the Kings', *CQ* 43 (1993) 420–7.

—— 'A New Macedonian Prince', *CQ* 44 (1994) 57–65.

—— 'The Historical Setting of Megasthenes' *Indica*', *CPh* 91 (1996) 113–27.

—— 'Ingenium und Macht: Fritz Schachermeyr and Alexander the Great', *AJAH* 13 (1988 [1996]) 56–78.

—— *Alexander and the East. The Tragedy of Triumph* (Oxford 1996).

—— 'Alexander, Euripides and Dionysos', in R. W. Wallace and E. M. Harris (eds.), *Transitions to Empire* (Norman, Okla. 1996) 140–66.

—— 'Calanus and the Brahman Opposition', in W. Will (ed.), *Alexander der Grosse. Eine Welteroberung und ihr Hintergrund* (Bonn 1988) 173–203.

—— 'Ptolemy and the Will of Alexander', in A. B. Bosworth and E. J. Baynham (eds.), *Alexander the Great in Fact and Fiction* (Oxford 2000) 207–41.

BOWERSOCK, G. W., *Roman Arabia* (Cambridge, Mass. 1983).

BRIANT, P., *Antigone le Borgne* (Paris 1973).

—— *Rois, tributs et paysans. Études sur les formations tributaires du Moyen-Orient ancien* (Paris 1982).

—— *État et pasteurs au Moyen-Orient ancien* (Cambridge 1982).

—— 'Note d'histoire militaire achéménide: à propos des éléphants de Darius III', in P. Brulé and J. Oulhen (eds.), *Esclavage, guerre, économie en Grèce ancienne* (Rennes 1997) 177–90.

BROWN, T. S., 'Hieronymus of Cardia', *American Historical Review* 52 (1946) 684–96.

—— *Onesicritus* (Berkeley, Calif. 1949).

BURASELIS, K., *Das hellenistische Makedonien und die Ägäis* (Munich 1982).

BURSTEIN, S. M., 'Bithys, Son of Cleon from Lysimachia: A Reconsideration of the Date and Significance of *IG* II², 808', *CA* 12 (1980) 39–50.

BURSTEIN, S. M., 'Lysimachus the *Gazophylax*: A Modern Scholarly Myth', in Waldemar Heckel and Richard Sullivan (eds.), *Ancient Coins of the Graeco-Roman World* (Waterloo, Ont. 1984) 57–68.

——*Agatharchides of Cnidus on the Erythraean Sea* (London 1989).

CALDER, W. M., 'The Seuthopolis Inscription', in R. W. Wallace and E. M. Harris (eds.), *Transitions to Empire* (Norman, Okla. 1996) 167–78.

CARNEY, E., *Women and Monarchy in Macedonia* (Norman, Okla. 2000).

——'The Trouble with Philip Arrhidaeus', *AHB* 15 (2001) 63–89.

COHEN, G. M., *The Hellenistic Settlements in Europe, the Islands and Asia Minor* (Berkeley, Calif. 1995).

COOK, J. M., *The Persian Empire* (London 1983).

CORRADI, G., *Studi ellenistici* (Turin 1929).

COURTWRIGHT, P. B., 'The Iconographies of Sati', in J. S. Hawley (ed.), *Sati. The Blessing and the Curse* (New York and Oxford 1994) 27–53.

DATTA, V. N., *A Historical, Social and Philosophical Enquiry into the Hindu Rite of Widow Burning* (New Delhi 1987).

DAVIES, J. K., *Athenian Propertied Families 600–300 B.C.* (Oxford 1971).

DEL MONTE, G. F., *Testi dalla Babilonia Ellenistica* I (Pisa 1997).

DESCAT, R., 'La carrière d'Eupolemos, stratège macédonien en Asie Mineure', *REA* 100 (1998) 167–90.

DEVINE, A. M., 'The Parthi, the Tyranny of Tiberius, and the Date of Quintus Curtius Rufus', *Phoenix* 33 (1979) 142–59.

——'Diodorus' Account of the Battle of Gaza', *Acta Classica* 27 (1984) 31–40.

——'Diodorus' Account of the Battle of Paraitacene', *AncW* 12 (1985) 75–86.

——'Diodorus' Account of the Battle of Gabiene', *AncW* 12 (1985) 87–96.

DREYER, B., 'Der Göteborger Arrian-Palimpsest (ms Gr. 1)', *ZPE* 125 (1999) 39–60.

——'Athen und Demetrios Poliorketes nach der Schlacht von Ipsos (301 v. Chr.)', *Historia* 49 (2000) 54–66.

DIMITROV, D. P., and DIMITROV, K., 'Le monnayage de Seuthès III selon les données de Seuthopolis', in Radu Vulpe (ed.), *Actes du IIe congrès international de Thracologie* (Bucharest 1980) ii.165–9.

DROYSEN, H., *Untersuchungen über Alexander des Grossen Heerwesen und Kriegführung* (Freiburg in Bresgau 1885).

—— *Heerwesen und Kriegführung der Griechen* (Freiburg 1888).
DROYSEN, J. G., 'Zu Duris und Hieronymos', *Hermes* 11 (1876)
458–65.
—— *Geschichte des Hellenismus*, 2nd edn., 3 vols. (Gotha 1877–8).
DUSSAUD, R., *Topographie historique de la Syrie antique et medié-vale* (Paris 1927).
ENGEL, R., 'Polyäns Stratagem IV 6, 8 zur "Seeschlacht am Hellespont"', *Klio* 55 (1973) 141–5.
ELLIS, J. R., 'The Step-Brothers of Philip II', *Historia* 22 (1973)
350–4.
ERRINGTON, R. M., 'Bias in Ptolemy's History of Alexander', *CQ* 19 (1969) 233–42.
—— 'From Babylon to Triparadeisos, 323–20 BC', *JHS* 90 (1970)
49–77.
—— 'Diodorus Siculus and the Chronology of the Early Diadochoi, 320–311 B.C.'. *Hermes* 105 (1977) 478–504.
—— *A History of Macedonia* (Berkeley, Calif. 1990).
FONTANA, M. J., *Le lotte per la successione di Alessandro Magno dal 323 al 315* (Palermo 1960).
FRASER, P. M., *Ptolemaic Alexandria*, 3 vols. (Oxford 1972).
FREDRICKSMEYER, E., 'Alexander the Great and the Kingdom of Asia', in A. B. Bosworth and E. J. Baynham (eds.), *Alexander the Great in Fact and Fiction* (Oxford 2000) 136–66.
GAWLIKOWSKI, M., 'Thapsacus and Zeugma: The Crossing of the Euphrates in Antiquity', *Iraq* 58 (1996) 123–33.
GOEDICKE, H., 'Comments on the Satrap Stele', BES 6 (1985)
35–54.
GOMME, A. W., ANDREWES, A., and DOVER, K. J., *A Historical Commentary on Thucydides*, 5 vols. (Oxford 1948–81).
GELLER, M. J., 'Babylonian Astronomical Diaries and Corrections of Diodorus', *BSOAS* 53 (1990) 1–7.
GORALSKI, W. J., 'Arrian's *Events after Alexander*', *AncW* 19 (1989)
81–108.
GRAF, D. F., 'The origin of the Nabataeans', *ARAM* 2 (1990)
45–75 (reprinted with original page nos. in *Rome and the Arabian Frontier from the Nabataeans to the Saracens* (Aldershot 1997)).
—— 'Aramaic on the Periphery of the Achaemenid Realm', *Archäologische Mitteilungen aus Iran und Turan* 32 (2000) 75–92.
GRAINGER, J., *Seleukos Nikator* (London 1992).
GREGORY, A. P., 'A Macedonian ΔΥΝΑΣΤΗΣ', *Historia* 44 (1995)
11–28.
GRIFFITH, G. T., *The Mercenaries of the Hellenistic World* (Cambridge 1935).

GRUEN, E., 'The Coronation of the Diadochoi', in J. W. Eadie and J. Ober (eds.), *The Craft of the Ancient Historian* (Lanham, Md. 1958) 253–71.

GULLATH, B., and SCHOBER, L., 'Zur Chronologie der frühen Diadochenzeit: die Jahre 320 bis 315 v.Chr.', in H. Kalcyk, B. Gullath and A. Graeber (eds.), *Studien zu Alten Geschichte. Siegfried Lauffer zum 70. Geburtstag...dargebracht* (Rome 1986) i.331–78.

HABICHT, C., *Gottmenschentum und griechische Städte*, 2nd edn. (Munich 1970).

—— *Untersuchungen zur politischen Geschichte Athens im 3.Jahrhundert v. Chr.* (Munich 1979).

—— *Athens from Alexander to Antony* (Cambridge, Mass. 1997).

HADLEY, R. A., 'A Possible Lost Source for the Career of Eumenes of Cardia'. *Historia* 50 (2001) 3–33.

HAMMOND, N. G. L., 'A Cavalry Unit in the Army of Antigonus Monophthalmus: *asthippoi*', *CQ* 28 (1978) 128–35 (=*Collected Studies* iii. 203–10).

—— 'Some Passages in Arrian Concerning Alexander', *CQ* 30 (1980) 455–76.

—— *Three Historians of Alexander the Great* (Cambridge 1983).

—— 'Alexander's Veterans after his Death', *GRBS* 25 (1984) 51–61 (=*Collected Studies* iii.131–41).

—— 'An Unfulfilled Promise by Alexander the Great', in W. Will (ed.), *Zu Alexander dem Grossen* (Amsterdam 1988) i. 627–34 (=*Collected Studies* iii.143–50).

—— 'Casualties and Reinforcements of Citizen Soldiers in Greece and Macedon', *JHS* 109 (1989) 56–68.

—— *The Macedonian State* (Oxford 1989).

—— 'Royal Pages. Personal Pages and Boys Trained in the Macedonian Style during the Period of the Temenid Monarchy', *Historia* 39 (1990) 261–90 (=*Collected Studies* ii.149–78).

—— *Collected Studies*, 3 vols. (Amsterdam 1993–4).

HAMMOND, N. G. L., and GRIFFITH, G. T., *A History of Macedonia*. ii: *550–336 B.C.* (Oxford 1979).

HAMMOND, N. G. L., and WALBANK, F. W., *A History of Macedonia*. iii: *336–167 B.C.* (Oxford 1988).

HANSEN, M. H., 'The Battle Exhortation in Ancient Historiography, *Historia* 42 (1993) 161–80.

—— 'The Little Grey Horse–Henry V's Speech at Agincourt and the Battle Exhortation in Ancient Historiography', in HISTOS 2 (1988).

HANSMAN, J., 'Elamites, Achaemenians and Anshan', *Iran* 10 (1972) 101–24.

HAREL. M., 'The Roman Road at Ma'aleh Aqrabim', *IEJ* 9 (1959) 175–9.

HART, S., 'Sela: The Rock of Edom?', *PEQ* 118 (1986) 91–5.

HARTOG, P., *The Mirror of Herodotus* (Berkeley, Calif. 1988).

HAUBEN, H., 'On the Chronology of the Years 313–311 B.C.', *AJP* 94 (1973) 256–67.

—— 'A Royal Toast in 302 BC', *AncSoc* 5 (1974) 105–17.

—— 'The Ships of the Pydnaeans: Remarks on Kassandros' Naval Situation in 314/13 B.C.', *AncSoc* 9 (1978) 47–54.

—— 'Who is Who in Antigonus' Letter to the Scepsians?', *EA* 9 (1987) 29–36.

HECKEL, W., 'On Attalus and Atalante', *CQ* 28 (1978) 377–82.

—— 'Kelbanos, Kebalos or Kephalon?', *BN* 18 (1980) 43–5.

—— 'The Career of Antigenes', *SO* 57 (1982) 57–67.

—— 'A Grandson of Antipater at Delos', *ZPE* 70 (1987) 161–2.

—— *The Marshals of Alexander's Empire* (London 1992).

HECKEL, W., and YARDLEY, J. C., 'Roman Writers and the Indian Practice of Suttee', *Philologus* 125 (1981) 305–11.

HERZFELD, E., *The Persian Empire* (Wiesbaden 1968).

HILLER VON GAERTRINGEN, F., 'Aus der Belagerung von Rhodos', *SBBerlin* 1918, 752–62.

HOLT, F. L., *Alexander the Great and Bactria. The Formation of a Greek Frontier* (Leiden 1988).

HORNBLOWER, J., *Hieronymus of Cardia* (Oxford 1981).

HORNBLOWER, S., *A Commentary on Thucydides* i– (Oxford 1991– –).

JACOBY, F., *Griechische Historiker* (Stuttgart 1956).

KANE, P. V., *History of Dharmaśāstra*, 5 vols. (Poona 1941).

KANGLE, R. P., *The Kauṭilīya Arthaśāstra*, (Bombay 1972).

KARTTUNEN, K., *India and the Hellenistic World* (Helsinki 1997).

KEBRIC, R. B., *In the Shadow of Macedon: Duris of Samos* (Wiesbaden 1977).

KENNEDY, D. L., *The Twin Towns of Zeugma on the Euphrates*, JRA Suppl. 27 (Portsmouth, R.I. 1998).

KLOFT, H., 'Kleomenes von Naukratis: Probleme eines hellenistischen Wirtschaftsstils', *GB* 15 (1988) 191–222.

KÖCHLY, H., and RUSTOV, W., *Geschichte des griechischen Kriegswesen von der ältesten Zeit bis auf Pyrrhos* (Leipzig 1852).

KROMAYER, J., and KAHNES, E., *Antike Schlachtfelder. Bausteine zu einer antiken Kriegsgeschichte* i (Berlin 1903).

LANDUCCI GATTINONI, F., 'Ieronimo e la storia dei Diadochi', *Invigilata Lucernis* 3–4 (1981–2) 13–26.

—— *Lisimaco di Tracia. Un sovrano nella prospettiva del primo ellenismo* (Milan 1992).

LASSEN, C., *Indische Alterthumskunde*, 2nd edn., 4 vols. (Leipzig, Bonn, London 1861–74).

LAUNEY, M., *Recherches sur les armées hellénistiques*, 2 vols. (Paris 1949–50).

LEFÈVRE, F., 'Traité de paix entre Démétrios Poliorcète et la confédération étolienne (fin 289?)', *BCH* 122 (1998) 109–41.

LEHMANN, G. A., 'Das neue Kölner Historiker-fragment', *ZPE* 72 (1988) 1–17.

LENS TUERO, J., 'En Catai y en reino de Sopites', in Jesús Lens Tuero (ed.), *Estudios sobre Diodoro de Sicilia* (Granada 1994) 23–31.

—— 'La réplica de los árabes nabateos a Demetrio Poliorcetes' in Jesús Lens Tuero (ed.), *Estudios sobre Diodoro de Sicilia* (Granada 1994) 117–25.

LE RIDER, G., 'Cléomène de Naucratis', *BCH* 121 (1997) 71–93.

LÉVÊQUE, P., *Pyrrhos* (Paris 1957).

LINDNER, I. M., *Petra und das Königreich der Nabatäer*, 3rd edn. (Munich 1980).

LOTI, P., *Vers Ispahan*, ed. K. A. Kelly and K. C. Cameron (Exeter 1989: first published 1904).

LUND, H. S., *Lysimachus. A Study in Early Hellenistic Kingship* (London 1992).

MA, J., *Antiochus III and the Cities of Asia Minor* (Oxford 1999).

MCKECHNIE, P., 'Manipulation of Themes in Quintus Curtius Rufus Book 10', *Historia* 48 (1999) 44–60.

MANNI, E., 'Tre note di cronologia ellenistica', *RAL* (Serie 8) 4 (1949) 53–85.

MARINOVIC, L. P., *Le Mercenariat grec et la crise de la polis* (Paris 1988).

MARSDEN, E. W., *The Campaign of Gaugamela* (Liverpool 1964).

MARTIN, T. R., 'Quintus Curtius' presentation of Philip Arrhidaeus and Josephus' accounts of the accession of Claudius', *AJAH* 8 (1983 [1987]) 161–90.

MASTROCINQUE, A., *La Caria e la Ionia meridionale in epoca ellenistica. 323–188 A.C.* (Rome 1979).

MEHL, A., *Seleukos Nikator und sein Reich* (Louvain 1986).

MEISTER, K., *Die griechische Geschichtsschreibung von den Anfängen bis zum Ende des Hellenismus* (Stuttgart 1990).

MENDELS, D., 'Aetolia 331–301: Frustration, Political Power and Survival', *Historia* 33 (1984) 129–80.

MERKER, I. L., 'Notes on Abdalonymus and the Dated Coinage of Sidon and Ake', I. L. Merker, *ANSMN* 11 (1964) 13–20.

—— 'Diodorus Siculus and Hieronymus of Cardia', *AHB* 2 (1988) 90–3.

MILNS, R. D., 'The Army of Alexander the Great', in *Alexandre le Grand; image et réalité* (Entretiens Hardt 22: Geneva 1976) 87–130.
—— '"Asthippoi" again', *CQ* 31 (1981) 347–54.
MØRKHOM, O., 'The Alexander Coinage of Nicocles of Paphos', *Chiron* 8 (1978) 135–47.
MOSSHAMMER, A. A., *The Chronicle of Eusebius and Greek Chronographic Tradition* (London 1979).
MÜLLER, O., *Antigonos Monophthalmos und 'Das Jahr der Könige'* (Saarbrücker Beiträge zur Altertumskunde 11: Bonn 1973).
NANDY, A., 'Sati as Profit versus Sati as a Spectacle: The Public Debate on Roop Kanwar's Death', in J. S. Hawley (ed.), *Sati. The Blessing and the Curse* (New York and Oxford 1994) 131–49.
NEGEV, A., 'The early beginnings of the Nabataean realm', *PEQ* 108 (1976) 125–33.
—— 'The Nabataeans and the Provincia Arabia', *ANRW* II.8 (1977) 520–686.
NIESE, B., *Geschichte der griechischen und makedonischen Staaten seit der Schlacht bei Chaironeia*, 3 vols. (Gotha 1893–1903).
NORET, J., 'Un fragment du dixième livre de la *Succession d'Alexandre* par Arrien retrouvé dans un palimpseste de Gothenbourg', *AC* 52 (1983) 235–42.
OGDEN, D., *Polygamy, Prostitutes and Death. The Hellenistic Dynasties* (London 1999).
OLDENBURG, V. T., 'The Roop Kanwar Case: Feminist Responses', in J. S. Hawley (ed.), *Sati. The Blessing and the Curse* (New York and Oxford 1994) 101–30.
O'SULLIVAN, L. L., 'Athenian Impiety Trials in the Late Fourth Century B.C.', *CQ* 47 (1997) 136–52.
—— 'The Rule of Demetrius of Phalerum in Athens' (Diss. Western Australia 1999).
OVADIAH, A., 'Macedonian Elements in Israel', in *Ancient Macedonia* iii (Thessaloniki 1983) 185–93.
PALAGIA, O., 'Hephaestion's Pyre and the Royal Hunt of Alexander', in A. B. Bosworth and E. J. Baynham (eds.), *Alexander the Great in Fact and Fiction* (Oxford 2000) 167–206.
PEARSON, L., *The Lost Historians of Alexander the Great* (Philological Monographs 20: New York 1960).
PELLING, C. B. R., *Plutarch Antony* (Cambridge 1988).
PODDIGHE, E., 'La natura del tutto censitario stabilito da Antipatro per accesso al politeuma di Atene nel 322 A.C.', *DHA* 23/2 (1997) 47–82.
POTTS, D. T., 'Madaktu and Badace', *Isimu* 2 (1999)13–28.

POTTS, D. T., 'Elamite Ula, Akkadian Ulaya and Greek Choaspes: A solution to the Eulaios problem', *Bulletin of the Asia Institute* 12 (2001).

PRANDI, L., *Fortuna e realtà dell'opera di Clitarco* (Stuttgart 1996).

PRÉAUX, C., *Le monde hellénistique*, 2 vols. (Paris 1978).

PRICE, M. J., *The Coinage in the Name of Alexander the Great and Philip Arrhidaeus*, 2 vols. (Zurich and London 1991).

PRITCHETT, W. K., *Essays in Greek History* (Amsterdam 1994).

RIST, J., *Stoic Philosophy* (Oxford 1969).

ROBERT, L., *Le Sanctuaire de Sinuri près de Mylasa* I (Paris 1945).

ROSEN, K., 'Political Documents in Hieronymus of Cardia', *Acta Classica* 10 (1967) 41–94.

—— 'Politische Ziele in der frühen hellenistischen Geschichtsschreibung', *Hermes* 107 (1979) 460–76.

SACHS, A., and HUNGER, H., *Astronomical Diaries and Related Texts from Babylonia I. Diaries from 652 BC to 262 BC* (Österreichische Akademie der Wissenschaften, phil.-hist. Klasse: Denkschriften 195: Vienna 1988).

SACKS, K. S., 'Diodorus and his Sources: Conformity and Creativity', in Simon Hornblower (ed.), *Greek Historiography* (Oxford 1994) 213–32.

SAITTA, G., 'Lisimaco di Tracia', *Kokalos* 1 (1955) 62–152.

SCHACHERMEYR, F., *Alexander in Babylon und die Reichsordnung nach seinem Tode* (Sitzungsberichte der Österreichischen Akademie der Wissenschaften, phil.-hist. Klasse 286.3: Vienna 1970).

SCHMITT, H. H., *Untersuchungen zur Geschichte Antiochos' des Grossen und seiner Zeit* (Wiesbaden 1964).

SCHMITT, O., *Der Lamische Krieg* (Bonn 1992).

SCHOBER, L., *Untersuchungen zur Geschichte Babyloniens und der Oberen Satrapien von 323–303 v.Chr.* (Frankfurt 1981).

SCHRÖDER, S., 'Zum Göteborger Arrian-Palimpsest', *ZPE* 71 (1988) 75–90.

SCHUBERT, R., *Die Quellen zur Geschichte der Diadochenzeit* (Leipzig 1914).

SCHÜRER, E., *The History of the Jewish People in the Age of Jesus Christ*, ed. G. Vermes, F. Millar and M. Goodwin, 3 vols. (Edinburgh 1973–87).

SCHWAHN, W., 'Die Nachfolge Alexanders des Grossen', *Klio* 24 (1931) 306–32.

SEIBERT, J., *Historische Beiträge zu den dynastischen Verbindungen in Hellenistischer Zeit* (Munich 1967)

—— *Untersuchungen zur Geschichte Ptolemaios' I* (Munich 1969).

—— *Das Zeitalter der Diadochen* (Darmstadt 1983).

SHERWIN-WHITE, S., and KURTZ, A., *From Samarkand to Sardis* (London 1993).

SIMONETTI AGOSTINETTI, A., *Flavio Arriano: gli eventi dopo Alessandro* (Rome 1993).

SIMPSON, R. H., 'The Historical Circumstances of the Peace of 311', *JHS* 74 (1954) 25–31.

SIROUX, M., 'Atesh-Gah', *Iranica Antiqua* 5 (1965) 39–82.

SWEET, W., 'Sources of Plutarch's Demetrius', *CW* 44 (1951) 177–81.

SYME, R., *Tacitus*, 2 vols. (Oxford 1958).

TARN, W. W., 'Alexander and the Ganges', *JHS* 43 (1923) 93–101.

—— *Alexander the Great*, 2 vols. (Cambridge 1948).

TATAKI, A. B., *Macedonians Abroad* (Meletemata 26: Athens 1998).

THAPAR, R., *A History of India* (Harmondsworth 1966).

THOMPSON, M., 'The Mints of Lysimachus', in C. M. Kraay and G. K. Jenkins (eds.), *Essays in Greek Coinage presented to Stanley Robinson* (Oxford 1968) 163–82.

THOMPSON, W. E., 'PSI 1284: Eumenes of Cardia vs. the Phalanx', *Chronique d'Égypte* 59 (1984) 113–20.

TORRACA, L., *Duride di Samo. La maschera scenica nella storiografia ellenistica* (Salerno 1988).

TRITLE, L., *Phocion the Good* (London 1988).

TURNER, E. G., 'A Commander-in-Chief's Order from Saqqâra', *JEA* 60 (1974) 239–42.

VEZIN, A., *Eumenes von Kardia* (Münster i. W. 1907).

WALBANK, F. W., *A Historical Commentary on Polybius*, 3 vols. (Oxford 1957–79).

WEHRLI, C., 'Phila, fille d'Antipater et épouse de Démétrios, roi des Macédoniens', *Historia* 13 (1964) 140–6.

—— *Antigone et Démétrios* (Geneva 1948).

WELLES, C. B., *Royal Correspondence in the Hellenistic Period* (London 1934).

WENNING, R., *Die Nabatäer—Denkmäler und Geschichte* (Freiburg and Göttingen 1987).

WHEATLEY, P. V., 'Ptolemy Soter's Annexation of Syria, 320 B.C.', *CQ* 45 (1995) 433–40.

—— 'Problems in analysing Source Documents in Ancient History: The Case of Philip', *Limina* 3 (1997) 61–70.

—— 'The Chronology of the Third Diadoch War, 315–311 B.C.', *Phoenix* 52 (1998) 257–81.

WHITEHEAD, D., *Aineias the Tactician* (Oxford 1990).

WINIARCZYK, M., 'Theodoros ὁ ἄθεος,' *Philologus* 125 (1981) 64–94.

WINNICKI, J. K., 'Militäroperationen von Ptolemaios I. und Seleukos I. in Syrien in den Jahren 312–311 v. Chr.', *AncSoc* 20 (1989) 55–92; 22 (1991) 147–201.

WIRTH, G., 'Zur Grossen Schlacht des Eumenes 322 (PSI 1284)', *Klio* 46 (1965) 283–8.

WIESEHÖFER, J., *Die 'dunklen Jahrhunderte' der Persis* (Zetemata 90: Munich 1994).

YARDLEY, J. C., and HECKEL, W., *Justin*. Epitome *of the* Philippic History *of Pompeius Trogus* Books 11–12 (Oxford 1997).

YOUROUKOVA, Y., *Coins of the Ancient Thracians* (BAR Suppl. 4: Oxford 1976).

General Index

Lamia, Athenian courtesan, mistress of
Demetrius 24, 273
Lamia, city in Central Greece 8, 61,
62
Lamian War 7–8, 9–10, 27, 61, 75–9,
86 n. 77
Lampsacus 248–9
Laomedon of Mytilene, satrap of Syria
57, 211
Laranda, Lycaonian city 11, 62 n. 122,
81
Leochares, sculptor 276
Leonnatus, Mac. marshal:
role at Babylon 7, 44, 48, 53
satrap of Hell. Phrygia 16, 58
in Lamian War 9, 62, 78–9
victory in Oreitis 54 n. 92
regal ambitions 57 n. 108, 78
Lycaonia 81, 90
Lycia, demanded by Cassander 214
Lydia 17, 19, 68
troops from 80, 134
Lysimacheia, royal capital 2
Lysimachus, son of Agathocles,
Mac. dynast:
career under Al. 275
regime in Thrace 8, 57, 269–72
in coalition against Antigonus 214
in Peace of Dynasts 218, 239,
241
assumes diadem 2, 246, 269, 275
in campaign of Ipsus 96, 248
campaign in Chersonese 247–50,
260
defeated by Getae 252
invades Macedonia (288) 96, 208
relations with Demetrius 252, 258,
265–6, 267, 272–5
hosts philosophers 185
lion hunts of 275–7
view of monarchy 2
coinage of 269, 272 n. 96, 277

Macedon, Macedonians:
recalcitrance at the Hyphasis 60
crush settlers' revolt 61–2
combined with Iranians 79–80
veterans under Craterus 6, 11–12,
60, 73–4, 77, 85, 101
in first coalition war 13, 17–18,
151
use of in Asia 3–4, 134, 151–2,
166

settlement of at Carrhae 231–3,
234–5
rejection of Demetrius 257–8
votes by army 59–60, 275
numbers:
at Hellespont 65–6
at Gaugamela 67, 73
at Opis (324) 74–5
at Al.'s death 75–84
in first coalition war 84–6
under Antigonus 92
under Arrhidaeus 88
under Ptolemy 88
before Ipsus 96
reserves 67, 92
reinforcements 68–73
attrition 86–90
repatriation 90–1, 94
Madri, epic queen 181, 184, 186
Mahābārata, Indian epic 181
Malli, Indian people 43 n. 56, 45, 104,
127, 145, 198, 255
Mallus, Cilician city 70, 216
Manu, Brahman authority:
on widowhood 180
on marriage forms 182
Maranitae, Arab people 199
Massagetae, Saca people 194
Media:
base for Antigonus 119, 124–5,
159–60, 161
Antigonus' settlement (316) 162
occupied by Seleucus 210, 218, 225,
237
cavalry from 124, 133, 148, 153, 158
Meleager son of Neoptolemus, Mac.
commander:
role at Babylon 7, 35, 38–9, 45–6,
46–7, 51
downfall of 54–5
Memphis 14, 87
Menander, Mac. commander, satrap of
Lydia 12, 16
Menyllus, Mac. garrison commander
85
mercenaries:
use of:
by Philip 66
by Al. 68, 72–3, 80–1
by Antipater 77, 91
by Polyperchon 92
by Lysimachus 248–9, 272 n. 96
training in Mac. weaponry 80, 107